Steeped in Murder

A Hilarious Tearoom Cozy Mystery

Kirsten Weiss

misterio press

About this Book

TEA, TAROT, AND TROUBLE.

Abigail's dream of owning a tearoom in her California beach town is about to come true. She's got the lease, the start-up funds, and the scone recipes. But she's out of a tearoom and into hot water when her realtor turns out to be a conman... and then turns up dead.

Not even death puts an end to the conman's mischief. He rented the same space to a tarot reader, Hyperion. Convinced his tarot room is in the cards, he's not letting go of the building without a fight.

But this unlikely duo will have to work together... With a little help from her quirky grandfather, Hyperion and Abigail steep themselves in the murky waters of the sham realtor's double dealings. But can they unearth the truth before murder boils over again?

Steeped in Murder is the first book in this Tea and Tarot mystery series with heart. Get cozy and download this hilarious caper today.

Tearoom recipes in the back of the book!

Copyright

Cover artist: Wicked Smart Designs

Visit the author website: www.kirstenweiss.com

Misterio Press mass market print edition / January, 2023

http://Misteriopress.com

ISBN-13: 978-1-944767-41-9

Contents

CHAPTER ONE

IN MY DEFENSE, THE day didn't *seem* that murdery.

The scent of salt air mingled with my herbal teas – mint and rosemary and roses. Whimsical stalls for the farmer's market lined each side of the broad pier. The scene was cheerful, colorful, and felony-free.

I couldn't wait to escape.

My first-of-the-morning customer adjusted the glasses on her nose and peered at the tin. Her graying hair tossed in the warm breeze. "The leaves look so beautiful. I'd think you'd keep them in glass jars."

A teenager in a black maxi-skirt and thick eyeliner drifted across the pier to stand beside her.

"Tea keeps better out of the light and heat." I glanced longingly toward the end of the pier, and the labyrinth of low, pastel buildings that climbed the hills encircling the bay.

My customer opened the tin and sniffed. "Mm. Olallieberry. This tea won't be around long enough for me to worry about storage."

The teen grunted and pointed at the bundles of dried herbs, dangling from the black canvas awning. "Do any of your herbs have, you know, magical properties?"

The woman rolled her eyes. "Beryl, you and your ideas."

Magic? I smiled. "Magic is as magic does."

"What's that supposed to mean?" the goth asked.

It had been a saying of my grandmother's. It meant we make our own magic, that dreams come true when you work toward them. But instead, I said, "When prepared and drunk mindfully, a good tea transports you to another world of peace and tranquility. If that's not magic, I don't know what is."

"No, you don't." Beryl slouched across the pier toward a Tarot reader who'd set up across from my stand. A giant tabby cat sat in a miniature throne beside his table, which was covered in a purple velvet cloth.

"Ouch." I laughed. Fifteen years ago, I'd *been* that girl. "Tough crowd."

"Beryl's going through a phase." My customer stuffed the tea tin into her carrying bag. "It's hard to believe she was such an adorable toddler."

"Have a great morning," I called to her departing figure. Because in that moment, I was certain it *was* going to be great. I'd learned not to trust my intuition long ago, but who can blame me for being buffaloed? I lived in an adorable California beach town. The sun was shining. And I was about to start my new and improved life and open an actual tearoom. Things couldn't be better.

A voice in my head chirruped that I'd just jinxed everything, I didn't deserve perfection.

I told the voice to shut up. This was my fairytale, dammit.

I rearranged tins on the shelves and surveyed my tiny kingdom of tea. Tea blends mounded in antique copper bowls lined the front table display. A pallet sign – *Abigail's Teas! Hand blended!* – leaned against the metal pole that held up my black awning.

An elderly accordion player wandered down the pier. He waved to my grandfather, seated on a folding metal chair behind my table.

"Go and bother Tomas!" My grandfather shouted and pointed to the black canvas wall on his left. They normally shared a table – Gramps selling his horseradish and Tomas his salsa. The two men had an informal competition over which of their wares could make more grown men cry.

Gramps popped a blueberry into his mouth and laced his fingers over the stomach of his beige sweater vest. It strained against his brown-checked shirt.

The accordion player paused in front of the Tarot reader and blatted out a tune.

The fortune teller, a slender, Eurasian man about my age, narrowed his eyes and shooed away the accordionist. The giant tabby stared at me from its throne.

Unnerved by the cat's unwavering gaze, I shifted my own to a vegetable seller with Alice-in-Wonderland-sized purple cabbages and reddish carrots. Beside her stall, a little girl and her father sold ducklings and baby chicks from an apple crate.

I wiped my hands on the front of my apron and checked the clock on my phone.

My grandfather chuckled and adjusted the brown plaid cap on his head. "You know you want to see your new building." His blue eyes twinkled. "Just go. I can manage your stall."

"You're supposed to be managing ours, Frank," a wheezy masculine voice drifted through the black canvas wall.

"What's the matter? You think I don't know how to make change?" Gramps lifted an untamed gray brow.

Maybe I *could* sneak away. "Are you sure you don't mind?" The market wouldn't get busy for another hour or so.

"I mind!" Tomas laughed. "If you expect me to flog your horseradish, Beanblossom, you've got another think coming."

A duckling the color of Amish butter escaped the apple crate. It waddled toward my tea stand, and Gramps tossed a blueberry the duckling's way. The berry bounced along the rough wooden pier.

"See?" Gramps motioned toward the black canvas. "Tomas is okay with it."

Tomas poked his head around the canvas. Tall, lanky and olive skinned, he was the Abbott to my grandfather's Costello. They'd been best friends for decades. "I'm just giving you a hard time, Abigail." He straightened his plaid bowtie.

The duckling beelined for the berry and snapped up the treat. The tiny bird tilted its head and gazed at Gramps adoringly.

On its throne, the tabby hunched its shoulders and eyed the tiny puff of down.

I scooted around the table and swooped up the duck. "I think this is yours." I handed the warm fluff of down to its owner.

The duckling peeped.

"Thanks." The man strode to the apple crate. Shaking his head, he said something to his pigtailed daughter, and she pinked.

I wiped my hands on my apron. "If you're sure you don't mind."

"I once killed a man with a bottlecap," Tomas said. "I can sell my salsa and your grandfather's horseradish without breaking a sweat."

Gramps snorted and rolled his eyes.

Ignoring the invitation to rehash Tomas's old war story, I glanced toward the Tarot reader. He spoke to a woman draped in filmy scarves and hooked a leash on the tabby.

The woman dropped into his chair and riffled a deck of Tarot cards.

I fingered the key in the pocket of my jeans. I'd been plotting and planning my tearoom since I was a little girl. A room that would be elegant, cozy and fun, filled with warmth and genteel laughter. The building of my dreams had been vacant for decades. I'd been certain someone would snatch it up before I could afford to. But the building had waited for me, like it was meant to be.

Whipping off my apron, I snatched up my purse filled with swatches and business plans. "Thanks. For everything." I kissed my grandfather's rough cheek, and my heart swelled with love. If it wasn't for him, none of this would be happening.

"Get out of here," he said.

Giddy, I strode down the pier, past stands of brilliant flowers and stalls flogging jam and honey, past stenciled signs proclaiming NO OVERHEAD CASTING to the fishermen who lined the railings.

My blouse's billowy blue-and-white sleeves rustled, tickling my arms. I swiped a curl of brown hair, streaked with gold highlights, out of my face.

To my left, a movement caught my attention. I glanced over my shoulder.

The Tarot reader paced me on the opposite side of the pier. He was handsome, with a straight nose, chiseled jaw, high cheekbones, and almond-shaped eyes. His shock of black hair was fashionably tousled. In spite of the morning's warmth, he wore a gray turtleneck above his elegant slacks.

The tabby tugged sulkily on its rhinestone leash and pulled back toward the pier.

California. Grinning, I strode down the pier's sloping deck to the cement walk. The spring air smelled of suntan oil and ice cream cones. Surfers plied the Pacific's low waves. But the beach was mostly empty at this early hour, as were the narrow streets.

And my new building was just around the corner.

Footsteps sounded behind me, and the skin between my shoulder blades prickled. I shot another quick look over my shoulder.

The Tarot reader was there, close, his expression intent. He crossed to the opposite side of the narrow road, and my muscles released. *Ridiculous.* He wasn't following me. There was only one way off the pier, and the town of San Borromeo was small. I was being paranoid.

I clasped my big portfolio bag to my chest and resumed daydreaming. My menu had been planned to the last scone. I'd drawn up sketches of the interior. But I needed to spend time inside to see if my dreams would fit the reality of a sixty-year-old structure that hadn't been occupied for thirty-plus years.

The kitchen would need new equipment. I'd have to strip the walls. New floors – wooden, of course, for warmth. Would green florals be too cutesy? Because they'd match my potted ferns perfectly and the drying herbs I intended to hang over the counter. Shelves behind it, where I'd sell tins of loose tea...

I glanced to my left.

The Tarot reader strolled past a shop selling beachwear. The tabby sneered.

I did a doubletake.

Yes, the cat was definitely sneering.

Lengthening my strides, I passed a restaurant and glanced in its broad, picture window. It was packed to the gills with diners eating leisurely breakfasts. In the reflection, the Tarot reader fell slightly behind me.

My new tearoom, a faded purple stucco building, stood on the corner of a pedestrian shopping area opposite. Art galleries and shops selling whirligigs and seashells lined the brick walkway. The owner of the t-shirt shop next door waved from his doorway. "Glad you got the place, Abigail!"

"Thanks!" Heart pounding with excitement, I fingered the key in the pocket of my jeans and jogged across the street. The building wasn't much to look at now, not with brown paper lining its dusty windows. But once I'd painted the stucco white, cleaned the windows and added flower boxes, the exterior would be perfect.

It was the sky-blue door that had captured my heart. Intricate molding. Tall, narrow windows at the top. A gorgeous doorknob with a poppy inset. Its siren song had been calling me for years, hinting at treasures hidden within.

The Tarot reader's footsteps padded behind me, and I dared another look over my shoulder. The enormous cat bounded forward. Its tawny eyes focused on my ankle.

Clutching my purse, I nodded to the man and promptly stumbled over a loose brick.

He nodded back as he caught up with me.

In awkward silence we walked side by side, weaving around potted plants. He pulled a key from the pocket of his gray slacks.

We reached the blue door at the same time and grabbed for the intricate knob.

"Hey!" We said in unison, twin keys extended.

"What are you doing?" he asked.

"What are *you* doing?"

"That's my building."

I blinked. "No, it's my building. I rented it starting today."

"I rented it starting today."

We eyed each other.

My stomach plummeted to the tips of my sandals. It was a mistake, that was all. A mistake. Something silly I'd laugh about with Gramps and Tomas later.

"My realtor," I said, "is Reince—"

"Briggs," he whispered.

"Oh, no." Something was seriously wrong, and my heart clenched. "I rented this building from Reince Briggs for a tearoom."

His skin turned a shade lighter. "I rented it for a Tarot parlor."

In a major earthquake, the ground is not your friend. The solidity of something beneath one's feet is so taken for granted that the shock of it confuses, disorients, terrifies. I felt that shock now, and the image of tiny white shoes floated into my mind.

A nearby whirligig rattled loudly.

"But... it's my new tearoom!" I bleated. "I have swatches!"

He glanced at the green and white fabrics spilling from my ginormous purse. "They're lovely swatches."

"You don't think... It has to be... Could it be a mistake?"

"Check your key."

I slid it into the lock, turned it. The blue door clicked open. Dust billowed from the opening on a draft of stale air. "Now yours."

He tried his key. It turned smoothly. His Adam's apple bobbed. "You didn't, er, pay up front, did you?"

"Six months' rent." My voice cracked. At California prices, it had been a lot of money. "I paid yesterday."

"I paid for three months yesterday too."

"How could Reince have rented it to us both?" I raked my fingers through my hair. Saint Borromeo *was* the patron saint of indigestion. Maybe I should have taken that as an omen before trying to start a tearoom here.

"Obviously, there's some mistake." A muscle pulsed in his jaw. "I should have known when I drew the five of swords. It's always trouble for me."

The cat stood on its hind legs and pressed its front paws to my knee.

"Ignore Bastet." The man's face cleared. "But I also drew the World card, and that means my Tarot room can't go wrong." He snapped his long fingers. "Who put you up to this? One of the gals at the Ren Faire? It was Winifred, wasn't it?"

"I'm not joking. This isn't a joke."

Oblivious to the drama, a family of three ambled past us in shorts and tees.

"No." I shook my head and stepped backward. The Tarot reader was right. It was a mistake, that was all. It had taken me years to save up the money for the tearoom, and in the end, I'd had to borrow some from Gramps, the man who'd raised me like his own daughter. But the image of those childish shoes rose again to my mind. I pushed the vision away. "There's got to be a rational explanation. I'll find out what."

"Good for you," he said briskly. "Let me know what you learn." He pushed open the door and stepped inside.

"Wait. What are you doing?"

"Going inside of course. World card!" He hauled the resisting feline inside.

"But I rented that building too."

"Look, you seem like a sincere sort of schmuck, so I say this with heartfelt sincerity, goodwill, peace on earth, and all that jazz. It ain't happening. You've made a mistake. This is my building."

"But—"

"The cards don't lie. I even consulted an astrologer, though I find that form of prognostication wooly at best, but she gave me a discount. And she assured me that today was my day. The stars are aligned. This is my tarot room, all's fair in love and Tarot, and you, dear lady, are SOL, even if you do look like an elf." He patted my head. "Buck up. You'll get through this." He shut the door in my face.

My hands clenched. "Oooh!" I blew out my breath. There was no sense in getting mad, even if he totally deserved it. And I might be height-challenged, but I do *not* look like an elf.

I'd just sort things out myself.

Forcing down my panic, I walked down the brick walk and around the corner to the parking lot. Parking was tight in the tiny beach town, and I'd figured now that I was a renter, I could use the building's rear lot.

My throat tightened. It was a little ridiculous how excited I'd been parking my car here this morning.

Unlocking my blue Mazda, I dumped the fabric swatches in the hatch-back.

I leaned against the warm car door and called the realtor. Maybe the Tarot reader had taken the wrong key or... something.

The phone rang twice before I noticed an answering echo nearby.

Brow furrowed, I scanned the lot, still near-empty at this early hour.

The ringing seemed to come from a dumpster near the bank's rear entrance.

Wary, I followed the sound, my head cocked, my phone loose at my side. "Hello?"

I passed the ATM and the glass door to the bank. A faint, unpleasant odor wafted from the dumpster, and I wrinkled my nose.

The ringing stopped.

I checked my phone. It had gone to voice mail.

I hung up and dialed again. An answering ring echoed off the concrete wall. Hand tightening on my phone, I walked around the dumpster. Reince's red sports car sat parked on the opposite side.

I sucked in my breath.

The realtor lay on his back beside the dumpster. His head rested against a concrete parking curb, stained brown-red with blood.

CHAPTER TWO

I SWAYED, STARING AT the dead man, at his blank gaze, at the cloud that had settled in his eyes. His chin was pressed to his chest, his lips parted. Dew glistened on his face, giving it a waxy, unreal look.

But this was real. Blood had dried on the parking curb, stained the shoulders of his charcoal suit, puddled on the asphalt. A dark bruise spread from the center of his neck.

A nearby phone rang. Rang again. Fell silent.

"Mr. Briggs?" I whispered, denial dulling my brain. He was definitely dead, and since I wasn't a medium, he couldn't answer me. But the frantic, irrational voice in my head asked me not to believe my eyes. "Reince?"

A morning breeze fluttered his red tie. The spotted tabby sniffed at the realtor's tasseled loafers.

I yelped and leapt backward, thunking against the dumpster.

The giant cat yowled, a funeral dirge, raising the hairs on the back of my neck. The cat's turquoise leash trailed along the fresh black asphalt.

I clutched my phone. "How did *you* get here?"

Ignoring me, the cat examined the corpse with professional detachment. His whiskers twitched. Or was it her whiskers? Bastet was an Egyptian goddess, wasn't she?

I wrinkled my nose, smelling dumpster and other odors I didn't want to think about too hard.

"Bastet!" The fortune teller jogged across the parking lot. "What are you...?" He trailed off, his gaze traveling from me to the dead man. "You killed our realtor!" He snatched the cat off the pavement.

The animal growled, offended.

"I did not," I said. "I just found him here. Look, the blood is dry. Mostly."

"What, are you a detective *and* a tea lady?"

"A man's dead. There's no need to be snarky."

His striking face rearranged itself. Outrage, anxiety, and chagrin flitted across his mobile features. Clutching the tabby, he edged backward, as if afraid I might attack.

"His phone was ringing," I said. "I called Reince, and I heard the phone, and I followed the ringing here."

"Or so you *say*."

"Well, yeah. I did just say it. Literally. I just said it."

"Now who's being snarky? I love snark, by the way, especially from elves."

"Not funny. Not with a dead body right there." I was only slightly height-challenged. "And some fortune teller you are. You couldn't predict this?"

"I can't believe you went there."

"Sue me. I speak in clichés when I'm rattled. Our realtor is dead!"

"Well," he said, "I tell jokes when confronted with corpses and crowded elevators. And I'm a Tarot reader, not a fortune teller." He swooped down and pressed two fingers to the side of the realtor's neck. "Cold as a morgue." He loosed a gusty sigh. The cat struggled beneath his arm. "You'd better call the police. If I put Bastet down, he'll probably start nibbling on him." He lifted the cat so they were face-to-face. "Remind me never to die when you're locked in a room with me."

"He? But isn't Bastet—?" I shook myself. *Moving on.*

I fumbled with the phone and called nine-one-one.

The dispatcher ordered me to stay where I was and not touch anything. We hung up.

"The police are on their way," I parroted.

"They'd better be." He gave me an appraising look. "I suppose you want to think I did it."

My shoulders jerked. *Want* to think he'd done it? He *could* have done it. "I haven't exactly gotten around to making a list of suspects."

He backed away. "Or maybe you and your partner killed Reince last night, and you only pretended to be surprised when you *found* his body this morning. Maybe that's why Bastet has been so fascinated by you." His eyes narrowed. "You carry the scent of death."

Wait. What? "My partner?"

"That old guy who looks like a mafia don."

"That's my grandfather."

"We can't help our relations, elf."

I shook my head. "Look, I didn't kill him. And who *are* you?"

"Hyperion Night." He motioned to the cat. "No wonder Bastet was stalking you. He has a sixth sense for violence. You know. Cats."

I nodded, hysteria batting against my brain. I needed to get a grip. Fast. I took a deep breath and slowly let it go.

"As for your partner—"

"I don't have a partner," I said more calmly, "and I didn't kill anyone."

"I sure hope not," a masculine voice behind us drawled.

We both jumped.

The stranger was tall and rangy. Beneath his blue suit jacket, his button-up shirt and jeans were anchored by a massive silver buckle. His face was bronzed by the sun, his maple-colored hair touched with gold. The newcomer shifted his weight, brushing his jacket aside with one hand to expose the police shield on his hip. But my gaze fixed on the large gun holstered beside it.

"Detective Chase," he said. "What have we got here?"

Hyperion gawped at the man. I couldn't blame him. If Apollo had fallen to earth by way of Texas, he would have looked a lot like Detective Chase.

"It's Reince Briggs," I said, stiffening. "The realtor. He's d-dead." I've got nothing against cops in theory. Society wouldn't function without them, and like any other group of people, most were good. But theory flies out the window when an authority figure is prepared to exert actual authority over you.

I hate it when that happens.

"Huh." The detective drew a pair of medical gloves from his pocket and pulled them on. He squatted beside the corpse. "So, you knew the man," he said, not touching him. "That makes things easier."

"Are you going to check his pulse?" I glanced at the gloves, at the body. Was Reince still alive? Because this was one of those few instances when I wouldn't mind being wrong.

"Why would I want to do that? I can see he's dead."

I bit the inside of my cheek. "Because you put on gloves?"

"We're standing next to a dumpster," he said.

Feeling foolish, I turned to study the green metal bin. "Right. There could be evidence inside."

He made a face. "Evidence is for the tech team. That thing's covered in germs."

But it seemed unlikely the germs would leap off the dumpster and down his throat.

"And who are you?" he asked.

"Abigail Beanblossom."

Hyperion made a choking sound that sounded a lot like *elf*.

"And this is Hyperion Night," I added, since the Tarot reader was still making gasping noises, his eyes glued to the detective.

A seagull wheeled above. Bastet tracked it with his gaze.

"Beanblossom." The detective stood and rubbed his square jaw. "You related to Frank Beanblossom?"

"He's my grandfather," I said, throwing an irritated look in the Tarot reader's direction. *Mafia Don. Ha.*

The detective looked over Hyperion, and his gray eyes flickered like a summer storm. "Hyperion. That's a name. What's your connection to this, Mr. Night?"

"I didn't do it." Hyperion clutched the cat more tightly to his chest. Bastet meowed, protesting.

"I didn't either," I said.

"Mm hm," the detective said placidly. "So, how do you know Mr. Briggs?"

"He was my realtor too," Hyperion said.

"And what did he sell you?" the detective asked him.

"He rented me that building." Hyperion motioned toward the rear of the purple stucco building.

Sirens wailed in the distance.

"And you?" He turned his wickedly gray eyes on me.

"Me? He rented me that building too." I cleared my throat. My mouth was dry, even though I'd gulped a can of diet cola an hour ago. *Stupid authority figures.* "Clearly, there's been some mistake."

"You're telling me he rented you both the same building? Did you pay any rent in advance?"

The sirens grew louder.

"Six months," I muttered.

"I only paid three," Hyperion said in a superior tone.

I scowled at the Tarot reader. So, I was a rotten negotiator. Did he have to rub it in?

"When did you pay this gentleman?" the detective asked.

"Yesterday," Hyperion and I said in unison and grimaced at each other.

"Well, that is a strange turn of events," the detective said.

"It's got to be a mistake," I babbled. "I've been planning to open a tearoom since I was five. I've even gone to cooking school. It's not that big of a building, but it's perfect for my tearoom."

"Or a Tarot studio," Hyperion cut in.

I clamped my jaw shut. I always talked too much when I got nervous. I'd make a terrible suspect in a police investigation. Authority figures made me nervous. Not that I had anything to worry about, being innocent and all. I folded my arms.

The detective brushed open his jacket and braced both his hands on his slim hips. "A Tarot studio," he said, voice flat.

"Tarot is an amazing tool for self-development," Hyperion said. The tabby clawed at his charcoal turtleneck. "The cards depict archetypes from our universal unconscious. They allow us to tap directly into our subconscious and superconscious knowledge. The psychologist Carl Jung did most of his work with synchronicity and archetypes around the I Ching and alchemy. But he wrote a bit about Tarot too."

My mouth crumpled, and I forced it into a more neutral position. That was exactly the sort of thing my mother would blather about.

"If you say so," the detective drawled.

"You sound like a skeptic," Hyperion said.

"I've been meaning to get that checked." The detective studied the body. "I thought the cards were used for fortune telling."

"That too," Hyperion admitted.

"Let me get this straight," he said. "You both paid the dead man rent up front for that building. The whole building."

Hyperion and I nodded.

The cat wriggled free of his arms and tried to crawl on top of Hyperion's head.

"Ouch! Get off!" The Tarot reader flailed and staggered against the dumpster. "That's my ear, not a stair climber!"

The detective eyed him askance. A police car skidded into the parking lot.

The detective glanced its way and groaned. "Rookies. You two, stop talking to each other. In fact, you." He pointed at me. "Go stand over there." He pointed to a spot on the other side of the dumpster. "And you." He pointed at Hyperion. "Stand over there." He pointed to a spot beside my blue Mazda. The detective waited until we'd gone our appointed spots, then he strode to the squad car and braced his hands on the rim of the open window. "The man's already dead. No need to endanger the public by speeding."

He said something more quietly to the uniformed cops. They nodded, exiting the car, and started toward Hyperion.

Sweat crawled down my neck. It wasn't because I was worried about being arrested for murder or anything. It was just a really warm morning.

I mean, this was San Borromeo. Nothing ever happened here. It couldn't have been foul play. Reince had probably just stumbled and hit his head.

I remembered the bruise on the front of his throat, and nausea swamped me. That bruise wasn't from a stumble.

Renting to us both had been a mistake. So, I wasn't a suspect, because you don't kill someone over a mistake.

But grudgingly, I acknowledged it would have been pretty damn hard for Reince to make a mistake that big. Unless he'd thought I only wanted to rent part of the building?

Another squad car drove into the lot at a more sedate pace and came to a halt beside the detective. Chase leaned in the open window and spoke to one of the officers. The cop, a woman with blond hair in a ponytail, nodded, and the squad car crawled toward me.

I wiped my forehead. Mistake. It was a mistake, not a motive for murder. I'd go to the realtor's office and get everything sorted out.

The police car glided to a halt in front of me. Two officers, a man and the woman, stepped out.

"Abigail Beanblossom?" the woman asked. She was only my height — five-foot-four — but she looked like she could take care of herself.

I nodded. "Yes."

"We'll need to take your statement." She opened the rear door. "At the police station, if you don't mind."

"The police station?" I asked weakly. Why the police station? I'd only found the body. I wasn't a suspect.

"If you don't mind," she repeated, her posture telling me it didn't really matter if I minded or not.

"You don't think I'm a suspect?" I couldn't be. I hardly knew the realtor. Besides, he was cold when I'd found him. Hyperion had said so.

"Ma'am," she just said, holding the door open.

Nausea swam up my throat. *Oh damn.* I was a suspect.

CHAPTER THREE

MUSCLES TIGHT, I PACED the interrogation room. It smelled of disinfectant. I wanted to think that was a good thing, until I considered all the reasons the room would need disinfectant. And Detective Chase gave me a lot of time to think. I'd watched enough police shows to know he was doing it on purpose – leaving me alone with my thoughts to shake me up.

It was working, and that was just irritating.

The door opened, and the detective strode inside carrying a file beneath one arm of his blue suit jacket. "Sorry to keep you waiting," he drawled and closed the door with his elbow.

I bit back a sharp remark. I'd been there over two hours and had already talked to the Texan detective twice. He'd somehow made casual intimidating, his questions pointed as a bowie knife. I glanced at the clock above the mirror.

The second hand clicked backward, thought about its next step, and made a tentative tick forward.

"Did you get everything you need?" I forced a smile.

He slid the manila folder onto the metal table in the center of the room and flipped it open. "Recognize this man?"

I came to stand beside him and looked at the page. A mugshot of an unsmiling Reince Briggs stared out at me. I sucked in my breath. "That's—"

"Roger Byrson. AKA Reince Briggs. AKA Reynold Bing. AKA—"

"Mugshots." I clutched the back of a metal chair to steady myself. This was happening. This had happened. "He's a criminal."

"Ran a standard real estate con. He'd rent houses and buildings that weren't actually for rent. He'd find empty ones, break in, and get new keys made. In the past, he managed to get out of Dodge before the actual owners showed up."

"You're saying, I bought—" My voice cracked. "I rented – a Brooklyn Bridge, a building that wasn't actually for rent."

"We can't know for sure until we talk to the owner."

"But... He worked out of an office. He had a partner."

"He's an identity thief. And the identities he steals belong to dead realtors. When did you say you paid Mr. Briggs?"

I released my death grip on the chair and straightened. "I gave him a check yesterday when we met at two o'clock." Had he cashed it? If I got to the bank right away, maybe I could stop payment. It would be all right. *Please, let it be all right.*

"And when did you find out he'd rented the building to Mr. Night as well?"

"Who? Oh, the Tarot reader. Just this morning. Wait. You don't think I—?"

"Thank you, Ms. Beanblossom. That will be all. For now."

"But what about the money I gave him?" I started to reach for his arm and dropped my hand. "If Reince was a conman, are you going to be able to get my payment back?"

"I'm sure someone will be working on that."

"Someone?"

"I'm just homicide, ma'am." Pulling down the sleeve of his suit jacket to cover his palm, he opened the door.

"Was my check in his wallet or in one of his pockets?"

"No, ma'am, your check was not on his person. Have a good day."

"Right. Right." I stumbled outside to stand on the station's concrete steps and blinked in the California sun. Adorable pastel buildings with scroll-like wrought iron balconies surrounded the station. Boutiques and burger joints in Caribbean shades tumbled over each other towards the Pacific. They made me want to vomit.

The money I'd paid Reince was just the first in a series of financial dominoes. My budget had been, to put it mildly, lean. If my money had been stolen and was gone, so was my tearoom. And not just the tearoom in *that* building, but in *any* building. It would take me years to earn enough back to start over in high-priced California.

Clutching my purse to my chest, I breathed heavily. The money couldn't be gone. I wouldn't let it be gone.

Across the street, a tourist couple paused in front of the windows of a candy shop with a wavy, shingled roof. Its decorative half-timbering exposed smooth, white stucco. San Borromeo had a dozen or so of these fairytale-style buildings – knockoffs of the famous Comstock homes of Carmel. *But just as good*, Gramps would always say. My grandfather lived in one, and I worried about him going up and down the narrow stairs.

I also worried about his reaction to learning I'd been tricked. Gramps had a heart condition. He'd also be wondering what was taking me so long.

I steadied my breathing and called my grandfather.

"Abigail! How's it going?"

"Um. There's been a small hiccup."

"Hiccup?"

I winced. I'd have to tell him eventually, but I'd rather give him the news *after* I got my money back. Because I had to get it back. "I need to go to the bank. Can you hold out for another hour?"

"Not a problem," he said stoutly.

"Tell her you have a new friend," Tomas shouted on the other end of the line.

"What?" I asked.

"A lady friend." Tomas guffawed.

"He's joking," Gramps said quickly. "Are you okay? You sound funny."

"I'm fine," I said. "Are you sure you don't mind managing the stall another hour?"

"I was planning on being here all day anyway. Don't you worry."

"Thanks," I said, relieved and more than a little guilty. We said our goodbyes and hung up.

I hurried to my bank. After a thirty-minute wait in the lobby, the manager gave me the bad news. Reince had been there yesterday afternoon and cashed the check. The manager remembered, because she'd had to sign off on it, and had been concerned about Reince carrying so much cash.

I tasted despair, which incidentally, is a lot like aspirin with a hint of lime.

Swaying, I tottered from the bank. *Okay. Okay.* Maybe the realty office where Reince had worked could help. Maybe he'd left the cash in the safe there.

I'd met his partner, Cyrus, and they had a secretary and everything. The realty, at least, was legit. It had been around for years, even if Reince hadn't. I checked my phone and jogged toward the realtors' office.

The sky had turned that flat blue-white color that sometimes comes on hot days. A trickle of sweat dampened my pseudo-peasant top as I huffed up a steep hill and past a mix of bungalows and B&Bs with colorfully-painted front doors, low, sloping roofs, and neat gardens.

I stopped in front of a gray stucco, foursquare-style home with a wide front porch and a wood-beam awning.

Two Mediterranean Cypresses, trimmed like spearheads, stood sentry on either side of the house. An elegant, coal-colored sign for the converted real estate office stood near one cypress.

Angry voices floated from the realty and over the cheerful garden of sage and desert agaves.

I strode down the flagstone steps to the porch. Flyers displaying homes for sale papered the windows. Behind the screen, the front door stood open. I pulled open the screen door and walked inside.

A shortish man and a brown-eyed blonde faced off in the gray-tiled foyer. A hanging spider plant swayed violently beside the wooden staircase, as if someone had swatted it. Glass-frosted doors bracketed opposite sides of the room.

A third person, a gray-haired receptionist in a yellow skirt and flowered, blue blouse braced her hand on the reception desk.

"—destroyed my kitchen tiles from Bologna," the man shouted in a thick Italian accent. His olive skin was dark with anger. A shock of near-black hair fell into his acorn-colored eyes, and he swiped it away angrily. He wore an expensive-looking blue suit. His white socks were jammed into loafers polished to a blinding sheen.

"I *live* there," the blond woman snarled. "I can make whatever changes I want. Those tiles were hideous."

The dark-haired man vibrated with rage. "It is *my* home!" He whirled on the older woman. "This is your fault."

"I don't know what happened, Mr. Peretti," the receptionist squawked. Her cat-eye glasses amplified her protuberant eyes, blue and watery. "But we'll look into it."

The Italian purpled and stepped closer. "Look into it? Look into it! I return from Roma and there is a strange woman living in my home." Peretti jabbed a stubby finger at the blonde. "Did you know she sold my furniture?"

"Not all," the blonde said. "Only the ugly pieces."

My stomach slithered onto the sisal throw rug. Two people in one house? Whatever had been left of my denial shattered, falling to pieces at my feet. I hadn't been the only victim of Reince's con.

"Please," the gray-haired receptionist murmured. "I'm sure it's all a misunderstanding."

If only that were true. Could one of these people have killed Reince? The Italian seemed angry enough.

"It's my home," the blonde said. "I don't see how you can misunderstand that."

"My home," the Italian, Mr. Peretti, shouted. "Mine!"

A low, hopeless noise escaped my throat.

"How dare you," the blonde shouted.

"Dare? Dare!" Peretti's chest swelled. "Of course I dare. It is my property!"

"Sir..." the receptionist's voice cracked.

"And you!" He stepped closer to her. "What do you know about this? Sneaking about and lurking in the background."

The older woman gasped and took a step back. She gripped her cat-eye glasses with one gnarled hand.

My neck tightened. I don't like seeing little old ladies picked on. "Hey."

The three turned to stare at me.

"And what is your role in this?" the Italian snarled.

"I don't have one," I said. "But I've never seen a situation calmed by shouting."

"I'll shout as much as I please," Mr. Peretti said. "This woman tore out my garden and replaced it with a desert!"

"It's a low-water garden." The blonde rolled her eyes.

"Who are you to tell me not to shout?" the Italian continued.

I took a prudent step backward. "Listen—"

"This woman is living in my house without my permission. And that man rented it to her. And she has a dog!"

The blonde pivoted toward the receptionist. "Where *is* Reince? I've left a dozen messages ever since this lunatic appeared on my doorstep."

"*My* doorstep," Peretti shouted. "Mine!"

"I don't know," the receptionist said, her voice shaking, "but as soon as I find him, I'm sure we'll straighten everything out."

"But he's dead," I said.

They goggled at me.

Whoops. "You mean... the police haven't come here yet?"

The older woman's legs folded. She slid to the ground, her back against the wainscoting beneath the stairs.

I hurried to kneel at her side. "Can I get you some water? Are you all right?"

Expression wan, the older woman shook her head. "The shock... Reince can't really be dead, can he?"

I rubbed my arms, suddenly cold beneath the thin fabric of my blouse. "I'm sorry."

"We've met before," she said, "haven't we?"

I nodded. "Briefly. Here, in this office." I motioned left, toward the plastic wall holders filled with flyers for homes for sale. "I was one of Reince's clients, Abigail Beanblossom."

"I'm Florence."

"He rented me the building at 2304 Laurel," I said, "and I paid him upfront. Another man, Hyperion Night, claims Reince rented it to him." I darted a glance at the Italian. He'd seemed surprised when I'd told them Reince was dead. They'd all seemed surprised. But had they been? "We can't both have the building."

"You're sure Reince is dead?" the receptionist asked.

"The police found his body this morning," I said. "He's dead." It wasn't a lie. The police had found his body after I had. But it bothered me a little that I'd instinctively veered away from that fact, as if I had something to hide.

"That's inconvenient," the blonde said.

"Good," Peretti said. "The man was either a fool or a criminal. He deserved to die. I hope it was painful."

"I wouldn't go that far," the blonde said.

"I do go that far," Peretti said. "Now get out of my house!"

"Under California law," she said, "you can't force me out."

"We'll see about that." He stormed out the front door.

I glanced between the receptionist and the screen door, swinging slowly shut. "About 2304 Laurel, I paid six months' rent up front. The bank told me Reince cashed the check. Could the money be here, by any chance?" Because if I didn't get that money back… I stood and swayed, suddenly dizzy. I told myself it was just money, just a building. But that was a lie. It was so much more.

"What on earth is that racket?" A woman, tall and muscular as an Amazon and with short, graying hair, walked down the stairs. A long, sheer kimono wafted about her ivory slacks and tunic. She spotted the receptionist, sitting on the gray tiles. "What's happened?" she asked coolly. Striding to the receptionist, she helped her to her feet.

"We'll look into your building," Florence told me and shot the newcomer a sideways glance. "And we do keep checks in the safe, but no cash. But I'll take a look."

"Thanks." I hurried after the Italian. I was clutching at slippery straws, but maybe he knew something about Reince that would help. "Mr. Peretti?"

He halted on the garden path and looked over his shoulder. "What?"

I trotted down the porch steps. "I think we may be in a similar situation."

"You and I are not in the same situation."

"We're not?"

"I was away. I came back. A strange woman was living in my house without permission. I am the homeowner! You, signorina, are the fraudster!"

"Fraudster? I'm not—"

"Now what's all this about?" a familiar voice drawled. Detective Chase stood on the sidewalk, his long arms loose at his sides.

My shoulder muscles tensed. Nah, I didn't look suspicious here. Not one bit.

"What this is about is none of your business," Peretti snapped.

The detective drew aside his navy blazer, exposing his badge. "I reckon it is, as you're disturbing the peace. What's going on here?"

"You are a police officer?" Peretti sneezed.

The detective stepped backward and raised a hand. "Whoa." A panicked expression crossed his chiseled face. "Are you sick?"

"Allergies." He whipped a handkerchief from his inside pocket. "Inside that house there is a ring of thieves."

The detective edged farther away from the Italian. "Are you seeing someone for that?"

"Why would I see someone? It is this foreign pollen." The Italian blew into the handkerchief.

The detective's mouth compressed. "How do you know it's allergies?"

The Italian glared. "What does it matter? You are a policeman, not a doctor. Arrest someone! Arrest all of them! But especially that woman."

The detective pulled a mask, like doctors wear, from the pocket of his jacket and slipped it over his face. "Ms. Beanblossom?"

Is not interfering in a police investigation. Had I been interfering? I hadn't been poking my nose into the murder, just into what had happened to my money. Though the Italian and the angry blonde did make two good suspects.

Peretti stuffed the handkerchief into his pocket. "Her?" He looked me up and down, his expression dismissive. "No, not that scrawny thing."

I straightened. "Hey!" If he was going to be like that, he could move to the top of my suspect list.

"I meant the blond she-demon inside," Peretti continued, motioning toward the realty. "She moved into my house without permission."

The detective cocked his head. "Now did she?" he asked, his voice muffled through the mask. "And what exactly are you doing here, Ms. Beanblossom?"

"Not interfering in a murder investigation!"

Detective Chase raised a brow. "Excuse me?"

Heh, heh. "Um, I rented my building from this company. The bank told me Reince cashed my check yesterday. I came to find out if maybe he'd left my money here."

"And I suppose you told them all about poor Mr. Briggs's untimely death."

Uh, oh. My gaze shifted to a poplar. A small brown bird hopped in its circle of shade. "Um, was I not supposed to do that?"

"All right then, I guess you've done enough damage. You can go."

"But... was my cash found at Reince's home?"

"No. You sure you don't have it?"

My jaw tightened. He thought I'd killed Reince to get my money back. I made a show of patting my pockets, rummaging in my purse. "Gee, no. Because I didn't kill Reince and take it."

"That's a relief. Now run along."

That was a little patronizing. But I was leaving anyway, so I smiled tightly and speed-walked down the street.

This was turning into a *really* bad day.

Nauseated, I returned to the farmers' market. Narrow flags snapped from the tops of stands in the warm ocean breeze. Shoppers in shorts and tank tops crowded the pier, their footsteps a hollow, arrhythmic drumbeat on the wooden planks.

I had to tell my grandfather about the building. But the thought of letting him down when he'd done so much – raising me when my parents were finding themselves at some new age commune, lending me money to fill the gap in my financing, rescuing me... I looked down, and for a moment I swear I saw childish legs ending in a pair of white shoes. And then the vision vanished, and I was looking at my own drag-queen-sized feet.

I walked past a stall selling white and purple cauliflower in short, slatted baskets, and my stomach twisted. And then there was my grandfather's heart. He wouldn't be worried about the money – he knew I'd pay him back - but he'd be furious with the realtor.

I was furious at myself. Why had I trusted Reince?

If I didn't get that payment back... My hands fisted.

Before I'd dreamed of a handsome prince, I'd dreamed of my own tearoom. A place of comfort. Doing what I loved. Independence. I could almost taste the scones, smell the brewing tea, and my heart ached with longing.

The accordion player drifted past. He played a sour note, and my fantasy evaporated.

I can do this. I inhaled deeply. I'd get the money back... somehow. I might have been conned, but the money I'd given Reince wasn't necessarily gone for good. Reince was dead. He couldn't have spent the cash *that* quickly. My face warmed at the uncharitable thought.

I stopped in front of my stall.

Gramps snoozed in the folding chair, his fingers laced over his broad stomach. A duckling nestled between his hands and chest.

Affection surged through me. I loved this man. How could I disappoint him with my mistake? "Gramps?"

He snorted and jerked upright. The duckling scrambled for balance, its unformed wings flapping helplessly.

"I'm awake!"

"Even the fish could hear you snoring," Tomas said on the other side of the tent canvas.

I worked to smooth my expression, which I guessed was somewhere between wanting to laugh and cry. "What's with the duckling?" I looked around the market. The little girl and her father were gone.

Gramps blinked. "Peking?"

"What?"

"Peking Duck," Gramps said. "He imprinted on me after I fed him that damn blueberry. Apparently, blueberries are like catnip to ducklings."

"It's a she," Tomas shouted.

"Fine, she," Gramps hollered back. "I had to buy the stupid thing. It wouldn't leave me alone, and a seagull kept trying to eat it."

Tomas pulled back the canvas flap that separated our booths. "How'd it go at your new building?" His brown eyes crinkled with concern. "Your grandfather told me there was a little problem."

And that was the moment. All I had to do was tell Gramps what had happened.

Or I could fix the "little problem" and *then* tell him. I swallowed. "Um, okay. You know. Nothing's ever quite what you expect when you move in."

Gramps laughed, the duckling jiggling on his stomach. "The course of business ownership never runs smooth. That's Shakespeare. Roughly."

A silver-haired man strolled to my table and eyed the copper bowls mounded with tea. "Have you got mint tea?" he asked, saving me from further explanation.

I dealt with the customer, and Gramps migrated to his and Tomas's booth of fiery pain.

We closed at four. My grandfather helped me take down my stand and load everything into a pushcart. I trundled it to my Mazda.

Police tape fluttered near the dumpster, where Reince's body had lain. A ponytailed woman in what looked like a white hazmat suit examined the crime scene. Uniformed police stood guard nearby.

I rubbed my face, remembering last weekend's CSI binge watch. What sort of trace evidence had I left when I'd found Reince's corpse?

Unimportant.

Shaken, I drove toward home, along winding treelined streets, the ocean glinting through breaks in the eucalyptus trees. I pulled into the driveway beside my sunshine yellow bungalow and slowed to a halt in front of the side yard gate. Above it, jasmine wound up the trellis.

A circular saw buzzed. Frowning, I stepped from the car into the gravel driveway. The full force of the noise struck me, and I flinched.

Fantastic. My new neighbor must be remodeling.

Rubbing my forehead, I trudged up the wooden steps to my front door and let myself in. Bamboo floors, soothing blue walls, and white crown molding. The bungalow had been my haven for three years now, when I'd started renting it from Tomas.

The saw screeched through the walls, drilling directly into my brain.

I gritted my teeth, dropped my purse on the dining room table and pulled out the business plan for the tearoom. The cover stared back at me. It was a watercolor I'd painted of the exterior, complete with swinging signboard that read: *Beanblossom's.*

A headache hammered at the back of my eyeballs, and my eyes warmed. I rubbed them ferociously. My dream couldn't be dead. Not yet.

Feet dragging, I walked into the cheerful blue kitchen and reheated some Mexican food. While the microwave hummed, I walked inside the pantry — my pride and joy. Drying herbs from my garden hung from ceiling racks. One shelved wall was lined with metal canisters of herbs. I opened a tin of dried mint and inhaled its crisp scent. I was *meant* to mix tea blends. Somehow, I'd make the tearoom happen.

The microwave dinged. I retrieved my plate and poured myself a glass of iced tea — my own blend of rosemary and horsetail (great for hair and skin).

I walked into the living room. And even though I felt like pulling the curtains and huddling on the couch with a bottle of wine and a box of tissues, the day was too beautiful to ignore. I opened the French door to the deck.

The roar of the saw made me take an involuntary step backward. I shut the door and leaned my forehead against a cool glass pane. Clearly, I should have stuck with my first instinct. But my instincts had never been good.

I drew the curtains, uncorked a bottle of wine, and flopped onto my couch. Turning on my TV, I slipped my headset over my ears. Soon I was killing Nazi zombies with Razzzor, the owner of the tech company I used to work at. After selling out to Microsoft, he spent his days gaming, getting analyzed and being rich.

"DIE NAZI SCUM!!!" I blasted an SS zombie horde and took down half a ruined church in the process.

"Watch it," Razzzor bellowed in my ears. "You nearly dropped that wall on me."

"Sorry," I muttered. "It's been a day."

"What's up?"

"It looks like..." My breathing turned ragged. "I think a realtor conned me out of a lot of money, my savings."

"I sensed something was wrong."

"Sensed?"

"My therapist says I need to show more empathy. What's really bothering you?"

"What's bothering me is without that money, my tearoom is DOA. On your right!" I shot a zombie, and it tumbled from the window of a French bistro.

"So, get the money back."

So much for empathy. "I can't," I snarled. "The realtor's dead."

"Whoa. Seriously? Nine o'clock!"

A zombie emerged from a pile of rubble and exploded.

"Where are you in all this?" he asked.

I lowered my head, recognizing more therapist-speak. "I can't go back to..."

"Working for me?" He laughed. "We did pretty well."

And that had been a once-in-a-lifetime stroke of luck. It wouldn't happen again.

"Just start over," he said.

A despairing sound escaped my throat. He had no idea how hard it was to earn the kind of money I'd just lost in a day. "I'd budgeted all my savings plus some money my grandfather had lent me for the tearoom. Losing six months' rent puts an impossible hole in my funding. I can't just start over, unless I can find a new location that doesn't require upfront rent *and* that's half the cost. Plus, I have to pay my grandfather back. Worse, I'm a suspect in Reince's – the realtor's – murder."

"Oh." He was silent for a while. "Do you need—"

"No." I was not going to borrow money from Razzzor. Bad enough I'd tapped my grandfather.

"Okay, but you know I'm here for you. And seriously, how bad can it be?"

"Right," I said dully.

But liberating Europe from the vile undead had eased some of the pain. The urge to throw heirloom tomatoes at my neighbor's house had passed, and the rough edge of panic from the morning's imbroglio had dulled.

Because Razzzor was sort of right. There was always a bright side. I mean, things couldn't get worse.

Right?

CHAPTER FOUR

MY NEIGHBOR'S BUZZ SAW jolted me out of bed early the next morning. Nerves officially jangled, I showered and slipped into white jeans and a matching tank. I grabbed an earring from my dresser.

The saw screeched. My hand jerked, and I stabbed my own earlobe. "Gagh!"

Swearing, I rummaged in the bathroom for a pair of earplugs and stuffed them into my ears.

The sound faded, and my shoulders relaxed. Then I remembered I was a suspect in a murder investigation, and pain crept up the back of my neck.

"I'm innocent," I said out loud. The cops would figure that out.

Because the day is always better when you start it with dessert, I decided to bake orange scones. Their flecks of orange zest never failed to cheer me up. And if I grated the orange and squished the butter into the dry mixture with more force than was absolutely necessary, well...

I glared out the kitchen window at the redwood fence blocking my neighbor's yard.

The scones totally deserved it.

Using my trusty pizza cutter (those babies are versatile), I sliced the dough into triangles, arranged them on a cookie sheet, and slid them into the oven.

I washed my hands and opened the pantry's white, bi-fold doors. What tea did I want with my orange scones?

I studied the shelves of metal canisters, the herbs dangling from the ceiling. Earl Grey would pair well with the scones, or maybe Lady Grey, but I felt like something brighter this morning.

I lifted bundles of dried spearmint and sage from their hooks on the ceiling. Returning to the kitchen, I set a pot of water on the stove to boil and retrieved a clear teapot from the glass-fronted cupboards. I crumbled the leaves between my fingers and dropped a pinch of spearmint and an equal-sized pinch of sage into the glass infuser. The crisp scent of the herbs drifted up to me, and I inhaled. *Heaven.*

The sweet, tangy smell of the baking scones filled the kitchen. Bowl in one hand, I whisked the glaze and wandered to the kitchen window.

A hummingbird paused beside the jasmine pouring over the high fence. It flicked its shimmering blue tail and zipped off.

I smiled. It was going to be a gorgeous day.

Hey. I wasn't annoyed at my neighbor anymore. I wasn't Zen enough to remove the earplugs, but still. The baking, contemplating what tea paired with orange scones, hand mixing herbs... I was *meant* to run a tearoom. Wild, glorious confidence zinged through me. It was going to happen. It *had* to happen.

The water boiled. The oven dinged. The scones popped with bits of orange-like confetti. I drizzled one with a zigzag of glaze. Then I added an extra heaping dollop for good measure. I'd done a lot of walking yesterday, so the calories wouldn't hurt.

Mouth watering, I plated a scone, balanced a mug of tea atop the plate, and walked out to my deck and a glorious California spring morning. The saw was only a faint background noise, and I grinned.

I could adapt, just like I'd adapt to whatever came next with my tearoom. I'd make my tearoom work. Somehow.

The sun warmed my shoulders as I ambled down the tanbark path. Passing lavender and sagebrush and my raised herb garden, I slowed at a wooden table and chairs beneath a blossoming dogwood tree. This was my sanctuary, and the knots in my shoulders loosened.

I brushed a scattering of white and pink petals off the table and set down my things. Because of the shade from my neighbor's ginormous eucalyptus trees, my dogwood bloomed later than most. But when it did, it was spectacular.

I sat in the surprisingly comfy wooden chair and leaned my head back, looking at the webwork of branches, inhaling the light, sweet scent of the blossoms.

The faint whine of the saw faded, stopped.

I sank deeper against the chair. *Ah.*

A massive cloud of acrid, black exhaust rolled over the redwood fence and across the table.

I leapt to my feet, coughing. My leg banged the table and the mug tipped, splattering tea across my scone. "Really? Really!"

Yanking out my earplugs, I stormed to the fence and banged my fist on the rough wood. "What's going on over there?"

"Construction," a rough, masculine voice shouted back. "What do you think?"

I sputtered. "A cloud of smoke just rolled through my yard."

"Do you think I'm happy about it? Something's wrong with my saw. It's stopped working."

The gods were smiling. "What a shame," I said with patent insincerity.

"It is for you, because any delay means the build's going to take longer."

"Build?" I bleated. That sounded like more than a simple fix-it job. "I thought you were remodeling."

"I'm modernizing the first floor and adding on a second."

"A second floor?" I asked, dismayed. The day was cursed. If my neighbor's house was two stories, would he be able to see into my yard? "Isn't there a height ordinance or something?"

"Oh," he said darkly, "you're one of those."

"One of what?"

"I've got all my permits, don't you worry."

"I'm not worried," I said. Did I sound worried? Frazzled, frustrated, and fractured, yes. Worried, no.

I bent to a knothole and peered through, catching an eyeful of his jeans — specifically, his well-formed crotch. A wash of heat flushed my cheeks, and I jerked upright.

"Nothing I can do about that," he said. "Construction is noisy. You'll just have to live with it."

What a... Oooh! Unable to come up with an argument – since he was right – I stormed to the dogwood tree, grabbed my mess of uneaten scone and undrunk tea, and retreated to my bungalow.

Rattled, I paced between the white brick fireplace and my dining table. The calming blue-painted walls failed to sooth, the racket from next door making my fingers twitch. Morning sunlight streamed past the curtained French windows. Beyond the glass, pink and white petals drifted lazily from the dogwood tree.

I gazed longingly at my gaming headphones, discarded on the ivory couch facing the TV. Killing zombie Nazis was satisfying, but it wouldn't save my business.

Detective Chase had seemed more interested in who'd killed Reince than where my savings had gone. In the rock-paper-scissors game of police priorities, murder beat theft. To Chase, I wasn't a victim. I was a suspect.

But what if the person who had killed Reince *had* also taken the money? If I could find my money, I'd solve two problems – save my tearoom and prove my innocence.

The question was, how? I paused and glared at my grandmother's collection of teacups on top of the entertainment center. And how could the realty not have known what Reince was up to? Someone must know *something*. My savings hadn't just evaporated into thin air.

Lacking inspiration, and because that damned saw was back in action, I shrugged into a pink blazer, grabbed my matching purse, and walked downtown.

I stopped in front of a brunch restaurant called the Wild Thyme and pretended to scan the menu in the window. It reflected the cheery pastel buildings behind me and my own figure. I smoothed my hair, which was coming loose from its ponytail.

I'd seen Reince in the Wild Thyme every morning for a month. I'd even met with him here a couple times myself. Maybe someone in the restaurant knew something.

I grabbed a morning paper from a gum-spackled kiosk and pushed through the glass and metal doors. My grandfather and I had eaten here often, and I recognized the tanned waitress headed toward me now.

Her straw-colored hair was done up in a loose bun. She wore a Hawaiian shirt, black slacks, and a green apron that matched the color of the carpet. She smiled. "You alone?"

I glanced to the section where Reince and I had sat, talking over the building. "Can I sit over there?" I pointed at a two-top jammed against a big, square window facing the street.

"Sure." She got me settled. The morning sun angled down the wooded hill and reflected off the napkin holders, the polished table.

Reaching across the table, I tugged down the blinds. I shrugged out of my lightweight pink blazer and hung it over the back of my chair. Spreading the newspaper on the table, I scanned its pages.

The article on Reince was tiny, jammed into a bottom corner of the front page. I guessed it hadn't made the headlines because the article didn't label his death murder. The only new info I gleaned was that he'd moved to San Borromeo ten weeks ago. It also confirmed my suspicion that he'd died the night before I'd discovered his corpse.

My fingers crumpled the paper. But it had to be murder, or else why had that detective questioned me so thoroughly? And what had caused that strange, dark bruise at the front of the realtor's neck?

A Hispanic waitress, her dark hair coiled in a bun, bustled to my table. "Good morning, Abigail!"

"Hi, Antonia." I smiled and folded the paper. "How's it going?" Antonia was the sort of person you just wanted to hug for no reason. The friendliest person in San Borromeo, she was nearly always wearing one of the rude t-shirts her multitude of nephews gave her on birthdays and Christmas. She was too nice to tell them to stop. Today's said: ZOMBIES EAT BRAINS - YOU'LL BE OKAY.

"I just got back from skiing at Lake Tahoe," she said. "It was gorgeous. There's six feet of snow up there, easy." Her shoulders hunched with delight.

Since I was more of a hot-chocolate-in-the-lodge person, I smiled and nodded.

"What can I get for you today, my dear?" She whipped a notepad from the black apron around her waist.

"Eggs Florentine and an iced tea, please."

"Anything else?"

"Um, this may sound a little strange, but there is something." I shifted in my seat. "You know that realtor, Reince Briggs? I think he usually came here in the mornings?"

"Oh, yeah. He's so sweet. But I haven't seen him yet today."

I flattened the newspaper in front of me and slid it toward the waitress. "Then you haven't heard. He's dead."

"What?" Paling, she grabbed the paper off the table. Her face contorted, and she took a quick step back, bumping into a passing waiter. "Oh, my God. I can't believe... Oh, my God."

Guilty heat rose to my cheeks. "I'm sorry. I didn't mean to..." *Ugh.* Clearly, I'd dropped a bomb on Antonia. But was this natural distress at a customer's death, or something more? "Did you know him well?" I asked cautiously.

"Yes. I mean, no. He ate here every day. I wondered why he was late this morning." Her breath hitched. "Now I know why."

"He was a friendly guy," I said, the corners of my mouth drawing down.

The jerk had been friendly enough to sucker me out of a big chunk of my savings. Some people had the touch – you just wanted to be around them, wanted them to like you. Reince was one of those people. I should have suspected something when I'd caught myself wondering why he hadn't gone into politics.

"This is terrible." She shook herself. "Sorry, what kind of bread do you want with your eggs?"

"I'll have today's muffin."

She scribbled the order on her pad, nodded, and hurried to the kitchen.

Pretending to read the paper, I wracked my brain for a way to pick up the conversational thread that didn't make me sound like a total jerk.

She whizzed back to the table with my iced tea. "Here you go."

"Thanks." Gazing at the paper, I tapped the newspaper article. "You know, this is weird."

The waitress paused. "How so?"

"The way they describe Reince's death is so vague. You don't think he could have been killed, do you?"

Her brown eyes widened. "N—" Her expression grew pensive.

"What's wrong?" I leaned forward, bracing my elbows on the table.

"I really shouldn't say. It's nothing."

It had looked like something to me. "Were there any people who came into the restaurant to meet him regularly?"

She edged away from the table, shaking her head. "Oh, I really don't think it's right for me to say."

"The thing is, I gave him some money," I admitted.

Her thick brows drew together.

"A lot of money," I continued. "My savings. I was going to use it to open a tearoom."

"Oh, no!"

"Worrying about money sounds terrible under the circumstances, but—"

The bell over the front door jingled. Antonia glanced toward it, nodded and smiled at the new customer.

Involuntarily, I looked over my shoulder. The Amazon from the realty yesterday stood in front of the register. She wore wide-legged gray slacks of some soft, swishy material and a sleeveless, silvery tunic. A long, tasseled necklace hung beneath a pair of reading glasses on a beaded string.

If anyone knew anything, it had to be someone from the real estate office. I realized I was staring and looked away.

The woman spoke to the hostess and sat at the window table in front of mine. The waitress sped off. I met the Amazon's gaze.

Ignoring me, she set her reading glasses on her nose, picked up the menu and looked it over.

I cleared my throat. She studied her menu.

"Excuse me?" I asked.

No response.

"Hello?" I asked more loudly.

An elderly man at a nearby table scowled. "The waitress will be back when she gets back. Hold your horses."

My face heated. "I'm not..." I scooted my chair back and walked to the woman's table.

In a nearby booth, a man in a baseball cap and dark glasses hunched low behind his menu.

"Excuse me," I said to the woman.

She looked up and frowned. "Yes?" she asked in a voice I reserved for telemarketers.

"Hi. We met yesterday? At the realtors'? How is Florence doing?"

Her angular face creased with puzzlement, then cleared. "Oh, yes. I remember you. You arrived at a bad time."

"That's me," I said, "mistress of bad timing."

She didn't smile.

"Sorry," I said. That joke had been bad timing, proving my point. "Reince. It must have been a terrible shock."

Heat prickled my back. I glanced over my shoulder. The man in the ball cap raised his menu higher. Sunlight glittered off his beaded bracelet.

She removed her glasses, her gaze running from my white tennies to the top of my head. "You knew Reince?"

"He was my realtor. For the 2304 Laurel building?"

Her brow puckered. "His body was found behind that building."

"Yes." I knitted my hands together. "I was the one who found him."

There was a choking sound behind me. I ignored it.

Her expression turned sympathetic, her shoulders relaxing. "How awful for you. What did you say your name was?"

"I guess I didn't. I'm Abigail Beanblossom."

"I'm Diana Archer."

"Archer — are you married to the realtor, Cyrus Archer?"

"He's meeting me here." She checked her watch. "Eventually. Possibly never. Are you dining alone?"

"Um. Yes."

"Since I most likely am as well, would you like to join me?"

Oh, yes. I would. "Thanks." I grabbed my purse, blazer, and iced tea and took the chair opposite. I squinted into the light.

"Is the sun bothering you?" She rose before I could respond, found the string to the blinds, and lowered them. "There. Better?"

"Yes, thanks." I smoothed the front of my loose, white tank. "Do you work at the real estate office?"

"Are you kidding? My husband and I would kill each other." Her smile faded. "A turn of phrase that's less funny since Reince's death."

"Did you know Reince well? The paper said he'd moved here around two months ago."

"He began working with Cyrus two months ago," she corrected. "I met him before then, at a charity function on the pier."

"The domestic violence fundraiser?" I asked. The town had closed the pier for the event.

"Yes, were you there?" She leaned forward and fixed me with a piercing look. "I would rather die than be a victim. And it simply isn't enough for us to talk about these things, you know, we women must *do* something."

"I agree, but no, I missed that one." I'd walked past that night and admired the paper lanterns, their light rippling off the water, but I hadn't been invited.

She relaxed against her seat. "When I learned Reince was a realtor looking for work, I suggested he meet my husband. The business has been growing so fast. You know how it is in the California real estate market."

I nodded. Too much money. Too many people. Too few houses.

"At the time," she continued, "it just made sense to bring the two together. I had no idea..." Her gaze clouded, and she coiled her tasseled necklace around one finger. She shook herself, the necklace slipping to her chest. "Have you completed your transaction on the building?"

"I thought I had, but there's a problem."

A waitress bustled past.

"Oh?" Diana canted her head.

"When I arrived yesterday morning to start work, I met another person who also thought he'd rented it, a guy named Hyperion Night."

Behind me, ice rattled in a glass.

"Quite frequently," she said, "these larger office buildings are rented to multiple tenants. You know — one tenant will get so many offices and others the rest."

"No," I said slowly. Hadn't she heard Reince was a conman yet? The detective must have spoken with her by now. "I rented the entire building."

She propped her elbows on the table, her chin on her hands. "How strange. And Reince was found dead behind that very building. What do you think he was doing there?"

"I wish I knew. He wasn't there because of me. I'd already paid him six months' rent in advance."

She raised a brow. "Six months? That's unusual."

"It's an unusual building. The owner let it sit empty for decades. And it's in a great location."

"And this Hyperion... Did he also pay six months in advance?"

"Three," I said heavily. What a sucker I'd been. Six months' rent! I'd been so greedy for that building, Reince must have smelled me coming from miles away. And now I might lose everything.

I straightened. Hyperion had said he'd also paid Reince money up front. Was that why Reince had been in the parking lot that night? To collect Hyperion's payment? Had Hyperion learned the truth about the building and killed him over it?

I glanced over my shoulder. The man in the baseball hat, who I was 99% sure was Hyperion, was gone. I rubbed my palms on the thighs of my white jeans.

"What is it?" she asked.

"Oh. Nothing." I smiled. "Freaked out and panicking is my natural state."

Her forehead creased. "That's no way to live."

I'd been kidding and opened my mouth to say so. But the waitress arrived and set down a cup of coffee.

"I'll take the fruit crepe," Diana said. "And not to confuse things, but we're eating together now. Separate checks."

"No problem," Antonia said. She wrote down the order and left.

"Do you come here often?" I sipped my tea.

"Why do you ask?" she said sharply.

"The waitress dropped off the coffee before you ordered. I mean, I know Reince practically used this place as his office." Which was strange, because he had an office with Cyrus. Of course, if he was trying to keep his shenanigans from Cyrus, doing business elsewhere made sense.

"I've always enjoyed this restaurant," she said, expression neutral.

"This must be hard on all of you, with him and Florence being such good friends."

She arched a brow. "Where did you get that impression?"

"I thought Florence might faint when she learned of his death." I'd also thought fainting had gone out of style with corsets and carriages. Had Florence been acting? But why?

"Florence is easily wounded. Her husband died recently, and she's only just gotten back on her feet."

And now I felt like a slug. "I'm sorry to hear that. I didn't know."

"Why would you? Florence keeps to herself. But we all knew she hadn't stopped mourning her husband. The office is like a family, my family. Though I don't work with my husband, I do have my own workspace there. And Reince's death..." She blinked rapidly, her knuckles whitening on the coffee mug.

I looked out the window to give her a moment. A purple VW Bug drifted slowly past, surfboards strapped to its roof.

"But about your little problem," she said, blowing out her breath, "what did Florence have to say?"

"She didn't know about the double rental until yesterday. But she said she'd look into it. I'm waiting to hear what she learns."

She set her mug on the table. "But that's not good enough. You must be crazy with worry, especially after that big down payment. Why don't I speak with my husband and see what I can do?"

"Could you?" I asked, hope rising in my chest.

"I don't see why not. When Cyrus and I first married, and he was getting started in the business, I did my share of reception work for him. I know where Florence keeps the paperwork."

"Thanks." I roughly tightened my ponytail. "This has been awful. The police told me Reince was a conman."

"What? That's ridiculous. It's typical, blame-the-victim mentality."

"They showed me mugshots. And I overheard the argument between that Italian man and his tenant—"

"Mr. Peretti and Ms. Halifax." She nodded, expression owlish.

"Right," I said. "What was that about?"

"I've no idea." She sipped her coffee. "But I'm sure it's a mistake, just like your little problem."

It wasn't a *little* problem. It had taken me luck and a lifetime to save that money. And if my grandfather hadn't chipped in...

But I leaned closer, bracing my elbows on the table. "If I don't have that building, or if I can't get my savings back, it's a stake through the heart of my business."

She cocked her head. "I hope you didn't tell the police that. They'll think it's a motive for murder."

I forced my grip on my iced tea to loosen. "Reince's death hasn't solved my problems. It's made them worse."

She gestured with one hand. "That was poorly worded. I simply meant that I'm certain it will all work out, and you don't need to do anything drastic."

"I would never do anything as crazy as kill someone over a tearoom."

"Of course, you wouldn't," she soothed. "You're obviously a sensible young woman."

Harrumph. I could be a *little* crazy. I was starting a new business, after all. "It was a lot of money. I probably shouldn't have paid so much up front, but..." But over eager and desperate, I'd let myself be fooled.

"Then trust in the universe."

Bile burned the back of my throat. *Trust?* She sounded like my absentee parents.

The universe wasn't going to get me my money back. But deep down I feared the universe *was* telling me something – that the money had come too easily, I didn't deserve it, and so it had been taken away.

We ate breakfast and made awkward conversation until the waitress brought us separate bills.

A tall, barrel-chested man in a business suit strode up behind her. His brown hair was graying at the temples. "Sorry I'm late." His blue eyes blazed in his tanned face. He bent and pecked her cheek.

"I figured you would be," Diana said, "so I invited Abigail to join me. Abigail, this is my husband, Cyrus. Or do you two already know each other? She was a client of Reince's."

He straightened. "Ah. And were you, er, satisfied with his services?"

"He rented me the 2304 Laurel Building. Reince also rented it to another man. The police think he conned us both."

"Ah."

"Is that all you can say?" Diana asked. "How can you *help* her?"

He shuffled his feet. "I'm not sure. Reince and I shared an office and a receptionist, but our businesses were otherwise separate."

My brow pinched. Reince had told me he and Cyrus were partners. But he'd also told me I could rent that building for a tearoom. If I had to decide which of them was a liar, I picked Reince.

"I doubt the community will see it that way," his wife said quietly. "You shared an office."

His complexion turned a shade lighter. "I'll look into it," he said, voice taut.

What impact would Reince's con have on the business? If Cyrus had found out what Reince had been up to, could he have killed him? Then he'd seen my money, and wanting to make it look like a robbery, or just wanting the money, taken it? And what about the receptionist? She'd worked with Reince. What if she'd been in on the scam?

Diana turned to her husband and launched into a longish discussion of an upcoming fundraiser for battered wives.

I'd become a third wheel, and I muttered goodbye, walking to the register to pay my share. I rummaged in my wallet and pulled out some bills.

Antonia hurried behind the register and rang me up. "You said you gave Reince some money?" she asked quietly.

I nodded. "Yeah," I said, depressed. "Most of my savings." But Gramps was getting his money back, no matter what. "It's kind of freaking me out."

She looked around. "He's got a condo over on Decatur Street," she said in a low voice.

I paused, hand in my wallet. "You mean Reince?"

She nodded.

"How do you know?"

Antonia flushed.

"Oh," I said, understanding dawning. She knew because she'd been inside. And she'd been inside, because... My face warmed. "Er, thanks."

I paid and walked out. Antonia had taken a risk letting me know about her relationship with Reince, and I was glad she trusted me. But knowing about his condo didn't really help. It wasn't like I could go to Reince's condo and break in. Though considering all the bone-headed moves I'd made recently...

I swallowed, the eggs Florentine doing unpleasant things in my stomach. Maybe breaking into that condo wasn't such a bad idea after all?

CHAPTER FIVE

BUT OF COURSE, I didn't break into Reince's condo. It was broad daylight, and I was no cat burglar. So to torture myself (because I can never get enough of that), I walked to the building on Laurel and gazed morosely at the blue door.

Tourists trooped in and out of the art gallery opposite, their heels clicking on the intricate brickwork. Whirligigs rattled and spun, glittering on the pavement in front of the shop next door.

I brushed my fingers across the elaborate doorknob and its inset poppy design. The metal was cool, though the morning had already grown warm, thick with the scents of sweat and suntan oil. If I couldn't rent the building, maybe the owner would let me buy the doorknob?

My reflection blurred in the dusty window, blocked with brown paper. In my pink jacket and white jeans, I looked like a strawberry ice cream cone.

A ripping sound. The brown paper inside the windows peeled away. On the opposite side of the glass, Hyperion's bark-colored eyes met mine.

He flung open the door. "What are you doing here?" He wore a navy t-shirt and elegant trousers. It was mildly irritating that he could make a t-shirt look sophisticated.

"You were spying on me in Wild Thyme." I pointed at the beaded bracelet circling his wrist.

"Was not."

"Was too. What are you doing in here?" I stood straighter, as if the extra quarter inch could make me more intimidating.

"Prepping, of course."

My mouth pinched with annoyance. Neither of us had the building. Why was he measuring for drapes? "So, you think this building is yours," I said flatly.

"Why wouldn't it be? It was in the cards, and the cards don't lie."

"Reince rented the building to us both, and he's dead."

"It's tragic, and I sent flowers to the realty. But aside from that, I'm not sure what I can do."

Damn. I should have sent flowers to the realty.

The massive tabby stalked across the concrete floor. His tail swished, menacing.

"I don't get it," I said. "Have you learned something new?"

He raised his nose. "World card, remember?"

"Did the World card tell you Reince also rented a house to someone without informing the owner?" I shifted the purse on my shoulder. "The police must have told you he was running a Brooklyn Bridge-type scam. Who knows how many people he conned?"

Hyperion's olive skin paled. He tossed his head. "I've examined all the angles, and in the end, whatever Reince was up to doesn't matter. The cards say this is my studio, and the cards are never wrong." He patted my shoulder. "Sorry, kid. I know you wanted the place. But this isn't necessarily the death of your dream. Look at it as a new beginning."

Kid? We had to be the same age or close to it. "It isn't a... We were scammed!"

The cat rubbed against my jeans, depositing brown and gold fur on the white fabric.

"The universe works in mysterious ways," he said. "Wretched, illogical and discordant ways, but mysterious."

If one more person quoted the universe at me... "And denial ain't just a river in Egypt. We can swap clichés all day, but that doesn't change the fact Reince illegally rented the building to us both, and our money has vanished—"

"I feel your pain."

I rolled my eyes. "Oh, come on."

"Look, I can't think that way, and neither should you. We won't get what I want if we dwell on the negative." He pinched his middle fingers and thumbs together and shut his eyes.

"We won't get what *you* want?"

"So, I am envisioning my Tarot studio. I am in my Tarot studio and surrounded by a bright, sparkly light of positivity. I am in the vortex."

Defeated, I crossed my arms over my chest. I was only arguing because I was mad he was inside and I wasn't. That wasn't getting me anywhere.

"Now," he said, "what were *you* doing in Wild Thyme?"

"None of your—"

"Excuse me!" A short balding man in a pinstripe suit stopped beside me on the sidewalk. Tufts of gray hair sprouted from his ears. "What do you think you're doing?" He huffed, pointing at Hyperion.

"He's in the vortex," I said.

"And *she's* coming to terms with a painful lesson about letting go," Hyperion said. "I, however, am revitalizing this fantastically abandoned building to become the first and only Tarot studio in San Borromeo."

"I think not, young man." He brandished his leather briefcase. "You have no right to be in this building."

"But I rented it," Hyperion said.

"So did I," I said.

"Both under fraudulent circumstances." He reached inside his breast pocket and drew out two business cards, handed them to me and Hyperion. Mine read: WILLIAM BONNET, ESQUIRE. "I represent the owner. Cyrus Archer called me to inquire about the status of the building. Imagine my surprise when I learned this building had been rented to you two without my permission. You'll both have to vacate the premises immediately."

Hyperion gaped like a koi fish that had just gotten stepped on.

"You represent the owner?" I asked, clutching at straws. "Would he like to rent the building? It's been sitting vacant for years, doing nothing." What was I saying? I had no money to pay for it now – not unless I got my savings back from Reince. But I floundered on, possibility making me reckless. "He must want to earn some income off it."

"It's not my fault the building's been vacant," the lawyer snapped. "It's been embroiled in a legal dispute. And that wasn't my fault either. The heirs were vultures," he muttered.

On the sidewalk, a golden retriever trotted past. His bronzed owner jogged behind him, leash in hand.

"Heirs?" I asked. Maybe they'd want to rent me the building.

"The point is," the lawyer said, "the estate's only recently been settled. Finally."

"I want to rent it," Hyperion and I said in unison.

The Tarot reader grimaced. "Who's the owner? I'd be happy to discuss this with him or her in person."

The lawyer's nostrils flared. "You can't. He's traveling. I told you, I'm responsible for the building."

"I want to rent it," we said again. Grimaced again.

"I'm not even certain how a property like this would be valued." The lawyer rubbed his hand over his balding head, slick with sweat. "The bottom line is, I must do what's best for my client."

"Wouldn't renting the building be best?" I asked.

"Yes, and I mean to get an optimal price," the lawyer said, his tone quelling.

I dug in my purse for my card and handed it to him. "Please let me know when you make a decision. I'd hoped to turn this building into a tearoom."

He stared at my card. "A tearoom, eh?" One corner of his mouth curved upward, and his gaze took on a wistful air. "I suppose you'll have scones? I could kill for a good scone."

"Yes to the scones. And crumpets and sandwiches and fresh jam."

"I intend to turn this into a Tarot studio," Hyperion said.

Mr. Bennet snorted and turned to me. "Have you a business plan for your tearoom?"

I wrenched it from my purse. "I do. With financial projections prepared by a CPA. You can keep it if you want. As you can see from the balance sheet, I have a strong cash reserve..." My mouth went dry. Or I'd *had* a reserve fund, until I'd given Reince six months' rent up front.

The lawyer gazed approvingly at my blazer. "A business plan *and* dressed for success."

Thank heavens I'd kept my blazer on. I might look like melting ice cream, but the white jeans almost looked like slacks.

The tabby chose that moment to attempt to climb my leg. Wincing, I unhooked his claws from my thigh.

"And a cat lover as well." The lawyer smiled. "I own a pair of Scottish folds."

"It's my cat," Hyperion said.

"And you let it wander about on the street," the lawyer said, "accosting strangers?"

A bead of sweat trickled down Hyperion's brow. "A Tarot studio is perfect for this area," he said rapidly, motioning to the art gallery. Paintings of beach scenes winked from its windows. "Not even Santa Cruz has anything like what I'm planning. There's tremendous interest in Tarot and metaphysics in this area. I've already had inquiries from nearly a dozen Tarot readers."

"Fortune telling." The lawyer's face pinched. "I can assure you, that whatever I decide, I will not be leasing this building to a business engaged in illegal activities."

I winced. Even though I wanted to beat out Hyperion for the building, the lawyer was obviously prejudiced against Tarot. It wasn't fair. I felt a little bad for my competitor.

"It's not illegal." Hyperion rubbed his palms on the thighs of his charcoal slacks.

"Do you have a license?" the lawyer asked.

Hyperion swallowed, his Adam's apple bobbing. "Tarot readers don't need a license in San Borromeo."

"In other words, you're taking advantage of the loophole."

"It's not a loophole." He wiped his forehead. "You don't need a license in most parts of California."

"Have you got a business plan?" the lawyer asked.

"I... have a decorating plan," Hyperion said.

The lawyer folded his arms. "So, you really have no idea if your business will be a success or not."

Hyperion's nostrils flared. He drew back his shoulders. "Of course it will be a success."

The lawyer lifted a single, gray brow. "I suppose you read that in the tea leaves?"

"In the Tarot cards," Hyperion said. "Tarot is an extremely useful tool for self-development and reflection. The cards depict archetypes from our universal unconscious. They allow us to tap directly into our sub-conscious and superconscious knowledge."

Uncomfortable, I shifted my weight and stared at a shiny blue whirligig. I was starting to recognize the spiel.

The lawyer blew out his breath. "Well, I can't ignore two offers on this property. I'll review the going rate for comparable buildings and get back to you, Ms..." He consulted my card. "Beanblossom? You're not related to Frank Beanblossom by any chance?"

I nodded, my lips parting with cautious hope. "He's my grandfather. He helped me with the financials in the business plan."

The lawyer beamed. "A good man, your grandfather. Chock full of common sense. A real straight shooter. We were on the church board together."

"When he was treasurer?" I asked.

"Exactly! This gives me an excuse to renew our acquaintance."

The tabby rolled onto his back and batted the hem of my jeans.

"What about my offer?" Hyperion bleated.

"How much are you offering?" the lawyer asked.

"Whatever she's offering plus a hundred dollars a month." Hyperion thrust a business card into his hand.

"That's not fair." How could I top that? I couldn't afford a bidding war.

The lawyer glanced at the card, and his nose wrinkled. "Hm. I'll be in touch." He smiled at me. "Good afternoon, Ms. Beanblossom."

"Bye!" I waved as he dodged a brick planter box filled with impatiens and strode down the sidewalk.

Hyperion shook out his arms. "It doesn't matter," he muttered. "The cards have never failed me before. I'll get this building."

I sighed. "I'm sure everything will work out for the best." Or at least I hoped it would. Maybe there was a better place for the tearoom. Maybe—

"Yes, I'm sure you'll find somewhere else for your tearoom." The Tarot reader retreated inside the building and slammed the door.

The tabby gazed up at me from the brick walk and meowed. Its amber eyes seemed to glow.

The door opened.

Hyperion reached out, grabbed the cat, and vanished inside. He slammed the door, rattling the windows.

So, good side: my odds of getting the building had just increased. Bad side: with my upfront payment in the wind, I probably couldn't afford it anymore.

And I was starting to feel guilty. It wasn't Hyperion's fault he'd been suckered like me. I stiffened my spine. And it wasn't my fault if the lawyer thought Tarot readers were crooks. All's fair in love and business.

"What does he expect me to do? Just give up?" I asked no one, then realized I'd spoken aloud.

Sweating, I shrugged out of my blazer and looped it through the handles of my purse. I strode towards home and up the shady side of a winding street, past boutiques and restaurants filling with customers.

Maybe there *was* a way I could rent the building. I groaned. Who was I kidding? I knew those numbers backwards and forwards, and I needed to get my deposit back if I wanted to rent anything in San Borromeo.

I turned up a hill into a leafy residential neighborhood. The scent of eucalyptus leaves mingled with lavender. I walked past a picket fence.

A faint buzz echoed behind me. I stumbled over a bit of uneven sidewalk and climbed on.

The buzz intensified.

I turned. Compact homes and dusty cars lined the road. Beside me, bright pink bougainvillea covered a low fence.

Uneasy, I shifted the purse over my shoulder and kept walking.

Heat prickled the space between my shoulder blades, and I got the sudden notion I was being watched.

Heh. Crazy.

I looked over my shoulder.

No one lurked beside the cars lining the street. No one stared from the lush gardens.

I bit my bottom lip. My imagination was running wild, that was all.

The buzzing grew louder, like a swarm of angry bees. I scanned the cloudless sky. People did keep bees around here. But they wouldn't attack unless threatened. Usually.

I lengthened my strides and turned the corner onto my street. The buzz of a saw echoed from the house next to mine, and I relaxed. So that's what I'd been hearing.

Finding a body had made me paranoid. Not that paranoia was totally out of line. My realtor/conman was dead. Feeling freaked out was perfectly normal.

But no matter how I tried to rationalize it away, I couldn't shake the feeling someone was watching. I unlocked my door and hurried inside, because I also got the feeling that the watchfulness was laden with malice.

CHAPTER SIX

KEEPING AN EYE OUT for angry bees, after lunch I walked to Gino Peretti's house. Lately, I'd been doing a lot of huffing around town, but there was a method to my madness. I needed to walk off my nervous energy. I also wanted to know more about Ms. Halifax's experience with Reince, assuming Peretti hadn't managed to evict her yet. Plus, I hate gyms.

Peretti's address hadn't been hard to find. He was listed in the phone book someone insisted on leaving on my doorstep every year. I was glad now I hadn't thrown it away.

Good manners dictated phoning in advance. But I wanted to see how the element of surprise worked.

Peretti's house sat tucked high on a hill. Glimpses of the Pacific peeked between eucalyptus trees. The clapboard California bungalow was painted white with green trim. A triangular, stained glass window wedged beneath the pitched roof. Spiky succulents and cacti dotted the gravel yard and cast spear-like shadows.

Buzzing filled the air.

Muscles tightening, I glanced up. This wasn't my neighbor's saw. I was too far from home. But the sky was blue and bright and bee-free, so I edged open the low, wooden gate.

Steeling myself, I walked down the zigzag path and up the short flight of steps to the front door. A cactus lurking on a wicker table snagged my pink blazer, still slung over my purse.

Muttering a curse, I untangled the fabric and pressed the bell.

A dog yapped on the other side of the door. I waited.

The barking was steady and insistent, high-pitched and irritating. Above the yips, that mysterious buzzing persisted, setting my teeth on edge.

Bouncing on my heels, I scanned the cactus garden. Where on earth was that sound coming from? It seemed almost mechanical now, and somehow thinner. It wasn't nearly as powerful as the saw or other power tools my neighbor had woken me up with this morning.

The jerk.

I knocked again. On the other side of the paneled, front door, the barking grew frenetic.

A door slammed to my left, and I jumped.

A curvy woman emerged from the forest-green craftsman next door. Her wavy, mahogany hair was streaked with frost. "No one's home." She clutched a laptop to her broad chest.

I hurried down the steps and made my way through the cactus garden to the white-painted fence. "Thanks for letting me know. Do you have any idea when she'll be back?"

"You a friend of Peretti's?" The woman wore jeans and a tee the exact color as her house. Its deep v-neck exposed a strip of black bra.

"No."

"Good for you. He's a monster. Not that his tenant's much better." She grinned.

"Sorry?"

"Don't be sorry. You're not selling something, are you?"

"Um, no." I glanced around. "I'm in kind of a weird situation — like Peretti's tenant. There was some confusion with my rental, and then my realtor died..."

She set her laptop on the hood of the Jeep and braced one hand on the low fence. "You knew the ill-fated Reince Briggs?"

"Slightly." I winced. "I think he may have swindled me out of six months' rent."

"But that's wonderful!" She clapped her hands together and immediately looked contrite. "Sorry. It's not wonderful for you. I'm a writer. Name's Allyson." She reached across the fence, and we shook hands. "It's the only thing that makes living next door to that woman bearable," she said.

"Excuse me?" What did her name have to do with anything?

"For the conflict. Writing is conflict, and she gives me oodles of it. I plan on murdering her."

I edged away from the fence. Maybe coming here hadn't been the smartest idea.

She smiled and covered her mouth with one hand. "On paper, of course."

"Of course," I said faintly.

"So, what happened? Don't worry, if I use it, I'll change the details — your name and the way you look and your entire personality in fact. How were you swindled?"

I explained the double-rental disaster, discovering the body, the incident in the real estate office.

"You found his body? I suppose the police think you're a suspect. The person who finds the body is always a suspect."

"I hope not."

"And then he ran off with your money, ruining your dreams of opening a tearoom?"

"Well, not after he was dead." Could he have transferred my money to an overseas account? "So, the fictional me had no reason to kill him." The real me didn't either.

"That's what everyone in prison says." She cocked her head, assessing. "If you were one of my heroines, you'd be in water so hot right now it boiled."

"I'm sure I'll get the money back," I said less confidently.

Allyson shot me a pitying look. "Highly unlikely. In the first place, con artists know how to hide cash. Even if the police do find the money, think of all the other people Reince must owe, and the tangle around any inheritance. It will be years before you see that money, if ever. I know, because I once wrote a book about a situation a lot like yours, and you were the killer. Well, someone like you. I suppose the police dragged you in for questioning? Would the tearoom have wi-fi?"

I rubbed my cheek. "I don't... know. I don't think so." The buzzing seemed to waver, as if the invisible bees had grown uncertain of their queen's direction.

Anxious, I glanced at the cacti behind me.

"If it *didn't* have wi-fi," she said, "I'd be there every morning writing. I can't write at home. I keep getting distracted by the blasted internet."

I took another stab at controlling the conversation. "You said there were conflicts with your neighbor? What's her name by the way? I only got her last name when I was in the real estate office."

Allyson's lips curled. "Kale. Kale Halifax. She's an artist. I wanted to take a look at her work, but she refused. Can you believe it? What if I was a potential buyer? Not that I actually was. Art these days. Can't anyone paint a decent sunset? But still!"

"And the fight with Peretti?" I asked before the conversation could zip in another direction.

She shifted her weight. "I think she set her dog on him. Not that he doesn't deserve it. Long story short — she shouted that he'd broken into her house, which is, of course, his house. He shouted that she had broken into *his* house. Nothing was said in an indoor voice, which was useful for me, because I got everything down — except for the Italian. Don't speak it. Honestly, good luck getting rid of a tenant here in California, even if they are squatters. Someone told me it was a six-month process. At least. And then, when he finally did get his property back, they'd wrecked all the doors and cupboards."

"Who?" I asked, confused.

The buzzing crescendoed. Allyson didn't react.

She waved her beringed hand dismissively. "Oh, no one you know. Nothing to do with Peretti. Anyway, if he thinks Kale is going to leave just because he asked her to, he's got another think coming. Do you think he killed that realtor? He's sure got a temper. Not that I'd put it past Kale. She's one of those *determined* women, you know the type, as tough and fibrous as her namesake."

"Um..."

She leaned closer, a few strands of her hair catching in a saguaro cactus. "They say he murdered his wife." The writer straightened, and her hair tore free. She yelped, wincing.

I blinked. "You mean... Peretti?"

She rubbed her head. "They lived here together last year. His wife was one of those hot-blooded Italian women, all fire and high-fashion. I couldn't understand a word of those fights. Completely useless. Though there was a lot of *basta*," she mused. "I had to call the police more than once. And then that Diana woman showed up—"

"Diana? Diana Archer?" My insides jangled — with nerves or excitement, I wasn't sure. Had I actually stumbled over a clue?

"That's the one. Talk about determined. She's worse than Kale. And then the wife disappeared."

Lost in her tangle of gossip, I massaged the base of my neck. "Wife?"

"The Italian job. Poof! She vanished. Some say he dumped her in the Pacific, but if he had, don't you think she would have washed up by now? Of course, he could have used weights. Or just buried her in the mountains. Burying her in the mountains would have been so much more effective. Animals. The weather. Bigfoot."

"What was Diana Archer doing here?"

"She's one of *those* women, always sticking her nose in and taking care of things." She shuddered. "I was on a committee with her once. Never again." She backed toward the Jeep in her driveway. "Well, you don't look like a murderer. I hope you don't get arrested." She waved and grabbed her laptop off the hood of her car, hopped in and zoomed off.

I stood beside the saguero and sifted through the mass of information she'd dumped. What was Diana Archer's connection to Peretti and his wife? Granted, San Borromeo was a small town. There were lots of opportunities to connect. But it wasn't *that* small.

My scalp prickled, and I scanned the yard, again feeling a presence. But no one was there.

Returning to the sidewalk, I walked down the steep, meandering road. I didn't like the sound of the wife's disappearance. But if Peretti was in the habit of making people disappear, why leave Reince's body out for me to find? Didn't murderers usually follow the same M.O.? Or was that just one more "fact" invented by Hollywood?

Buzzing filled the sky. A drone, a cross between a spider and a helicopter, zipped over the street. It hovered, swaying in place, as if caught in the act.

So *that* was the source of the noise. At least bee stings were not in my future. I relaxed and continued on.

The sound of the drone's motor swelled.

I glanced over my shoulder.

The drone stopped, weaving in mid-air.

Okay. That was a little weird. I turned, hands on my hips, and stared at the machine.

The drone stared back.

I stepped backward.

It edged forward.

I turned. Hurrying down the sidewalk, I glanced over my shoulder.

The drone followed.

The person directing it was probably just following the path of the road so it didn't get lost. No biggie.

Gulp.

The drone growled closer.

I broke into a trot.

It zoomed low, and I ducked, the breeze from its passage stirring my hair.

"Hey," I shouted.

The drone stopped, rotating one-hundred-and-eighty degrees to face me.

I stepped backward.

The drone zipped toward me, swooping low. I yelped and crouched beside a Prius. The drone swung about and started another run.

Heart banging against my ribs, I sprinted down the curving street, past recycling bins and pristine gardens and cars yellow with pollen.

The drone roared lower. Throwing my hands over my head, I dropped into another crouch beside an aged limo.

A pot-bellied, gray-haired man in a tank top, dingy slacks, and flipflops emerged on his porch. "Hey," he shouted. "Get away from my car!"

I half-stood. "I didn't mean—"

The drone swooped low. I screamed like a girl and dropped to a crouch. The drone circled behind the Lincoln.

"What are you doing fooling around with that drone?" he demanded. "Stop that!"

"I'm not fooling around." I hunched lower.

"You look like you're fooling around to me."

Cautiously, I raised my head. "The drone's—"

Something hard thunked onto the top of my head. Pain shot through my skull. My legs bent. I stumbled forward, smacked my forehead on the Lincoln. Stumbled backward. Fell on my butt.

Dazed, I sat in the road. Well. That was embarrassing.

My head wanted very badly to split in two and join up later for a drink. I slowly pitched onto my side, partly to avoid future drone attacks, and partly because it just felt good.

The man grabbed a newspaper off the porch and lurched into his yard. "Damned kids." He flailed at the drone with the rolled-up paper. "Get out of here! Scat!"

The drone zipped over the roof of a Victorian and vanished.

The man stormed around the car and scowled. "If you dented—" His chins pulled back. "You're bleeding."

Gingerly, I touched the top of my head, my face. Wet heat trickled down my forehead.

He helped me up and sat me on the sidewalk. "Wait here," he said. "I'll get something for you." He paused to glance at his car. The man wiped the edge where the doorframe met the roof with the side of his fist, and then he jogged into his house.

I braced my head in my shaking hands, and nausea swamped me. It was probably just kids.

But.

What if it wasn't?

CHAPTER SEVEN

"WHY DIDN'T YOU CALL the cops?" Razzzor bellowed in my headphones. "Look out!"

A Nazi zombie exploded atop a pile of Belgian rubble, and I winced. My head still ached from the drone attack. "I stood up pretty quickly. I might have hit the drone instead of it hitting me. And I wasn't badly hurt." A panda bandage on my forehead and an icepack on the top of my head had taken care of the damage.

"So? It had no business being around you at all."

I glanced at the wall clock above my white-brick fireplace. Seven o'clock.

Tentatively, I lifted a headphone from my ear. The icepack slid off my head, landing on my shoulder.

No hammers. No sawing. Silence.

I tossed the drippy icepack on the couch and readjusted the headphones. "Hey, Razzzor, I've got to go."

"We were just about to liberate Belgium."

"Save me some chocolate. It's Wednesday. I'm taking dinner over to my grandfather's."

"Whatever," he said in a disgusted tone. "I'll take out this zombie troop without you."

Sighing, I signed out of the video game. One thing I'd say for my new neighbor – he was punctual. I couldn't really blame him for the noise. He had to get the building work done sometime. At least—

Rock music blared from next door. I jerked upright to the pounding of drums and shrieks of...

"Judas Priest!" I ground my teeth. What was *wrong* with that man? Maybe I'd get lucky, and he'd flip the house to a nice big family with a pack of ten-year-old boys. Then things might quiet down.

I stalked to my bedroom. Champagne-colored duvet. Pale green throw pillows. Sand-colored walls. My bedroom is normally an oasis of spa-like calm, right down to the orchid beside my Buddha statue and the water fountain on the bedside table. But tonight, my necklaces on their small silvery tree rattled to the thump of bass.

I pressed my fingers to my eyes. It didn't matter. I was leaving anyway. Usually, my grandfather and I met earlier for dinner. But Gramps had asked to push our meal back to seven-thirty, because he had a surprise.

I dreaded delivering mine, and a tight, stretched feeling clenched my belly. *Surprise! My money was stolen, and that building's not really for rent!*

I grabbed my pink blazer and a matching pink-and-green scarf from the closet and threw them on over my tank and jeans.

In the kitchen, I placed the lasagna I'd baked into a paper bag and added a prepped loaf of garlic bread and a plastic container of green salad. It was enough for Gramps to eat for days. When he was on his own, his home-cooked meals consisted of peanut butter, cheese, and bologna sandwiches. Minus the bologna, they weren't half bad.

I'd hinted about moving in with him when I'd first returned to San Borromeo. But he'd promptly set me up with Tomas, who'd rented me the bungalow. Gramps liked his independence.

In honesty, so did I.

But my grandparents had been the mother and father my parents couldn't be bothered to be. Gramps had coached my soccer team, dealt with my teachers, and even joined my tea parties, hunching over my play table like a bear.

Heat seared the backs of my eyes. I couldn't let this man down.

I loaded the bag and my purse into my Mazda. Resisting the urge to peel out of my driveway, tires screeching angrily, I moved at a sedate twenty-five MPH down the road. It's not as if my neighbor would hear squealing tires over that racket anyway. Besides, there were kids on this street.

I turned the corner, and the noise receded. My death-grip on the wheel loosened, and I drove higher into the hills. Sunset turned the sky rose-petal pink, gilding the clouds gold.

I turned at a sleepy cul-de-sac and pulled into the sloped driveway of my grandfather's fairytale home. It had the typical wavy roofline and half-timbering over white stucco. One side of the house was completely covered in ivy. An octagonal tower joined the upstairs master bedroom.

The house was huge for one person. But he'd spent fifty years there and had no intention of downsizing.

I strode up the driveway, past the path to the front door and covered carport. The garage door stood open, and I walked inside, inhaling the scent of freshly cut wood. I loved that smell.

My grandfather's big circular saw was pulled slightly away from its corner, as if it had recently been used. I passed shelves filled with tools and went to the door to the home's interior.

"Gramps?" I rapped twice and walked into the country kitsch family room, decorated with my grandmother's collection of Hummels and souvenir spoons and decorative plates. A wide, tiled counter separated the family room from the kitchen.

"Abigail! Right on time." His back to me, Gramps burrowed inside the open refrigerator.

He straightened and smiled, his blue eyes crinkling. The overhead light glinted off his balding head. He was still in denial over the hair loss, carefully making a thin, wispy-white combover.

The sight made my heart surge with affection and some anxiety. When I was a kid, he'd always seemed ancient compared to the other parents. I'd spent a lot of time worrying about him dying. I still did.

Something honked by his feet, and I glanced at his tasseled loafers. The fuzzy yellow duckling gazed up at him adoringly.

"So, it's an indoor duck," I said, surprised. Gramps had grown up on a farm and had old-fashioned ideas about animals. He wasn't one for pets.

"He's too small to let run around outdoors. A raccoon will get him, and I'm too lazy to build Peking a cage right now."

"I can't believe you named your duck after a dinner."

"Ducks make good eating."

"You are not going to eat that duck," I said, laughing. Cooking the duck would be too much work.

"What else am I going to do with it?"

I rolled my eyes. He might have grown up on a farm, but he was a California guy now. He wouldn't eat something he'd named.

"I was looking for my blue cheese dressing." Gramps nudged the duckling out of the way with one foot. "Do you want some red wine?"

"Sure."

A semi-retired accountant who'd bootstrapped his way to success, Gramps understood frugality. The bottle wouldn't cost more than four dollars. He liked to believe a glass of red wine a day kept the Grim Reaper away, and I wasn't above a cheap glass of wine.

"What happened to your head?" he asked.

I touched the panda bandage. "I wasn't paying attention and banged it on a car door. How's it going?" I set my purse and bag on the white-tiled kitchen counter.

"Any day above ground's a good one." Gramps sniffed, his hand resting on the open refrigerator door. "Lasagna?"

"With extra meat and extra cheese." I turned on the oven and swallowed. *Get it over with.* "Gramps, there's something I need to tell you." My voice sounded high to my ears, and I coughed.

"Did you forget the garlic bread?"

"No." I pulled it from the bag. My mouth tasted like sawdust. "It's the tearoom."

He bent to the refrigerator. "There it is! In the door, I should have known." Triumphant, he brandished a bottle of blue cheese dressing and a plastic box of blueberries.

He tossed a berry to the duckling. It skittered across the kitchen floor, and the duckling waddled after it.

"He's nuts for these things." He popped a blueberry into his mouth and set the container on the counter. "Lots of antioxidants."

I rested against the counter, my hands reaching behind me to clench its edge. "Gramps."

"Wait just a minute." Setting the dressing on the counter, he bustled into the pantry. He returned with an unpainted, wooden sign that read: BEANBLOSSOM'S. The sign was at least three-feet across. Awkwardly, he balanced it on one knee. "What do you think?"

My throat squeezed shut. I stared, unable to speak.

That was why the garage had smelled of fresh-cut wood. He'd made me a sign. And he'd spent time on it too, each beveled letter carved in even, cursive script.

His broad brow creased. Gramps lowered the sign and bent to read it upside down. "What's wrong? I know I spelled our name right. Did I get the size wrong?"

"It's perfect," I choked out. "But..."

"But what?"

"My realtor was a conman," I blurted.

He blinked and set the sign on the floor, leaning it carefully against the closed refrigerator. "What's happened?"

I mastered my breathing and explained.

"And your advance rent payment?" he asked when I'd finished.

I shook my head, lead weighting my chest. "I don't know." *But the police think I might have stolen it after I killed Reince.* "The check cleared the bank, and Reince is dead. I'd like to think I'll get that money back, but—"

"But it could take months," he said. "Years." He shook himself. "That's all right. You'll get the money back eventually. I can loan you what you need to get you through this."

"No, I couldn't—" My eyes burned. "I should have told you right away, but I thought maybe there was some way I could fix this. Gramps, I'm not sure what to do."

Carefully, he set the duckling on the counter. It waddled to the plastic container of blueberries and pecked at its lid.

I studied the lasagna, the grooves between the counter tiles, anything to keep from making eye contact. A pile of dishes sat stacked neatly in the sink. I'd get to them after dinner. At least I could take care of *that* problem.

He gripped my shoulder. "Abigail, what would you do if you had a problem that you couldn't figure out? Let's say, you were giving away lots of coupons, but weren't making any money off them?"

"I'd probably talk to you about it. I'm pretty good with numbers, but you've forgotten more about finances than I'll ever know."

"And let's say you started getting bad reviews for your food. Then what?"

"That's not likely. My friend, Allie, is a chef. She's helped me pull together my menu."

"Exactly. You know what you don't know, and you know when to get help. That's why I trust you. Now, I'm offering you help."

I couldn't take more of his money, not when I already owed him so much. I *had* to track down our missing cash.

The oven beeped, and I turned and slid the lasagna and bread inside. "Thank you." I blew out my breath. "But I don't know what the situation really is yet. I may still be able to rent the building. The lawyer said he'd consider it. Anyway, let me find out what sort of rent he wants — if he's even willing to consider me." But there was no way in hell I was borrowing more money from Gramps.

"That makes sense. But I'm here, if you need me for anything." He shot me a sidelong glance. "And you always have a home here." He tugged on his collar. "With me."

"Do you... want me to move in with you?"

"Hell no. I'm just saying, if push comes to shove, you can. I love you, Abigail."

My eyes burned. I changed the subject. "He said he knew you. The lawyer, I mean."

"What's his name?"

"William Bonnet."

Gramps nodded. "Bonnet? We were on the church's finance committee. What about the other fellow who's involved in this mess? Your competitor for the building."

"Hyperion Night? I don't think the lawyer wants to rent to him."

"Why not?"

"Mr. Night wants to open a Tarot studio."

His face scrunched. "Tarot studio? What's that?"

Peking worked his beak into the groove of the plastic blueberry container and stuck. He backed away, the container dragging across the counter. The duckling jerked free, shook its tiny head, and quacked.

Gramps opened the box and gave him another blueberry.

"You know," I said. "Fortune telling."

"Sounds like something your—" He turned quickly away, opening a cupboard and peering inside. "Sounds sketchy to me." He drew out two wine glasses.

Sounds like something my mother would do. That's what he'd been about to say. And he'd have been right. I closed my eyes, seeing those damned white shoes. "I've been thinking a lot about that day in the airport."

The day my parents had abandoned me for the first time. The day they'd told me to wait quietly, and I'd get a treat. That I should not make a fuss and be a good girl. It was only much later I realized they hadn't lied – they'd never told me they were coming back.

He stilled, the wine bottle frozen over two small glasses. "Oh?"

"I never asked," I said casually, "how did you know to come get me?"

He poured two small glasses. "Your mother called."

"From the airport? That day?" Anger surged through me. "So, they blackmailed you into taking me in."

"Your grandmother and I thought they were taking you with them to India. I didn't like it – thought you were too young. Your grandmother argued a child your age shouldn't be separated from her parents. We thought they'd agreed."

"But they hadn't." They'd left me sitting in a waiting area, staring at my white shoes, until my grandparents had found me, stiff with fear.

"No. Your mother told us where to get you. Your grandmother – I thought she was going to have a heart attack before we reached the airport. But there you were, waiting calm and composed. I'd never seen a kid your age that brave."

Until my grandparents had scooped me up, my grandmother weeping, my grandfather's expression thunderous. I'm pretty sure I cried non-stop until the next morning. Even at the tender age of three, you understand when your parents don't want you.

"I was lucky," I said thickly. "You and Gran were the best."

He poured the wine, not looking at me. "We'll figure this out, Abigail. Don't you worry."

We ate dinner at the antique, dark-wood table in his dining room. Peking snoozed in a nest made of a scarlet cloth napkin at Gramps' elbow. Picture windows overlooked the sun sinking beneath the ocean. Lights from other homes dotted the hillsides, cascading toward the darkening Pacific.

But the garlic bread tasted like dust on my tongue, and the cheap wine made me headachy.

After dinner, we played a couple rounds of cribbage. Then I hugged him goodbye and walked to my Mazda. I stood in the cool driveway for a moment, remembering Christmases and Easter egg hunts and Independence Day picnics at this house. Tomas and his family had usually joined in the fun.

Gramps was my anchor, and I couldn't let him down. I certainly couldn't take advantage of his generosity. Not more than I already had. That would make me too much like my parents.

Something buzzed faintly above.

I tensed, searching the sky, my breath quickening. But if the drone had returned, it was hidden in the gathering darkness.

Fumbling my keys, I got into my car and drove.

CHAPTER EIGHT

San Borromeo neighborhoods aren't big on streetlights. So I drove slowly down the hill after I left Gramps. But my mind raced like a hamster in a wheel – round and round, going nowhere.

I forced my hands to unclamp from the Mazda's wheel. There was a bright side. At least I had someone in my life who cared about me as much as Gramps did. I hadn't told him how hard the police had grilled me about the murder. It would only worry him. Besides, I couldn't be a serious suspect.

I shifted in my seat.

Could I?

I turned onto my street. A wall of sound slammed the Mazda, and I flinched.

Cars filled every available space along the eucalyptus-lined road. Lights streamed from the windows of my neighbor's weathered bunga-low. Sacks of cement and piles of building materials littered his front yard.

I groaned. Of *course* it was too much to hope that his party would be over.

"Hello, earplugs," I muttered.

I slowed to a stop and stared, uncomprehending, at my driveway.

It was packed with strange cars. A gray F-150 had parallel parked in front of the entry, blocking the other cars in and me out.

I swore and smacked my hand on the steering wheel. *Seriously?* Who parks in someone else's driveway? Oh, yeah, friends of my stupid, loud neighbor did.

Teeth grinding, I drove around the block until I found an open space two streets away. I grabbed my purse off the passenger seat and stormed to my neighbor's house.

Frankly, I couldn't blame him for wanting to remodel. His was one of the more boring homes on the street - a pale-wood square with a gravel yard.

I didn't bother knocking on the seventies-orange door. The eighties rock music was too loud for anyone to hear me. Plus, the door was open.

I strode inside and gasped. The house was twice as big as I'd remembered it. A second, larger square room had been added to the back of the living area. A throng of people milled about clutching red plastic cups to their chests.

My shoulders pulled in, my jaw compressing. I'm not a fan of crowds.

To distract myself, I focused on the remodel. The interior walls had been removed, opening up the space. The exterior walls had been stripped to sheetrock.

Strings of lights in paper spheres hung from the rafters. There was no furniture. The kitchen had been upgraded to luminous wood cupboards and white granite counters piled with food and drink.

The rear wall had been replaced with open, sliding glass doors. These led into the backyard, where most of the crowd seemed to be congregating.

I could live in a house like this. Annoyed, I reminded myself I wanted to tell off my neighbor, not move in.

I pushed through the mass of people. Sexy twenty-somethings mingled with rough-looking construction workers and bearded millennials in low-slung jeans. A hipster compared tattoos with a shaggy, middle-aged man in black leather.

I walked onto the brick patio. Its wide steps cascaded down to a concrete deck. Off to one side stood a redwood pergola dotted with wicker lawn furniture.

Pausing, I scanned the crowd and realized the flaw in my plan. I didn't know my new neighbor's name. Worse, the only part of him I'd seen was his crotch.

The air was redolent of cigar smoke and barbeque. Figuring my neighbor would put himself in charge of the latter, I made my way to a group of men surrounding the giant grill.

"Hi," I shouted over the music to the man flipping burgers. He was dark-haired and burly, and looked like the type who'd be in construction.

He grinned. "Hey there. Can I get you a burger?"

"No thanks. I'm looking for the host. Are you the homeowner?"

"That depends," he said, waggling his thick eyebrows. "Is he in trouble?"

For Pete's sake. I rolled my eyes. "I live next door. I can't get into my driveway. Cars are blocking it."

He put a hand to his ear. "What?"

"I can't get into my driveway!"

"Oh. Sorry. I'm not the host."

"Then who—?"

"I am," a deep, masculine voice rumbled behind me.

I turned and valiantly forced myself not to drool. The man was tall, tanned, and muscular, with piercing blue eyes and hair that hinted at blond. He had a five o'clock shadow, which made total sense since it was after nine, and dammit, even my brain was babbling, because he was hot. I was still angry, but did he have to look like he'd fallen off the cover of a romance novel?

"Nice pandas." His gaze flicked to the bandage on my temple.

"Thanks." I cleared my throat. "I'm your neighbor—"

"Oh." He crossed his arms. "That one."

"What's that supposed to mean?"

"You wanted something?"

Oh. Right. "Your guests have parked in my driveway. I had to park two blocks away."

His bushy brows furrowed. "That's not right."

"And furthermore—" I fumbled to a halt, the wind leaking from my sails. "What?"

"I'll figure out who the cars belong to. But it might take a while in this mess." He motioned toward the crowd, which seemed, if anything, to be thickening. "Come with me." He turned and pushed into the crowd.

I followed close behind, using him as my personal linebacker. It was still slow going. Everyone we passed turned to speak to him. He had a joke or in the case of the women, a kiss, for each.

After an eternity of air kisses, we made our way inside and to the kitchen bar.

"Why don't you have a drink?" my neighbor asked. "They're engineers." He motioned to a cluster of pudgy men at the bar. "You'll like them."

"What? But—"

He vanished into the throng.

"I'm doing tiki drinks," the bespectacled man behind the bar said. "What can I get for you?"

"Do you know how to make a zombie?" Because zombified was the only way I was going to survive this party without screaming.

Another engineer, balding and in a lightweight plaid shirt, turned to me. "What do you think? Is *Die Hard* a Christmas movie?"

"What?" I hollered over the din.

"*Die Hard*? You know, Bruce Willis?"

I shook my head. "It may take place at a Christmas party—"

"See?" he said to the man beside him. "She thinks it is too."

The music thudded against my skull, and I rubbed my temple. It did nothing to ease the pain.

"But it doesn't really have a goodwill-toward-men Christmas message," I finished. Why were so many men obsessed with this question?

"Ha!" the second man said. "I told you. Women don't get *Die Hard*."

"It's an action movie," I said. "What's there to get?" More importantly, where was that drink?

The two shared a knowing look.

"Let me break this down for you." The second engineer leaned forward. Light from a chic kitchen lamp glinted off his balding head. "It's about never quitting. Never giving up, even if it seems like a lost cause."

"That's not what Christmas is about." Why was I arguing? More importantly, what was taking the bartender so long? "Do you know the name of our host?"

"It's also about the movie itself," he continued. "It is the epitome of action movies. The movie all other action movies aspire to."

"What's that got to do with Christmas?"

"Abigail Beanblossom!" Hyperion, in skinny charcoal pants and a light-weight, black knit top, bounded to the bar. "As I live and breathe. What are *you* doing here?"

I braced an elbow against the granite counter. *Perfect.* "Are you following me?"

"You wish. Excuse me, gentlemen," Hyperion said. "I need to have a word with this lady."

"She doesn't get *Die Hard*," the balding man warned.

Hyperion rolled his eyes. "Everyone knows it's a Christmas movie." He whisked a red, plastic cup off the bar.

"It is not a Christmas movie," I shouted over my shoulder.

Hyperion steered me into a quiet corner. "Don't you know not to talk *Die Hard* with a drunk engineer?"

"But he's so wrong. Bruce Willis even said it wasn't a Christmas movie, and he was the damned star."

"Er, right. Anyway, it looked like you needed rescuing." He thrust the drink into my hands.

"Thanks." I gulped the drink. It was the zombie, and I sighed with pleasure. At least one thing was going right tonight. "What are you doing here?"

"Abigail, *everybody's* here." He lowered his chin. "I mean, have you seen our host? He looks almost exactly like that actor, Chris Hemsworth, but with darker hair. What's with the bandage?"

"Just a little cut."

"And what brings you to this soirée?"

"He's my neighbor," I said glumly.

A blonde in a bikini top and pink miniskirt jostled me and smiled an apology.

"Tell me you can watch him sunbathing from your second floor," Hyperion said.

"I don't have a second floor."

"Rats. I would have invited myself over."

"Would you?"

"For a Chris Hemsworth lookalike?" he asked. "Duh. Though that detective was a tall, cool, glass of tequila too."

"Just don't cough in his direction." I knew a germaphobe when I saw one.

"What?"

"Never mind." Puzzled, I studied Hyperion. We hadn't exactly been hitting it off in our other encounters. What had changed? "Why are you making nice? We're still rivals, aren't we?"

"Yes, but that doesn't mean you're a bad elf. Just misguided."

How charitable. "You've got a suspiciously good attitude." The key word being *suspicious*. What was he up to?

"One must think positive," he said airily. "Act as if you have what you want, and you'll get it."

I crossed my arms, nearly spilling my drink, and uncrossed them. But I'd dealt with a lifetime of magical thinkers. I was fed up. "So, you're acting as if you have the 2304 building?"

"I may as well. The cards never lie. Would you like a reading?"

I blinked. "What?"

"I feel a *mite* guilty, taking your building away from you. A Tarot reading is the least I could do." He hauled me outside to the pergola and shooed a group of people off the wicker chairs. "I'm doing a reading," he told them. "If you're quiet, you can watch."

Bemused, I sat, sloshing orange zombie across the brickwork and narrowly missing my white jeans.

He pulled a small deck of cards from the rear pocket of his slacks and laid them on the redwood table. "Cut the cards."

Wary, I stared at the worn deck.

Hyperion adjusted the beaded bracelet around his wrist. "Let me guess. You think Tarot is bogus?" He lifted an elegant brow.

"You really are psychic. And yes, I think it's New Age folderol."

"Folderol?"

"Folderol. Bambosh. Ackamarackus."

"Are you summoning a demon or cutting the cards?"

I blew out my breath. What else was I going to do while my neighbor cleared my driveway? At least now I had a chair. I wiped my damp palms on my jeans and cut the deck.

"All right." He jammed the sleeves of his black top to his elbows and cracked his knuckles. "Let's find out what the cards say about your new tearoom, which will be in a different building, but nonetheless, delightful."

"Thanks!"

He turned over a card. A sun hung in the sky above a toddler riding a white pony. "The outlook is fantastic. The sun is about good fortune, positive things, standing out. Your tearoom will be a smashing success."

"Hm," I said. That would be nice, if I believed in Tarot or fortune telling.

His reading wasn't off though. I knew a bit about Tarot, though I'd never admit that to Hyperion. I'd gotten mildly obsessed with it during my dark, humiliating teen years. I'd thought maybe if I could be more like my parents, they'd take me with them on one of their New Age quests.

They never did.

"Now about the building..." He flipped another card, depicting a woman on a stone chair and holding a sword upright in one hand and a pair of scales in the other. "Justice." Hyperion frowned and rubbed his chin. "Hm... This one's a bit hazy. There are, of course, esoteric meanings to the card. It reminds us of the spiritual consequences of our actions." He shifted, the wicker squeaking beneath him.

The card also meant things going my way in a legal matter. "What's the non-esoteric meaning?" I asked innocently.

"Oh, that." He waved, dismissive. "The simplest interpretation here is that a just decision will be made." He glanced sideways at me.

"You mean the lawyer might choose me to get the building?"

"No, it means he'll choose me. That's justice, because the cards are clear that I will be in that building. It could also mean you won't be convicted of murder. That would put a serious crimp in your grand opening."

"Why would I be convicted of murder?"

He stared down his nose. "You did find the body."

"You were there too."

"Don't get huffy."

"I'm not—"

"Let's try one more card, just for clarification." He pulled another card and turned it over. Beneath a winged lion, a man and woman faced each other, each holding a cup.

Huh. Romance. Or partnership. I widened my eyes. "The two of cups? What does that mean?"

He swept up the cards. "Nothing. I'm not feeling the muse anymore."

"But it looked like a good card," I persisted slyly. "Does it mean I'm getting the building?"

"No, it does not mean that," he snapped.

"Then what—?"

"Driveway's clear." My neighbor appeared beside Hyperion's chair. "Are you telling fortunes?"

"Not anymore," Hyperion said. "The mood has been shattered." He stood, glared at me, and strode into the crowd.

"You just make friends wherever you go." My neighbor folded his arms.

"Thank you," I ground out, "for getting your guests' cars out of my driveway." I stalked from the patio, an effect that was somewhat ruined by the clots of people blocking my way at every turn.

Finally, I escaped the house and hurried down the street, rock music pounding at my back.

Something large rustled the tree leaves with its passing.

Involuntarily, I ducked.

A shadow skimmed above the trees and vanished.

I stared after it, my eyes straining in the darkness. It was probably just a night bird.

But I wasn't betting on it.

CHAPTER NINE

I DRAGGED MYSELF FROM bed the next morning. My eyes burned, my head aching and muzzy from a sleepless night.

I stumbled to the kitchen in my teacup PJs and stared, uncomprehending, at the cupboard's glass-fronted cabinets. Even deciding what to eat seemed like too much effort.

The cellphone on the butcher-block work island jangled. Yawning, I answered without checking the number.

"Ms. Beanblossom?" a man's voice drawled.

I tensed. "Yes?"

"This is Detective Chase from the San Borromeo PD. How are you this morning, ma'am?"

My stomach jittered unpleasantly. So much for justice and Hyperion's stupid Tarot cards. But like all suckers, I'd wanted to believe. "Fine," I said shortly. "What can I do for you?"

"I was wondering if you could come down to the police station this morning to answer some more questions."

Oh, damn. Damn, damn, damn. I stared out the kitchen window. Jasmine, ready for harvesting, crawled over the redwood fence.

"Sure." My voice cracked, betraying me. I cleared my throat. "When would you like to meet?"

"I'm outside your house right now."

I smothered a curse. *Now?* I glanced down at my cotton pajamas and gripped the phone more tightly, hands damp on the plastic. "I'm not actually dressed yet." The wall clock above the stove read nine A.M., and I grimaced. I was usually more of an early riser.

"I'll wait." He hung up.

"Son of a..." Racing to the bedroom, I threw on the first pair of worn jeans I could find and a blue and gray baseball shirt. He was trying to shake me up with this surprise visit, throw me off my game. Little did he know I didn't have any game.

After a quick-draw makeup application, I finger-combed my hair and knotted it into a bun. I grabbed my purse and hustled out the front door.

The lean detective straightened off the porch banister. I guessed the SBPD was going business casual, because he wore jeans, boots, and a starched white button-down shirt.

Detective Chase tipped his cowboy hat. "Thanks for making yourself available, ma'am."

Did I have a choice? "Sure."

A gray sedan sat parked in front of my driveway. Wire mesh blocked off the front seat from the rear.

"Should I follow you?" I asked hopefully. Because I really didn't want to sit in the back of that car.

"I reckon I can give you a ride. No sense in wasting gas at California prices."

My jaw tightened. "Thanks."

But to my relief, he opened the front passenger door for me. So at least I wasn't being taken to the police station behind the wire mesh like a criminal. Unless the seating arrangements too were meant to throw me off, drop my guard.

He strolled around the front of the sedan and took his time folding himself inside, buckling his seatbelt, starting the car.

"I assume this is about my realtor?" I asked. "Reince?"

"Yup."

My insomnia headache morphed into a cotton-like feeling behind my eyeballs. "Did you learn anything new?"

"I really can't talk about that, ma'am."

That left me at the limits of my sleep-deprived conversation skills. I rested my head against the seat back and closed my eyes.

At the police station, Detective Chase left me in a dingy gray room with a scratched mirror that I guessed was two-sided. They don't leave mirrors in interrogation rooms so you can fix your makeup.

I'm not precious about dirt, but I was careful not to touch the cracked linoleum table or the sides of my plastic chair. Folding my arms over my chest, I crossed my legs at the ankles and closed my eyes.

An hour later, the detective, sipping from a Styrofoam cup, deigned to join me. He repeated the same tired questions. I can't say if my answers changed between this interrogation and the last, I was that tired.

But I told the truth as I remembered it and tried not to think about how good he looked in his jeans and sports jacket. Chase was the enemy, dammit. But like I said, my instincts had never been helpful.

"What do you think he was doing behind your building?" he asked for the *nth* time.

"There's a good burrito place on the other side of the bank," I said, exasperated.

He stared at me over folded arms, his gray eyes glinting. "I'm not sure you're taking this seriously, ma'am."

"Are you telling me you don't like burritos?" It just wasn't possible.

His mouth twisted. "I prefer Tex-Mex, not this stuff they call Mexican food here."

"Then I guess I'm nacho type."

"See above regarding not taking this seriously."

I was. I really was. But Razzzor wasn't wrong. I had issues with authority, especially after being interrogated for two hours. "Trust me, I get it. It's all fun and games until you get arrested for murder."

He sighed and closed his folder on the metal table. "You can go, Ms. Beanblossom. We'll be in touch."

I practically flew from the station and emerged, blinking, in the sunlight.

I needed a drink. Coffee. Black. I gazed across the narrow street at a pink coffee shop. Tourists in shorts and bathing suits weaved around iron lamp posts and brick flower boxes. I wished I were one of them.

"Freedom!" Hyperion vaulted down the station's steps and punched his fist in the air. The Tarot reader met my gaze and stopped, quivering, on the edge of the sidewalk. "You!" He pointed.

I started with surprise. "And you." I pointed an equally dramatic finger.

He jammed up the sleeves of his navy button down shirt, open to the middle of his chest. "Don't tell me they dragged you in for more questioning too?"

"For three hours," I said.

"Me too. Three hours in that jangling, monolithic, concrete monstrosity. I'm starving, and I need sustenance."

I blinked. Was he inviting me out? "So do I."

"Let's go, elf." He tucked my arm inside his and hauled me down the sidewalk.

Too startled to protest, I didn't. Besides, I really was hungry.

"You realize they let us out at the same time so they could follow us?" he asked.

"There go my complaints about government inefficiency." I gnawed my bottom lip. "What did they ask you?"

"Hold that thought." He steered me down a narrow, cobbled alley toward the ocean and to a door hidden behind a potted Japanese maple. A sign on the gray stucco wall read, MORTAR AND PESTLE. He pushed open the door to a narrow hallway lined with unfinished wood. "It's hipster," he said, "but they have great tequila, in spite of the beards."

The dim room was half-full, people seated at rough, square wooden tables and eating lunch.

"This is a bar," I said.

"Wow, how did you deduce that?" He motioned toward a leather-cushioned seat on a wooden bench. "Where did you expect I'd take you after that ordeal? I'll get the drinks."

"But—"

"BRB!" He strode to the wooden bar.

My stomach rumbled, and I picked up a menu. Ahi tuna and Brussels sprouts? Stuffed artichokes with root vegetables and ahi tartar? What fresh hell was this? "Quail?" I asked aloud, outraged. This wasn't bar food. It wasn't even comfort food.

Hyperion set four shot glasses on the wooden table and dropped into the chair across from me. "Get the burger if you're hungry. They use locally-sourced beef. Skoll." He sipped the tequila and closed his eyes. "Mm. Nothing beats tequila for a tower moment."

"What?"

"Tower card. What appears to be a sudden and unexpected disaster but was actually a long time in the making."

"Huh." I searched behind the napkin holder. "Where's the salt and lime?"

His eyes popped wide. "Salt and lime? What are you? On spring break? This is Anjeo tequila. It's made to be sipped. Savored."

Hesitant, I raised the shot glass to my lips and took a sip. The tequila burned a trail down my throat. I coughed and struggled not to make a face. "Smooth," I croaked.

"The aging makes all the difference. Seven years, and that doesn't include the seven years it takes for the agave to grow." He gazed over his shot glass. "Have you heard from that lawyer?"

I rubbed my thumb against the side of my glass. "Not yet." I took another sip. Should I have had a lawyer at the police station today?

"What's wrong?" he asked.

"Oh. Nothing. Have *you* heard from Mr. Bonnet?"

"Not a word." He snorted. "William Bonnet. What kind of a name is that? Probably a shyster." He waved at a waiter in a white apron, and the slender man took our orders.

Hyperion knit his fingers together and rested his chin on his knuckles. "What did they ask you?"

"The same questions. How did I know Reince? When did I see him last? Why was I in the parking lot? Except..."

"Except what?"

I turned the shot glass on the table. "The detective kept coming back to you." I hadn't thrown Hyperion under the bus, but only because I hadn't anything to tell.

"They asked me about you." His dark brows slashed downward, and he slammed his empty shot glass on the table. "They're trying to play us against each other."

"Ha."

"Why, *ha*? You think I'm wrong?"

"I think they don't know us very well. We're already at odds over the 2304 building. And it's not as if we're in cahoots. We barely know each other."

"Cahoots? People still say that? You're so cute." He chuckled. "*Ackama-rackus*. I had to look that one up."

"The *point* is, if they were trying to play us off each other, doesn't that mean they think we did it together?"

"Killed Reince?" He angled his head. "I don't know about you, but I do not like the direction this investigation is headed. Why focus on us?"

"Because we found the body, and we had reason to rob him. He had our money."

"*You* found the body."

Uneasy, I shifted in my seat. What if Hyperion *was* involved in the murder? Had Hyperion just brought me here for drinks, or to find out what I knew? I slid my thumb along the lip of the shot glass. "I didn't kill him."

"Of course you didn't kill that reptile," he said.

I looked up, startled.

"You're half Reince's size," he continued.

But if the police thought Hyperion and I had done it together...

My appetite fled. This could be bad. Real bad.

CHAPTER TEN

ALONE OUTSIDE THE BAR, I squinted into the bright sunlight. Seagulls stared down their beaks from the tiled rooftops. A curtain shifted in the window of the tiny, pastel-colored building opposite.

I hurried down the narrow alley toward the beach. If I was a suspect, I needed a lawyer. But where was the money for that going to come from? And why hadn't William Bonnet, Esquire, called?

The alley dead-ended at a sandy trail. On the ocean, sunlight glittered hard as diamonds. Surfers, oblivious to the sharks just waiting for a snack, plied the low waves. The benches along the walk were filled, but I found an empty space on the low cement wall and got comfortable.

I dug through my purse for my wallet and found William Bonnet's number, dialed.

A woman answered. "Bonnet and Bonnet. How may I help you?"

"Hi, this is Abigail Beanblossom, calling for William Bonnet."

"I'm sorry, he's not available."

I left a message and hung up.

The scents of salt and suntan lotion eddied in the warm air. Dissatisfied, I stared at the lawyer's card. There was no address, only a phone number. I did a quick internet search on my cell phone and found an office address in nearby Santa Cruz, but no actual website for the lawyer.

Why no website? I tilted my head. And why hadn't he included his address on his card?

It seemed suspicious. But Gramps had known the lawyer, so he had to be legit. Assuming Gramps and I had been talking about the same William Bonnet.

But if we hadn't... That would be crazy.

I was losing it, paranoid.

But it wouldn't hurt to check out the lawyer. I'd already been fooled once by an imposter. I wasn't about to leave anything else to chance.

Rising from the low cement wall, I hurried home, where my Mazda gleamed in the driveway. It was stuffy with heat. I turned on the air conditioning *and* rolled down the windows to force the hot air out.

It's considered bad manners to just drop in at a professional's office. One makes an appointment first. But a seed of suspicion had sprouted in my chest that I couldn't yank free.

Highway One was already jammed with traffic, and I sighed with impatience, tapping the wheel. Rush hour used to happen around five; now it started at three. Soon it would last all day.

In Santa Cruz, the highway mutated into city streets. I crawled past burger joints and chocolate shops. Finally, I escaped the main road and turned onto a quasi-residential street with less traffic and a lower speed limit.

My Mazda glided past a mix of brightly painted, low, stucco buildings and Victorians.

I pulled to the curb in front of the lawyer's office — a sky-blue bungalow with a porch and white trim. It wasn't that different from my own house. A wooden sign staked into the lawn declared: BONNET AND BONNET, ATTORNEYS AT LAW.

I blew out my breath. Once again, my instincts had led me astray. The lawyer's office did exist.

Anyone can have a sign, paranoia protested.

Reince Briggs had had a legitimate business partner – Cyrus Archer. They'd shared a secretary and everything.

But the lawyer's sign was weathered, white paint peeling in strips from its face. It had been there a while. William Bonnet was for real.

And I was being an idiot.

My cell phone rang faintly in my purse. I rummaged for it, yanking it out after the fourth ring. "Hello?"

"Ms. Beanblossom, this is William Bonnet. My secretary told me you'd called?"

"Um. Yes." Guiltily, I glanced at the building. "I was wondering if there was anything else you needed from me before you made your decision?"

He chuckled. "You mean, you wanted to know if I'd *made* a decision."

"Well..."

"It's quite all right. I'm sorry to tell you I haven't, but I haven't forgotten about you either. I'm still waiting on my real estate agent to get a better sense of the building's rental value. I'll give her a call and prod her into action."

He stepped onto his office porch and shut the door behind him.

I slouched low in my seat. "Thanks, Mr. Bonnet."

"You can call me William." Phone pressed to his ear, he trotted down the wooden steps. "Please remember me to your grandfather. It's been ages since we've done business."

Sucking in my breath, I hunched lower, my knees pressed to the steering wheel. "I'll do that. And you can call me Abigail."

He strolled past, and I could hear his voice through the car window. "Have a good day, Abigail."

I waited a few minutes, then rose cautiously in my seat. The lawyer rounded a corner beneath an olive tree and disappeared from sight.

The bungalow's front door banged open. Gino Peretti, slick in a gray Italian suit, stormed onto the porch and down the steps.

My eyes narrowed, my suspicions roaring back. What was he doing here?

Peretti stalked past my car.

What could it hurt to ask? I bolted from the Mazda. "Mr. Peretti?"

His spun to face me. "You! What are you doing here?"

"I came to see Mr. Bonnet."

"Lawyers!" He shook his fist in the air and strode closer. "Do you know I have no rights? I cannot evict that... woman." He spat. "I am the owner, and yet she has more rights than I do."

"You mean, Kale Halifax?"

He stepped closer, and I edged away. "She can stay there for six months. Six months! She doesn't even have to pay me, and I still cannot evict her."

"I'm sure she'll pay you."

He took another step closer. "She says she won't. She already paid three months' rent to that criminal, Briggs. Where am I to live, I ask you?"

My hands turned clammy. My rear bumped against the Mazda. Me and my big ideas. "I don't—"

"And she says because she spent money renovating the house — my house — she wants to get her money's worth! Do you know what she did to my house? The Italian marble — gone!" He snapped his fingers beneath my nose. "She said it made her feet cold. My Italian tiles — gone!" Another snap. "I had those imported from Bologna. Do you know what that costs? What about *my* money's worth?"

I coughed. "Your wife must be upset."

"My wife? *Porca miseria*, what does that *puttana* have to do with it? She sits in Roma with a lover who is half her age and smiles at my agonies."

"I'm sorry."

"You should be sorry! You are a Californian. It is your fault the laws are outrageous."

Which just goes to show you should never apologize when you're not actually sorry. I leaned against my car. "Have you learned anything more about Reince Briggs?"

"What is there to learn? He is dead and good riddance. Ptah!"

I angled my head and pulled a coil of hair from my chignon, twisted it around one finger. Dumb. Innocent. Harmless. That's me. "The police have interviewed me twice now. They wanted to know where I was Monday night."

"Monday night? Why? Is that when he was killed? Good! Monday is a good night for me. This is Cyrus Archer's fault. He was that criminal's partner. He must have known what was going on."

So *much for the sideways approach.* "But Monday night—"

"I will sue him."

"Where were you Monday night?" I blurted.

"Monday night I was shouting at that woman in my house. I should burn it to the ground. Then where will she live? Eh?"

Uneasily, I shifted against the car. "You don't mean that." But I had the sick feeling he did.

"Do not tell me what I mean. I know what I mean!" He snapped his fingers and stormed to a red, vintage Alfa Romeo convertible. Peretti hopped over the door into his seat. The guy was nimble, I'd give him that.

Leaning back, Peretti banged his hand on the horn until doors popped open up and down the street.

A fit-looking man, his sleeves rolled to the elbows, stepped from the lawyer's office.

Peretti roared off, one digit raised in the air.

The man from the lawyer's office jogged down the steps. Shaking his head, he walked to the sidewalk. "Sorry about that. Did he give you any trouble?" He looked like a younger version of Mr. Bonnet – just under six-foot tall, with sandy brown hair and a face weathered by the sun.

"No. What's up with him? He seemed angry." *Crazy* angry.

He shrugged one shoulder. "You can't please everyone." He stuck out his hand. "By the way, I'm Northrup, Northrup Bonnet."

"Of Bonnet and Bonnet?"

"The younger," he said.

"I'm Abigail B—" I snapped off the word. I didn't need him telling his father I'd been lurking outside like a stalker. "Do you specialize in real estate law?" I asked, changing the subject.

"Yep, it's a booming business. Why? Are you looking for an attorney?" He eyed my worn jeans and baseball t-shirt. I probably didn't look like much of a client.

"No, no." I rubbed my arms. "I stopped here because I was lost."

"Oh, what are you looking for?"

"The yacht club," I lied. I knew very well where it was. Tomas was a member.

"That's south of here," he said. "You'll need to get back on One and then get on the freeway. Take the second exit." He rattled off a string of directions.

I thanked him and escaped.

Stuck behind a line of cars on El Camino, I drummed my fingers on the steering wheel. What if Peretti was serious about his threats? If he'd been crazy enough to kill Reince, would he set his own house on fire?

And what about his wife? He said she was in Rome, but what if he'd been lying? What if she really was dead, like his neighbor had suggested?

In fits and starts, I merged onto the freeway. I had to do something about Peretti. Go to the police? My shoulders tensed. Like they'd believe me. But I couldn't just let it go either.

The traffic crawled. "Come on," I muttered, bouncing my sandal's heel.

Finally, I reached the San Borromeo exit and whizzed down the off-ramp. I slowed to the residential speed limit, making my way up hills and shady streets to Peretti's white-painted bungalow. A sunshine-yellow VW Bug sat in his driveway.

I parked by the sidewalk and made my way along the zigzag path between the cacti to the porch.

A dog yipped behind the green front door.

I climbed the steps and pressed the bell.

The door wrenched open, and Kale Halifax, cradling a Chihuahua, glared out. "What?" She wore a brown tank top beneath a paint-spattered apron. Faded jeans hugged her slim figure.

I wrinkled my nose against the blistering paint fumes. "Hi, I'm Abigail Beanblossom. We met at Cyrus Archer's office?"

Her pale brow furrowed. "Did we?" The Chihuahua nipped at a long plait of blond hair hanging over her shoulder. A dot of red paint spattered the dog's tail.

"I'm one of the other people Reince scammed. A tenant." I smiled.

"And?" She shifted her weight.

So much for building rapport.

The Chihuahua yipped, a short, demanding bark.

"I just ran into Gino Peretti—"

She tossed her head. "So? I don't care what he told you. I have rights."

"He was talking about burning down his house. This house."

Her brown eyes hardened. "Did he send you? Are you threatening me?"

"No, I'm only telling you what he said."

"Then why say anything if you're not trying to scare me?"

"Because he scared *me*." Why had I stuck my nose into this? "I think—"

"I know all about Gino Peretti. He came here and shouted and stormed, but I'd had the locks changed. And I told Reince in no uncertain terms that he needed to sort it out."

The Chihuahua struggled in her arms.

"Wait," I said, leaning closer. "You told Reince?" *Dead Reince?* "About Peretti?"

"Yes, on Monday morning."

And Reince had been killed Monday night. "What time did you talk to Reince Monday?" My heart beat faster.

"Around ten or eleven. That lunatic, Peretti, was here at eight A.M. Can you believe it? I was in the middle of a still life. He was completely disruptive. It was unacceptable, which is exactly what I told Reince."

And that's when Reince had learned the jig was up. "What exactly did Reince say?"

"He said it was all a misunderstanding, and he'd take care of it." She rolled her eyes. "Obviously, he didn't. Men can be so incompetent."

I blinked. "Reince was a con artist. He had no interest in taking care of anything but himself."

"That's not my problem." She snorted.

"But what are you going to do?"

"I have three to six months to figure that out."

The Chihuahua yipped. One of its paws caught in the top pocket of her apron.

"Now you've upset Frito." She stepped backward into the house and banged the door shut.

I stared at the door. How could Kale be so blasé? Was she in denial, or was I taking Peretti's threats too seriously? And who names their kid after a vegetable?

Kale's curvy neighbor emerged from the craftsman next door. "You found her?" Allyson waved me closer.

I maneuvered through the cactus garden. "Hi, and yes."

"Poor thing." Twisting her mahogany hair into a bun, she ambled to the low, wooden fence. Wisps of hair stuck to her round face. "By which I mean poor *you*. So, what's happening now? Did she show you her paintings? Has anyone else been murdered?"

"No and no." I glanced toward Kale's — or Peretti's — bungalow. "Peretti threatened to burn down his house, but Kale didn't seem to take it very seriously."

She pressed a hand to her ample chest. "Good Lord. I'll need to trim the trees, just in case. Fires spread, you know."

"So, you think he could be serious?" She knew him better than I did. Maybe I *wasn't* overreacting.

"He killed his wife. Why not burn down a house?"

"He said his wife was in Rome with her lover."

She smiled, owlish. "Peretti *would* say that. No one's going to press that story too hard, are they? Best you stay out of it. He's got no reason to kill you, does he?" She braced her hand on the short fence.

"No," I said, disconcerted. "I don't think so."

"Now," she said, "if I were writing this story, Gino wouldn't have killed that realtor."

"Oh?"

She shook her head. "Too obvious. Of course, in reality, the killer is usually the most obvious person, and that's the spouse. That realtor wasn't married, was he?"

Was he? "Not that I know of."

"Then the insane Italian who murdered his wife did it. But it's all right. *You* don't have to worry. It's not like you're involved in this. No one's been following or threatening you, right?"

I edged from the fence. "Right," I said slowly. But I thought of the drone and wondered.

CHAPTER ELEVEN

I LOOKED FOR PARKING behind the purple building I still hoped would be my tearoom. The lot was packed, sunlight blazing off bumpers and windshields.

I circled, zipping triumphantly into a spot beside a battered blue pickup packed with construction equipment. Small victories. I'll take 'em.

Strands of hair from my chignon stuck to my neck. Peeling them free, I stepped from my Mazda and stretched, scanning the lot. Yellow police tape fluttered beside the dumpster where I'd discovered the realtor's body.

What *had* Reince been doing here? It must have had something to do with me or Hyperion or...

My gaze landed on an ATM machine. *The bank.*

When Kale had told Reince that Peretti was back in town, the faux-realtor must have known he was about to get caught. But he also must have known he couldn't get away with giving keys to both Hyperion and me for long. He must have been planning to escape Monday night or the next day. Had he been on his way to the bank to take his money and run?

A seagull alighted on the dumpster and gave me a hard look. It spread its wings, then flicked its tail disdainfully.

I made a face at the bird.

Maybe one of the conman's victims had taken their revenge here. Who had known that Reince was a crook? Kale Halifax and Gino Peretti, most probably. If Cyrus had found out, he'd certainly have reason to kill his crooked partner. Being associated with a con artist couldn't be good for his realty's reputation.

I leaned against my warm car. I'd found the body Tuesday morning. Reince had likely been killed late Monday night, or he would have been discovered by someone earlier. But the bank would have been closed by six, when it was still light out.

So, what was Reince doing in the parking lot so late? Sure, he could have taken cash from his ATM, but most ATMs had withdrawal limits. And there were always electronic transfers. Why go to the bank at all?

The seagull flapped his wings and lifted off the dumpster. It soared across the parking lot and landed on the rooftop of a bar.

I rubbed my chin. If Reince was a professional crook, would he have kept large sums of cash in a bank, where it could be seized by the authorities? Maybe he only kept a token account at the bank, and the rest—

"Excuse me," a masculine voice said from behind me.

"Sorry, I—" I blinked at my handsome neighbor.

Sunlight shimmered off his dirty blond hair. He wore jeans and a blue t-shirt with a hole in one arm. The shirt's cotton fabric stretched taut across his broad chest.

"What are you doing here?" I asked, shifting out of his way.

"Working." He opened the pickup's passenger door and grabbed a toolbox from the seat. Blue paint peeled away from the box in patches, revealing the bare metal beneath.

"You mean you're not working on your house?" That would make life quieter. Until he started up again.

He slammed the truck door. "I need to get paid and working on my own home doesn't do it." My neighbor turned and strode toward the rear of the purple building. He opened the door and walked inside.

What the...? "Wait, that's my building!" I hurried after him.

The rear corridor was dim and dusty, lit only by a small, square window high in the rear wall. The window was the single clean thing in sight.

A chill from the dust-covered concrete floor seeped through the thin soles of my tennis shoes. I wished I'd thought to grab a jacket this morning. But I hadn't, so I grit my teeth and followed the sounds of men's voices to the front of the building.

Hyperion and my neighbor bent over a table made of a piece of plywood laid across two wooden sawhorses. A brick lay on the concrete floor, not far from a gap in the wall it had fallen from.

"Bamboo's cheaper," the contractor was saying. "As long as you don't have to worry about water damage."

"In a Tarot studio?" Hyperion asked.

Dread pooled in my gut. "What's going on? Did you get the building?"

Hyperion pivoted and arched a dark brow. "Nothing's definite yet."

My knees went wobbly with relief for a moment, then I braced my hands on my hips. "You mean the lawyer hasn't contacted you either?"

"And I need to be prepared when he does." Hyperion ran his palms down the front of his black long-sleeved tee. He wore gray skinny pants and matching boat shoes — no socks, natch.

"Hold on," my neighbor said. "You don't have the building yet?"

"Don't worry," Hyperion said. "It's in the cards. Now I'm less worried about the floors and fixtures than I am about making this place ADA compliant."

The contractor shrugged, his muscles rippling. "As long as I get paid. And you're lucky. The bathroom's big enough for wheelchair access. It's simply a matter of getting the fixtures right and installing grab bars. We'll have to widen the doors of course."

"Even the front door?" I asked. I loved that door!

"Sure," he said. "How else is someone in a wheelchair going to get inside?"

I knew I'd have to fix up the bathroom, but I hadn't figured on the doors. "Oh, no."

"What's wrong?" my neighbor asked.

"Nothing." I got a grip on myself. "I'd just... The blue door was sort of a selling point for me."

"I can build something similar for you, salvage the doorknob and stained glass."

Hyperion nodded, then shook his head. "Not for her, for me. She's got nothing to do with the Tarot studio."

"Then what's she doing here?" the contractor asked.

I crossed my arms over my baseball tee. "I'm also in the running to rent this building."

The contractor rolled up his sketch. "All right. I'm done here. When you two decide who's in charge, let me know."

"Hold on," Hyperon said. "Brik, what's your estimate?"

A contractor named Brik? *Heh heh.* And then I noticed the play of muscles beneath his thin shirt, and I swallowed. *Hoo, boy.*

"Right." Brik opened a scuffed brown portfolio on the makeshift table and handed Hyperion a sheet of paper. "Here."

Hyperion's brown eyes widened. "That much?" he squeaked.

"How much?" I asked.

Hyperion handed me the estimate.

"Forty-five thousand?" My stomach cratered. "Dollars? Just to make the place ADA compliant?" There was no way I could afford that now.

"It includes the fixtures and flooring," the contractor said. "I'm giving you two a deal, since I'm new in town."

"I told you, we're not partners." Hyperion shot me a look I couldn't interpret.

"Whatever." The contractor zipped his portfolio. "Let me know once someone's in charge." He grabbed the blue toolbox and strode from the room.

The back door slammed, and my shoulders hunched.

"Thanks a lot," Hyperion snarked.

"It's not my fault the renovations are going to cost that much," I said hotly. "Can't you cut anything out?" Not that it mattered. But I couldn't stop myself from asking.

"I've already cut the remodel to the bare bones. We need new flooring and lighting. I know concrete is in, but if we kept this floor, it would be soulless. Tarot is magical, not industrial, even if there is that whole urban, chaos-magic scene."

"Well." I swallowed, disappointment sticking in my throat. "At least you don't have to worry about me outbidding you anymore. I'd need even more work done, to add a counter and shelving and upgrade the kitchen."

"Not really," Hyperion said, his delicate face glum. "Believe it or not, the kitchen is the one thing that's up to current standards. It's also the one thing I don't need."

"It might be *technically* up to standards, but—"

"Seriously?" he asked. "Are you really going to push for a twenty-first century kitchen? You probably can't even afford a twentieth-century floor."

"No." I sighed. "I can't afford any of it. The building's yours, if you can get it." I stuck out my hand. "Congratulations."

"Thanks, I guess." He hesitated, then took my hand.

Chin high and blinking furiously, I strode down the corridor and out the rear door. There was only one thing to do now — try to get my six months' payment back.

Okay, two things. Get my money back *and* find a new location. For either of those things, I'd need the realtor Cyrus's help.

I turned and stared at the building's rear window, high in the wall. It wasn't covered in brown paper, and it was sparkling clean. In fact, it looked brand new, and so did the fitting around it.

A dark idea blossomed in my mind. Could that have been how Reince had gotten keys to the place? He'd broken in, knowing the building had been empty for years, called a locksmith, and gotten a new set? And then he'd had to replace the window...

Shaking my head, I walked to my car. *Details.* Did they even matter at this point?

I opened my car door, and a wave of heat blasted me. Unthinking, I grabbed the steering wheel and yelped. It was just-out-of-the-oven hot. Stretching the sleeves of my tee over my palms, I rolled down the windows and drove to the real estate office.

Its sign swayed slightly in the breeze, which ruffled the branches of the Mediterranean cypresses. A yellow petal tore free from the desert agave and landed on a flagstone. It seemed to point toward the foursquare house.

I strode up the no-nonsense path, up the porch steps, and into the shade of the wood beam awning. The front door had been blocked open with an aloe plant, letting air flow through the screen. I pulled the latter open and walked into the gray-tiled entry.

The receptionist, Florence, looked up from her desk beside the stairs and peered over her cat-eye glasses. "May I help you?" Her white blouse was so crisp it had to be starched. Her hair lay in pewter curls tight against her head, impervious to the whirring ceiling fan.

"I hope so," I said. "It's about the 2304 building that Reince rented me. I'd like to get my advance rent payment back. As soon as possible."

"Oh!" The elderly receptionist's mouth made the same shape and seemed to freeze there. "Oh."

"Is Mr. Archer in?"

"Oh! I'm sorry, he's not." Her wrinkled hands fluttered above the papers scattered about her desk. "You really should have made an appointment, you know."

Yeah, yeah, yeah. But I was on a mission. "In that case, may I make an appointment?"

She pulled open a desk drawer and withdrew a wide, leather calendar, flipped it open. "He's not available tomorrow, and this weekend Cyrus is busy with open houses. Hm..." She flipped the pages.

Diana Archer descended the stairs. She stopped short on the landing. Her long, gauzy kimono swayed in the breeze from the overhead fan. It ruffled her close-cropped salt-and-pepper hair. Her mouth compressed into a determined line.

"Hi again," I said. "Diana, right?"

"Right." The realtor's wife descended the remaining steps, her silver necklace bouncing against her gray tunic. She shook my hand, her grip firm and no-nonsense. "This mess with Reince... It's unbelievable. The police still haven't resolved a thing, as far as I can see. You *are* here about Reince, aren't you?"

I nodded, relieved. If Diana wanted to be helpful, I wasn't going to stand in her way.

"Come inside." She motioned me toward a smoked-glass door on the right.

"Would you two like coffee?" Florence's hands trembled slightly, as if with palsy.

"That would be lovely." Diana turned to me. "Or would you prefer tea?"

"Coffee's fine," I said. "Thanks."

I followed her inside a large office with stained wood walls, a hardwood floor, and a desk. Two low chairs sat before it, an executive chair behind.

I paused to admire two colorful watercolors of San Borromeo. "Nice."

"Thanks. I painted those," Diana said.

They were good. I could almost imagine the sea grass swaying in the breeze. "I didn't know you were an artist." Diana had real talent.

"It's only a hobby," she said, dismissive. "Cyrus needed something on the walls."

"I believe Kale Halifax is an artist too."

"Mm." She sat in one of the cushioned chairs in front of the desk and waved me into the other. "This was supposed to be Reince's office. Not that he ever used it. Now we know why."

I lowered myself into the chair across from her. "Have you learned anything?"

"Only bad news. I'm afraid in addition to being a con artist, Reince was an embezzler. He cleared out the office's accounts."

"Oh. No." Suddenly finding it hard to breathe, I clutched the arms of the chair. If the realtor had been wiped out, he wouldn't be reimbursing me. My money was really gone. "Do you have insurance? Do the police have any idea where the money is?"

"Yes, and no." Her smile was cool. "Whether the insurance will pay or not is up in the air. They should pay. And I'm sure the police are trying to figure out what happened. So are our lawyers."

"He was killed near a bank. I doubt it was a coincidence."

She nodded, her eyes narrowing. "It wasn't. He died outside his bank, as it turns out. You believe he'd gone to get his money and run?"

"His money, your money, and my deposit." But he'd cashed my check right after I'd handed it over. "But he couldn't have been killed during bank hours, or someone would have found his body before I did the next morning."

She leaned closer, her silver necklace swaying. "I wonder if he kept most of his money in cash and only a small amount in the bank?"

"I wondered the same thing."

She dipped her chin. "That way, it wouldn't leave a trail. But it would look strange, wouldn't it, if he was always paying cash? No one really does anymore. So, he probably kept a small amount in the bank, so he could pay his credit cards and such."

"Exactly." Maybe I wasn't so bad at detecting. And maybe the police had already figured all this out too.

She tapped a finger on the desk. "In which case, where's our cash?"

Florence bustled into the office carrying a plastic tray. She set the tray on the desk, and the black mugs rattled. "Oh! I wasn't sure if you wanted sweetener, so I brought the bowl and spoons."

"Thanks." I took a mug.. "I don't suppose *you* have any idea where Reince put his money?" I asked the receptionist.

"Oh, no." She smiled, an oddly smug expression. "How would I know? He didn't confide in *me*. Why would he? Reince was rarely in the office." She cut a glance at Diana. "I told you we should have insisted he have his meetings here, but he wanted to be informal and meet in that café."

Diana's head lowered. "He said it put his clients at ease. And he did do some business here."

"Was he seeing anyone?" I asked, thinking of Antonia.

"No," Diana said. "I mean, I don't know, but I don't believe so. He never mentioned a girlfriend."

"I never trusted him," the receptionist said. "I told you I never trusted him."

Annoyance sparked in Diana's iceberg eyes. "Thank you, Florence. That will be all."

"Should I leave the tray?"

"Yes," Diana said, biting off the word. She took a mug from the desk.

Florence backed from the room and closed the door behind her.

"Sorry about that," she said. "Florence is a good person, but she's not always the most sensitive." Diana sipped from the mug and made a face. "I suspect the real reason Reince worked out of that café was because her coffee is awful." She set the mug on the nearby desk. "But she's a wonderful receptionist, devoted to Cyrus. And good help is hard to find."

I sipped the sludge and smothered a grimace. "I heard something odd about Mr. Peretti, the homeowner Reince scammed."

Diana canted her head. "Oh?"

"Someone told me— well, implied, that he'd killed his wife."

"Killed!" Her eyes widened.

"They said you might know something about Mrs. Peretti."

Her expression shuttered. "I assure you, if I had any evidence that a murder had been committed, I would have taken it straight to the police. Who told you this?"

"I think it was a neighbor," I said vaguely. So far, a nosy neighbor had been my best lead. What I needed were more gossips.

Her knuckles whitened on the mug. "That damned writer. She's the biggest blabbermouth in San Borromeo."

"Um..." I guess I hadn't been that vague after all. "*Did* you know Peretti's wife?"

She fiddled with her tasseled necklace. "Slightly. I heard she'd left town."

"Mr. Peretti said she'd gone to Italy to be with her lover, but—"

"Peretti?" She leaned forward in her seat. "You *spoke* with him?"

"I ran into him at a lawyer's office."

She coiled the necklace around one finger. "Interesting." Diana shook herself. "I don't know anything about the murder, but if I were you, I'd steer clear of Peretti. The man's unstable."

"Then you knew him too?"

"You saw how he behaved in this office. He nearly gave poor Florence a heart attack. I'd be careful about *running into* him again. He's unbalanced. You never know what someone like that might do."

Like murder?

Or arson?

Gulp.

CHAPTER TWELVE

I BAKED.

I had no job. I had no tearoom. I had no prospects. Pile on top of that the debt to my grandfather, the missing money, and the possibility I might be a murder suspect. But there were always cinnamon-chip coconut scones.

I'm a stress baker and a stress eater. People act like stress eating is ridiculous, but let's get real. Food does make you feel better in the moment. Later, you feel worse for eating too much, but in the moment, it helps.

So, I slathered clotted cream atop the warm scone, poured a cup of mint tea, and walked, head bent, into my backyard.

It was after six P.M., and my neighbor's saw had gone quiet. The sky was dusky blue, deepening the garden's shadows. The solar lights lining the tanbark paths around the raised herb garden flickered on.

I walked to the table beneath the dogwood and set down my plate. Dropping into a wooden chair, I breathed deeply, inhaling the sweet scent of its blossoms.

I'd thought I'd had a plan when I'd returned to San Borromeo. My surprise stock option windfall had been nearly enough to move back to the coast and open a tearoom. Gramps had filled in the financing gap.

My legs shifted. How was I going to repay him? My income from the farmers' market wasn't nearly enough. I'd started selling tea there more to get my name out and be productive than anything else.

I leaned back in my chair and stared into the lacework of branches. The dogwood flowers rustled, gleaming pink and white against the darkening sky, and more petals fluttered to the tanbark.

My chin lowered to my chest. I'd have to go back to my old job in Silicon Valley to repay Gramps. Would the new owners even take me back?

The thought of returning to being an executive assistant made me queasy. I'd been lucky with that company, getting those stock options, even if I had been pulling eighty-hour weeks. But I didn't think lightning would strike twice. I'd been good at my job, but I hadn't enjoyed feeling like the least important person in the room.

Lately, I'd gotten caught up in the dream of my own business. I wanted to live *here*, in San Borromeo, not in bustling Silicon Valley.

"Hey, elf!" Hyperion swaggered down the garden path in his black, long-sleeved tee and skinny gray pants. A silvery scarf was knotted around his neck. "There you are." He twirled a snippet of jasmine between his fingers.

"What are you doing here?" I asked, startled. I wasn't afraid of Hyperion – he didn't seem like a killer. But this was my yard, and it was dark, and we were alone. Maybe I *should* be afraid.

He sniffed the white blossom in his hand. "I didn't have your phone number, and you weren't answering your door. But your car was in the driveway—"

"How do you know what my car looks like?" I studied him. His free hand hung loose at his side, weapon free.

"There was a car with zero flair, style, or pizazz in your driveway. Who else would drive it?"

"What are you doing in my yard?" I asked, annoyed. That car got good mileage and was surprisingly roomy.

"Like I said, you didn't answer the door." He tossed the sprig of jasmine onto the wooden table. "You might have been lying dead inside. You're lucky I care enough to check."

I snorted. "Thanks."

He pulled out a wooden chair and sat across from me at the small table. "Aren't you wondering why I've graced your humble abode?"

"That was sort of the point of me asking what you're doing here."

"I've been ignoring the signs."

I arched a brow. "What signs?"

"The two of us, Empress and Magician, leasing the same building. Both being suspects in a murder investigation. The cards. The shock—"

"What are you talking about?" I had a bad feeling where this was going.

"You're the Empress card, and I'm the Magician. Of course, the Magician is a trickster, so maybe I'm *not* the Magician." He waggled his dark brows. "I *could* be the Fool, pure potential."

"I'm lost."

He heaved a sigh. "We're meant to do this together."

"Do what together?"

"Open a Tea and Tarot room." He reached for my scone, broke off the tip, and popped it into his mouth. He angled his head. "Hm."

"Tea and Tarot," I parroted.

"Of course, I'd prefer Tarot and Tea, but Tea and Tarot flows off the tongue more easily. And... alliteration!"

"I'm not a partnership person."

"You should be. People still read tea leaves — there's a grand old tradition of tea and fortune telling. Tearooms operate during the day. My Tarot classes will be in the evenings. We can share the space. And I can bring in Tarot readers throughout the day to read for your guests. We can advertise their services on the menu. It will be unique, and this way, we can pool our resources to fix up that building."

But I didn't want a partner. I wanted *my* tearoom. I wanted independence. I wanted to stamp my feet on the tanbark path and chuck him out.

Still, as things stood, I had zero chance of starting a tearoom on my own. But partnering with a Tarot reader? It would be like partnering with my mother. "I don't think it's a great idea."

"That's because you haven't had a chance to consider my proposition. This could be even better than working individually."

I closed my eyes and blew out my breath. This was wrong for so many reasons.

But maybe I wasn't being fair. After all, I barely knew Hyperion, though I could already see the guy was a chaos demon in training. What if he turned out to be a spendthrift too, or worse, a killer? He didn't exactly set off alarm bells, but the role of psychic psycho wasn't off the table.

"By pooling our money, we could fix up the building," he said. "And we'd get more usage out of the space. Plus, I'll stop calling you *elf*. Being in business with a mythological creature would be a little much."

I worried my bottom lip. The idea wasn't awful. And having Tarot readers in the tearoom would be an interesting twist, as long as they weren't too oddball. "I'll need to think this through."

"What other options do we have?" He broke off another piece of scone. "We're both out months of rent to that pestilent creep, Reince. We need to think creatively."

"That's true, and you seem like a decent guy, but that doesn't mean we're a good fit as business partners. Besides, I wanted something cozy and elegant for my tearoom, and I'm not sure Tarot—"

"Why not whimsical? A Mad Hatter's tea party? Oooh! Or dark and dramatic, like a Russian tearoom. We could have samovars! Or something modern. Sleek. Elegant. Refined." He snitched another piece of scone, and it vanished into his mouth. "This is delicious, BTW," he mumbled. "If the Tarot cards hadn't convinced me you might actually work out as a partner, this scone does. Do you have lemon curd?"

"I ran out this morning." My tearoom didn't even exist, and he was already taking over menu planning. But I ran my hand along the wide arm of my chair and considered his idea. "A tearoom. With Tarot readers." My mouth twisted.

"What's that look supposed to mean?"

"You're obviously modern and stylish," I motioned to his urban-chic outfit. "But I'm not sure some moony, turbaned Tarot reader will fit my tearoom."

"I'd never allow such a cliché. And that *is* a cliché – a bad one."

"Sorry," I muttered. "I guess that was unfair."

"Apology accepted. Don't worry, I'll screen the readers. We'll only allow cool people to work at our Tarot room. Leave it to me." He tugged on his bottom lip. "What look *are* you going for? Something English?"

"That was the original idea. But I understand if you don't want to do it," I said quickly, half-hoping he'd give up and leave me alone. *And the other half?* I shook myself. Was I really considering this?

He snapped his fingers. "I've got it. I'm thinking Tudor. An old English look with white walls and black windowpanes. We can put a stained-glass window in the new door but using clear glass. Herbs hanging behind the counter. But nothing kitschy — we'll keep it subtle, a mélange of modern and medieval. Was Tudor medieval? Never mind." He waved the question away with one elegant hand. "That way, you get English, and I get mystique."

Huh. That sounded kind of... cool. "Maybe. We'd need to develop a new business plan, work up some numbers to see if this is workable." But did I want it to work?

"Fantastic." Hyperion leapt from his chair and jogged to the redwood fence. He banged on it with the flat of his palm. "Brik! You there?"

My heart jumped. *Brik?* We were talking to Brik? What did my hair look like?

A masculine groan issued from the opposite side of the fence. "What now?"

"We need to talk to you about some new plans. The el— Abby and I are going into business together."

I shook my head frantically. "I didn't say—"

The olive tree on the other side of the fence rustled. Brik's denim-clad legs swung over the redwood fence, and he dropped to the ground in a crouch.

I gaped. *Whoa.* That was a six-foot fence. "How—"

"I used the tree branch to swing myself over." He brushed his broad hands on the jeans hugging his thighs. Actually, they hugged pretty much everything. I tore my gaze upward. He'd changed into a plain, white v-neck tee. Dammit, I was not going to crush on my neighbor, even if he did look good enough to devour.

I glanced down at my plate. The scone had vanished, and my mouth pinched. You shouldn't mess with a woman's scone.

"What's this about you two partnering?" my neighbor asked.

"Modern Tudor," Hyperion said. "Is it possible to lay out bamboo flooring in a herringbone design?"

"Wait," I said. "I'm not—"

"Sure," Brik said, "but it will take more time."

"That's fine," Hyperion said. "New colors: white walls, black trim. And we'll need to build a counter with shelves behind it for tea canisters."

I rose. "We haven't even—"

"And the kitchen needs to be modernized," Hyperion said.

I banged my hand on the table, and the empty plate rattled. "I haven't agreed to anything!"

The two men stared at me, looked at each other. Brik quirked a brow.

"We're only brainstorming," Hyperion said. "What's the harm?"

"Fine." Fuming, I trotted up the porch steps and into the house, found my business plan, and returned with it to the garden. I opened it to my own "artist's" rendering I'd sketched of the kitchen. "Like this."

"It's a little dark out here," Hyperion said.

I yanked a nearby solar lamp from the tanbark and handed it to him.

"We want to use as much of the original kitchen as we can to keep the cost down." Hyperion wielded the light like a torch "It *is* already up to code. You know, if this solar lamp was wood, you could kill a vampire with it." He made experimental staking gestures.

Brik pried the light from his grasp. "Give me that before you hurt someone."

"In that case," I said, "the most important part of the renovation is the front counter." What *was* the harm of a little brainstorming? It might give me a better idea if I really wanted to do this with Hyperion. "If we're going to spend money, we need to do it where the customers will see the results." *Sigh.* But I was dying for a new kitchen.

"Do you two even have the rental agreement?" Brik asked.

We looked at each other. The dogwood flowers shivered, and three more petals floated to the ground.

My neighbor shook his head. "Abigail's right. You shouldn't get ahead of yourselves."

"Tomorrow." Hyperion's brown eyes gleamed in the dim light. "The lawyer will contact Abby and let her know she's got the building."

"How do you know that?" I asked.

He folded his arms. "The cards never lie."

"But…" I sputtered. "We can't go into business without a plan."

"I've got mine. You've got yours. How hard can it be to put the two of them together?"

"You said you had a *decorating* plan."

"I was unnerved. Lawyers freak me out. I didn't know what I was saying. But I've got a plan."

"Well, then, okay." Fractionally, I relaxed. *Could* we actually pull this off? "Let's look at what you've got."

"It's at the Tea and Tarot room."

"Tea and Tarot?" Brik asked. "That's what you two are doing? Are you serious?"

"Deadly," Hyperion said. "But not enough to kill anyone," he added hastily.

"We wouldn't do that," I agreed.

"Right." Brik backed from the table. "Look, when you two get everything worked out, let me know."

"We should scope out the building now," Hyperion said. "I'll grab my business plan, and we can go over my modern Tudor ideas."

"Let's go." Excitement sparked in my chest. Had Hyperion thrown my tearoom a lifeline? I frowned, unsure how Gramps would react. Opening a Tarot studio was something my parents might do.

"What's wrong?" Hyperion asked. "You look like you swallowed a bad lime."

But my parents had never started a business, and my grandfather was practical too. Joining forces with Hyperion might be the answer to all my problems. I stood, the backs of my legs pushing the chair from the table. "My grandfather lent me money for the tearoom. I owe it to him to discuss it before we make any decisions."

"Oh, that's no problem," Hyperion said. "Older men think I'm adorable."

Brik snorted.

Hyperion broke into a jig. He bumped against the table, and the plate skittered to the edge. Brik caught it before it could fall.

"This is gonna be epic." Hyperion hooted. "Empress and Magician!" He winked. "Or Fool."

I led them through my house. Brik scanned the copper kitchenware from local garage sales, the geometric rugs, the collection of teacups. He stopped and stared at the tangle of cable and gaming headphones on the couch opposite the TV.

Grabbing my purse and keys off the dining room table, I shuffled the two men out the front door.

"I'll meet you there." Hyperion strode to a Jeep Wrangler, parked beneath a eucalyptus tree.

"We'll let you know about the remodel as soon as we get some clarity," I told Brik and slid into my Mazda.

"Sure," he said.

I started the car and pulled from the drive.

Brik's lips moved, and he took a step toward the sidewalk.

I shifted my foot to brake, but he shook his head and strode to his house next door. Whatever he'd meant to say could wait.

My heart thumped as I drove down the dark road, tree branches weaving into a tunnel above my car. Could we do it? Was this really happening?

If only I'd known what was about to happen, I'd never have left the house.

CHAPTER THIRTEEN

I PULLED IN BESIDE Hyperion's Jeep Wrangler. Stepping from my car, I glanced at the spot beside the dumpster, where Reince's body had lain.

An amber parking lot light flickered above me and went out. I shivered. No, that wasn't spooky. Not at all.

Careful not to stumble over a parking block, I made my way through the near-empty lot to the rear door. It swung open at my touch, its hinges creaking.

My flesh pebbled. "What? No bats?" I muttered. "Hyperion?" I shouted into the dark hallway.

"Over here! Stupid flashlight."

Eyes straining, I felt my way down the hall, my fingers trailing over the rough stucco walls. I stumbled over a box and stopped to dig my keychain with its mini flashlight from the purse over my shoulder.

Beneath my tiny spotlight, the hallway's walls looked dingier, the floor dustier. But this place had potential, I reminded myself.

I emerged in the front room and swung my weak beam. The sawhorse table. A garbage bin. Ancient-looking, water-stained boxes piled near the front door.

The keys bit into my palm. "Hyperion?"

"In the kitchen!"

How had I missed him? Relieved, I made my way back down the hall to the open kitchen door and peered inside. My light gleamed dully off metal counters covered in grime.

On the opposite side of a wide metal table, Hyperion banged a flashlight against his palm. The beam flickered across a 1960s-era refrigerator. He sighed and stared at the wall.

I walked around the table. A nail gun lay amidst scraps of paper and at least a quarter-inch coating of dust. "What's with the nail gun?"

"I used it for my business plan." He motioned to the wall with his flashlight.

On it hung a drawing of a purple interior littered with comfy-looking chairs and throw pillows. Beneath it, three bullet points in elegant script:

- *Invite Tarot readers — cut of daily readings*

- *Promote online*

- *Evening classes*

"That's your plan?" I asked, incredulous.

He sucked in his cheeks. "I believe in simplicity."

"Simplicity's fine, but where are the financials?"

He rolled his eyes. "I can have classes running every night and on weekends. At thirty dollars an hour per head, that comes to four-hundred-and-fifty dollars a day. Plus, we'll take ten percent off the top for any Tarot readers who use the space during the day, plus my online business—"

"Online?" I pulled a small, blue writing pad from my purse and jotted down notes.

"Selling Tarot decks and books, plus my own online courses." He pointed toward the poster and a drawing of a front counter. "I'd planned on keeping a supply of books and cards here, but that's out if you're going to be using the space as a tearoom during the day."

"We could add a bookshelf on the opposite wall. Then people can browse and buy." Books and tea weren't a bad combination. "We could even include books on tea, and maybe some cookbooks."

"You could produce your own cookbook. Oooh! The Tea and Tarot Cookbook. Recipes named after Tarot cards."

No, no, a gazillion times no.

"It's something to consider for the future," he said hastily. His flashlight flickered, and shadows shifted weirdly across the old kitchen. He banged the end of the light on his palm, and the beam steadied.

"All right," I said, "but how would your numbers change if this was a tearoom during the day?"

He canted his head and stared at the poster. "Not by much. We'd still have the evening classes. Weekends might be a problem. There is that small back room off the hall I could use for group classes on weekends though."

"You mean, the storage room?"

"Is that what it is?" he asked. "Because we don't need one."

"Sure we do. To *store* things."

"We can convert it into an intimate classroom."

"Then where will I keep my supplies?" I asked.

"There's plenty of space in the kitchen — what about the pantry?"

We discussed kitchen upgrades, and I shook my head. "We don't even have the building yet."

"We will, and it will be dazzling."

"Assuming neither of us gets arrested for murder."

"Ha ha, and ha," he said. "You're a laugh riot."

"Hyperion, the killer had to be in Reince's circle. And that means a client or someone he worked with."

The space around me darkened, the linoleum floor vanishing into a pool of black. My flashlight had gone out. I clicked it a few times.

Dead.

"Are you a tearoom owner or a detective?" he asked.

"Right now, neither." I blew out my breath. Hyperion really was my best chance at opening a tearoom, curse it all.

He shot me a look, as if satisfying himself I was done. "All right," he said, "I've got twenty thousand left to invest — assuming I don't get my upfront rent back."

We talked more numbers, and my excitement grew. This was looking more and more possible. I still wasn't thrilled with sharing my tearoom with a bunch of fortune tellers, but it would make the place... different.

And people *were* looking for more than tea when they came to a tearoom. They wanted an experience. Hyperion could provide novelty.

The Tarot reader stilled. He looked toward the kitchen doorway. "Did you hear something?"

"No, I was too busy thinking."

"Does your head hurt?"

Shifting, I closed my notebook. "If what you're saying is correct, this is all upside. We'll need a written agreement though."

"Sure." He shrugged languidly. "Know any lawyers who'll do it pro bono?"

"Maybe," I said slowly. "And my grandfather's a CPA. He can review it too." A draft wafted through the kitchen, and I shivered. Had I shut the rear door properly?

He stuck out his hand. "Good faith deal until we iron out the details?"

We shook, his hand firm and cool. That sensation of being watched spread across my upper back, and I stiffened.

"What's wrong?" Hyperion released my hand.

"I don't know." I turned toward the open doorway and the yawning darkness beyond.

Something clunked outside the kitchen door.

"Did you hear that?" he whispered.

My breathing quickened. "Maybe it's the building settling," I whispered back.

"Someone's here." Taking my arm, he dragged me away from the door.

I grabbed the nail gun off the table, and he pulled me into the pantry. Shelves layered with dust and random bits of electrical wire lined the walls.

"Turn off your flashlight," he said, hoarse.

"It is off."

"Whoops. I'll turn mine off." There was a click, and the darkness was absolute.

Straining my senses, I scented something acrid. "Do you smell smoke?" I asked in a low voice.

"No, but—"

Something rattled in the hallway outside.

"Oh-my-God-it's-the-killer," he whispered, yanking me closer.

My hands turned clammy. Someone was in the building. And if whoever was here meant well, they'd have called out to us. It wasn't as if we'd been quiet. Whoever it was *had* to know we were here. The scent of smoke grew stronger. "I really think I smell smoke."

"No—"

"Yes." On shaky legs, I pulled away from him and toward the pantry's entry. I fingered the trigger on the nail gun. "And smoke means fire. We can't wait in here."

"That's probably what Reince thought," he hissed, turning on his flashlight. He aimed it up at his chin, casting his face in demonic shadows. "Right before he was beaten to death. And may I remind you, Reince was bigger than the both of us put together."

"Turn that off." I peeked from the pantry.

"You are not the boss of me."

A faint, flickering glow illuminated the kitchen doorway.

"Fire," I said, mouth dry. "The building's on fire. We have to go." I fumbled, lurching forward. My unlit flashlight clunked onto the floor and vanished in the darkness.

"Wait!" Hyperion grabbed my arm, spinning me into his chest. "Give me that gun." He released my arm and grabbed for the nail gun.

I jerked away.

His flashlight wobbled. Shadows sped across the shelving.

I gasped, and the barrel of the nail gun bumped into something.

Ka-chunk! The gun jumped in my hands.

Hyperion shrieked and crumpled to the floor.

Horrified, I stared at the nail gun in my hand.

I'd shot Hyperion.

CHAPTER FOURTEEN

"YOU SHOT ME!" HYPERION rolled on the pantry floor and clutched his thigh. His flashlight clanked to the linoleum, spiraled lazily into a corner, and flickered. The room went black.

Oh, my God. I'd shot a man. "I'm sorry," I wailed. Hold on. I *hadn't* actually shot him. "You shot yourself."

I dropped to the floor. Hands shaking, heedless of the dust and bits of wire and plaster, I felt for his flashlight. Finally, my fingers touched metal, and I clicked it on.

An arc of light bounced around the filthy pantry. I aimed it at his leg. His hand gripped his gray trousers. Blood seeped between his fingers.

Hyperion gasped. "How bad is it?"

"I can't tell when your hand's covering the wound."

"You shot me!" He clenched his jaw. "Take it out. Take it out. Take it out!"

"What if the nail's nicked an artery? It could be the only thing keeping you from bleeding out." I was no expert on first aid, but I knew that much. It was about the only thing I remembered from my first aid class. That and not to worry about counting out the chest compressions.

He groaned.

I glanced out the pantry door. Light flickered on the wall outside the kitchen. The smoke thickened, burning my throat and eyes. "Can you walk?"

He glared. "Are you kidding me?"

Carefully, I set the nail gun on the concrete floor. "Lean on me." I wrapped my arm beneath his and tried to stand.

He collapsed against me, knocking me to the linoleum floor. Something hard and sharp stabbed my back.

"I can't believe you shot me." He moaned. "These trousers are brand new."

I coughed. "You can live in the past and die in this fire, or we can get out of here, even if you have to crawl."

"Easy for you to say. You weren't shot in the leg." But he rolled onto his stomach and crawled toward the kitchen on his elbows. He dropped his head to the floor and coughed. "I won't make it. Go on without me."

"Don't be such a drama queen." I grabbed the arm on his uninjured side and tugged.

"Is that a crack—"

"No, and it's only a flesh wound," I snapped, fear arcing through me. *Please let it only be a flesh wound.*

"I can't."

"Are you giving up?" I asked. "What about your Tarot studio?"

He groaned. "Leg. Hurts."

A flashlight beam blinded me.

"What the hell's going on in here?" a man asked.

"Brik?" I squinted at his muscular silhouette.

"Who else?" he asked.

I gulped. "There's a fire, and Hyperion's hurt—"

"She shot me!"

"It was an accident," I said.

"The fire's out," Brik said. His black jacket rustled as he moved. "Come on."

"It's out?" I asked stupidly.

"Upsy-daisy." Brik scooped Hyperion into his arms.

Hyperion groaned, his head lolling on Brik's broad shoulder. The contractor grunted and carried him from the kitchen.

Baffled, I trotted after the two men, down the hall and into the parking lot.

He set Hyperion against the stucco wall and examined his leg. My neighbor glanced up at me, his blue eyes glacial. "My nail gun?"

"That was yours?" Hyperion's eyes bulged. "Why would you leave something like that lying around for her to pick up?"

"I thought someone was in the building," I said to Hyperion. "You heard them too. And the fire—"

"Is out." Brik dug a phone from the back pocket of his jeans. "It was mostly smoke." He dialed. "This is Brik Jacobs. I'm in the parking lot behind the building at 2304 Laurel. We'll need an ambulance and the police." Brik walked a short distance away from us, stopping beneath a yellow streetlight.

"You're a menace." Hyperion hissed and clutched his thigh. A dark stain spread across his gray skinny pants.

I splayed one hand across my chest. "I told you, it was an accident. You grabbed the nail gun, and it went off." This was not my fault, because I would never shoot someone.

"The nail gun *you* were holding," he snarled.

Guilt tightened my midsection. *Dammit*. Maybe it *was* my fault. I hated it when it was my fault.

Pocketing the phone, Brik walked to us. "All right. This I've gotta hear. What happened?"

"We were in the kitchen," I said.

"The pantry," Hyperion said.

"But first we were in the kitchen," I said, "and we both heard someone in the building and smelled smoke. Hyperion panicked and dragged me into the pantry."

"I did not panic." A muscle pulsed in Hyperion's jaw. He pressed the back of his head against the wall. "You panicked, and then you shot me."

Brik shook his head. "I really didn't think you were the type to get nailed by a woman."

"Really?" Hyperion glared. "You're going there?"

"I'm telling you," I said, "he nailed himself."

One corner of Brik's mouth quirked upward. "That I can believe."

The Tarot reader huffed.

"I only grabbed the nail gun in self-defense." I pointed at Hyperion. "You yanked my arm, and it went off. It was an accident. But I'm sorry.

I shouldn't have—I'm sorry." Because in fairness, I had been holding the nail gun. I didn't *think* my finger had been on the trigger, but it had been dark, and I'd been... Well, not panicked. But I hadn't exactly been at my best.

"Was there much damage?" Hyperion asked, anxious.

"You tell me," Brik said. "You're the one who was shot."

"Fire damage," he clarified. "We've got enough problems to worry about without a burned-out building to repair. How bad is it?" he asked, straining forward.

I stared. *We*? We were still a "we" after he'd accused me of shooting him in the leg?

A siren sounded in the distance.

"There was a small bonfire of boxes in the room at the front of the building," Brik said. "There was another garbage fire in the hallway. I put them both out before there was any real damage, aside from scorch marks on the concrete."

"Two fires?" I asked. "But that means it wasn't accidental. We aren't crazy. Someone set those fires. Someone else was in the building."

"No sh— kidding, Sherlock." Hyperion gripped the contractor's hand. "You saved me. Thank you, even if it was your fault she picked up the nail gun in the first place."

The siren grew louder.

"Someone was in the building with us," I said. "Picking up the nail gun was a perfectly logical thing to do after Reince was killed right outside." I only hoped the police saw it that way. And what was Brik doing here?

I opened my mouth to ask, but a Jeep Commander with a blue light on the dash pulled slowly into the parking lot. I snapped my mouth shut as it rolled to a halt beside us.

The headlights cut. The driver's door opened, and a booted foot stepped onto the pavement.

Detective Chase emerged from the Jeep. He rubbed his chin and shifted his weight, planting one hand on his hip to reveal the gun beneath his blazer. "What do we have here?"

"Someone broke into our building," I said.

"And tried to kill us," Hyperion said.

"Is that a nail in your thigh, Mr. Night," the detective asked, "or are you just happy to see me?"

"Oh." Hyperion coughed. "This is nothing. An accident."

My muscles relaxed. Hyperion wasn't ratting me out. Not that I didn't deserve it.

The detective's eyes narrowed. "Are you sick?" he asked Hyperion and edged away.

"Paranoid much?" Hyperion coughed again. "It's smoke inhalation."

"I've never taken a sick day in my life," the detective said. "And I don't intend to start now."

"Stoic." Hyperion winced, tightening the grip on his leg.

An ambulance wailed into the parking lot, red and blue lights cascading across the pavement.

"And what's your role in this circus?" the detective asked Brik.

He raked a hand through his blond hair. "I realized I'd forgotten my nail gun inside. Hyperion had asked me to give him an estimate on work for the building. I knew these two would be here tonight, so I dropped by to pick it up. When I arrived, there was a small fire going near the front door and one in the hallway. I extinguished both and found Hyperion and Abigail in the kitchen. Hyperion had been injured." His eyes glinted. "I helped him outside and called you."

"Now, see?" The detective turned to us. "Simple. Clear. That's the way to give a statement. It's almost as if you've had some practice at this." He glanced at Brik.

The contractor's eyes narrowed.

Black cases in hand, two paramedics bustled to us. They knelt beside Hyperion. "What happened?"

"Nail gun." Hyperion's head lolled against the stucco building.

The red-headed paramedic grimaced. "Not another one."

I blinked. Were nail gun accidents common?

The second whipped out a pocketknife and sliced Hyperion's slacks to the thigh.

Hyperion whimpered. "Those were new."

They patched him up, then bundled Hyperion onto a stretcher and lifted him into the ambulance.

I bit my lip and looked uncertainly to the detective. "Is it okay if we follow him to the hospital?"

"By all means," Chase drawled. "Let's all go. In fact, I'll drive."

Brik's jaw clenched.

I motioned with my thumb over my shoulder. "But I have my car—"

"I'll drive," Detective Chase said.

I locked up, and a silent Brik and I piled into the detective's enormous Jeep (I got stuck in back). We followed the ambulance up San Borromeo's winding streets to the highway.

"Do you normally leave your nail gun lying around?" the detective asked.

"No," Brik said shortly.

"The nail gun was an accident." I leaned between the seats. "But someone really was inside the building. What if that person was connected to Reince's murder?"

"Have you got your seatbelt on?" the detective asked me.

I slid back in the seat and snapped on the belt. "Yes."

"You could get me a ticket if you don't."

"But the intruder—"

"You sure there was one, and you didn't just *accidentally* set the fire yourselves?" Detective Chase asked.

"I saw someone leaving the building when I drove into the parking lot," Brik said. "I didn't get a good look and assumed it was Abigail or Hyperion. But someone else was in there."

I shot him a grateful look, which he missed since I was sitting behind him. The detective would have to believe us now.

"Hm." Detective Chase cut a quick glance at the contractor. "How did you say you know these two? You're bidding for contracting work?"

"Yes."

"You from around here?"

"No."

"When'd you move here?"

"Last month," Brik said.

"A man of few words." The detective was silent for a minute. "I suppose that construction work would be nice to have, you being new in town."

"Not nice enough that I'd commit perjury," Brik said.

"Not even for a nice young lady like Abigail here?"

Brik growled something inaudible. It sounded a lot like, *blech*. But I'd take *blech* if it meant confirming my story with the cops.

We pulled into the hospital parking lot. Peppering us with questions, Detective Chase led us to the Emergency Room's waiting area. It was a surprisingly comfortable room with soft faux-leather chairs and couches in muted pastels.

The detective dipped into his pocket. Extracting one of those face masks doctors wear, he slipped it over his face.

Wow. He really did come prepared for anything.

Brik's lips curled with scorn.

"Sneer all you want," Detective Chase said. "Do you know who comes to hospitals? Sick people."

Thirty minutes later, I slouched deeper in my mauve chair. "I'm telling you, someone else set that fire."

"Why?" the detective asked, his voice muffled by the mask. "Why your building? Why you?"

I bit my bottom lip and glanced longingly at the wall clock. The second hand ticked forward, hesitated, as if stuck, and then ticked backward once and stopped.

The glass doors to the parking lot swished open, and I did a double take.

Clutching a bulky purse to her chest, the receptionist from the realty walked into the waiting room. The older woman looked around, licking her lips, and smoothed her pale green skirt and matching floral print blouse. Spotting us, Florence's eyes widened behind her cat-eye glasses. She minced to our grouping of chairs.

The detective and Brik stood.

"Oh, my goodness!" She toyed with the green plastic beads hung around her neck. "The police called and told me that Mr. Night had been hurt at the building, so I came here right away. Is he going to be all right?"

"The police called you?" The detective's brow furrowed.

"Oh," she said, "they called Mr. Bonnet, and he called me."

I smothered a groan. What must the lawyer think of us? Neither of us should have been inside the building yet. And the fire! He'd never let us rent the place now.

"Mr. Bonnet said there was an assault," the receptionist said, her voice quavering. "Is it true?"

Surprised, I raised my head. Assault and not arson?

Hold on. Was I guilty of assault with a nail gun?

"Mr. Night was injured in an accident," the detective said. "But it looked to me like he'll be all right."

Florence turned to me. "From now on, if there are any problems, please contact me directly. Here, let me give you my number."

I handed her my phone. The flash went off, and she yelped. "Oh! Did I just take a selfie?"

I glanced at the screen, and an image of Florence's surprised face. "Um, yeah."

"Sorry. I'll just... I don't even know how to delete it."

"Don't worry about it," I said.

She tapped on the screen. "There you go." She returned the phone. "I included my email address too, just in case. Say, whenever a friend of mine calls, her picture shows up on the screen. How do you do that?"

I demonstrated, using her photo on my phone, while the men shifted impatiently.

"Ma'am, what exactly are you doing here?" the detective finally interrupted.

Florence's gray lashes fluttered. "Someone was hurt in a building we were renting! True, we weren't *really* renting it. How were we to know what Reince was up to? But that still makes us responsible." She sighed. "Or at least, that's what Mr. Bonnet seems to think. He was quite angry when the police called him at this hour."

"I can imagine," I muttered, tasting something sour at the back of my throat.

"Why are you at the hospital rather than Mr. or Mrs. Archer?" the detective asked her.

"Oh!" Her bulging eyes widened. "I'm the emergency number for the realty. The Archers are too busy in the evenings to deal with issues like these. They work so hard, especially Diana. It takes a lot of energy to run your own business. That's why Diana is getting me on her new healthy eating plan. Do you know Diana lost eight pounds on it last month? She had to buy all new clothing." The older woman beamed. "Isn't that something!"

"Fascinating," the detective said. "If you all will excuse me, I think I see someone I know." He wandered into a corner to speak with a doctor in a white coat.

Conspiratorial, Florence leaned toward me. "Though I don't think Cyrus was too happy about Diana's latest credit card bill. All that new clothing, and dinners at that fancy restaurant with the cable car!"

"Elegy?" I asked, confused. It was a quasi-famous local spot with views overlooking the ocean.

"I think I see someone too." Brik edged away.

"She only went to celebrate her accomplishment with a friend. Diana always says it's important to celebrate our victories, even the small ones." Florence frowned. "I wish she'd invited me, but I've only just started my eating plan."

"Um, did Mr. Bonnet say anything else to you about the building?"

"He was shouting, so I didn't quite get it all. That lawyer does have a temper, doesn't he?"

My heart plummeted. We were so doomed.

CHAPTER FIFTEEN

GRAMPS PEERED AROUND THE café and lowered himself into the pale-green booth. "I don't know why you wanted to sit here." He set his checked, cabbie-style hat on the table. "The lighting's better by the window." He waved to an elderly man hobbling down a narrow aisle.

The scents of Wild Thyme bacon and potatoes wafted through the air. Something sizzled in the open kitchen at the far end of the restaurant.

I scooted into the booth and leaned across the table. "Because—"

"There you are!" Tomas slid into the booth, and my grandfather shifted over to make way. Tomas's brown eyes twinkled. "Switching up our morning routine?" His blue plaid shirt lay open at the collar and his trousers hung loosely on his lanky frame. He stretched a long, bronzed arm across the back of the booth.

"I invited Tomas," Gramps said.

"I was hoping you would," I said. Tomas was a retired lawyer.

"You look lovely," Tomas said, nodding to my red sleeveless dress. "Not a bad choice. Of restaurant, I mean. This place does a good huevos rancheros."

"It's my favorite," I said in a low voice. "But the real reason I wanted to meet here is because this is where Reince did most of his business."

Gramps' white brows lowered. "That con artist?"

"Yeah," I said. "He met most of his clients here. This was his favorite booth."

Tomas laughed. "And you think the waitresses might know something."

"Antonia told me a little bit, but she seemed uncomfortable talking about a customer. I thought we could try again."

I'd been amazed Antonia had told me as much as she had. Reince – her presumed lover – had been murdered, and she was too nice to gossip. But Gramps was my secret weapon. He looked as sweet and twinkly and harmless as Antonia, and waitresses thought he was cute.

My grandfather nodded. "If the police won't find that money, maybe someone here knows something. You were never the sort to let the grass grow under your feet."

Tomas sobered. "Your grandfather told me about your troubles. Real shame." He shot a quick glance at Gramps. "Now don't you worry about the rent. We'll figure something out."

I felt heat rush to my face. "Thanks, but... if I can't make the payments, I'll move out so you can find a new tenant." And I really hoped that didn't happen, because I loved that bungalow. But I wasn't about to take advantage of Tomas's kindness.

Tomas frowned. "Now, Abigail—"

Antonia bustled to the booth and flipped open her notepad. Today's t-shirt read: I'M NOT ALWAYS RUDE – SOMETIMES I'M SLEEPING. "Good morning gentlemen and lady!" She pointed. "My grandfather had a hat just like that! I love it!" Smiling, she pulled a pen from the bun of gleaming black hair piled atop her head. "Can I get you started with coffee or juice?"

We ordered drinks and watched her zip to the kitchen.

"Is she the one?" Gramps asked. "She's too sweet. I don't think I can ask."

"Yes, and we have to," I said. "She seemed to know Reince, er, well, but I didn't get far."

"What did you tell her?" Tomas asked.

I explained.

Gramps shook his head and frowned. "You dodged the truth a bit, don't you think?"

"About finding the body?" And being a suspect? Heck yes, I'd dodged the truth. I shifted, and my thighs squeaked against the faux-leather seat.

"You were taken advantage of," Gramps said. "You've got nothing to be ashamed of. It wasn't your fault."

Oh. That truth. My gaze dropped to the table, because I should never have agreed to six months' rent. Maybe getting conned wasn't my fault, but I shouldn't have lost quite so much.

Antonia returned, and we ordered while Gramps chatted her up about the weather, her work, her family.

"I'll be back with your food." The waitress patted my grandfather's hand, turned on her heel and strode to the kitchen.

"Now I'm feeling guilty." Tomas fiddled with his collar. "She's adorable."

"You're a heartless lawyer, remember?"

"I *did* once kill a man with a bottlecap," he mused.

I laced my hands around my glass of iced tea. "There's something else I need to tell you. I still haven't heard from the lawyer about the building. But I've spoken with a contractor, and the repairs are going to cost more than we expected."

My grandfather grimaced. "You're going to have to find a new spot, aren't you?"

"Maybe not." My hands slid along the cool glass, damp with condensation, and I tried to swallow. "I've been talking to the other man who rented the building — or thought he had — Hyperion Night."

My grandfather's brows drew downward. "That psychic fellow?"

I braced myself. "He suggested we work together and provide Tea and Tarot."

Tomas choked on his coffee. "Psychic? Tarot cards?"

"It's not such a crazy idea," I said rapidly. "There's a history of telling fortunes with tea leaves."

Gramps gave me a look. "You sound like your mother."

"I know, I know, but it makes sense. Hyperion can bring in Tarot readers during the day, and we'll put their services on the menu." I explained our idea.

"Interesting," Tomas said.

My grandfather's shaggy brows rocketed upward. "You think?"

He shrugged. "You know my grandmother was a *curandera*. Folk magic isn't going away, and in this area, people are especially interested in that stuff."

I smiled, grateful. If Tomas didn't hate the idea, my grandfather might warm to it. And with his money on the line too, my grandfather got a say.

Gramps cocked his head. "I do like the idea of earning money off that space in the evenings, when your tea shop is closed. But don't you want to do this on your own? You were always an independent girl. I didn't think you'd want to work with a partner."

"If I want this tearoom, I don't have much choice."

He shook his head. "You know what you want. But I think you've overlooked a flaw in your plan."

A cold, lead weight thudded inside my midsection. "What?" That I sounded like my feckless parents, and neither had a nickel to their names?

"Here you are." The waitress appeared beside our table and unloaded the food. "Is there anything else I can get you?"

Gramps scooted from the booth. "Can you tell me where the men's room is?" He stumbled, and she caught his elbow before I could move.

"I'll show you," she said. "This way." She walked him to a hallway at the rear of the restaurant.

I watched Gramps, moving more slowly than usual, vanish around the corner. "Is he okay?"

"He's just acting frail for the waitress."

I gnawed my bottom lip. "I really hope I can make this tearoom work. I don't want to disappoint him."

"You're not your parents," he said quietly, his acorn-colored eyes serious. "Your grandfather knows that. And you'll never disappoint him."

A hard lump formed in my throat, and I looked out the window. On the sidewalk, a young father lifted his toddler over his head and sat him on his shoulders. The boy squealed with delight and gripped his father's hair.

"Do you think I should move in with Gramps?" I asked.

"There will come a day when you may have to. But don't rush it. He'd hate being taken care of, and right now, he's fine on his own." He paused. "Are you going to invite your parents to your grand opening?" Tomas asked shrewdly.

My hand tightened on my spoon, and I rubbed my thumb along its edge. "Last I'd heard, Mom was at some ashram in India, and Dad was in Fiji." Their quests for personal development had finally led the couple to drift apart too.

"Forgiveness isn't for them, Abigail. It's for you."

"If they ever come back to California, maybe I'll get a chance." I knew he was right. But I didn't want to think about it now. There were too many other, more immediate, problems to solve.

My grandfather returned to our booth five minutes later and shook his head. "She lent that scoundrel two-hundred dollars."

Tomas sipped his coffee. "Some fellows have all the luck."

"That's all she told you?" I asked, dismayed.

"It's enough," he said. "What kind of monster could take advantage of a sweet girl like that?"

"Con artists tell themselves their victims deserve it," Tomas said, "that they're greedy."

"Well, thanks for trying," I said. "You said there was a flaw in my plan for the tearoom?"

Antonia stopped by the table. "How is everything?"

"Excellent," Tomas said.

The phone rang in my purse. Hoping it might be William Bonnet, I pulled it from its pocket. Florence's face popped onto the screen, her expression frozen and wide-eyed.

"It's from the office where Reince worked," I said. "Is it okay if I take this?"

"Go ahead." Gramps nodded. "They might have information about the stolen money."

I put the phone to my ear. "Hi, this is Abigail."

A garbled sound, as if from underwater.

"Hello?"

More scratchy noises and gabbling.

"Hello?" I asked more loudly. "Uh, Florence, I think you've butt dialed me." I hung up and pressed redial. The phone rang and went to voicemail.

"Hi, Florence, this is Abigail Beanblossom. I just got a call from you. But I couldn't hear anything, so I'm assuming it was an accidental call. Anyway, if I'm wrong, ring me back." I disconnected and set the phone on the table.

"Is everything all right?" Tomas asked.

"Fine," I said. "She must have dialed me by accident."

"I recognize her," Antonia said slowly, pointing at the phone on the table. "That woman."

"She's the receptionist where Reince worked," I said.

Antonia's brows knit. "Receptionist? That's weird."

"What do you mean?" Gramps asked.

The waitress's cheeks flushed crimson. "I try not to listen in on customers' conversations."

"Of course not," Gramps said stoutly.

"Never," agreed Tomas.

"But I do remember that woman," she said, "because she lent Reince money too. Or at least, she promised to lend him money. I don't know if she actually went ahead with it. I thought she might have been his mother."

"Why his mother?" I asked.

"It was just the way they were together. She was... protective?" She scratched her chin with the edge of her notepad. "That's not quite the right word. Reince wouldn't talk about her, and I didn't ask."

Strange. I was sure she'd told Diana that she hadn't trusted Reince. "Did you hear how much she was lending him?" I asked.

"Ten thousand, I think? It's why I stopped— Well, when I heard that, I started to get worried about the money I'd given him. I mean, it wasn't so much, but I try to save money for my family." Her head jerked up, and she nodded to another customer. "I've got to go. If you need anything else, just let me know. I'm sorry about your money." She hustled to another b ooth.

"Ten thousand dollars." Tomas shook his head. "It's enough to kill over, if you're angry enough."

"I don't know," I said, thoughtful. "Florence didn't strike me as the vengeful type." But she might have felt ashamed if she'd given him money and realized she'd been taken for a fool. Would the humiliation have been enough for her to kill over?

Antonia had said she'd only lent Reince two hundred bucks, but they'd been involved. And hell hath no fury, etc., etc. "Could Antonia have—?"

"No." Tomas and Gramps said in unison.

"Okay, okay. I'm just trying to cover all possibilities."

"Antonia wouldn't hurt a fly," my grandfather said, and I sort of agreed. "What do you know about this Florence person?" he asked.

"Not much," I said. "But it was a little weird she called me this morning. And she showed up at the hospital last night."

"Hospital?" Tomas asked. "Why were you at the hospital?"

Gramps smirked. "She shot someone with a nail gun."

"You what?" Tomas's brown eyes bulged. "You have to be careful with those."

"Oh, stop. You once killed someone with a bottlecap. And I didn't shoot him. He grabbed the nail gun, and it went off."

"Huh. Whose finger was on the trigger?" Tomas poured Tabasco sauce on the mound of huevos rancheros and potatoes.

"I'm not sure." My chin sank to my chest. *Had* I pulled the trigger?

He gave me a skeptical look and dug into his huevos.

"Which brings us back to this Hyperion fellow," my grandfather said. "I trust your judgment. But you should think carefully before making any decisions about partnering with this guy."

"I know this is happening fast, but we've got some good ideas."

"I'm not worried about your ideas." Gramps wooly brows drew downward. "That psychic was a victim of this conman too. The body was found behind your building, where he was working. Abigail, he's a suspect in the murder."

CHAPTER SIXTEEN

OUTSIDE THE CAFÉ, I leaned against my Mazda. Though the metal door of my car was cool, the morning was warming, and I was glad I'd chosen a sleeveless dress.

Teenagers in board shorts slouched down the crooked sidewalk toward the beach. Mrs. Honeyfoot, a retiree from my grandfather's church, emerged from a wine tasting room and set up a sandwich board beside a green-painted lamp post. She waved to me, and I waved back. Seagulls wheeled overhead, cawing, and the scent of fresh-baked pastries from a nearby bakery flooded the narrow street.

I couldn't politely wait for William Bonnet to call anymore. I needed to know if we had the building or not. Heart thumping in my ears, I made the call.

"William Bonnet," he answered briskly.

"Hello, Mr. Bonnet. This is Abigail Beanblossom."

"Ms. Beanblossom! I was just about to call you."

"Oh?" I crossed my fingers and my toes.

"My client has agreed to rent the building, as is. If you're willing to deal with any repairs, it's yours." He named a price.

I bounced on my toes. Together, Hyperion and I could just pay it. We had the building! My tearoom was going to happen!

"The first three months will need to be paid up front," he warned.

My stomach twisted. Of course they would. But after having lost my first upfront payment, the idea made me a little sick.

A white Hyundai cruised hopefully past my parking spot. The car stopped, and an Asian man in glasses leaned out the open window. "Are you leaving?"

"Um. Yeah," I said.

"What?" the lawyer asked.

"Sorry." I fumbled with my car keys and opened the door. "That should work."

"Shall I email the paperwork to the address on your card?"

"Yes, please." I slithered into the driver's seat. "Though there has been a slight change." I closed my eyes. The lawyer had not liked Hyperion, and I hoped it wouldn't be a problem. But it was better to tell him now. "I have a new business partner — Hyperion Night. Both our names will need to be on any documents."

He paused. "Mr. Night? The fortune teller?"

"Since my tearoom is open only during the daytime," I said, talking fast, "he suggested using the space for his Tarot classes in the evenings." Biting my lip, I put the phone on speaker and set it on my dash.

"Wouldn't you rather sub-let it to him?"

An uncomfortable flush of heat rolled across my skin. I hadn't even considered sub-letting – an option that would have given me more control. What else hadn't I considered? "We're working out the details now. But on the whole, this should make the business more profitable," I said more confidently and started the car.

"Adding another name to the agreement is an easy correction," he said slowly. "I'll send it to you for review."

My heart started beating again. "Yes. Yes! Thank you so much! I'm so excited about this building!" I punched my fist in the air, banged it on the car roof, and repressed a shout of pain.

"I expect to be invited to the grand opening."

"You will be." Rubbing my injured hand on my thigh, I pulled from the spot, and the Hyundai zipped into my place.

The lawyer and I said our goodbyes and hung up.

Feeling optimistic, I drove to the 2304 building. I unlocked the rear door and propped it open with the kick-down stopper. The electricity wasn't on yet, and the windowless rear hallway was sunk in gloom. But it was *my* gloomy hallway, and elation fizzed in my veins.

Bone-colored light drifted from the front room and faintly illuminated the passage. Black smoke stains smeared the wall and floor where the fire had burned last night.

I toed the ashes with my red sandal, and a shiver crawled up my spine. No incriminating matchbooks or lighters rolled from the charred mess of burnt cardboard.

So much for clues.

I picked my way to the front room. Sunlight shone through the streaked and dusty windows. It turned the spiraling dust motes to gold and spotlighted every pile of dirt and scrap of trash on the cement floor.

I sighed. The arsonist had had a lot of flammable material to choose from.

A matching scorch mark crawled up the wall near the blue front door. I knelt and brushed my fingertips through the ashes. All I got for my sleuthing was gray fingers.

Dropping my crimson purse on the sawhorse table, I stood in the center of the room and turned slowly. The counter would go against the left wall. Behind it, shelves where metal tins of loose tea would be displayed for sale. Above, a chalkboard menu.

My vision wavered. The plans would have to change if I was partnering with Hyperion. Why *hadn't* I considered sub-letting? But my anxiety was mingled with excitement and possibility.

Returning to the windowless kitchen, I felt for the wall switch before I remembered there was no power.

I studied the dim, blocky silhouettes of counter, stove, table. We could make this work. Nodding, I walked outside to the parking lot, jammed the doorstop up, and gave the door a push closed. It shut with a satisfying c lang.

I reached for my purse. It wasn't on my shoulder.

I stared at the heavy metal door. "Augh!" I'd left my purse inside.

Frantic, I tugged on the handle.

Locked.

I patted the pockets of my red dress. Phone? In my purse. Car keys? Ditto.

I swore, kicked the door, and pain shot from my toes to my shin. Grimacing, I leaned against the building and took deep breaths. Note to self: don't kick down doors in open-toed sandals.

I blew out my breath. Okay. This wasn't a total disaster. Hyperion had told me Brik would be stopping by in an hour or so. He had Hyperion's key and could let me inside.

He'd think I was an airhead, but I couldn't blame him for that. And I really needed my purse.

Heat radiated off the black pavement. I pressed against the stucco wall and its thin line of shade. Sweat beaded my hairline.

Desperate, I reached into my pockets again. Eureka! A crumpled and faded five-dollar bill. Which goes to show there's always a silver lining. Or in this case, a five-dollar bill that had gone through the wash.

Optimistic once more, I walked around the buildings to the sidewalk. The whirligigs in the shop entrance beside my soon-to-be Tea and Tarot room stood motionless in the still air. Beach-themed windcatchers drooped around a tin mermaid with a green and gold tail.

I aimed for the coffeeshop a block away. I could grab a seat and a glass of something cold while I waited for the contractor.

Cyrus Archer emerged from the post office. The realtor paused beneath its limp American flag. His gaze darted up and down the crowded street.

He gave the street another up-and-down look and strode off.

Huh.

It was almost as if Cyrus was worried about being followed.

This really made me want to follow him.

I leapt into the entryway of a comic book shop, its windows plastered with superheroes, and I peered around the corner.

He walked away, his arms swinging.

Why *not* follow him? It wasn't like I had anything better to do. I hurried after the realtor and swerved around a brick planter filled with impatiens.

Cyrus stopped short. Looked over his shoulder.

I turned, framing my face with my hands, and peered into a shop window. Inside, a woman arranged a filmy scarf over a mannequin. She gave me a startled look.

Smiling, I edged from the window.

Cyrus was moving on.

I needed something better to hide behind. Like a newspaper, or...

"Ice cream!" A vendor pushed his cart, bell jingling, down the sidewalk.

Cyrus glanced over his shoulder again.

"I'll have an ice cream," I said, digging the money from my pocket.

"What flavor?"

"Your biggest. And one that costs less than five dollars including tax."

A trio of high school-aged girls in shorts and tanks drifted between Cyrus and me.

The ice cream man frowned but fished inside his cart.

Cyrus turned a corner.

"Never mind."

"Wait. Here." He handed me a ginormous ice cream treat.

"Thanks." I handed him the bill and trotted off.

"Wait. Your change!"

"Keep it!" I hurried around the corner.

Cyrus strode down the sidewalk, and I blew out my breath, relieved. I hadn't lost him.

I stopped by a garbage bin and unpeeled the wrapper from my ice cream. *Oooh! Chocolate.* Which I couldn't eat because ice cream is the single dairy product I have an intolerance for. It's cruel and unfair, but at least I still have frozen yogurt. I could really go for one right now.

Cyrus looked over his shoulder.

I angled myself away, raising the ice cream to hide my profile. After a moment or so, I risked a peek.

He strode away from me, past a vintage record store and clothing boutiques and down the sunny sidewalk.

I followed him all the way from downtown to a leafy condominium complex on Decatur Street.

Something cold dripped along my hand. I glanced down. Chocolate ice cream slithered down the cone and coiled in brown rivulets around my knuckles. Napkinless, I licked it off, imagining a burning sensation starting in my gut.

The realtor punched in a code at the pedestrian gate. He walked into the complex.

My heart leapt. This was Decatur Street. Antonia had told me Reince had a condo on Decatur Street!

The gate swung slowly closed.

I raced forward and grabbed it before it clicked shut. Ha! That was one door I hadn't been locked out of. I waited a few moments and walked through.

Hands sticky, I trailed Cyrus along the winding paths. We passed a club house and swimming pool, Japanese maples and pink camellia bushes. He seemed to know where he was going, because he didn't hesitate, and the place was a freaking maze.

He opened a latticed gate and walked inside.

I paused beside a matching, latticed window that overlooked a small patio.

Inside, Cyrus squatted beside a flowerpot overflowing with spider plants. He pulled out a dirt-covered metal box. The realtor opened it, walked to the door, fiddled with the lock, and went inside.

Now what?

"What are you doing?"

I high jumped about a mile.

Brik stood, arms crossed over his ripped white tee, and frowned.

"How did you...?" I sputtered. "What?"

"I tracked you from the tearoom."

"How?"

He pointed to the cement walk. A splatter of chocolate marked the spot. "I followed the ice cream."

"I'm following Reince's partner," I whispered, "Cyrus Archer."

"Why?"

"Because he was behaving suspiciously."

He lifted a single blond brow. "*He* was behaving suspiciously?"

"Also, I might have locked my purse in the tearoom."

"Why didn't you call me?"

"Duh." I rolled my eyes. "My phone was in my purse."

"And you didn't have anything better to do than follow a realtor?"

Just what was he implying? "Wait here and see if he comes out," I hissed. "I'm going to find out who this condo belongs to."

"This should be exciting," he said dryly.

I jogged to the complex's front gate. As I'd hoped, there was a listing of names beside the condo numbers. I ran my finger down the list. Yes! The condo belonged to Reince Briggs. "I *knew* it." I hurried back to Brik.

"He's still in there," he whispered loudly.

"Good. He's breaking and entering. That's a dead man's condo." I grabbed the knob on the lattice gate.

Brik touched my arm, halting me. "What are you doing?"

"I'm going to talk to Cyrus. We've caught him red-handed."

"That's not a good idea."

"He can't kill me. Not when you've witnessed me going inside."

"Uh..."

I walked into the patio. The door to the condo stood open, a strip of yellow police tape hanging off one side and billowing in the breeze.

Hey, the police tape had already been broken, and an open door is practically an invitation to investigate. By going inside, I was just being neighborly, making sure things were okay. Right?

I stepped inside the most boring room ever. No pictures on the white walls. A card table with a single folding metal chair. A discarded pizza box. No throw pillows on the gray couch. A TV. All it needed was a camera on a tripod, and I could believe cops used this place for stakeouts.

Brik stepped inside. "Huh. The minimalist approach."

There was a crash from another room. I moved toward the noise.

"Hold on," Brik said. "Who's there?" he shouted.

"It's okay," Cyrus hollered. "I have permission." He emerged from a back room, and his face turned gray.

I stared.

The realtor had lost weight since I'd seen him last. His sports jacket seemed roomier. The bones in his face stood out more prominently. Maybe he was on Diana's diet too. "You," he rasped.

"Hi." I waggled my fingers. "Um, are you okay?" Because he didn't look good.

He stared back, his eyes hollow in their sockets. "What are you doing here?"

"What are *you* doing here?" I asked. "This is Reince's apartment. And that was police tape outside."

"I was..." He collapsed onto the sofa arm. "Hell."

"The police have already searched the place," I said slowly. "What do you think you'll find?"

"Think?" He laughed, voice strained. "Hope. I hope I'll find my money."

"Don't you think the police would have told you if they'd found a pile of cash?" I asked.

Cyrus shook his head. "Reince said he had a secret hiding place. I thought maybe I could find it. He stole from the company too. We're insured, but... I can't let it go."

I sighed. "Tell me about it."

Brik's eyes glinted. "What sort of secret hiding place?"

"No idea," he said. "But options are limited in a rental."

Brik scanned the floor. He disappeared into the kitchen.

"How did you find me?" Cyrus asked.

Thumps emerged from the kitchen.

"Someone told me Reince had a condo on Decatur," I said. It wasn't a lie, and admitting I'd gone stalker didn't seem like a good idea. I wondered how often Antonia had been here. "Was Reince seeing anyone?"

"We didn't discuss his love life. Why?"

"Just grasping at straws." Antonia had volunteered the information that they'd been involved. It didn't seem like the action of a killer. Plus, I *liked* Antonia.

Frowning, Brik walked into the living area. "Nothing there." He studied the brick fireplace and cocked his head. The contractor paced to the fireplace and ran one finger across the grout. He pulled a knife from the small sheath at his hip and flipped it open.

"Did you find something?" Cyrus asked excitedly.

In answer, the contractor stuck his knife into the grout and levered out a brick.

We crowded behind him. I don't know about the others, but I was holding my breath.

Brik reached inside the hole and ran his fingers along the back. "Empty."

My breath hitched with disappointment.

Cyrus scrubbed his hands over his face. "This is a nightmare. This *has* to be the hiding place he was talking about. But where's the money?"

"Whoever killed him must have taken it," I said. Maybe Reince's murder *had* been a simple robbery gone wrong? "But how did they know he had money on him?"

"Maybe he didn't," Cyrus said. "Maybe the killer just saw Reince withdraw cash from the ATM and thought he'd take it."

I sagged. If Cyrus was right, if the murder had been random, the odds of catching the guy had just dropped to near zero.

My money was gone.

CHAPTER SEVENTEEN

BRIK WALKED ME TO the tearoom.

I told him the good news about the building. "So, you can start work for real."

"Groovy," he said, and I was pretty sure he was using the word unironically. The contractor unlocked the rear door. "And congratulations."

"Thanks!" I retrieved my purse and called Hyperion from the front room, the bare cement cool through my sandals.

Brik propped open the blue front door. A cross breeze scented with sea air flowed into the room. It fluttered the hem of my red dress.

The phone rang five times, and a machine picked up. "This is Hyperion Night. *Someone* shot me in the leg with a nail gun, but I'll be working today in spite of my disability. Leave a message."

I winced. "It's Abigail." And then I blurted. "We got the building!"

Brik glanced at me and unclipped a retractable measuring tape from his belt.

There was a click and an answering squeal. "I knew it! I told you we would! Wait, does that lawyer know about me? Forget it, it doesn't matter."

The contractor measured a window.

"He knows," I said. "How's your leg?"

The measuring tape rattled back into its casing, and Brik made a note in a small pad.

"My leg hurts like hell," Hyperion said. "But at least my tetanus shot is up to date."

"Um, speaking of up to date, Mr. Bonnet wants three months' rent in advance."

There was a long silence. "I guess we had to expect that. But you ran the numbers, didn't you? We can do it, right?"

"Y-es." But Hyperion should have known the answer without asking. True, not everyone is a numbers person. I was lucky to have my grandfather to advise me. But our Tea and Tarot room would be Hyperion's too.

"Then it's settled," he said.

Brik measured another window.

My brows drew together. "Maybe we should go over the numbers again? Together?"

Another clatter of measuring tape.

"Why?" Hyperion asked. "You and your grandfather checked them over."

"Yes," I said, "but this is your money too. It's important you understand everything. I don't want to have any misunderstandings down the road." *Or to find out I'm working with a snarky version of one of my parents.*

He blew out his breath. "Fine. Come to my studio. I'm free for the afternoon. We can go over whatever it is you want me to look at."

"I'll come now. Bye."

He hung up.

"You going somewhere?" Brik asked.

"To Hyperion's office. No more trailing suspects. Promise."

"Are your fingers crossed?"

"Funny, funny."

In the parking lot, I searched for Hyperion online and found his address on his website — sleek, colorful and simple. At least he knew design, or he knew to hire someone who did.

I dumped the phone in my purse, opened the Mazda's door, and hesitated. Retrieving my phone, I returned to the internet and an online review site.

Hyperion was listed. His reviews averaged four and a half stars. There was one complaint, from a woman who said he was self-righteous, talked nonsense, and was obviously cold reading.

Biting my lower lip, I shifted against the hot car. But that was only one review out of fifty-two. Most of his clients were happy, and that was a good sign.

Hyperion's address wasn't far. Unwilling to give up my parking spot, I left the car where it was and started walking.

A fishy smell arose from the bridge over the estuary, where the river met the ocean. Balconied restaurants and tiny, stucco, pastel bungalows overlooked its banks. A salty breeze tugged free a wisp of my hair, and I tucked it behind my ear.

I climbed higher, panting up a steep, treelined hill, and then turned east, away from the ocean and into a low valley. The air was still and stuffy in the bowl-shaped depression.

Unenthusiastically, I gazed at Hyperion's office — a squat, unlovely building with zero view of the ocean. No wonder he wanted to move.

Hitching my purse over my shoulder, I strode to a pair of glass doors. They opened onto a seventies-style hallway. White plastic letters in a corrugated sign board listed the tenants in the two-story building. Someone had removed the last three letters of Hyperion's first name, so it read: HYPER   NIGHT 203.

I smothered a grin.

Ignoring the elevator, I climbed the concrete steps and walked down a dingy hall. In the ceiling, a fluorescent light flickered, pinging metallically. I was no psychic, but even I could tell this place had bad mojo.

I rapped softly on the scuffed wooden door to room 203 and walked into a reception area. A thin, brick-colored carpet covered the floor. Three closed office doors branched from the waiting area. In an alcove on the left, a woman labored at a computer.

Without looking up, she pointed to a placard on the wall above her: DEVON REYNOLDS - FINANCIAL PLANNING.

I scanned the three closed doors. Hyperion's wasn't hard to deduce. An arc of twinkle lights blinked above his name, in sparkly gold letters.

I knocked.

Hyperion, in a navy suit, blue-striped shirt, and purple cravat, peeked out the door. "Are you armed?"

"Of course, I'm not—"

He pressed a finger to his lips, motioned me inside, and shut the door. "The reiki master next door has a client. We have to be quiet."

"Nice outfit," I whispered. Not a lot of men can pull off a silk cravat.

"I told you, Annie Oakley, I'm meeting clients. And you don't have to whisper inside my office."

I rolled my eyes, my gaze coming to rest on the gauze-draped ceiling. The ivory fabric probably hid pipes or something equally unsightly. Matching gauze worked as drapes over big, square windows.

The tabby dropped from a side table decorated like a pagan altar with flameless candles, crystals, and driftwood. The cat bumped his head against my shin.

I bent to pet Bastet.

"Have you got the contract?" Hyperion limped to a wide, round table covered in a black cloth. He rested his hand on one of the red velvet armchairs beside it.

I dropped into the chair opposite, setting my purse on the beige carpet, and pulled my phone from my pocket, checked my email. "Yes. I'll forward it to you."

"Here." He snapped his long fingers.

I handed him my phone, and he sent himself the document.

Bastet hopped into my lap, and I grunted. The cat weighed at least twenty pounds.

Hyperion eased into a velvet chair and stretched out his injured leg. "Now, what did you want to talk about?"

I ruffled the cat's fur. "If we're going to be more than co-tenants and work as actual business partners, it's important we both agree on the business side of things."

"The business side is boring. That's why I became a Tarot reader and not an accountant."

I arched a brow. "You find money dull, do you?"

"It does come in handy," he said, grudging. "Don't worry. I'm not one of those New Age types who thinks money is the root of all evil. Unlike you,

I just find accounting tiresome. That's why we're such a good fit. You play to your strengths, and I'll play to mine."

That was a relief. "Fine, but we should still agree on what the other is doing. For example, I wouldn't like it if you launched an expensive advertising campaign without telling me."

He rolled his eyes and crossed his arms, the fabric of his suit jacket rustling. "Show me your plan."

I drew my updated business plan from my bag and slid it across the table. "I worked on this last night."

He arched a brow. "When did you find the time?"

"I couldn't sleep much after—"

"You shot me?" He lowered his chin and raised his brows.

"You yanked the gun. It was an accident."

"That's *your* story." His brown eyes glinted.

"How many times do I have to say I'm sorry?"

"I'll let you know when you get there. At least last night wasn't a total disaster." He pressed the back of his hand to his brow and pretended to swoon. "Brik got to carry me from the burning building like an action hero. And we have the building!" He bounced on his heels with glee and blanched, grabbing his thigh. "Ow."

"Can I get you anything?" I asked.

"World peace? But I'll settle for my calendar." He pointed to a plain desk against the wall opposite the altar.

"Sure." I'd meant get him something for the pain, but I stood.

Bastet dropped to the carpet with an indignant yowl.

A day planner lay open on the desk. "Did you mean your day planner?" My back to him, I flipped the pages to Monday, the night Reince had been killed. Hyperion had seen two clients in the afternoon, and there was a seven P.M. appointment that said, *Wine Bar*.

A cold knot hardened in my stomach. A wine bar backed onto the parking lot where I'd found Reince's body.

"What are you doing?" He lurched from his chair. "Are you...? You're snooping!"

Hastily, I shut the book and handed it over. "No, I just wanted to make sure I was grabbing the right—"

"Oh, come on. You wanted to know where I was on Monday night, when Reince was murdered."

My face heated. What had gotten into me? First tailing Cyrus, then reading Hyperion's datebook? Forget Nancy Drew. I'd turned into a Nancy Don't. "Can you blame me? We're about to become business partners, and Reince was found dead behind our building."

"That's right," he said. "*Our* building. And none of this 'Reince was found,' business. *You* found him. How do I know you're not the killer?"

"You said it yourself. I'm too small to have killed him."

"We don't know how he was killed. Or if *someone* had an accomplice."

"We know he had bruises on his throat."

"Have you ever been punched in the throat?" he asked.

"No."

He rubbed his neck, his fingers whispering over the purple silk. "It doesn't take much power, and it's surprisingly debilitating. You can't breathe. Hit someone hard enough, you can crush their windpipe and it's night-night forever."

"How do you know?"

"I looked it up online."

"You were checking to see if I could have done it?" I asked, outraged.

The cat's head swiveled between us, his ears flicking.

"Duh." He rolled his eyes. "Of course, I was checking up on you. You shot me."

"Well, then... Good. We're both suspicious, and we've both been cleared. Now maybe we can trust each other."

Though Hyperion *could* have met Reince at the wine bar and killed him afterward. But I just couldn't see him as a killer. Hyperion was too... optimistic. Homicide is for pessimists who don't think they have other options.

Or for optimists convinced they can get away with murder.

"Fine." He fell heavily into the red chair. "What did you want to show me?"

"The budget." I hurried to his side and flipped open the business plan. "This is our budget. If you want to change any of these numbers, let me know, because everything's connected. The numbers all tie together."

He whipped a pen from the inside pocket of his navy suit jacket and made notes in the margins. "I'll need time to review this. Let me get back to you later."

"All right." I edged toward the door. "Take your time."

He grunted and didn't look up. "Sit."

"What?"

He shuffled a deck of Tarot cards "You tortured me with your business plan — or you will when I read it. Now it's my turn."

I sat, gripping the arms of the chair. "You're going to read my cards? But you already did that."

"That was for a different question. With your permission, I'd like to do a partnership reading for us both."

He laid out two sets of three cards, one above the other. Hyperion flipped the bottom left card — the Knight of Pentacles. "This is you. Stubborn, plodding, meticulous. But you get stuff done, and keep moving forward, even if you prefer a slower pace." He flipped the card above it — the Queen of Wands. One corner of his mouth lifted. "And I'm the queen. Dynamic, passionate, someone who can bring others together to accomplish tasks. Budget aside, I'm your marketer."

"Okay," I said, "but—"

He wagged a finger. "Uh, uh. My turn." He turned over the bottom middle card. It was the Magician. "Hm. And one of your strengths is being able to bring different elements together to create something new. You make things happen. And I..." He flipped the card above it — the Sun. "Am the Sun. I shine brightly. I attract attention, and good luck follows me wherever I go."

"Murder and con artist aside," I said dryly.

"Oh, we'll get out of that. I hope," he said beneath his breath and turned the last bottom card. It was the Ace of Pentacles. He leaned back in his chair. "A card of good fortune in the material realm. You have all the powers of the pentacles suit at your fingertips. This is a card of new beginnings, of growth, of wealth." He turned the card above it, revealing the Ace of Cups, and his brows rose. "And to your ace, I bring the Ace of Cups. My power is love, and the passion I bring." He sat back in his chair. "Interesting."

"It seems straightforward to me. It was a good reading, right?"

"More than good." He ran his fingers above the top row of cards. "Don't you see? We match. There are three types of Tarot cards — the court cards, by which I mean the kings, queens, knights and pages, the major arcana, like the sun and magician, and the pip cards."

I knew this already and didn't get the point. "And?"

"And look. For your knight, I have a queen. For your major arcana card, I have a major arcana card. You have an ace, I have an ace. We're a perfect match. As partners. Just don't start thinking I'm your new gay best friend."

"Fine by me. I've already got a best friend."

He goggled. "You've got a friend? Who? What's her name?"

"*His* name is Razzzor," I said, offended. I have friends. Not a lot, but I value quality over quantity.

He laughed and pressed a hand to his chest.

"What's so funny?"

He wiped his eyes. "Razor? You're a secret biker babe. Thank God! For a while there, I thought you were a boring hermit type. Do you wear leathers? Can I try them on?"

I folded my arms. "Razzzor's an engineer."

"Oh." Sobering, he cocked his head. "Oh, no. This is an online friend, isn't it?"

"It is not—" *Damn.* He sort of was. "He's mildly agoraphobic!"

"Keep telling yourself that. Have you ever met him IRL?"

"In real life? Yes."

"At a gaming convention?"

We *had* met at a convention. It was how I'd gotten hired at his startup. "Look over those numbers." I walked out and did not slam the door behind me.

I hurried from the building.

Did I trust Hyperion or not?

My fists balled. I wanted to trust him. He felt like a person I could trust, even if he was a Tarot reader.

I knew my prejudice against everything New Age was unfair. Hyperion wasn't my parents. And if he believed in what he was doing, and his clients were happy, and we were making money, who was I to judge?

I huffed up the tree-lined sidewalk and crested the hill. Sunlight sparkled, blinding, off the ocean, and I paused, breathing it all in. Tiny figures of surfers plied the waves.

My heart lightened. I — we — had the building, and everything would work out. Swinging my arms, I strode down the hill.

A crowd of people clustered on the concrete bridge over the estuary. Diners leaned over the carved, wooden railings of a nearby seafood restaurant.

The bridge was a common spot for photography, and I smiled. The view of the pastel buildings, like square blocks of ice cream reflecting in the water, was picture perfect.

I paused on the edge of the crowd and leaned over the railing, the rough balustrade pressing into my elbows.

A few people *were* taking pictures, but not of the pastel rentals or the ocean. They leaned over the parapet and aimed their phones down, toward...

I followed their gazes and sucked in my breath.

Florence floated face-up in the stagnant water, her arms outflung, her lips blue, seaweed tangled around the receptionist's neck.

CHAPTER EIGHTEEN

SHOCKED, I REELED FROM the railing and stumbled off the edge of the sidewalk. My heel twisted beneath me.

A horn blared. Someone grabbed my arm and yanked me forward, against the parapet.

My ribs struck the concrete edge and I gasped, bent over the balustrade. Below, Florence floated in the sluggish water, her face gray, her eyes staring.

"Careful," Brik said.

"Ow." Bracing my hand on the rough concrete wall, I straightened, turned.

A red pickup zipped past on the winding road.

"Sorry about the rough handling," he said. "That truck was moving fast."

"And I didn't leave a trail of ice cream this time," I said shakily. "Were you following me?"

"I finished measuring your rooms and got hungry. There's a great taqueria at the top of the hill. What's going on here?"

I glanced toward the railing. "A woman's down there. Dead. It's Florence from the real estate office. She— she..." I closed my eyes, nausea swimming in my throat. She'd called me only this morning. How could she be dead this afternoon?

He peered over the balustrade. "Dammit. Has anyone called the police?"

A cruiser drifted to a halt beside the crowd, and a uniformed officer stepped out. A second police car stopped behind the first, and a policewoman emerged. The crowd's mutters and exclamations grew louder.

The female cop walked to the end of the parapet and jumped the low ledge, skidding through the tall, brown grasses. She disappeared into the gully.

I turned from the ledge and gripped my elbows. It couldn't have been an accident. For Reince to be murdered and then the woman who worked with him... I shuddered.

"Do you have any evidence for the police?" Brik asked, his voice low and rumbly.

I shook my head.

"All right. Let's get out of here." Hand firm on my arm, he steered me across the street and into a cheerful yellow coffee shop. He smelled like clean sweat and sawdust, and for a wild moment, I wanted to lean against his broad chest and just breathe him in.

"What's your poison?" He led me through the side doors to a blue-tiled patio overlooking the river and pulled out a lemon-yellow chair.

I slung my purse over the back of the folding chair and sat. "Black coffee."

"Huh. I figured you for tea." He returned inside the coffee shop.

From my chair, I watched the crowd across the street. The policeman said something to the bystanders. Gradually, they drifted away.

I tore my gaze from the bridge and watched the slow-moving river at the bottom of the slope to my right. The foliage was thick along its banks, which were dotted with homes and restaurants.

Had Florence gone in upriver? Or had someone dumped her into the ocean, and the tide had carried her in?

Brik emerged with two paper coffee cups and set one on the yellow table in front of me. He scraped back a chair, its metal legs shrill on the blue tiles.

We sat for a long moment, not speaking.

I sipped the coffee. It scalded my tongue, and I hissed.

"You knew her?" he asked gently.

I turned the paper coffee cup in my hands, letting its warmth soak into my palms. "Not well. She was the receptionist at that office where Reince — the murdered realtor — worked. She was..."

"Nice?" he asked.

My gaze fixed on a hole in the arm of his white tee. Honestly, I wasn't sure if she'd been nice or not. She'd been tremulous, saccharine sweet, and a part of me hadn't quite trusted that. "You met her last night," I reminded him. "She came to the hospital."

"Oh. I should have known." He sipped his coffee. "She was wearing the same clothes as last night, I mean."

I nodded. That meant she'd been killed after she'd met us, late last night or early this morning. Before or after the phone call I'd gotten? I felt suddenly too hot and put the coffee on the table.

Had the call come from the killer? Or someone who'd found her cell phone? Where had Florence gone after she'd left the hospital?

"Her death wasn't an accident," I said. This was a small town, and we didn't have much crime. The coincidence was impossible to ignore. "I should talk to the police."

He looked away. "They'll figure it out. If you tell them you were at another crime scene, it could make trouble for you. But if someone identifies you as being at the crime scene and you don't report it, that could make trouble for you, too."

I brought a shaky hand to my forehead. I had to tell the police about the phone call, but not right now. They were busy with the body. With Florence.

Poor Florence.

"How did your meeting go with Hyperion?" he asked.

"Good." I said, relieved by the change of topic. "We're going to make the Tea and Tarot room work."

"I hope so." He checked the silvery watch on his wrist. "I've got some time. Do you want to return to the tearoom, talk things through?" His face reddened. "About the project, I mean."

I wanted to do anything that would stop me from thinking about the body under the bridge. "That would be great. Let me phone Hyperion. He'll want to come."

I called my new partner, and he agreed to meet us at our future tearoom. But I didn't say anything about Florence. It seemed too raw and strange to announce over the phone. Rising, I dropped the phone into my purse.

A gray Jeep stopped on the bridge. Detective Tony Chase unfolded himself from the car.

I hesitated. Should I say something to him about the call now?

The detective strode to the end of the bridge, vaulted the parapet, and disappeared beneath.

Later. That decision made for me, I walked with Brik past the gathering emergency vehicles. We wound along the close streets to my purple stucco building.

I touched the front door, and its uneven stained-glass windowpanes. "Do you really think you can save this?"

"Remake it," he said. "Don't worry, you'll like the finished product. I promise."

Unlocking the door, I walked inside the concrete front room. Brik followed.

I rubbed my bare arms. The scorch-marks on the wall seemed uglier than they'd been this morning. Remnants of burnt cardboard lay scattered beside the sawhorse table. Had the person who'd set the fire killed Reince and Florence?

"It wasn't much of a fire," Brik said, following my gaze. "Wouldn't have done any serious damage — there's nothing much to burn. But it made a lot of smoke. There was another small fire in the hallway, by the kitchen door."

"You didn't report the fire when you called the police," I said, half-grateful, half-guilty. If the lawyer, Mr. Bonnet, had found out, he might have had second thoughts about leasing us the building. But if the arson was connected to the murders...

"The fire was out," he said. "I didn't see any point to calling fire trucks to the scene. And I told the detective at the hospital."

Why had someone set those fires? To scare us? To make sure we didn't get the building? Had it been a spur-of-the-moment idea, or had the arson been planned in advance? "Well, thanks. At least someone kept a clear head last night."

The front door opened. Hyperion limped inside, his giant, spotted tabby beneath one arm.

The cat meowed, and Hyperion set him on the floor. Bastet beelined for me and rubbed against my leg.

"Bastet! Leave her alone," Hyperion snapped, brushing white and orange cat hairs from his navy suit jacket.

Ignoring him, the cat rolled onto his back. Oblivious to the dust covering the floor, he batted his paws in the air. But I knew better than to try to rub a cat's belly. They hate it.

"Florence is dead," I blurted. "From Reince's office."

Hyperion stared. "The woman with the bad perm who said, *Oh?*"

"They found her in the estuary," I said.

"OMG. I want to take that nail gun and shoot myself with it, because I do not want to live in a world where this is happening. That poor woman."

Brik edged the nail gun to the side of the sawhorse table.

"She was wearing the same clothing as last night when she was found," I said.

Hyperion adjusted his purple cravat. "A fashion faux pas, true. But really, Abigail, you shouldn't speak ill of the dead."

"More importantly, she must have been killed after she left us at the hospital," I said. "But I got a butt-dial from her this morning."

The fortune teller's brow furrowed. "Hold up. She was at the hospital?"

"I forgot to mention it before," I said. "You were getting stitched up."

"Don't remind me." Hyperion brightened. "Does this mean I have an alibi?"

"We don't know when Florence was killed," I warned.

Bastet rubbed against my bare ankle.

"Maybe her death was an accident," Hyperion said.

"What are the odds?" I asked.

Brik coughed. "Maybe we should discuss the building."

"Not yet," Hyperion said. "This is important. We need clarity." He drew a pack of cards from his suit jacket pocket, and my spine stiffened.

He laid three cards on the sawhorse table and frowned. "This isn't over. The troubles, I mean."

"That's clarity?" The contractor raised a skeptical brow.

Hyperion's long finger glided along the tops of the cards. "The seven of swords, the Tower, the eight of wands — whatever's about to happen next, we won't like it, and it's coming fast."

My insides quivered. "Not another murder?" I mentally slapped my head. *Come on, Abigail. Tarot isn't real.*

He shook his head. "It's impossible to tell. The Tower refers to a sudden, unpleasant change. A shock to the system. Disaster. And this spread isn't about what's already happened. It's about what will happen."

Great. "At least there wasn't a death card."

"The death card rarely means death. Though it can." He sighed. "And Brik, I owe you a reading after you saved my life last night." He scooped up the three cards and laid down ten more in an elaborate pattern, then looked up. "With your permission, of course."

Brik shrugged. "Since I don't believe in fortune telling, it can't hurt."

A pained expression flitted across Hyperion's face. "Not fortune telling. Tarot reading. There's an enormous difference."

I shifted, impatient. "But Florence—"

"I promise this won't hurt," Hyperion said, expression puckish. "Much."

He touched the first two cards, one crossed on top of the other. "This is the current situation. A fresh start, crossed by the queen of pentacles. Court cards like the queen of pentacles usually represent other people or aspects of our own personality. Given what I know of you, I'll go with other people. So, who is this sensitive soul in your life?" Hyperion waggled his eyebrows. "A romantic interest?"

For no good reason, a wave of heat washed up my chest and neck. "I don't think this is the time—"

"Beneath you," Hyperion continued, "the four of pentacles. You've closed yourself off. The question is, can you open yourself to new people and experiences?"

The contractor grunted. "I moved to San Borromeo, didn't I?"

Hyperion pointed to a heart pierced by three swords. "You came here because of a past heartbreak, and..." He pointed to a card displaying a man pierced by ten swords. "A tragedy. A death. And this card is you, the king of pentacles—"

"Abigail's right," Brik said. "We've got enough to worry about, and this is upsetting her." He swept up the cards and deposited them in Hyperion's hand. "Let's talk about your building."

Embarrassed, I shook my head. I hadn't been upset, just irritated. "It's okay, but—"

"Fine," Hyperion said. "What about my Mad Hatter's tea party idea? Crooked empty frames on the walls. Bold colors. Mismatched furniture and whimsical chaos?"

Urgh! Why were these two so interrupt-y? "I thought we'd agreed on something more sedate," I said, trying to go with the flow. If they wanted to talk business before murder, fine. "Whatever happened to the Tudor look?"

"Look at the front of this building," Hyperion said. "It's purple stucco. We can't afford to give it a Tudor facelift. What about Moroccan? We can paint the exterior salmon and put a tiled fountain in the center, here."

"And belly dancers?" I asked, caustic. "Morocco makes delicious mint tea, but no. I'd have to change the entire menu to middle eastern, and that's not what I had in mind."

"Japanese?"

"It will limit the market," I said, "and don't you think that would clash with the fortune telling?"

"Tarot reading," he corrected absently and sat against one of the sawhorses. He rubbed his chin.

"What about something more modern, less Tudor?" Brik glanced at the black tangle of pipes beneath the ceiling. "You can keep the ceiling unfinished — that's popular now. And there's brick behind that stucco. I can remove the stucco on one of the walls. If I pick up some salvage wood, I can use them to build the counter and shelves. Add Edison lights—"

"Muted, neutral colors," Hyperion said.

"Framed herbariums on the walls," I said, my enthusiasm growing. "And plants to warm the space. Bundles of dried herbs hanging over the counter."

"And private groupings of tables," Hyperion said. "I suppose salvaged wood is cheaper?"

"If you know where to go," the contractor said. "And I do."

"That's a great idea," I said to him, impressed. There was more to Brik than met the eye.

He shrugged, his muscles rippling beneath his tee. "I may be new here, but I've been doing this a long time."

"Can you figure out a new estimate for the work?" I asked.

He nodded. "I'll have it for you by tomorrow."

Bastet pawed at my sandal.

"Did you roll in catnip before you came here?" Hyperion scowled and snatched the cat from the floor. "Okay. We're done here, and I've got an online Tarot class to prep for. Let's talk tomorrow." He limped outside.

Brik and I parted at the door, and I drove home. But once I was alone in my kitchen, I couldn't stop thinking about Florence. Her staring eyes. Her blue lips. The seaweed tangled around her neck. I blinked rapidly, my shoulders tightening.

I called the detective.

Voice mail.

"This is Detective Chase. Leave a message."

I stared through the kitchen window at the jasmine cascading over the redwood fence. "Hi, this is Abigail Beanblossom. I saw Florence beneath the bridge today. She called me this morning. Or someone did, using her phone. No one was on the line. It sounded like one of those accidental—"

Beep. The line disconnected.

I tossed my phone on the butcher block island. Well, I'd tried. If it meant anything, Detective Chase would call.

Trying to get my mind off murder, and because it was well past lunchtime, I decided to bake blueberry scones. I always ended up making too much for one person, but maybe my new neighbor would like a batch. Brik had been kind on the walk back to the tearoom because I'd been upset about Florence. A thank you...

I froze, the measuring cup hovering over the flour canister on my gray granite counter.

There were more and cheaper lunch places closer to the tearoom. Had Brik's presence been coincidence, like he'd claimed?

Now I really was being paranoid.

I folded in frozen blueberries — frozen to keep them from bleeding all over the dough when they baked. Then I rolled out the dough and cut it into triangles with a pizza cutter.

While the scones baked, I paced the cozy living room. I glanced past the ivory couch and through the curtained window to the street.

As secretary, Florence had to have known all the dirt at the Archer Realty. Maybe that was why Reince had insisted on doing most of his business from the café — the café where he'd talked Florence into giving him a loan.

A loan for what? Another scam?

Flipping on the ceiling fan, I opened the French doors to my backyard and stepped onto the porch. I surveyed the raised beds of herbs, the flowering dogwood tree, the winding tanbark paths.

Why Florence? Had she somehow threatened the killer? Could Florence have helped Reince with his scam? Working in the office, she'd have been well positioned to help embezzle funds.

Above me, something buzzed, low and persistent. Involuntarily, I stepped backward, into the house.

A dark shape vanished behind the trees.

CHAPTER NINETEEN

"DROP THE LANDMINE! DROP the landmine!"

Frantically jamming the paddle forward, I raced in front of the German tank. Bombs exploded in the village around me. "I can't get far enough in front of it. Zombies move a lot faster when they've got wheels."

"Treads," Razzor corrected. He shot an undead Nazi emerging from the burnt-out shell of a patisserie.

My avatar clambered over a pile of rubble.

The tank kept coming.

I glanced toward my garden. A misty Sunday twilight streamed through my French windows. "Why don't *you* plant a mine?"

"I don't have any more."

The tank got hung up on a pinnacle of broken stone. I dropped and rolled, blasting the Nazi zombies emerging from it. "Gaaaaaaaaaaah!"

"Nice. So, in summary," Razzzor said, "over the last week you found another body from the realty, and you're going into business with a psychic."

"In summary, the police found another body from the realty, and I'm going into business with a Tarot reader."

Someone knocked at the door. "Just a sec," I said. "Someone's at the door."

"Wait—"

But I was already ripping off my headset and hurrying across the wood floor. I peered through the peep hole. Detective Chase stood on the step, and I yanked the door open.

"Detective Chase?"

He whipped off his cowboy hat and extended my phone. "It's all yours."

"You're done with it already?" Detective Chase had waited until yesterday to contact me about Florence's call. After a round of light questioning, he'd confiscated my phone. I'd thought I wouldn't see it for weeks.

"Long story," he said. "But I can take your phone back to the station, if you want."

I clutched the phone to my chest. "No, no. Thank you."

"Ms. Beanblossom, where were you between eleven o'clock Thursday night and one A.M. Friday morning?"

"Is that when Florence was killed?"

"Ms. Beanblossom?" he asked pointedly.

"Right, I was at home. Alone." At least now I had a general time of death for Florence, for all the good it did me. I also had no alibi.

"And Mr. Night?"

"After you left us, we called a taxi and dropped him at home. I can't imagine he could have gone anywhere. He talked a nurse into giving him excellent painkillers. He was pretty loopy when Brik and I dropped him off."

The detective replaced his hat on his head. "Thank you. Have a good day." Straight-backed, he turned and strode down the steps and to his car.

I returned to the couch and the game. Putting my feet up on the coffee table, I sipped a glass of iced chai. Most of the ice had melted, leaving a watery concoction.

"What happened?" Razzzor asked. "Who was it?"

I explained.

Razzzor sighed through the mic. "Murder, psychics... You were never this interesting when you worked for me. I don't know why you're opening a tearoom. Food service is hard work. You could come back to Menlo Park and be my new executive assistant. It's easy street. All you have to do is make appointments, schedule stuff, get me coffee—"

I whipped around and shot him in the chest. His torso exploded in a shower of red gore.

"Hey!" He sputtered. "We're going to have to start this campaign all over again. I'm sick of Belgium."

"Do you really think I don't have bigger dreams than serving your coffee? And I did a hell of a lot more than that for you. Besides, you don't have a company anymore, remember?"

"Apologies," he said gruffly. "I couldn't have done it without you. But I'll have you know I might be starting another company. And don't act like I'm being sexist. You said you *want* to serve people tea."

"In my own business!"

"Honestly, Abs, do you think you're being fair?"

I rolled my eyes, recognizing more therapist-speak.

"Because having an executive assistant was *my* big dream," he continued. "Don't I get a dream?"

"Oh." I thought about that. The truth was, he'd been a great boss, and I'd been more than fairly compensated. "Maybe I overreacted." I shifted my headset and rubbed my ear, sore after six hours of play. "Sorry I shot you," I said, grudging.

"I'll just bet you are."

~ elle ~

Monday morning, after checking the sky for drones, I scurried to my Mazda and into town. Florence's death had made the weekend paper, but the article hadn't gone much beyond "body found in estuary." I hoped Monday's paper would be more enlightening.

Parking beside a green kiosk dotted with gum, I grabbed a paper. I laid it flat against my steering wheel and flipped through the pages. There was a short article on page three.

GRIM MURDER ALONG SAN BORROMEO RIVER

Local woman, Florence Deebles, was found dead in the estuary beneath the Ransom Bridge in San Borromeo. Police received a call around eleven A.M. Friday morning about a woman spotted floating in the water beneath the bridge.

Responding officers found the woman dead. Police are treating the death as foul play.

A dive team and search-and-rescue unit was dispatched to the scene to search for any possible evidence.

"It's likely Ms. Deebles was killed elsewhere, and her body dumped somewhere more secluded, upriver," said Detective Tony Chase. "Later, her body floated downstream. Anyone with information about the death is urged to call the SBPD."

I tossed the paper to the empty passenger seat. No kidding it was foul play. What sort of help was that?

But it *was* interesting that they thought Florence's body had been dumped upriver. Lots of homes and businesses backed onto the river, and the area was dense with trees and brush — perfect for hiding misdeeds.

A man in shorts and a striped tee crossed the street with his terrier. The dog strained at its leash toward an iron lamppost. His owner hauled it away and into a peach-stucco coffee shop.

San Borromeo was so idyllic, it was hard to imagine someone taking Florence to a secluded, woodsy spot to kill her. But we did have lots of secluded, woodsy spots. Uneasy, I glanced in my rearview mirror.

Secluded, woodsy spots like the park by the river. Late at night the park was closed, but it wasn't gated. Anyone could get inside.

And so what? Was I going to search the park with a magnifying glass for clues? Hardly.

But I *could* pay my condolences at the realty. I checked my outfit: narrow, navy slacks and a blue-and-white peasant top. It wasn't mourning, but at least I didn't look like I'd just left a yoga studio.

I stopped at a sidewalk florist, its shelves overflowing with flowers. Selecting a pink and yellow bouquet of asters, daisies, and roses, I paid the cheerful woman behind the register.

"Aaaabigail, for me?"

I started and turned.

Hyperion pressed a long hand to his chest and batted his eyelashes. His white, button-up, collarless shirt accentuated his clavicles. His skinny jeans accentuated everything else.

"How's your leg?" I asked.

"Fine. My lawyer has checked the contract and didn't have any changes. I'm ready to sign, whenever Bonnet adds another signature line for me."

I squealed. "Perfect! I'm so excited!" I steadied myself and took the change from the flower seller. "Did you review the budget?"

He rolled his eyes skyward. "Yes. And I think I can manage to restrain my spending within expected parameters."

"Expected parameters? Were you watching *Star Trek* last night?"

"Since you shot me in the leg—"

"Come *on*." He was never going to let that go.

"I've been watching more TV than usual, even if it does dull my third eye. So, what's with the flowers?"

"They're for Cyrus and Diana. Condolence flowers."

"Condolence or snooping?"

I scowled.

"Don't get me wrong," he said. "If you're playing amateur sleuth, I'm all in."

"I'd planned to go alone," I said stiffly.

He just looked at me.

We drove to Cyrus's office in my car.

Cyrus stood beside the desk in the foyer. If possible, he'd lost even more weight, his rumpled navy suit hanging off his frame. Gray hairs flecked his temples. He glanced up, his tanned face worn. The hanging fern beside the stairs seemed in much the same state. "I haven't found the money," he said.

"I figured as much. I only wanted to..." Realizing I was mashing the flowers to my chest, I extended the bouquet. "For Florence. I mean, my condolences to you and Diana on your loss."

He blinked, as if bewildered, then stepped forward and took the flowers. "Thanks," he said, gruff. "She was a good woman. A friend."

Hyperion wrung the realtor's hand. "We were very sorry to hear about her death."

"Florence had everything organized, my entire schedule." He rubbed his forehead, and his large hand trembled. "And now... I'm a little lost. Did you know Florence?" he asked Hyperion.

"No," the Tarot reader said, "but she was kind enough to come by the hospital on Thursday—"

"Hospital?" Cyrus's brows lowered.

"Hyperion had a little accident at the building we're leasing," I said quickly.

"I wouldn't call it *little*," Hyperion grumbled, rubbing his leg.

"The police called the lawyer," I said, "and Mr. Bonnet called her."

"Oh." Cyrus's brow furrowed. "Was it serious? The accident?"

"No," I said.

"Yes," Hyperion said.

I forced a smile. Hyperion wasn't going to let me forget about that nail gun any time soon. "I guess she didn't have a chance to tell you about it." *Before she'd been killed.* "Have the police said anything to you about what happened? To Florence, I mean?"

The realtor's face darkened to the color of a brick. "All the cops did was throw around a load of innuendo. Two murders in one office — how was I supposed to know what Reince was up to? He was rarely here, so it wasn't like I was watching him. He had people skills. He had a license. He had references. I wasn't going to micromanage the guy, especially when his numbers looked so good."

"Did Florence organize Reince's numbers?" Hyperion asked.

His hands tightened on the flowers. "She—" His Adam's apple bobbed. Abruptly, his shoulders folded inward, and he sat against the desk, the bouquet dangling between his knees. "Look, I get it. You're worried about your money. But there's nothing more I can tell you."

Ouch. We might have been here partly for mercenary reasons, but were we that obvious?

"The police will get in touch," he continued, "if they track the money down. Are you insured?"

"Not for something like this." I tugged at the hem of my blouse. "But I'm worried about more than the missing money. First Reince's death, now

Florence's... Whatever happened to her *has* to do with Reince. And the police have been questioning me too. Is it possible Florence and Reince had more than a working relationship?"

Cyrus goggled. "Reince and Florence? You think they were having an affair? No. No. She was a lovely person, but a cougar she was not."

"That wasn't exactly what I meant," I said.

"Then what? That they were somehow colluding? Florence would never betray us." Cyrus clawed one hand through his graying hair. "None of this makes sense. I mean, Florence!" He opened his arms and dropped them. A mauve petal fluttered to the sisal rug. "She's the last person you'd think would be up to no good."

"Maybe she wasn't," Hyperion said. "Maybe she figured something out about the killer, and that's why she died."

Cyrus laughed shortly and dropped the bouquet onto the desk. "You're not making me feel better."

"One of the detectives was at the hospital when Florence stopped by Thursday night," I said.

He eyed me wearily. "So?"

"So," I said, "they know where she was right before she died. But what was her schedule like earlier that day?"

"Thursday?" Cyrus twisted on the desk and picked up a leather-bound planner. He handed it to me. "She was here all day."

I opened the planner to Thursday, and Hyperion peered over my shoulder. The book was blank aside from a notation at noon: *Thursday lunch!* "Who was she having lunch with?"

"Oh." Cyrus straightened off the desk. "That. She and Diana had lunch every Thursday. It was a thing. You said you were leasing that building." He smoothed his navy suit jacket. "Does that mean you worked something out with the owner?"

I returned the calendar. "With the owner's lawyer."

"At least that's one bright spot," Cyrus muttered and returned the planner to the desk. "Though I don't suppose I can bill you our usual fee, since you got the place after all."

"No," Hyperion said. "You can't."

"I'm still out Reince's six-month payment," I said.

"And I've no idea where that money is." Cyrus looked toward the plastic brochure holders on the wall. "I'm sorry."

"What are you apologizing for, Cyrus?" Diana strode through the front door, her loose ivory slacks swishing about her long legs. She wore a pale-blue tunic and a long leather necklace hung with golden hoops.

The screen banged shut behind her. "You know what the lawyer told us," she said. "You're not responsible for Reince's actions." Ropes of muscle stood out on her neck. "If you're thinking of suing," she said to me, "talk to our insurance company."

Her husband waved his hand in an indifferent gesture. "They brought flowers. For Florence."

Diana stopped short and grimaced. She smelled faintly of sweat, and I wondered if I did too. The day was hot.

"Florence." Her mouth curled downward. "If I hadn't suggested you hire her..." She blinked rapidly, her blue eyes glistening. "It's as if someone has a grudge against us — first Reince, now Florence."

"The police asked us if we had any enemies," Cyrus explained to me.

"Like Gino Peretti?" I asked.

They looked a question at each other.

"He was angry," I said. "I ran into him a couple days ago. He threatened to burn down his own house, with Kale — the tenant — inside."

And someone had set a fire in the tearoom. Was arson Peretti's M.O.? My insides quivered like mint jelly at the thought. But why would he come after me? I hadn't been *that* irritating.

"We remember Kale Halifax," Diana said stiffly. "Did you tell the police about the threat?"

"Of course," I said. Detective Chase hadn't seemed impressed. "And I contacted Kale. She didn't seem to take the threat seriously. You warned me Peretti was unstable," I said to Diana. "Do you think he might follow through?"

She shrugged. "Anything's possible."

"You knew his wife, you said?" I asked.

The realtor started. "Diana? You know Peretti's wife?"

"Chiara came to the local women's shelter one day," she said. "I was there, donating clothing. We got to talking."

Cyrus's eyes bulged. "No wonder the man's— Why didn't you tell me?"

"You know what happens at that shelter is confidential." Diana picked up the bouquet and sniffed the flowers.

He gaped. "I'm your husband. Two people who worked here are dead. Don't you think this is something I should know?"

"This isn't my fault!"

I squirmed, embarrassed by the squabble.

Cyrus blew out his breath. "No." His gaze shifted over her head, to the hanging spider plant. "But you still should have told me," he muttered.

"How exactly did you help her?" Hyperion asked.

Diana sighed and laid the bouquet on the desk. "Advice, mostly. And I shouldn't even be telling you two that. Chiara ended up returning to Italy."

"Did Peretti know you were helping his wife?" Hyperion asked.

She tossed her short hair. "I don't care if he did. He should be ashamed of himself for how he treated her."

"Are you sure she returned to Italy?" My phone rang, and I reached into my pocket for it.

Her eyes widened. "Y— I mean, I assumed she did. We haven't been in touch. Are you suggesting she didn't?"

"I don't know." But my skin pebbled. Gino had two reasons to hate the real estate office — Diana's aid to his wife and Reince leasing his home. Had it pushed him over the edge?

CHAPTER TWENTY

My phone rang a second time. Pressing it to my ear, I smiled an excuse to Diana and Cyrus. "Hello?"

"Abigail," my grandfather said. "I wanted to check in. I heard about that woman's death."

I should have called him. "I'm fine. Hyperion and I are actually talking to the realtor now."

"That fortune telling fellow?"

"Is that your grandfather?" Hyperion hissed, grabbing for the phone.

I jerked away. "Why don't you and Tomas come over for dinner, and we can talk?"

"Hello, Mr. Beanblossom," Hyperion bellowed.

I covered the receiver and glared. "Do you mind?" I hissed.

"What was that?" Gramps asked.

"Dinner." Quickly, we made the arrangements, said our goodbyes, and hung up.

I smiled at Diana and Cyrus and edged toward the office's front door. "That was my grandfather. Hyperion and I should be going."

"But what about Gino?" Diana asked.

Cyrus jaw tightened. "Peretti's all talk. I know the type."

I hoped he was right.

Hyperion and I returned to my Mazda. "You haven't told your grandfather about me yet, have you?"

"Of course, I did."

I started the ignition.

"Hm," he said doubtfully.

"I *did*. Now, where to?"

"Back to Tea and Tarot, *tout suite*."

I drove to the parking lot behind the tearoom. The lot had already grown crowded. I was about to give up, when a violet VW backed from a space in front of me. *Huzzah!* I zipped into the space.

I followed Hyperion down our tearoom's cool, dark hallway and into the kitchen.

Gingerly, Hyperion sat atop the now-clean metal table and moved the nail gun on it so it lay near his hip. He probably wanted to keep it handy in case I tried anything.

"Now," he said. "About that new contract—"

"I'll call Mr. Bonnet now."

Hyperion listened, one foot swinging, while I told the lawyer that the contract was fine.

"I shall correct the signature lines and email the amended contract to you today," the lawyer said. "Will that be all?"

"I think so."

We said our goodbyes and hung up.

"He'll do it," I said.

"That's that then. We have the building." He slithered off the table and stuck out his hand. "Howdy partner!"

We shook.

"We don't have the building for sure until the contract's signed," I warned. "And we're not partners until we have a signed agreement."

"Don't be a Nelly Negative. I've been telling you from the start, this building was destined for us."

I hitched my ginormous bag over my shoulder. "Actually, I think you said it was destined for *you*."

"How was I to know the universe had a business partner in mind?" He rubbed his flat stomach. "I'm going to grab lunch."

"Okay," I said, bemused. "Then why did you want to come here? I could have called Mr. Bonnet from the realty."

"I have some things in the back of my Jeep I need help carrying. I can't put extra weight on the leg you shot."

"I didn't—" I ground my teeth. The nail gun so wasn't my fault. "Fine. I'll help you carry your stuff."

Hyperion limped dramatically to his Jeep Wrangler, parked in the furthest possible space from our building. He swung open the rear door and pointed to three cardboard boxes. "Samples."

"You had time to get samples? We only decided on a modern look on Friday."

"Which gave me the whole weekend. I don't let the grass grow under my feet."

"I guess not." Whatever I was getting into by partnering up with Hyperion, at least he was hard working.

I hefted a box. "Ooof. Heavy."

"You can set that one in the bathroom. I'll wait here." Grinning, he sat on the bumper.

I staggered across the parking lot, edged open the rear door with my hip, and speed walked to the bathroom. I set the box down, and something hard and heavy clanked inside.

Uh oh. What had I just broken? I let my purse slide to the concrete floor and opened the box. It was filled with different shapes and shades of undamaged gray and white tiles. *Whew.*

Brushing off my hands, I returned to the Wrangler.

"That one," Hyperion said, pointing. "Front room."

My mouth pinched. "You're enjoying watching me fetch and carry, aren't you?"

"Are you fetching and carrying? Because all I see is you wasting time flapping your jaw."

I grabbed the box, which was, if possible, even heavier. Huffing, I wound through the lot and into the building. I set the box beside the sawhorses near the front windows and opened it. Sample paint cans. Lots of them.

"How many different shades of black and white can there be?" I muttered. I returned outside and grabbed the final box.

"Thanks so much." Hyperion made a kissy face.

"You're welcome, *partner.*"

"That goes into the small classroom," he said.

Pasting a faux-smile on my face, I lugged it into the storeroom and returned to Hyperion. "Satisfied?"

He checked his watch. "I will be once I get a roast beef sandwich from the deli. Want anything?"

"Egg salad, thanks," I said, surprised by the offer. "But I left my purse in the bathroom—"

"I got this." He said, waving dismissively. "I'll be back in thirty. In the meantime, you can lay out the sample tiles and put some test paint on the walls. There are brushes in the box."

Resigned to playing Hyperion's minion for the day, I returned to the bathroom and set the tiles in groupings near the wall. I stood back and studied them. I wasn't a huge fan of the whitest tiles, or the darkest gray ones.

Hyperion hadn't bothered getting samples for the kitchen. But that was my domain and my problem.

I returned to the kitchen. Shoving aside the nail gun, I opened my purse, pulled out the business plan, and flipped to the sketches I'd made of the kitchen. My back to the door, I braced my hands on the metal table. Even if I hired an outside bakery to make my scones, I'd still need a new stove.

In the hallway behind me, something shifted.

My head jerked up. I hadn't locked the back door.

Mouth dry, I glanced at the nail gun on the table. "Hyperion?" I whispered.

Silence.

My heart banged against my ribcage. I reached for the gun.

The kitchen door behind me creaked.

I grabbed the nail gun and spun, arms extended like a TV detective's.

"Whoa!" Brik ducked.

I lowered the gun, my pulse pounding. "I could have shot you! What are you doing here? Why didn't you say anything when I called out?"

"No, you couldn't have, and I didn't hear you." Brik edged sideways. He wore his usual white tee and faded jeans. "And I didn't think you'd try to shoot me with my own nail gun."

I stepped backward, and my hip bumped the table. "I didn't— My finger wasn't even on the trigger."

"It looks like it is to me."

"It isn't—" *Whoops.* Tingling swept from my chest to my temple. Carefully, I lowered the nail gun to my side. "What are you doing here?"

"Hyperion asked me to look at his samples. I assumed he was referring to flooring."

"What else..." I felt myself flush more deeply. "Oh. The tile samples are in the bathroom."

"I also came to collect my nail gun." He took it, his big hands clasped over mine, and I jolted at the contact. "It's all fun and games until someone gets nailed."

"Ha ha." I smoothed the front of my peasant top.

Grinning, he stepped away, the nail gun tucked beneath one muscular arm. "So, after all the drama, you two got the building?"

I checked my phone and smiled. "The lawyer just emailed the contract. All we need to do is sign, and the building's ours."

"Quick work."

"Renting the building?"

"You and Hyperion deciding to go into business together."

"Oh." Uneasy, because it *had* been quick, I rested against the metal table. "I would have preferred to go it alone. But this business with Reince threw a wrench into both our plans. We lost our advance rent payments, and then with the unexpected extra costs of renovation..."

"You should have been expecting them."

"The extra costs wouldn't have mattered, if I hadn't lost six months' rent," I said coolly.

"So, you were desperate."

"Yeah," I admitted, "but that wasn't the only reason. Joining forces makes sense. We have complimentary businesses." Though desperation *had* been the primary driver. I wondered for the hundredth time if I was making a mistake.

"I saw the police car in front of your house Saturday," Brik said.

"Oh. Right." I looked down at my brown leather sandals. "The detective asked about Florence."

"Did you tell them you were at the bridge?"

"I had to."

"Yeah," he said heavily. "I guess you did."

"You think I did the wrong thing?"

He crossed his arms, muscles bulging, and leaned one hip on the grimy stove. "I think I should keep my opinions to myself."

"Why start now?"

He laughed, his voice a seductive rumble. "Did you decide on your design?"

"We're going with your suggestion of modern. I just want to make sure it's cozy too. I think as long as there are comfortable chairs and plants to give it life, it'll work."

"That brick wall will give the place color too," he said. "And distressed wood beneath the counter will warm up the room."

We talked wood grain and Edison lights. His arctic eyes lit with excitement, and my own enthusiasm grew.

I was starting to like the idea of working with my neighbor. Brik could be annoying, but he could be kind and funny too. More importantly, he seemed to know what he was doing.

"I have food!"

I gave a little jump.

Hyperion breezed into the kitchen.

This was ridiculous. I couldn't freak out every time Hyperion surprised me. Our business plan was solid. We'd develop a clear and workable partnership agreement, and Hyperion totally wasn't a killer.

Was he?

CHAPTER TWENTY-ONE

LEAVING HYPERION TO DEAL with Brik, I crossed the parking lot behind our building and strolled to the rear of the wine bar. I needed to banish my doubts about Hyperion once and for all.

Hyperion's calendar had said he'd been at *a* wine bar the night Reince had died. If he'd been at this one, he would have been suspiciously close to the scene of the crime.

The wine bar's back gate opened into a covered, outdoor patio. Past it, in the restaurant proper, oversized paintings decorated bare wood walls. Rows of tables lined the area between the patio and the black granite bar.

Though it called itself a wine bar, it was a restaurant. And I came here often enough to be on a first name basis with the owner, Barry.

Unfortunately, Barry wasn't in, and I was left quizzing a suspicious waiter.

He jammed up the long sleeves of his black tee. "What do you need?" The waiter cocked his head, expression wary.

"Do you know Hyperion Night?"

"Who?"

I dug out my phone and found a picture on Hyperion's website. "Him," I said, handing him my phone.

He shot me a quick, suspicious glance. "I've seen him around. Why?" He returned the phone.

I stiffened my spine. "This may sound weird, but was he here Monday night?"

The waiter arched a brow. "Are you a private detective or a jealous girlfriend?"

"Neither. I'm thinking of going into business with him."

"And you need to know if he was here Monday night to make your decision?"

"It's complicated."

His hazel eyes bored into mine.

Crumb. Was he going to make me tell him everything? "You know the man who was found dead in the parking lot Tuesday morning?"

"Uh, huh."

"Hyperion told me he was here that Monday night. I only want to know if he was with the man who was killed, or if he was with someone else. And what time they left, if possible."

"Fine. Yeah. This Hyper guy was here. I waited his table."

My stomach plummeted all the way to my sandals. So, Hyperion *had* been at this wine bar. "Who was he with?"

He cocked a brow. "Really?"

"Okay, was he with…" I did another search on my phone and found Reince's photo. "Him?"

The waiter glanced at the phone. "Nope. He was with someone else."

"What? Are you sure?"

"Yeah, I'm sure. It was another guy."

Relief flooded my veins, and my gaze flicked to the ceiling fan. Hyperion hadn't killed the faux-realtor. "Do you remember what time he left?"

"They left together at ten, when we were closing. I didn't think they'd ever leave."

"Fantastic! Thank you." If Hyperion had left with someone who was not Reince, then it was unlikely he'd bumped into Reince in the parking lot and killed him. Murder gets awkward in front of a witness. True, he *could* have returned to murder Reince later. But the timing made it a lot less likely he was the killer. I'd take less likely. I needed that tearoom. And as much as I hated to admit it, I needed Hyperion.

"And I'll have a glass of the Paso Robles Zinfandel." Hey, I had to show my appreciation somehow, and I'd already eaten an egg salad sandwich.

Besides, the wine by the glass was half-off before four P.M., and the bar was quiet.

I ran my palm along the smooth, black counter. Wine racks lined the opposite wall. Our tearoom would be cooler.

Sliding onto a barstool, I called Tomas. As I'd hoped, he had good suggestions for partnering with Hyperion, and even offered to draw up a draft agreement.

That done, I finished the wine guilt free and paid the bill, leaving a hefty tip. I returned to the parking lot. Brik's pickup was gone.

Hyperion limped from the tearoom toward his Jeep Wrangler.

"Hyperion!"

He turned and waited for me beside a Prius.

"I spoke to my lawyer," I said. "He's going to draw up our partnership agreement."

His brown eyes narrowed. "How much will your lawyer cost us?"

"We're old friends, and Tomas is semi-retired. He's doing it as a favor."

Hyperion's shoulders relaxed. "Good. After talking to Brik about the remodel, all I can think about is the money I don't have. It's ruining my vibe. And I need a drink."

I didn't, since I'd just polished off a glass of red wine. But in the interests of a positive partnership, I followed Hyperion to the Mortar and Pestle, and we found a quiet, corner table.

Hyperion ordered two shots of tequila.

"I'll have iced tea," I said.

"Keeping hydrated is important when you're drinking tequila. Two shots," he repeated to the waitress.

She bustled to the bar.

He folded his long arms on the table. "Now, what should we talk about?"

"The murders."

Hyperion arched a brow. "Must we?"

"These murders might be a real problem for us."

"For you, you mean. I have an alibi for Florence's murder. I was home in bed, recovering from a nail gun wound."

"You're welcome," I said, waspish. "I don't have an alibi, and someone tried to set my tearoom—"

"Our Tarot studio."

"Tea and Tarot on fire. Don't you think the fire's connected to the murders?"

He leaned back in his chair and crossed his arms over his loose white shirt. "The fire could have been set by kids."

"You don't really believe that, do you?"

He made a face. "No."

The waitress set down two shots of tequila and my iced tea. "Can I get you anything else?"

"Not right now," Hyperion said. "Thanks."

I waited until she was out of earshot. "Somehow, we — or our building — are tied up in these murders."

"The building?" His brow arched. "How can a building be linked to murder?"

"Reince *was* found in our parking lot."

"Technically, the lot isn't ours. It belongs to the city."

"You know what I mean."

He sighed unhappily and shoved a tequila shot across the table to me. "I know."

Wanting to get it over with, I threw back the shot and gulped iced tea as a chaser. "How well did you know Florence Deebles?"

"Not at all."

"Did you notice anything odd or unusual at the real estate office or when you met with Reince?"

He sipped the tequila. "There was that too-good-to-be-true price for our building."

"Aside from that."

The waitress appeared at our table with two more shots and placed them in front of Hyperion. "From the gentleman at the bar."

Hyperion twisted in his chair and waved.

A handsome man in a business suit raised his glass in a toast.

"Do you know him?" I asked.

"Yeah. Don't worry. He won't bother us. You were saying?" He shoved a glass across the table to me and shot back his own.

"What about Reince?" I asked. "Did he say anything that struck you as strange?"

"No. He told me everything I wanted to hear." He scrubbed his hands across his face. "I should have been more suspicious of the whole setup. What are you driving at?"

"Gino Peretti."

"That guy you mentioned at the realtor's today? I've been meaning to ask – who is he?"

I drank the shot. It burned a trail down my throat. "Reince rented Gino Peretti's house. Peretti was on vacation or out of the country at the time, and he didn't know about the rental. When he returned and found someone living in his house—"

"He went bananas?"

"That's one way to put it. Peretti threatened to burn down his own house out of spite."

"Yikes." Hyperion sipped the new tequila and canted his head. "This isn't bad."

Two more shots appeared on the table in front of him. "From the other gentleman at the bar." The waitress cocked her head toward a tanned, forty-something blond in jeans and a chambray shirt.

Oh, come on. Hyperion got more attention from men than I did. This was just demoralizing.

Hyperion saluted him and turned to me. "You were saying?"

"Do you know him?" I asked.

He shrugged, a languid motion. "He's just someone I met at Brik's. So. Gino Peretti."

Two more shots appeared in front of Hyperion. We downed them. I shuddered.

"Don't you see?" I asked. "He threatened to burn something down, and then someone set our building on fire."

"They didn't really set it on fire."

"But they might have."

"With all that concrete?" He wrinkled his nose. "I don't think so."

"Can we agree that someone set a fire in our building?" I asked, exasperated, and tossed back the shot. My stomach lurched, and I shook my head, dizzy. Ugh. Too much. Too soon.

"We're not getting anywhere." He gulped down the tequila and banged the shot glass on the wooden table. "We need facts. Evidence. Data!"

"I've done internet searches on all the sluspects—"

"Sluspects?"

"Cyrus, Gino, Diana and Kale—"

"Who's Kale?" he asked.

"Kale Halifax. She's the woman Reince rented Gino's house to without telling him."

"Why is she a suspect?"

I hiccupped. "Because I don't like her."

He nodded gravely. "Follow your feminine intuition. Look, cyber stalking is well and good, but if you're serious about getting the dirt on someone, you need to go old school."

"How?"

"I do not know," he said gravely.

"We can stake out the real estate office." I was a genius. "They'll never expect it, since we were just there."

He dropped some bills on the table and stood, knocking over his chair. "Come on."

Weaving, I followed Hyperion outside and bumped into the potted Japanese maple. I blinked in the blinding daylight. "Ow." I shoved a slim branch aside and shielded my eyes. Did the sun have to be so darned... sunny?

"This way," Hyperion caroled.

I followed him down the narrow, cobbled alley, past tiny pastel tourist apartments. "And then there's the drone."

"What drone?" He paused on the busy sidewalk and darted across the street.

I followed, edging around a trio of elderly tourists exclaiming over a jewelry store window. "The drone that's been following me. It even divebombed me once. It was like something out of a Hitchcock film."

"*North by Northwest*. I adore Cary Grant." He turned right on a residential side street and strode up the hill.

"Me too!"

"We have so much in common. We make perfect partners." He paused beside a massive lavender bush on the corner and snapped off a stalk. "Now which way..."

"That way." I pointed right, past a blue bungalow, the garden behind its picket fence bursting with lavender and foxglove and black sage.

"Of course. Thataway."

"You know who uses drones?" I asked, panting to keep up with his long strides.

"Perverts?"

"Realtors." My sandals flapped on the hot sidewalk, and I hurried to the shade of an olive tree. "They use them to take aerial shots of homes they're selling."

"That's less interesting than perverts."

"But it points to someone at the realty following me."

"Why would they want to?" he asked. "I mean, no offense, but what do those realtors have against you? You, like me, fell for Reince's scam. Neither of us are threatening to sue the company he worked at, though now that I think of it, it's not such a bad idea. How could Cyrus have not known what Reince was up to?"

My thoughts clouded. "Or Florence," I said slowly. "She was Reince's secretary too, and she's dead." Sweat dampened the back of my peasant top.

"There is something else we need to discuss." He shot me a sidelong glance.

"Oh?"

"Your attitude towards my half of the business."

"What are you talking about?" My words seemed to slur, and I shook my head.

He dropped lightly from the curb, and we crossed the street. "Oh, come on. Do you think I haven't noticed?"

"Noticed what?"

"The way your mouth pinches every time I bring out my cards. White lines form around your nostrils."

"Oh. That." I kicked a stone, and it skittered into the street. I hadn't thought it was that obvious. "It's not you."

"Then what is it?"

Cheeks burning, I tugged at my shirt. "It's my parents," I mumbled. "I mean, I know it's a cliché to blame your parents. But they're into crystals and Buddhism and Tarot and meditation and wicca and—"

"Buddhism *and* wicca?"

"There's nothing they haven't tried. They're on a lifelong spiritual quest." I waved my arms expansively and stumbled into a rosemary bush.

"So, what's wrong with that?" He grasped my arm, hauling me upright.

My heart burned with remembered pain. "What's wrong, is they abandoned me when I was three because I was killing their spiritual buzz."

He stopped short. "What?"

"I was in the way, ruining their groove. And I guess I was too big to sit for free on my mom's lap anymore when flying to Katmandu, or wherever the hell they were going next. So, they left me behind to complete their spiritual quest, abandoned me at SFO. My grandparents were forced to raise me. That was over twenty years ago." More like thirty years, but potato po-tah-to.

His face darkened. "That is bullshit. Raising a child is *the* most important spiritual practice. Of course, I don't have any kids, but—"

"It's not as bad as it sounds." I hiccupped. "They felt it wasn't fair to drag me around the planet. They wanted me to have a normal life and education. And I see them at the holidays every two or three years."

"Abigail—"

"It was okay," I said quickly. "My grandparents were amazing. I had a great childhood." Pre-abandonment, I'd also been blessed by the Dalai Lama, the Pope, and a bunch of other shamans and holy persons whose names I didn't remember. "Stupid white shoes."

"You're wearing sandals." He stopped across from the real estate office, and I stumbled into him. He grasped my arms, steadying me. "Abigail, I had no idea. You know that's not what—"

On the opposite side of the street, Cyrus emerged from the office. The wood-beam awning cast prison bars across his face. He turned to fiddle with the slowly closing screen door.

"Quick! Hide!" Hyperion leapt behind a dusty, red Honda.

I froze like a deer blinded by a semi.

"Abigail?" Cyrus jogged down the steps and stopped beside the realty sign. A monarch butterfly flitted lazily around the tall agave's yellow flowers.

"Oh... Uh. Hi." Torn between fight or flight, I did neither and stood woodenly on the sidewalk.

"What are you doing back here? If you're looking for your money – again – I haven't learned anything new in the past three hours. I'm sure the police will let you know when they learn anything."

"My money?" Yeah! My money! Suddenly angry, I plowed across the street and stumbled on the curb. I shook my finger at him. "About that—"

"I'm on my way to the police station for another interview." He spun a set of keys on his finger. "I've really got to go."

"What about your drone?" I blurted. He wasn't getting away from me... with it... *Whatever!* It wasn't going to happen this time.

He blinked. "Drone?"

"You do have a drone, don't you?"

"Yes, we have a drone. My wife insists I only bought it because of my toxic masculinity. But it's useful for photographing homes and land-scapes."

"Ah, ha!" I pointed a wavering finger. "I knew it." The bastard! Bastardo! It was funnier in Italian, and I fought back a giggle.

"What's this about our drone?"

"It's been following me."

"Following you?"

"Following. Me." The Mediterranean Cypresses tilted. I pushed against a nearby Mercedes to straighten the sidewalk.

"Are you okay?" Brow furrowed, Cyrus stepped off the path and studied me.

"Never mind me. What's it look like?"

"What's what look like?"

"Your drone!" *Duh.*

"It's one of those helicopter-style drones with four legs for easy landings."

"That's it!"

"What's it?" His gaze darted up and down the street, as if seeking escape. But there was no escape from me. Huzzah!

"That's the drone that's been following me."

"Are you drunk?"

Indignant, I drew myself up. "No." Not after two... four... five(?) shots. *Huh.* "Who controls your drone?"

"Florence did. She loved playing with the damn thing, so it's got nothing to do with masculinity."

"But you knew how to use it and where to get at it."

"Of course, I did," he said, exasperated. "It's my drone."

"Then why have you been following me with it?" And where the heck was Hyperion? I whirled and staggered, looking for him. When I couldn't find him, I shrugged.

"I haven't been. If someone's been photographing you, it's probably some teenager."

"Photographing? I didn't say anything about photographing."

"Well, what else would you use a drone for?"

The front door opened, and Diana stepped onto the porch. "I thought you were going..." She paused on the steps, then hurried toward us, her loose clothing fluttering about her tall frame. "Abigail, what are you doing here? Again?"

"Harassing me about our drone." Her husband folded his arms.

Her eyes widened. "Our drone?"

"Someone's been following me with a drone," I muttered, less certain of the righteousness of my cause.

"Men!" She planted her hands on her hips and glared at her husband. "There's no good reason for the average person to own a drone. I've heard story after story of rogue drones being used as remote... peeping Toms!"

"They're for aerial photography," Cyrus said wearily.

"How many people are serious aerial photographers?" she asked. "Because I can assure you, most drone owners are not. It's all to do with this culture's toxic masculinity."

Cyrus shook his head.

Her arms dropped. "I hear you and Hyperion Night are going in together on that building."

"Yes." I spoke slowly, careful to enunciate. "It looks like we are. I get to have my tearoom. Hyperion gets to use it for his Tarot studio in the evenings and bring in readers during the day for people who want a reading with their tea." I realized I was swaying and braced my legs wider. "It's the perfect solution."

"Well," she said, "be careful. Partnerships can be tricky, and I've heard..." She glanced across the street. "Is someone hiding behind that Honda?"

"What?" I asked. "No, I don't think—"

"Come out from there," she bellowed, striding across the road.

Hyperion popped up from behind the car. He brandished a deck of Tarot cards. "Found them!"

"What are you doing back there?" Diana scowled.

"I dropped my Tarot deck," he said airily. "Cards everywhere, and this pack is my favorite. It's been broken in, perfectly soft and worn. It took me years to get it this way. Would you like a daily draw?" He held up a card.

"Daily draw?" She crossed her arms, feet set apart.

"Tarot card of the day. I do one every morning."

"No, thank you," she said. "Cyrus, you're going to be late if you don't get moving."

Her husband started. "Right. Well, good luck with the drone. I'll let you know if the police tell me anything about Reince's hidden money." Cyrus squeezed into a blue Prius and zoomed off.

I stared after the car.

"Well?" Diana asked.

My shoulders twitched. "What?"

"Move along," she said. "We don't like loitering on this street."

"Oh. Right." I crossed to Hyperion, and we slunk away.

"That went well," he said.

"I can't tell if you're being sarcastic or not."

"Definitely sarcastic."

CHAPTER TWENTY-TWO

I COVERED MY FACE with my hands and groaned. "Why didn't you stop me?" My lower back pressed against my kitchen's gray granite counter.

"I'm not your gay best friend," Hyperion said. "I'm not responsible." He sat on a bar stool, one elbow on the butcher-block work island, hand gripping his head.

Late afternoon sunlight slanted through the window above the sink. A hammer banged on the opposite side of the redwood fence.

I groaned. *Tequila.* I'd made a fool of myself in front of Cyrus and Diana. Worse, I'd confessed my childhood trauma to Hyperion.

"Don't get your knickers in a twist," he said. "At least we learned the real estate company owns a drone."

"Cyrus was right. Lots of people have drones." I retrieved a water glass from one of my cupboards, filled it from the tap, and gulped the good stuff down.

"Lots of people don't lose two coworkers to murder inside of a week."

True. I gulped more water to dilute the alcohol. An electric saw screeched outside, and we flinched.

"Look," he said. "Since you, uh, revealed something personal to me, maybe I should tell you something personal?"

"That's okay." I grabbed a dishtowel off the stove handle and wiped my hands in it. "You don't need to."

"No, really. Things haven't always been easy between me and my parents either. It wasn't easy telling them..." He drew a long breath. "When I told them the truth about who I really am."

Oh. Oh *wow.* "You mean, when you came out—"

"As a Tarot reader."

"Oh!" *Right.*

"They're astrophysicists. If it's not science, they've got no time for it. I'm a huge disappointment."

"That's... um. I'm sorry to hear that." I dropped the towel on the counter and picked up the glass again, took a drink.

"Eh, they'll get over it. I mean, it's not quite as dramatic as your story, but—"

"No, no. I'm glad you told me." I set the glass beside the sink and gripped the sides of my head, trying to squeeze out the headache.

"You okay?"

I motioned toward the kitchen window. "Brik's home renovations have been driving me crazy. And why didn't you help me at the real estate office? You left me flapping in the wind with Cyrus and Diana."

"We were supposed to be following suspects, not interrogating them, remember?"

If our adventure had had a point, I'd forgotten what it was.

"Don't worry about Cyrus," he continued. "We have bigger problems. Brik won't start construction on Tea and Tarot until we've got everything signed, including a partnership agreement."

"Why does he care about that?"

He rolled his eyes. "I suppose he wants to make sure he's paid."

"I don't see what—" The saw screamed, and an answering throb echoed in my temple. "Tomas will get something to us soon," I ground out.

I walked to my laptop on the butcherblock work island, and I tapped the mouse pad. The computer flickered to life. Opening a search engine, I entered *Kale Halifax artist* into the search box.

Nothing came up.

"That's weird," I said.

"Hm?" Hyperion lounged over my shoulder.

"The woman who's living in Gino Peretti's house. Her neighbor told me she was an artist, and I smelled paint fumes when I visited. You'd think she'd have a website."

"Maybe she's not a very good artist. Look up Peretti."

I did and found a one-page website with contact information for an almond-exporting company.

"I told you the internet was overrated." Hyperion slid off the barstool and stretched, his skinny jeans tight against his lean form. He limped to the pantry door, opened the white, bifold doors. "What's in here?" The Tarot reader flipped on the light and walked inside. His dark head brushed a bundle of drying herbs hanging from the ceiling.

"Teas," I said, irritated.

"Why do you dry herbs in here? Do they need the dark?"

"They need somewhere dry," I said. "The kitchen's too steamy."

Hyperion leered. "That's what *he* said."

I ignored him.

He rolled up the sleeves of his white, collarless shirt. "Do you know the magical properties of these herbs?"

"No."

"That's all right. I've got a book."

"Why—?"

Hyperion limped from the kitchen and into my blue-painted living area.

I trotted after him. "I don't need to know the magical meanings of herbs."

He paused and squinted at my entertainment center. "Hold on." Hyperion hobbled around the couch and grabbed one of my grandmother's teacups off the shelf. "These are fortune telling teacups."

"My grandmother collected them." I snatched it from his grasp. "They're antiques."

"I know they're antiques, but—You! Fortune telling. You know more than you let on. Your grandmother, your parents... You've got a history of magic running through your family."

"Don't remind me." It was why my parents had left. My grandmother had always wondered if that teacup collection had spurred my mother's interest in everything New Age.

He stared at me a long moment and nodded. "Okay."

My muscles unclenched. At least he knew when to drop a subject.

Hyperion made his way to the front door. "They might make a nice addition to our tearoom though." He waggled his fingers at me and exited, limping down the wooden steps.

"You do Tarot reading," I called after him, "not fortune telling."

He waved over his shoulder.

"We're supposed to be adding to each other's market," I shouted over the roar of the electric saw. "If the tearoom is all about magic, we'll be limiting the market."

He shambled down the street.

Augh! I shut the door and leaned against it. If the tearoom was too magically themed, that was the only sort of people we'd attract. Even in California, that was a limited universe.

But we were partners — or we would be — and... I gnawed the inside of my cheek. And I had a good feeling about Hyperion. But I'd had a good feeling about the building too, and so far it had presented one problem after another.

My lips pulled in a tight smile. This would be a test. If Hyperion agreed that we wouldn't *completely* magic-up the tearoom, then it proved he could compromise. We could be partners. And if he didn't... My stomach twisted. If he didn't, we couldn't be partners.

The sound from the saw cut out, and I relaxed against the door. I checked my watch. Six o'clock. "*Thank* you."

Still jittery and not at all hungry, I walked to the kitchen and drank another tall glass of water. What I needed was an herbal boost after all that tequila.

I filled my plain, metal teapot and set it on the stove to heat.

Inside the pantry, I studied the metal canisters lining the walls. I shouldn't drink caffeine at night, but I had a sudden craving for Earl Grey. I opened the labeled tin. A few black leaves lay scattered on the bottom.

I piled three more canisters — china black, lavender, and dried bergamot peel – into my arms. The latter two came from my own garden. Carrying the tins into the kitchen, I placed them on the butcher-block work island. From the cupboard, I took an indigo ceramic bowl and laid it beside the tins.

Earl Grey is made by adding bergamot oil to black tea. But bergamot leaves contain the oil, and in small doses, lavender has a similar, complimentary flavor.

I mixed the herbs by hand. The bergamot and lavender added sparks of color to the black tea, giving it a more exotic look. I added a teaspoon to a strainer and carefully poured the rest into the tin.

I gazed through the cupboard at my teacup collection. *Exotic...*

A shiny burnt brown ceramic mug called to me. It had no handles and was shaped like an urn, primitive, and mysterious. *Like Brik.*

Heat flared across my cheeks. Like Brik? Where the heck had that come from? Obviously, I still had tequila in my system.

The teapot whistled. Dropping the strainer inside the shiny ceramic mug, I poured the water. I cradled the mug, the warmth seeping into my hands, and inhaled the steam. Even the scent was delicious.

Setting it on the counter to cool, I returned the metal canisters to the pantry, turning the labels so they faced outward. My foot crunched on something.

A few stray leaves lay on the bamboo floor. Kneeling, I crushed them between my fingers, and inhaled a tart, lemony scent. I removed a bunch of lemon balm from its hook in the ceiling and examined the dried leaves beneath the overhead light. They'd been here a week and looked dry enough for tinning.

I brought them into the kitchen and extracted an empty tin from a drawer.

Sitting on the barstool Hyperion had vacated, I plucked curled leaves and dropped them into the canister. I was always tempted to crush them, but they preserved better intact.

I shook the half-filled tin, enjoying the rustle of leaves.

Something crashed – shattering glass. I shrieked, jerking backward.

Dried lemon balm exploded into the air. Tiny leaves drifted onto my shoulders and the tile floor.

Clutching the container to my chest, I raced into the living room. A warm breeze drifted through a hole in my front window. Broken glass glittered on the cream-colored sofa, across the bamboo floor, the throw rugs. A brick lay on one of the sofa cushions.

My jaw slackened. I stared in disbelief at flapping blue curtains.

Someone had thrown a brick through my window.

Why—?

A fist pounded on the door.

"Ack!" I jumped again, scattering more lemon balm.

"Abigail?" Brik shouted. "Are you all right?"

"We're here to save you," Hyperion called. "Even if you did shoot me in the leg."

Tottering to the door, I swung it open and braced my weight on the knob. My legs wobbled. "Someone..." Unable to continue, I pointed at the wreckage.

Brik, handsome in jeans and a plain white tee, brushed past me. His jaw clenched. "Are you all right?"

I nodded guiltily. *Primitive like Brik. Sheesh.* Good thing Hyperion wasn't a mind reader.

Unless he was.

The Tarot reader winked at me.

And what was he doing with Brik? "I was in the kitchen when it happened," I said.

"In other words," the contractor said, "you didn't see who did this."

"I didn't do it." Hyperion jerked his head toward Brik. "I have an alibi."

"I didn't think you..." I swallowed, having a hard time completing sentences.

"The police aren't going to be able to do anything about a broken window," Brik said. "But I think you should call them anyway." He picked the brick off the sofa and frowned. "Huh." A corner of the brick had broken off and rolled into the crevice between the ivory cushions.

"Huh?" Hyperion asked. "What's huh?"

Brik shook his blond head. "Probably nothing."

"Probably?" The Tarot reader's voice rocketed upward.

"It's an old brick, that's all," he said. "Look how this corner has crumbled off."

"So?" Hyperion asked.

"So, it looks a lot like one of the bricks from your building," he said.

"Oh, my goddess." Hyperion lurched and grasped the back of the couch. "It's our stalker."

"Calm down, Hypertension," the contractor said.

Hyperion drew himself up. "You think I've never heard *that* before?"

Brik frowned at me. "What's on your head?"

Confused, I brushed my hand across my hair. Lemon balm fluttered to the floor.

"Tell me that's not dandruff," Hyperion said.

"I'll call the police." I stormed into the kitchen.

Since this didn't seem like a job for emergency services, I looked up the phone number for the local P.D..

The dispatcher promised they'd send someone within the next hour, and I reported back to the men.

"An hour?" Hyperion's jaw dropped. "Are you kidding? What if this was an emergency? They say when seconds count, the police are only minutes away, but this is ridiculous."

"It's not an emergency," Brik rumbled. "I'll get plywood." He strode out the front door.

"Can you believe it?" Hyperion asked in a low voice.

"No. I don't know why anyone would throw a brick through my window."

"I didn't mean your window problems. I've never felt such sexual tension with a straight man in my life."

"This isn't about you," I sputtered and stamped my foot. Glass crunched beneath my sandals. "And what were you doing with Brik?"

He waggled his brows. "Wouldn't you like to know?"

"Yes, that's why I asked."

"All right. I stopped by his place to say *hi*." He looped a long arm over my shoulders. "I've been thoughtless. I can only imagine how awful this feels, knowing someone with evil intentions, probably a vicious murderer, not only knows where you live, but is trying to frighten you with drones and bricks. I mean, obviously, the vandalism is connected to the murders.

That means, in the killer's mind at least, you're connected to the murders. You might be the next target. It must be terrifying."

"Thanks," I said dryly. "I feel loads better." And weirdly, I did.

The Tarot reader winked. "Any time."

CHAPTER TWENTY-THREE

THE NEXT MORNING, I lounged beneath my dogwood tree and reveled in the silence and a mug of tea. A light breeze stirred the branches, and giant pink and white petals drifted lazily onto the table. The building was ours, the papers signed, and the world was good.

Which is usually right when the rug gets pulled out from beneath you.

Tiny gray and brown birds hopped along the tanbark paths. A shadow swooped low. The birds took wing, scattering.

My shoulders tensed, and I scanned the sky. But no drone hovered above the trees. Thoughtful, I sipped my tea.

Someone pounded on my front door, and I sucked a mouthful of tea down the wrong pipes.

Hacking, I hauled myself from the garden chair and staggered into the house. I set the mug on the dining table, knotted my hair into a quick bun, and peered out the peephole.

Hyperion's brown and gold eye stared back at me.

I yelped and jerked away.

"It's your favorite Tarot reader," he caroled. "Are you home?"

Gritting my teeth, I opened the door.

He bustled inside.

"Hyperion, I have—"

"I know where Gino Peretti is," he announced, beaming. Then his dark brows slashed downward. He planted his hands on the hips of his skinny camel-colored slacks. "What on earth are you wearing?"

I was wearing comfort clothes - soft, drawstring pants and a matching blue tunic. "What's wrong with these?"

"What's wrong? You look like a frumpty dumpty. Get changed. We can't interrogate Gino with you looking like that. He's Italian."

I eyed his sharply pressed white shirt, the gray jacket, the pocket square. "Is that why you're dressed like a nineteen-forties movie star?"

"You *get* me, partner. Now go change." He shuffled me into my bedroom and stopped in the doorway. "Oooh! Love it. You *do* have a sense of style."

Flattered, I let my frown ease into something more neutral. Hyperion had style, and I didn't mind his approval. I loved my bedroom's soft gray walls, crystal chandelier, and gauzy blue curtains. The coverlet was brown with white stripes, and blue, brown and gray pillows were strewn near the headboard. I'd painted a silhouette of a brown and barren tree on the wall. A white tree silhouette stood at the opposite corner. The bamboo flooring in this room was darker, with an unfinished look.

He walked to the white, louvered closet doors. "Now let's see if you're a secret slob." He pushed them open and stood, arms wide, hands on the handles. Neat rows of clothing, arranged by weight and color palette, hung from hangers. "I knew it. You're a control freak."

"I'm organized."

"Control freak. Why else would you be investigating a murder when there's a perfectly good detective around to do it for you?"

"Me? Why are *you* so gung-ho on investigating?"

"I'm naturally curious," he said. "So, shall we?"

"What's with this *we* business? Yesterday, you hid behind a car while I talked to Cyrus."

He waved his slender hand carelessly. "Oh, that. I'd been drinking, and so had you. Shame on you for leading me astray. But this morning I'm sharp as a tack fresh from the factory." He pressed a long finger to his lips and studied my closet. "No slacks. Peretti will respond to something more feminine. Ah, ha!" He swooped on a rusty-rose, floral print wrap dress, sleeveless and tea-length, and tossed it on the bed. "Now shoes..." He grabbed a pair of champagne-colored low-heels and frowned. "Don't you have anything with more of a heel on it?"

"No." Stilettos made me wobble. Plus, they hurt.

"It's all right. I'll still be able to run faster than you."

"What does that mean?"

"It's about the bears."

"What bears?"

He rolled his eyes. "How fast do you have to be to outrun a bear? Faster than the slowest person you're with. And Peretti *did* threaten to firebomb his own house."

"I should never have told you about that," I grumped. "How do you even know what he looks like?"

"Because he came to our Tarot room this morning and shouted. Lots of dramatic gesturing. The man turns cursing into a flamenco dance."

"He... what?" I pressed my hand to my lips. "Why didn't you lead with that? Are you all right?"

"Do I not look all right? Your handsome neighbor turned up and scared him off." He snaked out a white marabou scarf and tossed it over his shoulders. "Abigail! You have hidden depths."

Cheeks warming, I dragged the scarf off him, leaving tiny feathers on the shoulders of his gray blazer. "It was for a Halloween party."

"You should wear it. Peretti will go nuts."

"Hyperion, why are you here?"

He blinked. "Justice, of course."

"We all want justice, but the police—"

"No, not the concept, the Tarot card." He pulled a card from behind the pocket square in his blazer. "This card keeps turning up in my readings. We won't be able to have our tearoom until justice is done. Besides, I need to prove my dependability."

"You what?"

"After what your parents did, you've got abandonment issues—"

"I do not."

"And I am in this with you to the end."

No more tequila. *Ever.* I folded my arms. "You want to interview Peretti to prove yourself?" Dubious, I studied Hyperion.

"And because the cards told me to."

Great. Was this what working with him was going to be like?

Fun? a small voice inside me asked.

"Can you think of a better reason?" he continued. "Besides, I just saw him walking into that breakfast place on Sandhill Road. He'll be there at least an hour. You know how slow the wait staff is. But you need to hurry." He tossed the dress at me, and I clutched it to my chest. "Go! Shoo!" He waved me toward the bathroom.

Bemused, I changed. Soon we were bulleting down the winding roads in Hyperion's Jeep Wrangler.

I clung to the grab bar as we skidded around a corner and into a parking spot someone had just exited in front of the restaurant.

"There's one thing you should know about me." Hyperion unbuckled his seatbelt.

"Eeep." I unclamped my fingers from the grab bar and extracted myself from the Jeep.

He stepped from the car and stretched. "I am one with the parking gods."

"Hyperion, your interpretation of that justice card might be wrong. This morning I got the—"

Gino Peretti emerged from a restaurant with terracotta walls and French flags fluttering beside the door. Through its windows, diners ate beside a trompe l'oeil of a French village worthy of a Nazi-zombie apocalypse.

Peretti paused beside a planter bursting with impatiens. He checked his cell phone.

"Oy! Peretti!" Hyperion waved and bounded past a store selling Asian antiques. A blue parrot outside its door adjusted its grip on its high metal perch and squawked at Hyperion's passage.

Peretti, in a gray suit and white socks, scowled. "You again! You are here to torture me. You are in league with those villains."

"I told you this morning I'm not," Hyperion said, soothing. "She is." He pointed at me with his thumb.

"What?" I edged past the parrot.

Peretti did a doubletake. Then, incredibly, he laughed. He took my hand and bowed, kissing it. "You, dear lady, are no villain." He glared at Hyperion. "You, I am not so sure of."

I frowned at my new partner. "We're as much in the dark as you about what happened. Both of us lost money to Reince."

"Please forgive my passion." He released my hand, and his jaw tightened. "Those thieves. And that... woman in my house. They are enough to make anyone mad."

"He means crazy," Hyperion whispered loudly in my ear.

"I know what he means," I said. "Mr. Peretti, have you learned anything more about Reince?"

"Reince is no longer the problem." He snapped his fingers. "Reince, a small part of me even admires."

"You do?" I asked. "But he was a common thief."

"Quite uncommon. He understood the ladies. He had that simpering old fool who worked for him wrapped around his finger."

My eyes widened. "Florence? Florence Deebles? What do you mean?"

"They were together when I found him."

"You saw her with him the day he died?" And if she'd been with Reince when Peretti had caught up with him, she'd had to have known or at least suspected what was going on.

"Yes, the old one." He stepped closer. His breath smelled of stale coffee and cigarettes. "I think she was in on it."

"You think Florence helped Reince's scam?" I asked. "But she seemed so... harmless."

"Women can be foolish when it comes to love. But so can men, eh?" He nudged my arm.

Florence and Reince? An item? No way.

"I don't know," Hyperion said, rubbing his chin. "That woman seemed far too meek to be a con artist."

A Tesla hummed past, top down. The driver's blond hair streamed behind her.

"Then why did I see her at the Mercedes dealership last week?" he asked. "Eh?"

"Florence was buying a car?" It could mean nothing. Or it could mean she'd come into money. Our up-front rent payments?

"I saw her getting into a silver Mercedes," Peretti said. "Now, I have spoken to a lawyer. Together we will sue Cyrus Archer—"

"But the Archers didn't know what was going on," I said. "It doesn't seem fair—"

"Of course he knew!" Peretti's eyes bulged. "It was Archer's job to know! They were sharing an office. Reince worked for him."

A seagull fluttered onto the sidewalk and picked at a crust of bread. The parrot shifted on its perch and eyed the bird.

"I don't know about a lawsuit," I said, uncertain. "It sounds expensive, and I've already lost so much—"

"It isn't about the money," Peretti shouted. "It is about vengeance!"

Startled, the gull flapped off.

"That doesn't sound very healthy," I said, edging away.

Hyperion looped an arm over my shoulder. "We'll think about it. Have your lawyer call our lawyer." Like magic, a business card materialized between his fingers. "My number."

The Italian grabbed the card. His eyes narrowed with suspicion. He grunted, turned on his heel, and strode down the sidewalk.

"Strange man," Hyperion said.

"Why did you tell him I was working with Reince?"

"I wanted to get a reaction from him."

"He's nuts. What if he'd believed I was one of the bad guys?"

Hyperion laughed. "Not in that dress he wouldn't. You look too innocent. What do you think about him seeing Florence at a car dealership?"

"A new Mercedes can't be cheap." I frowned. "How much do receptionists make in real estate?"

"Maybe she's independently wealthy," he said.

"There's only one Mercedes dealership in San Borromeo," I said. "Why don't we ask them?"

"Ask what?"

"Whether she was planning to lease or buy. I mean, it is a little strange, isn't it? If she was buying, did she get the money from Reince? Maybe she *was* helping him." But getting money from Reince didn't make sense, because she'd supposedly given him ten-thousand bucks. "If she was leasing... Well, maybe she could have afforded to lease on her salary, and none of it means anything. Though I don't suppose the dealership will tell us that sort of information."

"Leave it to me." Hyperion ushered me into his Jeep, and we roared to the outskirts of town.

The Mercedes dealership was on a wide street, across from a Ford dealership with trucks jacked up on angled ramps.

Hyperion zipped into the lot. A Mazda pulled from a spot in front of the glass and steel showroom, and Hyperion whizzed into the space.

"Told ya." He grinned. "Parking gods."

That was going to get irritating fast.

He yanked up the parking brake and unbuckled his seatbelt. "Okay, you're looking for a new car, and your friend Florence recommended a Merc. Can you be dithering?"

My hand twisted in the seatbelt. "Why would I—?"

"Of course, you can. You're dithering, and I'm pushy—"

I arched a brow. "You? Pushy?"

"Meow. Claws in." He opened the car door. "I'm going to prove myself to you. And, justice! Remember?"

"Hyperion, your Tarot card was wrong. We have the—"

He jumped out and slammed the door.

"Building," I finished, annoyed. *Fine.* If he was going to be ruled by a Tarot card, that was his business. I followed Hyperion's long strides into the dealership.

We walked through the automatic doors. Air conditioners hummed, pumping out cold air and new car smell. The glass doors whooshed shut behind us.

A saleswoman materialized besides a Mercedes SUV. "Hi! I'm Angela. How can I help you today?" She had old-school glam – wavy hair and a tight red suit that emphasized every curve.

"My friend's looking to buy a Mercedes," Hyperion said.

"No, I'm not," I said, flustered. "I mean, I'm not sure. A friend of mine is buying one, and she raved about your service."

The saleswoman's face lit. "Oh? What was her name?"

"Florence," I said. "Florence Deebles."

A startled expression flitted across her face and as quickly vanished. She must have heard of Florence's death. *From the police or the paper?* My stomach wriggled unpleasantly. Were we interfering in an investigation?

"She was here only last week," I said. "Maybe you remember her?"

She swallowed. "A lovely woman. A friend of yours, you say?"

"I can't remember the type of Mercedes she was looking at," I said. "Can you, Hyperion?"

"She didn't tell me." He pinched my arm. "Ix-nay on the ame-nay," he murmured, bending toward my ear.

Oh, that wasn't obvious. Not at all.

I smoothed my expression. "Can you show me that one? I mean, the car Florence was planning on buying?"

"Certainly." The saleswoman crossed the showroom floor and stopped in front of a silver convertible. She stroked one hand along its hood. "The C-Class Cabriolet. Ms. Deebles wanted this car, because she was looking for something she could drive around town. But what do *you* need from a car?"

All I needed was to get off this lot before I signed something.

"Is it turbo charged?" Hyperion asked.

"Of course."

"Seat warmers? You want seat warmers," he told me. "And neck warmers. And back warmers. The entire seat should be warming. She has sciatica," he whispered to the saleswoman. "Really uptight."

I glared.

"You're in luck," she said smoothly, "because it has all those features."

"What are the miles per gallon?" I asked, not meeting her gaze. As a soon-to-be-entrepreneur, I sympathized with her need to make a sale. And she wasn't going to get one from us.

Hyperion laughed. "You don't buy a Mercedes for MPGs. You buy it for style. How much?"

She named a figure, and I swallowed a yelp. I could buy a lot of industrial oven for that price.

"Florence told us there was a cash discount," I croaked.

Her expression turned bland. "Did she?"

"She told me that was why she'd paid cash," I said.

"We offer zero-interest financing," she said. "But Florence chose to take advantage of our cash rebate."

So, Florence *had* paid cash! Ha! I wasn't a bad detective after all.

The saleswoman's eyes gleamed with misguided avarice. "Are you looking to buy today?"

"Never make a snap decision on a purchase over forty-thousand dollars. That's your rule, isn't it darling?" He steered me from the convertible. "Thank you so much. She'll think about it."

"Here's my card." She jogged to catch up with us and handed one to me.

I stuffed it into my purse. "Oh, thanks—"

"No time," Hyperion sang out. He ushered me from the showroom and into his Jeep. "Nicely done, Nancy Drew." He snapped on his seatbelt. "Hm. Where do you think our poor departed Florence got all that lovely cash from?"

"We don't know there's anything suspicious about it," I said. "Maybe she inherited the money. Maybe she'd had it in savings."

"She was trying to buy a car last week, *after* Reince was murdered, and now she's dead? The timing alone makes it suspicious. Who buys a car when they're in mourning?"

"I don't know if she was in mourning, but she did seem upset by his death." *Could* they have been having a relationship? "What did you think of what Peretti said, that Florence was in love with Reince?"

"He could have been into older women. But given what we know of the man, odds are he was working some angle."

My nose wrinkled. "That's awful, if true. Though it *was* weird she showed up at the hospital after you were, er, got hurt."

"After you shot me, you mean." He started the car. "You said she came to the hospital, right? What excuse did she give?"

"She said she felt responsible because of the realtors' connection to the building."

"What connection?" He whipped the Jeep into the street. A horn blared. "Cyrus's company *had* no connection. That was the entire point of Reince's scam. How did she even know we were there?"

"She said the police had called Mr. Bonnet, and he called her. Hold on." I dug my phone from my purse and called the lawyer.

"Ms. Beanblossom! Did you receive the rental agreement I sent?"

"Yes, thanks. It looks good. Say, did the police— Did you call Florence Deebles last Thursday night about the building?"

We passed a surfer, his wetsuit peeled to his waist. He braced a banana-yellow surfboard on his head.

"Call who?" the lawyer asked.

"Florence Deebles, from the realtors."

"Why would I call her? They have nothing to do with the 2304 building. If they're trying to get some commission—"

"No. Sorry, it's not important. I must have misunderstood."

We said our farewells, and I hung up.

"What was that about?" Hyperion asked.

"The police didn't call Mr. Bonnet. He didn't call Florence on Thursday about the accident." There'd been no good reason for Florence to lie, and that only left bad reasons.

"We need more answers, and I am here to help you get them. To Cyrus's office!" He hallooed and darted through a gap in traffic, narrowly avoiding a bicyclist. "Watch the road," he shouted out the window. "Did you see that idiot?" he asked me.

I gripped the door handle. "Hyperion, we have the building!"

He whooped. The Jeep lurched forward, hurling me against the seat. "What? Why didn't you tell me? That's marvelous! We need to celebrate. Drinks all around. No, we need to do more than that. A party! We'll have to have it at your place though, because my apartment's too small."

"I can't throw a party. My house—"

"Is perfect."

"Hyperion—"

"It's marketing. We need to start creating buzz about our business."

The last thing I wanted was a bunch of strangers tramping through my private space. "You're missing the point. As much as I want to learn the truth, we don't *need* to solve the crime to get the building. We already *have* the building. We don't need to harass Cyrus again." Because if I kept this up, he'd get a restraining order.

"Abigail, you can depend on me to see this through. And our business will run a lot more easily if we get our cash back."

"Well, yeah, but—"

"We can invite Brik and his sexy friends to your party."

I thought about that. *Primitive and mysterious.* "Well. I guess. If you insist."

CHAPTER TWENTY-FOUR

WE WALKED ALONG THE garden path, past sand-covered gravel and low-water plants. The afternoon sun made slanting shadows of the wood-beam awning above the realtor's porch. Unseen birds chirped, hiding in the cypresses.

Hyperion opened the screen door. "After y—"

Kale Halifax stormed from the realty, her blond braids flying behind her. Her overalls were paint stained, her eyes blazing with fury.

I sprang away from the door, narrowly avoiding getting knocked off the porch and into a sage brush.

She turned to the open doorway and shook her fist. "This isn't over. You're responsible!"

A door slammed inside the two-story house.

Brushing past us, she leapt down the steps and stormed through the garden to the street.

"That was unexpected," Hyperion said.

"That was Kale Halifax."

"Peretti's squatter?" He turned to watch her march to a yellow Bug.

She roared off, tires squealing.

"And people call *me* a drama queen." He motioned me toward the door. "As I was saying, after you."

"Chivalry? Or are you afraid someone else will charge out and flatten you?"

"The latter." He shuffled me into the gray-tiled and empty reception area. "Halloo," Hyperion called. "Let me handle this," he said to me in a quieter voice.

The hanging spider plant by the stairs drooped, the edges of its long leaves brown. A frosted glass door on the left burst open.

Cyrus, looking harried, strode into the room. "I can't— Oh." He blinked. "It's you again. I thought—" He jerked down the hem of his rumpled blue blazer.

"Thought it was another angry client?" Hyperion asked.

Was it my imagination, or had the realtor added a new thatch of gray hair around his temples?

"I guess you ran into Ms. Halifax," the realtor said. "And she's not a client. Can I help you?"

"What's got her so hot and bothered?" I asked.

"She claims Reince owes her money, ergo, so do I." His gaze drifted to the wall of brochures in their plastic holders.

"For the rent?" I asked. "But I thought she was staying in Mr. Peretti's house until her upfront payment ran out?"

"She said she is. But she claimed she had some kind of private arrangement with Reince. In any case, the insurance company has ordered me not to pay anyone anything until this is straightened out." He shot me a quelling look.

"What sort of private arrangement?" I asked.

"No matter," Hyperion said. "The good news is we're not going to sue you. Or at least I'm not going to. I can't speak for Abby."

I scowled at the interruption. This private arrangement might not have anything to do with the murder or our missing money, but it would have been nice to know.

Cyrus's gaze ping-ponged between the two of us. "Sue?"

"We heard Florence was buying a new car," Hyperion said. "Did you give her a bonus?"

I rolled my eyes. *Subtle.*

"What?" The realtor rubbed his forehead. "What does that have to do with you not suing?"

"It has to do with us trying to figure out where our money went," Hyperion said. "Florence bought a Mercedes and paid cash. Those aren't cheap."

"And you think she paid with your money?" Cyrus asked.

"The timing seems odd," I said.

"Yes," the realtor said, "I suppose it would. But I did give Florence a bonus recently." He glanced toward the matching smoked glass door on the right. "With everything that's been happening, she'd been a real trooper. I'm surprised she put it towards an expensive car though." Cyrus frowned.

"Why?" Hyperion asked.

"It's none of my business," he said quickly and tugged at his open collar. "I'm not monitoring her finances. But I thought the death of her husband had left her in dire straits. That's why she took the job here. A Mercedes seems frivolous." He shook his head. "Diana would know."

"About being frivolous?" I asked.

"Hardly." One corner of his mouth curled upward. "About Florence's plans. Those two were thick as thieves. My wife helped Florence with her finances after her husband died. But you shouldn't bother my wife. She's devastated by Florence's death. She feels responsible."

"Responsible?" I prompted.

"Because she brought Florence into the office." He sat against the wooden reception desk and folded his arms.

"Is it possible Florence knew what Reince was up to?" Hyperion asked.

He pursed his lips and angled his head back. "If she'd known, I'd like to think she would have told me."

"But did she have access to any... I don't know, contracts or documents or appointment books that might have pointed to what Reince was doing?" I asked.

"You don't understand," he said. "Florence was devoted to Diana. She was grateful for everything my wife did to help her in her difficult time. If she knew anything that would have hurt the agency, she would have told Diana. Or told me."

Hyperion's brows lifted. "Then what connects Florence's murder to Reince's aside from sharing an office?"

"I don't know." Cyrus sagged against the desk. "I don't understand any of it. First Reince's betrayal, now Florence's death. They have to be connected, don't they? Could Florence have killed Reince?" He looked up, expression hopeful.

It didn't seem likely, and I bit my lip. Because if Florence had killed Reince, then who had killed Florence?

Gramps grilled chicken on my patio. Smoke from the barbecue drifted over a gibbous moon, hanging above the tops of the dogwood tree. "The farmers' market was hopping today. Too bad you missed it."

"I thought I'd be busy with my new tearoom." Instead, I'd been playing detective.

I handed my grandfather and Tomas cold bottles of their favorite local beer and filled them in on my day.

Standing next to Gramps, Tomas cradled Peking in one hand and pointed at chicken that looked like it needed turning with the other. In the dim light from the French doors, Tomas's striped button-up shirt looked gray and white, like prison wear. He wore a matching bowtie.

"So, all we have are more questions," I said, concluding my report.

Gramps prodded a chicken breast with a pair of metal tongs. The warm evening breeze tossed his white hair and the short sleeves of his blue-check shirt. "You've taken this as far as you can, Abby. Let the police handle it from here. It's their job. And did you know a board in your fence is loose?" He pointed with the tongs to the redwood fence.

"No," I said, "but the murder—"

"You're going to need all your energy for starting up that tearoom," Gramps said. "Now if you need me to do it, I can come over next weekend and fix that fence."

"Thanks, but I can do it." I didn't want Gramps over-exerting himself, especially not when the weather was so warm.

Tomas lowered himself into a patio chair and set the duckling on one knee of his khaki trousers. "Your grandfather's right. You've got your building. Focus on your business."

The duckling turned twice, then sat and closed his tiny eyes.

"I know I should," I said, frustrated, "but I can't. The building is connected to Reince and to Florence, and they're both dead." It was about more than the money now. I needed to *know*.

"You don't know if they're dead because of your building," Gramps said.

Tomas twisted off the bottlecap. "We have too many chicken breasts."

The breeze shifted and barbecue smoke billowed toward Brik's redwood fence.

"If there are leftovers, you both can take them home." It had been my plan all along to keep Gramps well fed. "Why did Florence come to the hospital to check on Hyperion after his accident?" I asked, before they could tell me again not to investigate. "She said the police called the lawyer, and he called her, but Mr. Bonnet denied it. So how did she know? Was she a witness? Was she involved?"

Beneath his bushy white brows, Gramps gave me a penetrating look. "Or was she a gossip with her nose in someone else's business?"

My cheeks burned. I was so not a gossip.

Tomas chuckled. "Now, now. Abby isn't like that. Of course, she's curious. But you know what curiosity did to the cat, young lady." He took a long pull of his beer.

"Someone set fires in our building," I said. "Why? To scare off Hyperion and me? To destroy evidence? And Reince's body was found right outside."

"Outside and on the other side of the parking lot, as I recall," Gramps said. "That conman was probably getting money from the ATM machine, and a robber killed him. I never trusted ATMs. People should look each other in the eye when they exchange money. And what happens if the ATM makes a mistake? Good luck getting your money back. I had a client who lost five hundred bucks that way."

"But then why kill Florence?" I asked. "She didn't just fall into the estuary and drown. She must have known or seen something that made her a threat to the killer — most likely the person setting that fire. But why would Florence be lurking around our building at all? Maybe she followed the arsonist there, which meant she'd suspected that person all along. And why has someone been—?" I bit off my words. Gramps would only worry if he learned about the drone.

Hyperion limped around the corner of the house. "There you are. Is that chicken?" He hobbled up the porch steps and stuck his hand out to Gramps. "Hyperion Night. You must be Abigail's grandfather."

I sucked in my cheeks, nonplussed. What was *he* doing here?

Tomas cocked a brow.

"And you must be that fortune telling fellow," Gramps said, giving Tomas a meaningful look.

"I'm Tomas." The older man raised his beer bottle in greeting. "What do you do? Read people's palms?"

"Entrails," Hyperion said.

Muffling a groan, I briefly squeezed my eyes shut. After everything my grandfather had gone through with my parents, there was no way this was going to go well.

Hyperion rubbed his hands and angled himself closer to the barbecue. "Just kidding. I read Tarot cards."

Gramps' eyes narrowed. "And you tell the future with them?"

"Oh," he waved his hand airily. "The future is easy once you know the past. People just keep doing what they've always done."

Unbelievable. Hyperion was *admitting* his fortunes weren't on the up and up?

Incredibly, Tomas laughed. "Ain't that the truth. I'd tell my clients over and over not to do something, and they'd just keep right on doing it, because that's what they'd always done."

Gramps nodded. "And then they wonder why they keep getting the same results. It's nuts, but what can you do? People are going to be people, and habits are hard to break."

"Did Abigail tell you I once killed a man with a bottlecap?" Tomas asked.

My shoulders relaxed. Everyone was smiling. Gramps wouldn't smile if he didn't like you.

"The trick," Hyperion continued, "is to realize your pattern and then break it. That's where a Tarot reading can help. It takes you outside the mundane, gets you out of your head. Is that a duckling?" He clapped his hands together.

"Peking," Gramps said.

"We're house training her," Tomas said.

"Ducks make good eating." Gramps brandished his tongs.

"Cut it out," I said. "You know you're not going to eat that duck. You've named it."

"Named it after a meal," Tomas said.

I glared. They were going to give Peking a complex.

"Hm." Gramps squinted at Hyperion. Barbecue smoke drifted between them. "I suppose that realtor got your money too?"

"Three months' rent," Hyperion said mournfully. "May I?" He pointed to the duckling in Tomas's lap.

"Take 'em."

Hyperion swooped onto the duckling and cradled it in one hand.

"How are you planning to manage things if you don't get your money back?" Gramps asked.

Hyperion stroked the duckling with the back of one long finger. "I might need to cut back on the blood sacrifices, but with Abigail's help, I'm sure I'll be able to make ends meet."

I covered my face. Not happening. Not *happening.* I peeked through my fingers.

The two older men looked at each other.

Hyperion's nostrils quivered. "That's a lot of chicken."

"You hungry?" Gramps shot Tomas another sideways glance. "We got plenty. Beer's in the fridge." He angled his head toward my lit bungalow.

"Excellent. BRB!" Still holding the duckling, Hyperion let himself in through the French doors and beelined for the kitchen.

Tomas looked over his glasses at me. "Blood sacrifice?"

"Um, I'll just go..." I hurried after Hyperion.

Hyperion leaned inside the refrigerator, one hand braced on the door. The duckling sat on my butcherblock island and looked confused.

"Got any radler?" Hyperon asked.

"Human sacrifice?"

"Ew. Go straight to the dark place, will you?" His voice echoed in my fridge. "I said blood sacrifice, and I was referring to that poultry massacre on your barbeque. Even the duck looked disturbed. If I come back as an animal, I'd like to be a duck. They can fly *and* swim – the best of both worlds. Plus, they're sociable. Have you ever seen a depressed duck?"

"Hyperion."

He heaved a sigh and emerged with a honey-wheat blend. "Your grandfather and his friend knew I was joking."

"What are you doing here?" I ground out.

"I came to check out our party pad." Retrieving Peking, he wandered into the living room and pointed with the bottle at the plywood covering the window behind the couch. "You'll need to get that fixed. Can Brik do it?"

"I don't know," I said distractedly. "I haven't asked."

"Then I will." He made for the front door.

"You can't just show up on his doorstep."

He halted and rubbed the lip of his bottle against his temple. "Mm. I suppose not. BTW, I called him earlier. Now Brik wants us to sign a contract with *him*. In your grandfather's day, a handshake was good enough."

"He's got no reason to trust us."

"I suppose not. After what happened with Reince, I want everything in writing too."

"Everything *was* in writing with Reince." I dropped into a chair beside the dining table. "But it was all meaningless, because he was a crook."

"Don't beat yourself up over Reince. He's a *was*."

"What?"

"Reince is a *was*. I don't waste time thinking on wases, only ises." He strode onto the deck.

I trotted after him. The scent of barbeque coiled in the air, and my stomach rumbled.

"I understand you'll be a part of our Tea and Tarot room," Hyperion said to Gramps.

My grandfather gave Hyperion a hard look and set his jaw. "Yes, and as a lender, I plan on keeping an eye on the tearoom's accounts."

I tensed. *Uh oh...*

"Good." Hyperion gingerly lowered himself into the empty chair beside Tomas. "I know enough about accounting to understand we'll need professional help. Abigail told me you think an LLC is a better choice than a partnership?"

Gramps, Tomas, and Hyperion engaged in a lively conversation on the benefits of pass-throughs and depreciation, and I started to relax. Hyperion was talking like a businessman – a smart-ass businessman, but a businessman – and my Gramps had a soft spot for entrepreneurs. From the jokes and laughter, it seemed they might actually *like* each other.

I brought plates, rolls, and potato salad to the patio table. We ate, Hyperion feeding bits of lettuce to the duckling and keeping the older men laughing. Gramps and Tomas swapped stories about their youthful travails in the Air Force.

I cleared the dishes, and Hyperion outlined his plans for promoting the Tarot side of the business.

"And people really pay to get their fortunes told?" Gramps asked, his voice thick with skepticism.

"People have always paid for that," Hyperion said. "Fortune telling is one of the world's oldest professions. Though I prefer to call myself a Tarot reader rather than a fortune teller. Fortune tellers get a bad rap, fairly or not. But I really do try to help people move forward in a positive direction."

Gramps looked as if he might say something, then glanced at me and clamped his mouth shut.

Tomas pushed away from the table with a groan and stared wistfully at the crumbs of peach pie on his plate. "I can't do it. I can't go on."

Hyperion rubbed his stomach. "You do know how to bake, Abigail. I'll give you that. I don't suppose you'll be baking pies for the tearoom though?"

I shook my head. "Scones and tiny sandwiches." I did plan on making my own jam though, because, yum!

"Rats." Hyperion collected the plates and took them into the kitchen. I took my time following him and found him loading the dishwasher.

"Thanks," I said.

"For what?"

"For making nice with my grandfather and Tomas."

"I do know how to be a good guest."

We cleaned up, and I packaged leftover chicken and potato salad for my grandfather. Tomas, who always had a well-stocked refrigerator, declined the offer of leftovers.

I walked with the older men out the front door, and we paused at the top of the wooden stairs.

Cradling Peking, Gramps took a careful step down. "Now don't forget to send Tomas that—"

The step creaked.

My grandfather pitched forward. His body twisted.

"Duck!" Gramps thrust the duckling toward me.

Automatically, I grabbed Peking from his hands. My heart seized. "Gramps!"

Tomas and I lunged for him, too late.

My grandfather thudded awkwardly down the final two steps and landed hard, unmoving.

CHAPTER TWENTY-FIVE

GRAMPS LAY SPRAWLED, EYES shut, at the foot of my stairs. Light from my open front door knifed across his still form.

"Call nine-one-one." Holding my breath, I cradled the squirming duckling to my chest and crouched beside my grandfather. I checked his pulse. It throbbed faintly in his wrist.

"I'm calling," Hyperion said.

"Gramps?" I ran my free hand lightly over his head, his fragile tufts of white hair. No blood darkened the walk. *Let him be okay, let him be okay.*

Tomas, his brown eyes worried, crouched beside me. "That looked like a bad fall."

Hyperion paced at the top of the steps and murmured into the cell phone.

"I know," I choked out, running my hands along my grandfather's arms, limp beneath his lightweight jacket. "I don't feel anything broken, but—"

Gramps' eyes blinked open, and his legs twitched. "What? Where's my hat?"

I rocked back on my heels and gulped a relieved laugh. "Don't move. You might have hurt something."

He groaned. "I'm fine. How's Peking?"

"The damn duck's fine!" Tomas snapped. "You got knocked cold."

"That must be why my head hurts. Where's my hat?"

Tomas handed him his checked, cabbie's hat. "Here."

His arms flailed. "Help me up. Or maybe..." His expression slackened. He drifted backward, and his eyes closed.

"Gramps? Gramps!" My knee hit the ground hard, and I gasped.

And then Brik was beside me and dropping a gray throw over my grandfather. "I saw his fall from my front window." He glanced at the stairs.

I looked over my shoulder. The second to the top step had levered up, pitching Gramps forward. My stair. My fault.

"I'm so sorry, Gramps," I whispered, my throat compressing. "You're going to be okay." He'd been conscious for a moment, so he had to be, right?

Brik squeezed past us and aimed a pocket flashlight at the wooden stairs. The contractor knelt, his brow furrowing. "Someone's tampered with this step."

"What?" I grasped Gramps' cool hand.

Tomas clambered up the stairs and examined the damage.

"Look," Brik said. "All the nails have been pried out. If anyone stepped close to the edge, the stair would flip forward. And it did."

"Abigail could have been hurt," Tomas said indignantly.

I fought back tears. "Gramps *was* hurt."

Tomas hung his head. "Your grandfather is tough. He'll be okay."

Hyperion slipped his phone into his camel-colored slacks. "An ambulance should be here soon. I'll get a pillow." He hurried indoors and returned with a throw pillow from my couch.

Gently, we slid the blue cushion beneath my grandfather's head, and we waited.

The ambulance arrived ten minutes later. Five minutes after that, a totally unnecessary firetruck and police car pulled to the curb.

A familiar looking Jeep Commander double-parked beside the squad car.

Detective Chase extracted his tall form from the vehicle. Striding to the sidewalk, he hooked his thumbs in his belt, drawing back his navy blazer to expose his gun. His handsome face wrinkled with concern. "What happened here?"

The ambulance crew braced my grandfather's neck and lifted him onto a stretcher.

"My grandfather fell," I said, my voice thin. "Someone sabotaged my step. He could have been—" *Killed.* I clenched my jaw.

The detective eyed the duckling. "Did they now?"

"She's right," Brik said, pointing. "You can see fresh marks where someone dug out the nails."

The detective lanced me with his gaze. "That doesn't tell us who was responsible."

A wave of heat roared from my chest to the top of my head. "Are you kidding me?" Did he think I'd done this? To my own grandfather?

"Well, then maybe you should figure out who did," Tomas snarled. "You're a cop, aren't you?"

Detective Chase climbed the steps. Unclipping a flashlight from his belt, he squatted, examining the wooden boards. He shined the light around the other steps, the pavement. "Find any nails?"

"No," Brik said, "but I wasn't looking either."

"There's one," Hyperion chirped, pointing at the cement walk that ran along the side of my house.

Chase hopped the banister. With a handkerchief, he carefully deposited the nail in an evidence bag from the pocket of his blazer.

"Never leave home without it?" Hyperion asked. "The evidence bag, I mean."

"Not when I'm on duty." The detective scanned the pavement with his flashlight and located two more nails.

Still clutching the downy Peking, I followed Gramps to the ambulance and watched anxiously as the paramedics loaded him inside.

"Which hospital are you taking him to?" I asked a paramedic with a blond ponytail.

"Mercy," she said. "Emergency room."

I nodded. Mercy Hospital was close. "Thanks."

The ambulance pulled from the curb. Its sirens howled, its blue lights reflecting off the cars parked along the side of the street.

"I'll drive you to the hospital." Tomas's skin looked faded, his skin sagging.

"No," I said. "It's all right, you must be tired."

"You're distraught." He crossed his ropy arms. "You shouldn't be driving."

The ambulance turned the corner.

"I'll give her a lift," Brik said. "It's no trouble."

My jaw clenched so hard it ached. Who cared who drove? I could drive myself. I just wanted to go. *Now.*

"You sure?" Tomas asked.

"It's what neighbors do," the contractor said.

Come on, come on.

"Okay, you take good care of her now." Tomas kissed my forehead. "Call me when you get word."

"Maybe you should take the, uh, duck," I said. "I don't think they'll let him into the hospital."

"I'll take good care of Peking," Tomas said, gruff. He extracted the tiny bird from my arms.

I hurried inside and grabbed my purse and a cardigan. Squeezing past Hyperion at the top of the stairs, I clambered over the broken step and trotted to the sidewalk. I glanced over my shoulder.

The detective's flashlight beam arced across the narrow path along the stairs.

"It's all right," Hyperion called. "I'll hold down the fort here."

"Thanks," I said, grateful.

While Tomas watched, I let Brik usher me into his dented blue Ram. He carefully edged the hem of my wrap dress out of the way, then shut the door and got in on the driver's side.

"Thanks for this," I said. "Tomas would have insisted if you hadn't—"

"I know." He turned the key, and the engine rumbled to life. "It's okay. I'm sorry about your grandfather."

My hands fisted in my lap. "Thanks." Gramps would be okay. He had to be.

— *elle* —

The ancient oven inside the tearoom's kitchen was nearly as heavy as my heart. Bent double, I scraped the oven across the linoleum floor.

From the front of the tearoom came the sound of heavy blows. Something crashed, and I winced.

Bastet, perched atop the stove, meowed.

I scowled at the giant cat. "You're not helping." I grunted and gave the stove another tug.

Gramps was still in the hospital, and his condition was serious. I'd visited him that morning, but Hyperion had urged me out of the hospital and into our new building.

Hyperion was right; I needed to keep my mind off Gramps. But even dragging a stove across the floor, I couldn't stop thinking, and a cold, hard knot of worry coiled in my stomach.

Someone had tried to hurt me. It was unlikely a fall like that would have given me more than a sprained ankle. But it had badly hurt my grandfather. The message was clear: stay away from the murders.

Message received.

My neck corded. If Gramps died because of me...

"Let me do that." Brik strode through the old building's kitchen doorway and edged me aside. "What are you trying to do anyway?"

"Clean out whatever's behind this stove." I straightened and wiped away the hair stuck to my face with the back of my hand.

"Any word on your grandfather?" Brik asked gently.

I studied my palms and brushed the grime from the skin. "Same as an hour ago." Giving up, I wiped my palms on my worn jeans. "His condition's serious. And that's better than critical, right?" *Right?*

"This wasn't your fault." His expression darkened. "Someone tampered with your stairs. They meant for you to get hurt."

I laughed, a harsh sound. "What are the odds the police will figure out who's responsible?"

He shook his head and pulled the stove away from the wall, its legs screeching against the concrete. "Is that far enough?"

"Yes, thanks."

He nodded and left to join Hyperion.

Another loud crash sounded from the front room. Briefly, I shut my eyes. Hyperion had a talent for tearing things down, even going at one wall with a sledgehammer. I was a little jealous – I wouldn't mind smashing things right now.

I grimaced at the kitchen's grease-covered walls. If only we had enough money to rip out the tiles and start fresh. But we didn't, so I collected my bucket and brush and returned to work. Gramps was counting on me to make this tearoom happen.

An hour later, Hyperion stuck his head into the kitchen and whistled. "Looking good. The kitchen, not you. You're a disaster. Mind staying out of sight while I interview a reader in the back room?"

Hyperion's concession to physical labor had been narrow-legged olive-green sweats and a white tee. And he *still* managed to look like he'd stepped from the pages of a men's magazine.

Irritated, I sat back on my heels and dropped my brush into the bucket. Sweat-caked dust and grime made my face itch. "What?" I wiped my brow with the back of my hand.

Bastet placed his paws on the bucket's rim and sniffed the gray water.

"A reader for our tar— tearoom." He shrugged into a denim jacket.

"You can say Tarot room," I said. "I'm having a hard time adapting as well."

"There's no sense in wanting what you don't have, and I'm delighted to add tea to the Tarot menu. Or Tarot to the tea menu. It's like that old candy commercial. *You got your Tarot card in my tea! No, you got your tea on my Tarot card.*"

I forced a smile. Gramps loved that candy.

"Too soon for jokes?" He swooped into the kitchen and picked up the cat. Bastet meowed a protest. "If it makes you feel any better, I did a reading for your grandfather last night. Normally, I don't read about other people — it's an invasion of privacy. But this was a special case. He's going to be all right."

That would be great news if I believed in Tarot readings. I stretched my smile wider. "Thanks. I appreciate it." How could I have ever thought Hyperion was self-centered and pretentious? Oh, right. Because I'd been projecting my parents onto him. "And I'll stay out of the way of your interviewee."

He brushed a fleck of dirt off the shoulder of my worn, blue t-shirt. "Good. If she sees you in that condition, she may think I'm an abusive employer. And keep the noise down in here."

I glared. He'd been the one making all the racket.

"There's no door on that back room," he continued, scooping up the cat. "So, I can't help it if I hear everything that happens in here."

"I'll be quiet," I said.

A bell trilled, and I started.

He punched his fist in the air. "There's the reader."

"We have a doorbell?"

But he'd already zipped from the kitchen.

When did we get the doorbell? A door opened, shut. Hyperion and an unseen someone tramped past the kitchen door.

I called the hospital for news about Gramps, and finally got patched through to the correct nurse's station.

"I'm sorry," a nurse said, her voice sympathetic. "There's no change."

My shoulders slumped. "Thanks. I'll call again later." I hung up.

No change.

Murmured voices drifted into the kitchen.

Heartsick, I moved into the oversized pantry. Its shelves were thick with dust, but at least they were relatively grease free. I sponged off the shelves and swept the linoleum floor.

"Ow!" Hyperion yelled.

I paused, leaning on the broom.

"That's it...?" Hyperion's voice climbed, thick with disbelief. "And your clients *like* that...? No... No. Absolutely not! That's ludicrous! Absurd! Out! OUT!"

A door slammed.

Footsteps clomped into the kitchen.

"Can you believe it?" Hyperion asked. "Where are you?"

I stuck my head from the pantry. "It didn't go well?"

"You could say that. She reads with the cards..." He drew a deep breath. "Face down."

"Huh?" I leaned the broom in a corner and stepped into the kitchen.

"Exactly!" He braced his hands on his hips. "And then, when I tried to turn the cards over..." His brown eyes bulged with outrage.

"What?"

"She slapped my hand!"

"She did not."

"Did too." He massaged his brow. "Of all the pretentious twaddle."

I raised a brow. "Twaddle?"

"Can you imagine if she slapped a customer? She had the nerve to tell me she was a psychic. If she was a real psychic, she'd have known not to pull that garbage with me." He snapped his fingers.

"Do you have any more readers lined up?"

"Oh, tons. Everyone who's anyone wants to work here. Well, everyone who's anyone and doesn't have an office."

"So, you'll go on to the next person. It's no big deal."

"No big deal? Didn't you hear me? Face. Down. Are you even listening?"

I pocketed the phone. "No, I'm sorry. It's just..." I motioned to the kitchen. I'd been working in it for hours, and it was still a disaster.

His forehead wrinkled. "Of course, you're not listening. You're worried about your grandfather."

"Worried and sweaty and frustrated." I retrieved the broom and bucket from the pantry and dumped dirty water into the industrial sink.

"Let's talk about something else," he said. "What about art?"

Bastet strolled into the kitchen and rubbed against my ankle.

Baffled, I set down the mop. "Who's Art?"

"Not who. Art. For our walls. I was thinking we could feature local artists on the walls and sell their work. That way, we don't have to pay for the decor."

It was the sort of moneysaving idea my grandfather would love. My eyes watered.

Panic widened his eyes. "Don't cry. Please don't cry. He'll be all right, I promise."

The big cat meowed.

"I'm not going to cry." I sniffed.

"Good. Come with me." He thrust Bastet into my arms and maneuvered me from the building. Pausing to lock the rear door, Hyperion bundled me and the cat into his Wrangler. We roared off.

I brushed a strand of hair from my face. "Where are we going?"

"To see a local artist."

Bastet coiled in my lap and purred.

"Like this?" I asked. "I'm a wreck."

"So are most artists."

He turned up a hill, and my stomach bottomed. "Oh, no. Not Kale Halifax?"

"You said she's an artist. We need art." He placed a hand over his heart. "And I am here for you," he said solemnly.

"Thanks, but we can't investigate anymore. My grandfather is in the hospital because of what we've been doing."

"Because of what the killer's been doing. And your grandfather strikes me as the kind of man who wouldn't want him to get away with it."

"Gramps asked me to stop." I needed to honor his wishes, especially now he might... My throat turned to a lump of stone.

I stared out the window at the homes and gardens zipping past. There was no getting around it. Gramps might not get better. He was old, and when you got older, recoveries got harder.

"Your grandfather asked you to stop because he didn't want *you* to get hurt."

"How do you know that?"

"I didn't spring full-grown from the forehead of Zeus you know. I have grandparents too."

I braced my elbow on the open window and squeezed my bottom lip between my finger and thumb. Gramps wouldn't want me to get hurt now either. "I appreciate what you're trying to do, Hyperion. But let's face it, the police are professionals. We're not. I'm done."

"You're just feeling responsible."

"Because I am responsible."

"And the best way to get over it is to jump right back onto that horse and ride like the wind."

"But—"

"Too late. We're here!" He swerved into an open parking spot in front of the white clapboard bungalow and bounded from the Jeep. Hyperion walked backwards into the succulent garden. "It's art. What could possibly go—"

A high, thin scream cut the air.

Hyperion froze.

"Wrong?" I scrambled from the Jeep and scrabbled in my purse for my phone.

Another long, shrill scream. A dog barked wildly from inside the house.

The door to the nearby Craftsman banged open. Kale's middle-aged neighbor, Allyson, shot into her garden. "Is someone being disemboweled?"

Gino Peretti, covered in foam, stumbled around the corner of the bungalow. Clutching a gasoline can, he plowed into a cactus. Peretti shrieked again and dropped the plastic can. Clots of foam dripped to the ground.

"Serves you right!" Kale, wearing a paint-spattered apron over her tank top, rounded the corner. She brandished a fire extinguisher.

"You witch! You fiend!" He ripped off a stream of Italian. It would have been more intimidating if Peretti didn't look like a fro-yo.

Hyperion's eyes crinkled. The Tarot reader clapped his hands to his mouth.

Kale straightened, tossed the extinguisher to the ground, and replied in kind. And in Italian.

The two shouted in violent Italian and gesticulated wildly.

Expression avid, her round-faced neighbor edged to the low, wooden fence. "Oh, my goodness. Should we call the police?"

"No police," Kale and Gino shouted.

The two combatants stared at each other.

One beat.

Two.

Inside the house, the dog yipped, frantic.

Kale folded her arms over her paint-stained apron.

"I will be going now." Foam quivering on his business suit, Peretti collected his gas can and lifted his chin. He strode to his Alfa Romeo parked on the street. With quick, angry motions, he brushed off the worst of the foam, hopped inside the sports car, and roared off.

"Well," Allyson said. "That's something you don't see every day."

Kale pointed. "Write about this, and I'll sue."

Allyson smiled and returned inside her house.

Kale rounded on Hyperion. "What are you looking at?"

"We're interested in selling your art at Tea and Tarot," he said.

"I already have an agent for my art sales," she said.

"Oh?" I asked and edged closer to Hyperion. "Who? We'd love to contact him. Or her. Or do you mean Reince? I heard you had a private arrangement with him."

Kale's fists clenched. "That's a lie. Who told you that?"

Whoops. I couldn't rat out Cyrus. What if Kale was the killer? What if she turned on the realtor next? "I can't remember where I heard it," I said. But at least I had an admission that she and Reince had been partners in... art?

She advanced on me. "Who told you?"

"Florence," I blurted. "Florence Deebles."

Her face turned white, then red. "She was wrong."

"But—"

"But what? What do you think you're doing? Playing amateur detective? You're not a cop. You don't know what you're doing. You're just nosy and pedestrian and have no taste."

Hyperion gasped.

"Keep this up," she continued, "and you'll be the next person found dead under a bridge." She made a rude gesture and stormed into her house. The door slammed, the dog barking madly.

"We are not pedestrian," Hyperion shouted after her. "And we do too have taste." He put his hands on his hips and studied me critically. "An argument that would carry more weight if you weren't dressed like a Russian peasant after a hard day picking cabbage."

"It doesn't matter." My chest caved inward. She was right. I didn't know what I was doing.

CHAPTER TWENTY-SIX

"DON'T YOU THINK IT'S suspicious? Because I think it's suspicious." Hyperion forked a buttery wedge of crab into his mouth, closed his eyes, and made yummy sounds. "I love living near the ocean."

Unenthusiastic, I poked at my Caesar salad with a fork. After the fiasco with Kale and Peretti, Hyperion had insisted on taking me to lunch. We sat in rattan chairs in a Mexican seafood restaurant of chic lines and trendy pastels. An aloe in a turquoise wall planter hung beside me. Our open window overlooked the water and the estuary where Florence had been found.

I imagined her body, gray hair floating like seaweed, and I pushed my plate away, rumpling the cloth placemat.

What if the person who'd killed Florence had succeeded in killing Gramps? And then there was Kale's threat about finding my body in the estuary. It was probably just talk, but—

Something brushed my neck, and I jumped two inches in my seat before I realized it was only hair that had escaped my chignon. I smoothed the front of my faded blue tee and tried to look like I'd meant to go airborne.

"Peretti was totally trying to commit arson," Hyperion said. "Or else why bring the gas can? I get why he didn't want us to call the police, but why didn't Kale? He tried to burn her house down."

"His house."

A warm breeze fluttered the white curtains. I hoped it wasn't blowing my sweat stench over the neighboring tables.

"Whatever." He shrugged. "Kale was living in it. She could have been killed. And why didn't she want to sell us any paintings? Have you ever met an artist who wasn't interested in showing their work?"

"It doesn't matter," I said wearily. "We're not the police. We're just nosy. Let's concentrate on launching our business. Isn't that enough?"

A seagull skimmed low outside our window, and I tracked its path. It landed on the bridge over the estuary and spread its wings wide.

He shook his head. "You forget the justice card."

"Maybe it was telling you to let the police do their job."

"That was not my interpretation," he said stiffly. "What's wrong with you today?"

My throat closed. "I need to call the hospital." Scraping back the rattan chair, I rose and walked to the tiled entry area, made the call.

A nurse answered, and I gave her my grandfather's information.

"Oh, yes," she said. "Good news. He's awake."

My eyes squeezed shut with relief. "He is?"

"They're moving him to another room. The transfer will take a couple hours. You might want to wait until three or four to stop by for a visit."

"I will! Thank you! Thank you!" I hurried to our table. "He's awake."

Hyperion beamed. "I told you so. Do you want me to drive you to the hospital?"

I shook my head and sat. "They said they're moving him to a new room, and it will take a couple hours." Suddenly hungry, I dug into my salad and speared a grilled shrimp.

"So, about Peretti—"

"No." I pointed my fork at him. "Let the police handle it."

"You're going to let a killer hurt your grandfather and scare you off? The best thing you can do for your grandfather—"

"Is make sure his investment in the tearoom—"

"Tarot studio."

"Tea and Tarot room is a success." I stuffed more salad into my mouth.

He folded his arms. "That doesn't sound like justice to me. We should at least tell the police about Peretti."

"Fine. You do that."

We finished lunch in awkward silence.

Hyperion dropped me in the parking lot behind our purple building. "See you later," he said, leaning out the Jeep's door. "I'm going to the police station to tell Detective Chase about Peretti and that gas can."

"You know you can call the station?"

"Have you *seen* that cowboy?" He hummed the chorus to *All My Ex's Live in Texas*, revved the engine, and drove off.

I watched his Jeep zip from the lot and shook my head. We weren't detectives. We were getting in the way, and the consequences for Gramps could have been deadly.

I walked down the tearoom's narrow, rear hallway. A metallic clank echoed off the bare walls, and I stilled.

I edged open the bathroom door.

Brik, in his paint-splattered jeans and tee, held a tablet computer in his hand. A thin black plastic pipe snaked from the computer into the toilet. He'd rigged a temporary light on a hook against the sickly green wall.

That paint had to go.

"What's going on?" I asked.

He raised his blond head and handed me the tablet. "Take a look at this pipe."

The tablet showed a grainy black and white image. The pipe looked scaly, like a snake turned inside out. "What exactly am I looking at?"

"This is the pipe that runs to the sewer. The old pipes, like this one, were made of clay."

"And?" I asked, dread tightening my gut.

"You see those cracks, where it looks like scales?"

"Yeah."

"That's a problem. When the water was turned on today, I tried flushing, and the toilet clogged."

A fresh bead of sweat formed on my brow. "How big a problem?"

"These pipes are at least seventy years old. They need to be replaced."

I gulped. No *problem*. I could deal with this. "How much will that cost?"

"It depends on how far away the sewer line is. I don't do plumbing, but in this part of California, it can be anywhere from ten to forty thousand."

I felt the blood drain from my face, the lawyer's words echoing in my brain. *As long as you pay for all the repairs.* "How long do you think it will take to fix?" I asked, my voice hoarse.

"My experience is a week or two, depending on how far you have to dig out. But that doesn't include permits, lining up a plumber..."

He rambled on, but I'd stopped listening. I stared blankly at the green chipped wall. This was a disaster. We didn't have an extra ten to forty thousand.

Worse, this would push back our launch, and we'd be stuck paying rent without earning any income. "Does it have to be repaired now?"

"It does if you want people to be able to use the bathroom."

Damn, damn, damn! "Okay." I cleared my throat. "Thanks for letting me know."

"Are you all right?"

"It's okay," I lied. "We'll figure this out." Maybe if we sold our cars... We'd be able to pay half. "I need to go to the hospital." And get out of here before I started in on the wailing and gnashing of teeth.

His brow creased with concern. "How's your grandfather doing?"

"Better. He's awake." And that, I reminded myself, was all that mattered.

"That's great news. Listen, I'm going to keep going with the tear-down, if that's okay?"

"Right. Sure." I stumbled from the bathroom and down the hall, pushed the backdoor open.

A uniformed delivery man stood frowning at a clipboard. He rested one suntanned hand on the handle of a dolly loaded with square boxes. The cardboard flaps of the top box hung open.

"Hi," I said, surprised. "Are you looking for 2304?"

"Yeah, is this it?"

"It is. Do you need me to sign for something?"

"This tile delivery." He nodded his head.

"Sure." I took the clipboard and peered into the open box. The tiles gleamed deep, psychedelic purple. "Wait a minute. These aren't ours."

"Well, talk it over with the store. Just sign the form."

I shook my head. "No, if I sign, I'm saying I accept the delivery. I can't sign for a wrong delivery."

"Look, lady, I just—"

"No, dammit, you look," I exploded. "Take it back. I'm not signing for the wrong tiles. No one is signing for these. Take them back!"

"Whoa." Hyperion strolled to us and cocked his eyebrow. "What's going on?"

"Talk to Brik," I snarled. "And don't you dare sign for those tiles!"

Hyperion raised his hands in a warding gesture.

Chest heaving, I wove through the lot to my Mazda and leaned against the door. Trying to get me to sign for tile we hadn't ordered? Did the delivery guy think I was a pushover?

My face heated with shame. Because it wasn't the deliveryman's fault he'd been given the wrong tiles. I shouldn't have gone ballistic.

And the sewer. Ten-thousand dollars. Forty-thousand dollars. Could we get a bank loan to see us through?

But banks don't like to lend to people who actually need money — and especially not to startups. New businesses were too risky. And I couldn't go to Gramps for more. I also couldn't let the business fail. We'd signed the rental agreement, and Brik had already started work. It was too late to back out now.

Dammit!

Okay, today I'd do a Scarlett O'Hara and think about it tomorrow. Today was about Gramps.

Gingerly, I slid into my sweltering car and rolled down the windows with my fingertips. I drove to the store for some magazines and a flower arrangement and then on to the hospital.

My cell phone rang. *Hyperion.*

I declined the call and turned the phone to silent.

As hospitals went, the one Gramps had been sent to was decent, with modern tiles and lots of natural lighting. Even better, there were no visiting hours. Or at least, not for someone in my grandfather's condition. Visitors could come and go as they pleased.

My grandfather's door stood open, a gray curtain on a curved track blocking the view. I rapped lightly on the door and pushed the curtain aside.

Gramps lay in bed beneath a tawny blanket. He smiled. "Abigail! Come in."

The TV muttered in the corner, a national newscaster talking about the latest disaster. A watercolor of San Borromeo – pastel buildings, ocean and palms – hung on one wall.

"Hi!" I set the flowers on a dresser opposite his bed. A massive pink and yellow bouquet dwarfed my own offering. I jammed my hands in the pockets of my bootcut jeans. "Nice flowers."

"I don't know who they're from," he said. "I guess the old memory's fading."

I plucked the card from the bouquet. *Get well soon, Diana.*

"They're from the realtor," I said. How had Diana known about my grandfather's fall?

"You know her?"

"Slightly. I'll call and thank her for you, if you like. How are you feeling?"

"I feel like I want out of here, but the doctors say I should stay another day for observation." He made a face. "Bedrest is boring." He brightened. "How's Peking?"

"Tomas has introduced her to fresh peas."

"Tomas always did eat healthy. Well, that'll just make Peking better eating."

"Come off it," I scoffed. "You risked your life for that stupid duck. You're not going to eat her."

His expression turned sheepish. "She's not a bad duck. I guess I could keep her around. I hear geese make good guard animals. Maybe I could train Peking?"

Good luck with that. "I brought you some magazines." I set them on the narrow table over his bed.

"Thanks." He turned off the TV and set the remote on the swivel table over the bed.

"I'm so sorry about what happened." My voice cracked.

He waved away my apology. "Don't worry, I won't sue. And now you've got steps and a fence to fix? Or have you already fixed that fence of yours?"

"Not yet." It was just like Gramps to worry about the fence.

He shifted on the bed, the sheets rustling. "When I get out of here, I'll take care of it."

"I can do it. Have the police talked to you?" I asked, changing the subject.

"The police? Why?" He laughed. "Do they think you're criminally liable?"

"No. It looks like someone tampered with the stair." I looked out the window at a stand of Monterrey pines. "The nails were pulled out. If anyone stepped on the edge, the stair would flip up."

He raised himself on his elbows. "Sabotage? Whoever did that should be horsewhipped. That was aimed at you, Abigail."

I perched on the edge of a tan lounge chair. "The police took fingerprints. They'll catch whoever did it."

"Sure, if the person is in their system. You had the right idea, Abigail, taking things into your own hands." His hands fisted in the sheets. "I'll be damned if I'll let someone get away with this. Why would anyone do that to you?"

"I think because I was asking questions about Reince. But I don't think the person was trying to kill me," I said quickly. "It was a warning, a warning I'm taking seriously. If I could take it all back—"

"Don't you dare take it back. When I get out of here, I'm helping you."

Oh, boy. This was not the conversation I'd had in mind. "What did the doctors say? You must be on the mend, if they're letting you go soon."

"Forget about me. How are things at your new building?"

"Good." I choked on the lie, the word creaking out. "Brik's started the tear-down." I couldn't tell him about the sewer. Not until I had a full view of the situation, and he was out of the hospital.

There was a knock at the door. Tomas sidled into the room. "He lives!" Today's bowtie was bright red against a brown button-up shirt.

"I hope so," Gramps said. "It beats the alternative."

"And I've got news for you," Tomas said. "Peking is a he!"

Gramps raised himself higher. "What? The guy who sold it to us said it was a girl. That means no eggs."

"Well, I took a closer look, and she's definitely a he. And you call yourself a Pennsylvania farm boy. You can't even tell the difference between a boy duck and a girl duck."

"I lost my reading glasses."

I listened to their genial bickering for another thirty minutes, then I rose. "Well, I'd better get back to work."

"You take good care of my investment now," Gramps said, laughing.

I schooled myself not to wince. "Will do!" I edged from the room. To my surprise, Tomas followed.

"Abigail?" he asked in a low voice. "Is there something going on?"

"Why?"

"I stopped by your building on my way here to drop off the partnership agreement. That fortune teller was shouting at someone in the parking lot."

"Oh. Right." I grimaced and steered him away from the door and into a bland waiting area. "It turns out the pipes that run out to the sewer may need replacing."

Tomas whistled softly. "That's not cheap."

"I know I have to tell Gramps. But I'm hoping I can figure something out, or maybe the contractor's made a mistake or— We only paid a three-month advance. What happens if we just leave after that?"

"If memory serves, you'll have to keep paying until the owner finds another tenant. And he hasn't been looking for one for years."

I rocked slightly, my shoulder brushing the corridor wall. "You mean I'd have to find a tenant for him or be stuck paying rent for two years?"

"Let me take another look at your contract."

"Why? Do you think there might be a loophole?"

"Just let me take a look at it again this afternoon." He patted my arm. "You never know."

My heart thudded dully in my chest. But I did know. Whatever could go wrong, would go wrong.

"Oh, and here's your copy of the partnership agreement to review." Tomas handed a sheaf of paper to me and vanished into Gramps' room.

What was the point of a partnership? My dream was doomed.

CHAPTER TWENTY-SEVEN

Afternoon sunlight slanted through the redwoods. In the hospital parking lot, I checked my phone. I blew out my breath. Three missed calls from Hyperion. I leaned against my Mazda and phoned.

"Abigail! The sewer! The bathroom! We need to talk."

I scraped my hand through my hair, damp and gritty with sweat. "Yeah," I said heavily. "We do." And this sort of discussion was better done in person. "Where are you?"

"At the Mortar and Pestle. I needed a drink after this catastrophe."

"I'll meet you there."

I drove down the hill into San Borromeo and parked on the street. The ocean glittered, the scent of seaweed and freshly baked ice cream cones teasing the air. Another perfect California beach day mocked my personal dark night of the soul. I couldn't see a way out besides cutting our losses and running.

Steeling myself, I trudged down the cobbled alley and into the dim bar.

The air conditioning was running full blast. Hyperion sat in his denim jacket, his elbows braced on a rough, wooden table. Limply, he stirred a mixed drink in a mortar.

I sat on the leather-covered chair opposite. "Hi."

"Low is more like it. The sewer! How were we supposed to know it needed to be repaired? Where are we going to come up with forty-thousand dollars?"

"It might not cost that—" I shook my head. *Not the point.* "We aren't."

"Then how are we going to pay for the repairs?"

"We can't," I said, sickened. "I didn't even think to check the sewer line before renting the building."

"Now what?"

"Tomas is reviewing the rental agreement this afternoon to see what he can do. But we need to prepare for the worst."

He braced his head in his hands. "I can't believe this."

"I can't either. But what choice do we have now? We need to cut our losses."

He looked up. "The problem with the sewer I can believe just fine. It's you I can't believe."

My hand flew to my chest. "Me?"

"You'll do anything to get out of this partnership. I knew you were a loner, but I didn't figure you for a quitter."

"Be realistic. We can't afford these repairs."

His jaw set. "I thought you had abandonment issues. But you're the one who's doing the abandoning. Our first roadblock, and you give up."

"This isn't our first roadblock. It's one of many roadblocks. Maybe this tearoom isn't meant to be."

He stabbed a long finger at me. "I'm disappointed, and your grandfather will be too. We have a great business plan. The perfect location. And then a few things go wrong, and you just throw in the hookah."

"What does that... Someone tried to kill my grandfather."

"Someone tried to scare you off, and your grandfather got in the way. Are you going to let them win? Don't you want this tearoom? Or is the real problem that you don't want to go into business with me?"

"It isn't easy giving up control," I admitted slowly. It was harder putting my trust in someone. Hyperion and I may have bonded over murder, but I'd learned the hard way that if I wanted to make things happen, I had to do it on my own. But Hyperion had brought a lot to the table. "But I admit, partnering with you makes the tearoom better."

"So, what's the problem?"

"So, the sewer. The murders. My grandfather."

"Toughen up, buttercup. And if you can't, maybe you're not the sort of person I want to go into business with." He rose, his leg bumping the table, and limped out.

A waitress slapped the bill on the table and sailed to the bar.

Perfect. Another unexpected expense. Growling beneath my breath, I dug my wallet from my purse.

Was I giving up too easily?

Tossing the money on the table, I walked from the bar.

A woman strolled past wearing one of those *Keep Calm and Carry On* t-shirts. My parents would have said it was a sign. Of course, my parents would have also given up on the tearoom a week ago.

I stopped short, and a kid on a push scooter shouted, swerved around me.

Dammit, my parents *would* have given up. They'd have cut and run at the first chance, like they did whenever life got uncomfortable. I couldn't abandon Hyperion when he needed me most. That would make me *exactly* like my parents.

My jaw hardened. I wasn't my parents. And I wasn't giving up on Hyperion and our Tea and Tarot room. I was too angry. That tearoom was going to open and whoever had hurt my grandfather was going down.

Even if it killed me.

Hyperion wasn't answering my calls, so I drove to his office. His Jeep sat in the lot in front of the squat, cement building.

I rode the rickety elevator to the second floor. The doors shuddered open, and I leapt into the hall before the cable decided to snap.

It had just been that kind of day.

The door to room 203 stood open, and I hurried into the reception area. The financial planner wasn't at her desk. The twinkle lights over Hyperion's door weren't on. His door wasn't open.

I knocked gently, one hand clutching my purse.

After a moment, the door opened. Hyperion, expression lofty, stared down at me. "Yes?"

A woman murmured in Spanish behind him.

"Are you with a client?" I asked.

"What do you want?"

"To apologize," I said.

He edged the door wider. "Come in."

I stepped into his office. A small television sat on the altar between the flameless candles, driftwood, and crystals. A red-velvet armchair sat angled toward a telenovella playing on the TV.

"I'm still not sure I was wrong about the money," I said. "But we shouldn't make a snap decision."

"We?" he asked pointedly.

"I shouldn't."

"All right," he said. "I admit, I pitched a fit too when I heard about the sewer problem. We all react in our own way. Just don't quit on me, okay? We need each other if we're going to make this work — now more than ever."

"You're right. I'll sign that partnership agreement if you will."

"I already did."

"But you said—"

"I read Tarot. Do you really think I didn't intuit where you'd land?"

Intuit my... The TV drew my eye. Two women in tight fitting short dresses shrieked and grabbed each other's hair.

He waved towards the screen. "Maricella is having an affair with Linda's husband. Linda just found out, and she is *mad*. Maricella should have known you do *not* mess with Linda's man."

"Right. That's not..." I stared. *An affair.*

"What's wrong?"

"Nothing. I just..." I shook myself. "I have to go."

Hyperion straightened. "Are you investigating?"

"No," I lied.

"You're a terrible liar."

"Gramps was nearly killed. I don't want to get you hurt just because I'm obsessed with that damn realty."

"You just don't want to let me in," he said. "Are we partners or not?"

"Partners in the tearoom."

"Don't be selfish. I'm a suspect too. I'm going."

"Fine," I said, exasperated.

We hurried as fast as Hyperion's limp could carry him from the office and to my car.

Thoughts jumbling, I drove to the real estate office as fast as I dared — which wasn't very much in a residential zone.

I parked in front of the building. Hyperion and I walked through the neatly graveled yard and past the Mediterranean Cypresses. On the front porch, I rattled the knob.

Locked.

"What now?" Hyperion asked.

I stepped away from the door and checked my watch. It was only four-thirty. Were they closed? But a light shone through the closed blinds. I knocked, waited.

"Maybe someone's dead inside," Hyperion said.

I glared at him.

A car door slammed.

"Or they're around back," I said.

We walked down the steps and through the garden to the driveway that ran along the side of the house.

Dress shirt rolled to the elbows, Cyrus was loading real estate signs into a black SUV. His red power tie was askew.

"Tally ho," Hyperion shouted.

The realtor jerked, and the signs cascaded to the pavement. "Oh," he said, his look haunted. "It's you. I'd ask how I can help you, but that would only encourage you to return. You both need to stop coming around here."

I glared at Hyperion. "Diana sent my grandfather some flowers. I—"

"We," Hyperion said.

"We wanted to thank her," I muttered.

"Your grandfather?"

"He's in the hospital."

"I'm sorry to hear that, but the flowers sound like Diana. Involved to a fault." He dug in the inside pocket of his blazer and pulled out a card case. "Here." Cyrus handed me a business card, and his hands trembled slightly. "Her cell phone." He collected the signs and dumped them in the open back of the SUV.

"How did you two hear about my grandfather's accident?" I asked.

"I didn't," Cyrus said, "until you told me now. Diana has friends at the hospital though. She used to volunteer there. Sometimes she still pitches in."

"Right. That must be it." I ran my fingers along the edges of the business card.

"Are you off to an open house?" Hyperion asked brightly.

"No," Cyrus said. "Why? Are you looking?"

"Sadly, no." Hyperion heaved a dramatic sigh.

Cyrus fiddled with a cufflink. "Was there something else? If you're here to ask about Reince, I still don't know anything, and at this point, I don't *want* to know anything. Ignorance is bliss."

"We're not here about Reince," I said quickly. "Well, we are. But—"

"Look," Cyrus said, "I thought I was making my life easier by bringing Reince into the business. I even thought I was doing him a favor. Now clients are pulling their listings. Guilt by association. The word's out that he was a crook. I can't help you."

"We don't blame you for what happened," I said.

Hyperion snorted.

"But the money Reince stole was a big loss for us," I continued.

"You want to talk about loss?" The realtor's nostrils flared. "Diana blames me for what's happened, for Florence's death, and—" He clamped his jaw shut, as if he'd regretted saying that much.

"For Florence's death?" Hyperion asked.

"She and Florence were close. My wife's taking it hard."

"Florence and your wife knew each other for a long time," I said, "didn't they?"

"For years. They were thick as thieves. Though between you and me, I think part of the reason she brought Florence in was to make sure I didn't have a younger, sexier receptionist. Not that it would have mattered," Cyrus said quickly. "I love Diana."

Then why bring it up? "So, she thinks Florence's death is connected to Reince?"

"It has to be." One of the signs jammed, and he worked it up and down until it slid between the others. "And they both worked for me, and Florence helped Reince with his appointments, ergo it's my fault. He had references. A history. Licenses. How was I to know I needed to hire a private detective before hiring a licensed realtor?"

"You couldn't have," Hyperion said, his voice dripping faux-empathy.

The hollows of the realtor's cheeks darkened. "Tell that to my lost clients."

"It's not your fault," Hyperion said. "You were taken in like everyone else. People will come around."

"Will they?" Cyrus laughed starkly. "Life isn't exactly fair, as my wife is so fond of reminding me." He shook his gray head. "No, that isn't fair. Diana's worried, and who can blame her? We've spent years building up this business. She doesn't want to lose it any more than I do."

"Is that a real possibility?" I asked. "That you'll lose the business?"

"I hope not. Look, I'm sorry, I've got to go." Cyrus slammed the rear of the SUV shut and stepped into the driver's side.

"Wait," I said, "I—"

He backed from the driveway, swerving to avoid me.

We walked to the street and watched his car vanish over the crest of the hill, and I wondered.

CHAPTER TWENTY-EIGHT

I THREW MYSELF INTO my work at the Tea and Tarot room. Maybe it was Hyperion's influence, and his insistence that our business was in the cards. Maybe I was just tired of worrying. Okay, I *still* worried, but I was a big believer in faking it until you make it.

My forced optimism seemed to work. Thursday night, they released my grandfather. Friday, he was well enough for me to take him and Tomas out for a celebratory dinner at Elegy. It perched on a hill so steep you had to park in the lot below and take a gondola to the restaurant.

We sailed high above the trees, the warm air heavy with the scent of eucalyptus. The lights of San Borromeo winked off the darkening ocean. A near-full moon sank low over the Pacific, leaving a mercury trail on the water.

"We live in Shangri-la, my friend." Gramps clapped Tomas on the shoulder. In spite of the warmth, he wore a lightweight dove-colored jacket over his checked shirt and khaki slacks.

Tomas shoved his Giants cap up with the tip of his thumb. He wore a matching baseball jersey over his black shirt and slacks, and an orange-and-black Giants bowtie. "Is that your way of thanking me for talking you into moving to California?"

They bickered good naturedly, and I leaned against the gondola's rails. Crossing my legs at the ankles, I admired my low, sparkly flowered heels. My grandmother would have loved them. The pink almost exactly matched my button-up dress.

The gondola bumped to a halt at the restaurant. We emerged, and a hostess greeted us. I'd made reservations, and she showed us to our seats on the flagstone patio overlooking the water. It was cooler here, a breeze stirring the white tablecloths. Gas heating lamps glowed with orange flames between the tables.

We ordered. The waitress left.

Tomas leaned forward, his dark eyes serious. "I have news about your rental agreement."

Uh oh. I squeezed my hands together.

"What's wrong with her rental?" Gramps asked.

My stomach roiled. Here it came. I'd have to confess the real situation to Gramps. I drew breath to speak.

"Did I say something was wrong?" Tomas asked.

"If everything was right," Gramps said, "you wouldn't be reviewing the agreement."

"Everything is fine," Tomas said. "The building owner handles everything outside the walls."

My breath caught. "You mean—?"

Tomas grinned. "Anything that runs outside or underground – like pipes – is covered by the owner."

I sagged in my chair. Hyperion and I wouldn't have to pay for the new sewer line! I frowned. But would the new owner?

"And I took the liberty of contacting that lawyer," Tomas said, "Bill Bonnet. He's going to take care of everything."

"He is?"

"What does he need to take care of?" Gramps asked.

I squeezed his hand. "Just some plumbing." I turned to Tomas. "That's wonderful news. Thank you. Do you mind if I send a quick text to Hyperion?" I asked them.

"Go ahead," Gramps said.

The waitress arrived with our drinks, and I shot a text to Hyperion: BUILDING OWNER PAYS FOR PLUMBING. BONNET IS ON IT.

A moment later I got a text in reply: JUSTICE! U R A POET AND U DON'T KNOW IT.

I smiled. *Typical Hyperion.*

"What did he say?" Tomas said.

"He said he knew it would all work out."

My grandfather laughed. "I'll bet. You sure you know what you're doing jumping into business with a fortune teller?"

"Tarot card reader," I corrected, tearing off a slice of the bread. "And no, I don't know, exactly, but Hyperion's solid." I bit into the bread. It was perfect – warm and tangy. It didn't even need butter.

"I think so too," Gramps said. "I'm glad you've got a partner. He seems like a good egg, and going it alone is hard work." He tore a piece of sourdough bread from the basket. "Have the police gotten closer to figuring out who sabotaged your front steps?"

"No." I glanced about the deck. "But one of my suspects ate here."

Tomas raised his brow. "So that's why you've dragged us to this fancy place."

I felt a flush work its way up my cheeks. The truth was, I *liked* hanging out with Gramps and Tomas. And Gramps had said he wanted to help. This seemed harmless. "I owe you for helping us with the legal stuff. Besides, it's beautiful up here." And after being stuck in the hospital for days, Gramps was itching to get out on the town.

Tomas braced his elbows on the white tablecloth. "All right, Columbo. What's your plan?"

I set my phone on the table. "To show the waiters pictures of everyone involved — Reince, Florence, Gino, Kale, and Diana."

Gramps unfurled his white napkin and placed it in his lap. "Won't work. This is a fancy joint. They know better than to gossip."

I shifted in my seat. "It's not really gossip."

"He's right," Tomas said. "What you need is a ringer."

"A what?" I asked.

"A frail and innocent old man they can't deny." Tomas angled his head toward my grandfather.

"I'm not frail," Gramps said. "But I do want payback for that rigged step. Gimme that." He plucked my phone from the tablecloth, and his bushy, white brows drew downward. "Now, how do you see the pictures?"

"Luddite." Tomas snatched the phone from him and pulled up the pictures. "Here."

"Huh." My grandfather scraped back his chair and stood. "Watch and learn." He toddled to the hostess stand.

The young woman beamed at him and looked at the phone. She guided Gramps into the bar.

Tomas cleared his throat. "So, what do you think of your new partner? Really?"

I laughed shortly and rubbed my damp palms over my skirt. "Why?"

"Your grandfather would never say it to you, but he's worried about how quickly you jumped into business with this fellow."

"Ah." I looked down at my hands, folded on the table. "It was one of those necessity-being-the-mother-of-invention situations. But..." I met his gaze. "Hyperion's serious about making our business work."

"Do you trust him?"

Slowly, I nodded. I didn't know why I trusted him. I *shouldn't* trust him. But there was something deeper to Hyperion than I'd ever seen in my parents. And though my wounded heart told me alone was best, my head told me I couldn't do this without the Tarot reader.

Gramps huffed back to our table and dropped onto the chair. "Well, they recognized two of 'em."

He showed me the photos.

"Are you sure?" I asked, my excitement growing. I'd been right.

"I'm sure that's what they told me. What do you think it means?"

The waitress materialized at our table. "Hi, are you ready to order?"

Tomas glanced at me, and I nodded. "I think we're ready."

We placed our orders, and she walked away.

Gino Peretti and Kale Halifax strolled into the restaurant. She adjusted the ivory, fringed shawl draped over the shoulders of her floral-print dress.

I sat up straighter. My knee bumped a table leg, and I winced.

The Italian leaned closer to Kale. He raised himself on tiptoe, exposing the white socks beneath his blue slacks. Peretti whispered in her ear.

She jerked away from him and smiled tightly.

"What's wrong?" Gramps' white brows pinched.

I ducked behind a wine menu the waitress had left. "That's Gino Peretti and his unwanted tenant," I whispered, "the two I told you about."

"The lunatic who tried to set his own house on fire?" Tomas swiveled in his chair and squinted. "He could have burned her alive. What's she doing with that idiot?"

Gramps shook his head. "Some women can't resist trouble."

I peeked over the top of the wine menu.

The couple paused beside a landscape painting by a famous California artist. Kale gestured animatedly.

"What are they doing?" Tomas asked.

"Dining out, I guess," I said. "She's an artist."

Gramps snorted. "I've never heard of her."

"What artists have you heard of?" Tomas asked.

"Well, there's that fellow who draws all the English cottages."

"What's his name?" Tomas asked.

Gramps scowled. "I don't need to know his name. I know his paintings."

Putting down my menu, I scooted my chair from the round table. My bracelet caught in the tablecloth, and the candle wobbled. I disentangled myself. "I'll be right back. I have to wash my hands."

Gramps frowned. "Didn't you wash 'em before you came here?"

"The gondola railing might have been dirty."

The hostess guided my two suspects deeper into the restaurant.

"What's wrong with a little dirt?" my grandfather asked.

"That's not why she's going to the ladies' room," Tomas said.

The hostess seated Kale and Peretti in a crescent-shaped booth. Behind the booth's vanilla-colored leather seat, a curving walk led to the bathrooms.

Face averted, I strolled behind their booth and knelt to adjust the strap on my floral heel.

"I have buyers in Italy," Gino was saying. "Much lower risk, eh?"

Buyers?

"Unless they don't pay," Kale said.

Was Peretti her agent? I'd thought she already had one.

He laughed softly. "Oh, they'll pay. If I can sell almonds to Italy, I can sell—"

"Can I get you anything to drink?" a waitress asked them.

They hemmed and hawed over the drink menu.

A pair of long legs stopped beside me. I looked up at an auburn-haired waitress.

"Are you okay?" she asked.

Embarrassed, I leapt to my feet. Crouching behind the booth might have looked a *little* weird. "Um. Yeah. Fine."

Cursing beneath my breath, I moved on to the ladies' room. Checked my makeup. Checked my hair. Tugged up the v-neck of my dress.

Taking my time, I wandered into the hallway and paused behind their booth. I faced away from the couple and rummaged in my clutch.

"What about Fiorello?" Peretti asked.

"His works are ludicrously simple," Kale said. "But he's dead, so everybody loves him. There's also Mignoni."

"A fine Italian name. What does he do?"

"Did," Kale said. "He was inspired by Modigliani."

"Who?"

She sighed. "He painted geometric shapes in primary colors."

"Perfect! They will offend no one. I suppose the paintings are large?"

"Oh, yes."

"Hi!" Smiling broadly, the hostess strode to me. "Are you looking for the ladies' room?"

I fumbled in my purse. "My hand sanitizer." I lifted the thin spray cylinder from my purse. "Got it." I hustled back to the table, sat, and reached for another slice of sourdough. "Sorry it took me so long."

"Hear anything good?" Gramps asked.

I grimaced. "You saw me?"

Tomas laughed. "I love you like a daughter, but spy you are not."

Why did I even try? I repeated the fruits of my eavesdropping.

"I don't get it," Gramps said.

"That's because all your taste is in your mouth." Tomas pointed with his butter knife at my grandfather. "Fiorello. Mignoni. They were great Italian-American artists. Italian-Californian, actually."

"You know them?" I asked.

"I knew Fiorello. Have one of his paintings." His eyes misted. "Mariella wanted me to sell it and take her on a trip to the Galapagos."

Mariella was his late wife, and I nodded. She'd been full of love and laughter, and I still missed her like my Gran.

"Why the Galapagos?" Gramps asked. "All that's there are a bunch of turtles."

Tomas shrugged. "She was my wife. How could I say *no*?"

"But you haven't sold it?" I asked.

"No. When I had it appraised, Mariella reconsidered. She wanted to keep it for our grandchildren. I won't go against her wishes now."

"Is it worth much?" Gramps asked.

His friend swallowed. "Enough. The appraiser said fifty thousand. Mariella thought he was lowballing us, because we're old."

I stared sightlessly at the bud vase centered on the table. The rose leaned at an angle, its petals a bloody red. "Where would Kale get her hands on a quantity of paintings like that to resell?" Or had I mistaken their conversation?

"Museums?" Tomas asked. "Private collectors? Fiorelli and Mignoni are both dead. It's not like they can paint any more."

"No." I tapped my fingers on the tablecloth. "I don't suppose they can." I thought about my encounter with Kale and Gino two days ago. "Unless..."

"Unless what?" Gramps asked.

I shook myself. "Nothing. I've been reading too many detective novels."

"Lately," Tomas said, "your life has *been* a detective novel."

"More like the Keystone Cops." I sighed. "It's so confusing. I found Reince Tuesday morning, but I think he'd been in that parking lot all night. There was dew on his face and clothes. He must have been killed there late Monday."

"Why?" Tomas asked.

"Because if it had been earlier, someone would have seen his body and reported it." I rubbed my collarbone. "At first, I thought he'd come to my building for some reason, but his body was near the bank and its ATM machine."

"He was taking out money," Gramps said.

"More than that," I said. "I think he was about to leave town. Something spooked him. Probably Gino Peretti. Peretti had returned from Italy to find Kale living in his house, and then he went to confront Reince."

"Why?" Tomas asked. "If Kale's presence was a surprise, why find Reince?"

"Kale told Gino who she'd rented the house from when he showed up on her doorstep," I said with more certainty. "Once Peretti turned up, Reince knew he was finished. He must have had money elsewhere — you can't withdraw that much money from an ATM all at once, can you? But he wanted to clean out his account. Someone followed him there and killed him."

"Someone who knew he was bugging out?" Tomas asked.

I shredded my sourdough bread. "I guess. Otherwise, the timing is too coincidental, don't you think? And Florence must have known something about it all. Otherwise, why kill her?"

"Why sabotage your front step?" Tomas asked.

"The killer's running scared," Gramps said. "He's not a pro. He's worried."

"That makes me feel better," I said.

"It shouldn't," Gramps said, grim. "There's no one more dangerous than an amateur."

CHAPTER TWENTY-NINE

BRIK'S PICKUP SAT PARKED beside the open rear door of the purple Tea and Tarot room. Saturday afternoon sunlight reflected off the truck's windows, and I adjusted my sunglasses. The weatherman had promised a storm tonight. I could feel it in the air. A thickening, a pressure, a sense of expectancy.

With a shiver, I studied the open door, then walked into the cool hallway. I hadn't been able to resist the urge that drew me to my new business.

I stopped short in the front room and coughed. Three walls had been covered in fresh sheetrock. The fourth, brick, had been cleaned. Sunlight glowed through the filmy windows. It heated the already uncomfortably warm room and set the billowing clouds of dust alight.

"How do you like it?" In dusty jeans and a worn, white tee, Brik set his nail gun on the sawhorse table. He stooped to pick something off the floor, his jeans hugging his butt.

Having no business looking at his jeans or his butt, I tore my gaze away and fingered the collar of my black top. My sandal crunched, and something sharp dug into my instep.

I shook the chunk of sheetrock free of my sandal. Maybe wearing shorts and silk and sandals hadn't been the best idea today.

"It already looks fantastic," I said.

Even though the white walls were unfinished, they brightened and expanded the space. For the first time, I could *see* the new tearoom.

"Should I open the front door?" I asked. "It's an oven in here." Yeah, that was why I was sweating. It had nothing to do with the hot contractor.

He straightened and flicked a long nail into a bucket. "Nah. Too many nosy neighbors interrupting my work. But thanks for asking. Don't worry, once we get air conditioners in here, the place will be fine. The walls are thick, and they're well insulated."

"I guess that will keep the electric bills down."

He smiled, wry. "Not so much in winter. Check out your new counter." He nodded to a slab of white quartz propped against the brick.

Marveling, I ran my hands across the stone's surface, gritty with dust. "How did you get a counter piece so fast?"

"Do you like it?" Twin lines formed between his brows.

"Are you kidding? It's perfect. I thought I'd have to spend hours in a supply store looking for the right piece."

He raked a hand through his blond hair, damp with sweat. "About that. Listen, I got you a deal. The counter had already been cut, but the person who originally bought it changed their mind."

"Why?"

"Because there's a chip, here." He pointed to a nick in one edge. "But we can face that away from the customers. Since I'm building the counter anyway, I can make this piece fit. It seemed about the right size," he said, his blue eyes anxious.

My heart warmed. Brik was looking out for me. Or at least for the tearoom. "It's perfect. Well, not technically, since it's got that tiny chip, but I wouldn't have even noticed if you hadn't pointed it out."

His broad shoulders relaxed. "Great. I figured you'd be okay with it, especially since it's half the price we budgeted. But if you don't like it, I can cut it and use it somewhere else."

"Where else could you use this much countertop?"

His face reddened. "My bathrooms."

"Wait, was this originally for your house?" I asked, chagrined.

"No," he said. "Not originally. Some guy in Santa Cruz ordered it, then rejected it when it arrived at his coffee shop. When I saw it, the price had been knocked down so much I decided to see if I could bargain it down a little farther."

"For your own remodel. Brik, I don't want to take your counter. It isn't fair."

"Don't worry about it. It was a little too much for me. It works better here."

I grinned, relieved. I liked the stone, and I *definitely* liked saving that money.

"I picked up the flooring you ordered." He nodded toward the long, stacked boxes against an opposite wall.

I examined the top box, peering through its plastic lid at the fake wood inside. This was happening. Our Tea and Tarot room was coming into being. It felt... magical.

Hyperion strolled into the room from the rear of the building. He looked like he'd just stepped off a yacht in his longish navy shorts and crisp white shirt. "You won't believe what..." He moved his sunglasses to the top of his head and pointed at the slab of quartz. "Is that a chip?"

"No one will see it," I said. "It will be on the work side, and—"

"I see it," Hyperion said.

"And it's half the price of a counter without a chip," I said.

He heaved a sigh. "I hate being poor."

"We're not poor," I said. "We're opening a Tea and Tarot room."

He folded his arms over his pressed white shirt, and the navy sweater over his shoulders slipped sideways. "Then I hate being on a budget."

I doubted that would change — not on the income from a Tea and Tarot room. Unless we somehow managed to franchise. Or Hyperion became one of those super-famous TV psychics.

"So, are you okay with the counter?" I asked. None of our arguments so far had amounted to much, and I hoped that wasn't about to change. Because getting a discount on the counter would relieve our budget pressures.

He waved his hand, dismissive. "I'm the Tarot side of the business. It's your counter. Besides, it will all work out. Fame is literally in the cards."

"What about fortune?" Brik asked.

"The cards don't show me more than three months ahead," he said, "and our breakeven date is well past that."

I smiled. He'd read my projections. "Hyperion, I want to tell you about last night."

He leered. "Oooh. Did you meet someone? Do tell."

I explained about what I'd overheard at the restaurant.

Brik raised a brow. "I don't think I should be hearing this."

Someone pounded on the front door, and I nearly jumped out of my sandals.

"You expecting anyone?" Brik's brows lowered.

"No." *What now?*

"I'll deal with it." Hyperion strode to the door and flung it open. "If you're going to bang on something, you'd better mean—"

Gino Peretti stormed inside, jostling Hyperion's shoulder. "So. It all works out for you! You have your building, while I am still homeless!" He trembled with fury in his Italian suit.

"How did you know we were here?" Hyperion rubbed his shoulder.

"I followed you," Peretti said. "Criminals! Charlatans!"

"That's enough." Brik's expression darkened.

"Hold on." I shifted my weight, and something crunched beneath my sandal. I hoped it wasn't a rusty nail. "What are you talking about? I saw you and Kale last night, and you two looked like you were getting along."

"Her!" He snapped his fingers and ripped out a stream of Italian. "I thought I could reason with the woman. I offered her..." He sputtered. "How did you get your building? Was it Cyrus? Did you bribe him?"

"It had nothing to do with Cyrus," I said, indignant. "And I've never paid a bribe in my life."

"Really?" Hyperion peered at me. "Never? What sort of sheltered life have you led?"

Peretti quivered with rage. "None of my business? I have lost my home because of that idiot, Cyrus. He should be shot! I should shoot him!"

"You don't mean that." I slipped my hands into the pockets of my shorts and edged closer to Brik.

"And here you are," he ranted, "building your... your... What are you building?"

"A Tarot and tearoom," Hyperion said. "And we're not open. So, you'll either have to be more interesting or leave."

"Interesting?" Peretti's dark eyes narrowed. "You want interesting?"

"No," Brik said. "We really don't."

"You think you know what's going on?" Peretti asked. "You know nothing."

Brik's head lowered like a bull readying to charge.

I placed a hand on the contractor's muscular arm. "What don't we know?"

"Kale Halifax is a fraud. Just like the dead Reince. They were in cahoots."

Hyperion yawned, covering his mouth. "Cahoots? Were the bums selling stolen ice? Running a racket?"

Peretti's brow creased. "Why would someone steal ice?"

Brik's mouth quivered.

"Just tell us what you came to tell us," I said sharply.

"The Halifax woman..." He drew himself up. "Is an art forger."

I glanced at Hyperion. "That would explain a lot."

"You are not surprised?" Peretti asked, flushing.

"Of course, I'm surprised," I said. "It's not every day you meet an art forger. But it explains why she refused to call the cops after you tried to burn down her house—"

"My house!"

A horn blared on the street outside.

"Sorry." *Not sorry.* "Your house."

"And it would explain why she doesn't have a website," Hyperion said. "An artist her age would definitely have a website."

"Why haven't you told the police?" I asked the Italian.

"It is not my business," he muttered.

"But you told us," I said. "Why?"

"I thought *you* might want to tell the police."

"It's interesting." Hyperion rubbed his jaw, then shook his head regretfully. "But it's not our business either."

"Why don't you want to tell the police?" Brik asked. "What are you hiding?"

"You Americans are all alike. Just because I am a foreigner, you think I am a criminal."

Hyperion rolled his eyes. "We think you're a criminal because we caught you trying to commit arson, and your wife has gone missing. Duh."

"My wife is in Italy!"

"I see you're not denying the arson." Hyperion's nose twitched.

"I admit nothing."

"But you want us to snitch on Kale on your behalf?" Hyperion asked. "I don't think so."

"Unless it has something to do with Reince's death?" I asked.

"Yes." Peretti nodded vigorously. "Reince was helping her sell her so-called works."

Which Kale had sort of already admitted. "That's old news."

"She is a murderess. It is your duty to go to the police."

"No," Hyperion said, "it's your duty. It's our duty to tell the police we saw you trying to commit arson."

Peretti waved his hands in the air. "What is wrong with you people? A killer is in your midst, and you talk about arson."

"Kale was *in* the house when you tried to set it on fire," I said tartly. "She could have been killed. And her dog. Where were you last Thursday night?"

"Why Thursday? What is Thursday?"

"The night someone tried to set this building on fire," I said.

His brown eyes widened. "You think I...?" He drew back his shoulders. "No. I was at your police station Thursday night, arguing with a stupid policeman. He would not remove that interloper from my property. He said I could file an eviction notice, but it would take at least two months to evict her. Two months!"

"What time were you there?"

His dark brows lowered, his lower lip jutting forward. "All night."

"You argued all night?" I asked, disbelieving.

"No." He looked toward the slab of white stone, leaning against the counter, and his voice dropped. "I was in jail all night."

Brik raised his brows. "What did you do? Punch a cop?"

"No." His arms flailed in a helpless gesture. "It is not important. Your police will not believe me about Kale Halifax. You must tell them."

"They'll want confirmation from you," I said.

"You cannot tell them I told you." He backed toward the front door. "I will deny it. I said nothing! I did nothing! It is my own house!" He fled out the door. It banged shut behind him.

"Well, that was some full-tilt weirdness," Hyperion said.

I pulled my cellphone from the pocket of my shorts and dialed. "I'm calling Cyrus's office. Peretti practically threatened to shoot him."

"I don't think so," Brik said. "He was just blowing off steam."

"Still," I said, pressing the phone to my ear, "they need to know."

Brik shook his head. "I know the type. He's all bark, no bite."

The phone rang once, and an answering machine suggested I leave a message.

"Hi," I said. "This is Abigail Beanblossom." I bit my lip, hesitating. What if Brik was right? But I hadn't thought he'd try to set his own house on fire either. "I just talked to Gino Peretti. He threatened Cyrus, and I think he may be dangerous. Please call me as soon as you can. It's urgent."

I hung up.

Hyperion eyed me. "Vague enough?"

"I told them Peretti threatened Cyrus."

"Hm." Hyperion pursed his lips. "I'm loving this story about art forgery. It's so Danielle Steele."

"Peretti might not be the best source," I said. "Not when he wants revenge on Kale. But his story fits with the other things we know." I made the mistake of leaning against the sawhorse table. It lurched sideways, legs screeching against the concrete floor, and I jerked away. I brushed off the seat of my olive shorts. "I mean, it's plausible. And if Peretti was in jail, he's got an alibi for the fires in the tearoom."

"Tea and Tarot studio," Hyperion corrected.

"But would Kale kill Reince over... What exactly was he accusing her of?" I asked.

Brik shook his head. "I've got work to do in the back. You two figure this out." He strode down the hallway.

"Okay." My brain fumbled for answers. "Reince is helping Kale with her scam on the side — helping her sell fake artworks. She was upset because he had something that belonged to her. What? A painting that he hadn't sold? Money that he hadn't paid her?"

"If he was willing to rip us off," Hyperion said, "it would be easy to steal from her. Kale could hardly go to the cops."

"But is a fake painting worth killing over?" I asked. "Couldn't Kale just paint another one?"

"Maybe it was money then," he said.

"The proceeds of a sale? And she killed Florence, because Florence knew about their deal? But Kale wouldn't get her money from Reince if he was dead." I shook my head. "Look at how Kale handled Peretti when he tried to burn down her house. She stayed pretty cool under pressure. I can't see her killing Reince out of revenge or anger. She'd make sure she got her money — or whatever she wanted — first. But apparently, she didn't."

"You think she's innocent? I thought you didn't like her."

I braced my fists on my hips. "I can't accuse someone of murder because I don't like them."

"You can't *not* accuse someone because you feel guilty about not liking them."

"I don't feel guilty." My mother would say Kale's soul was out of alignment, and I should feel sympathy rather than dislike. And she'd probably be right, but come on.

I motioned to the renovation work. "What do you think of what Brik's done?"

"I think he sold you a chipped counter. It's a bad omen."

"Us, partner. He sold us a chipped counter."

"Like I said, *partner*." He folded his arms. "A bad omen."

I glanced uneasily at the white stone. "There are no such things as omens." But were there?

CHAPTER THIRTY

THE WEATHER HAD TURNED muggy by the time I returned from my quest at the monster home improvement store. I pulled into a spot beside Brik's pickup. Pewter clouds, the bleeding edge of a monsoon moving north from Mexico, lowered over the parking lot.

A tepid breeze tangled my hair. I tugged the boxes free of my rear seat and shut the car door with my hip.

Propping the boxes on my closed trunk, I checked my phone. Neither Cyrus nor Diana had returned my call about Peretti yet.

Beside the propped-open door to the tearoom, Brik lowered a toolkit into his truck bed. "Find everything?"

"Yep." Though I'd needed all my indoor tracking skills and directions from two different sales clerks. "Where do you want this stuff? In your truck or the tearoom? Tea and Tarot room," I corrected myself.

Thunder rumbled. I glanced at the clouds.

Brik grunted. "Inside." He took the boxes from my hands and lugged them into the building.

I trailed after him into the hallway. Shadows fell like cobwebs along the bare, concrete walls.

"Hey, can I borrow your nail gun tonight?" I tugged on the charm at the end of my necklace.

He stopped and turned, his eyes widening with alarm. "What for?"

Annoyed, I dropped the charm. "To nail things." Was he still holding the nail gun incident over me? Even Hyperion had stopped nagging me about it, and he'd been the one I'd hospitalized.

The contractor's true-blue eyes narrowed. "What sort of things?"

I heaved a breath. "A board's fallen out on my redwood fence."

"It's supposed to rain tonight. I'll fix it for you tomorrow."

"I'm not talking about the fence bordering your yard. It's the side bordering my other neighbor. I can do it. The board doesn't need replacing or anything. All I need to do is nail it back in place."

"Maybe you should stick with a hammer," he said. "Though on a fence like that, you'd be better off using screws."

"You think I can't handle a nail gun?"

"I've seen how you handle a nail gun." He put air quotes around the word, "handle."

My lips crimped. "Look, if you don't want to lend it to me, fine. Technically, our relationship ends here at the tearoom."

He cocked a brow. "Does it?"

Hoo boy. That question led to all sorts of interesting possibilities.

"We're neighbors," he said. "And I'll fix your fence."

My neck stiffened. "I can fix my own fence." I wasn't a total incompetent with power tools. I'd helped Gramps around the house when I was a kid. And I knew in this instance, a nail gun would be a lot easier to handle than a hammer. "I think it's better if we keep things professional. You don't need to do me favors around the house." If possible, my face grew even hotter. That had not come out the way I'd intended.

"All right."

I blinked, surprised. "All right?"

"Let's see how you manage the gun." He turned and walked into the main room. The muted sunlight streamed through the paper covering the windows, turning it amber.

He took the nail gun from the sawhorse table and pointed to a piece of newly installed drywall. "Go for it."

I pressed the gun against the wall.

"Stop!"

My arm jerked, the barrel scraping the thick white paper. I ground my teeth. "Why are you shouting?"

"Put on safety goggles first." He tossed me a pair, and I caught them one handed.

Dropped them.

And I'd almost been on the verge of looking cool.

Casually retrieving them from the floor, I strapped the plastic goggles over my eyes.

I found a stud, pressed the tip of the gun against it, and thunked a nail into the wall.

He grunted. "At least you didn't try to shoot it from a distance."

"Oh, come on." The nail could have gone anywhere if I'd done that. How dumb did I look?

"But you need to push the gun against the surface of the wall." Pressed against my back, he wrapped his arms and hands around mine. He smelled of sweat and sawdust, and I forced myself not to react. Or at least not to show my reaction, which was something along the lines of, *oh, yeah!*

Brik pressed the gun hard against the drywall.

My heartbeat accelerated.

He squeezed the trigger, and my hands vibrated with the force of the shot. "Like that." His breath was warm on my neck, the planes of his muscles firm against my thin top. He stepped away and rested his hands lightly on my shoulders. "You try."

"Sure." My voice cracked, and I cleared my throat. "No problem." I pushed the tip of the gun against the wall and fired.

"Okay. The gun's yours. Bring it back on Monday."

"Thanks." I turned off the gun and whipped off the goggles, extending them to him. "Here."

"You got a pair at home?"

"Um, no."

"You can bring those back on Monday, too."

"Right. Thanks. Safety first." Ugh, how lame could I get? I backed down the hallway. "Oh, hey. You know the rear window in the hall, at the back?"

"Yeah."

"It looked kind of new to me. What do you think?" *Could* Reince have made his first foray into the building that way?

"Yeah, it's new. Why?"

"No reason." It didn't mean that was how Reince had gotten inside to make keys, but I couldn't see the owner installing a random new window. It must have been Reince. "See you Monday!"

I fled to my Mazda. Leaning inside, I dumped the nail gun and goggles on the passenger seat.

"Abigail!"

I jolted, banging my head on the door frame. Skull throbbing, I rubbed my head and backed out of the car.

Kale Halifax strode toward me. She wore a tank top and low-rider jeans, her blond braid dangling over one of her shoulders.

I glanced toward Brik's pickup, near the open door to the tearoom. "Hi, Kale."

"What are you doing here?" she asked.

"Running errands. You?"

Her gaze flicked sideways, and she folded her arms. "I heard Gino Peretti talked to you."

"Where did you hear that?" I asked, wary.

"One of your business's nosy neighbors." She rolled her eyes. "Look, Peretti's trouble. You need to stay away from him."

I forced a smile. "I could give you the same warning." Kale cared about herself, not me. What was she really doing here?

Her jaw tightened. "What does that mean?"

"I saw you at Elegy with him the other night."

She sucked in her breath. "Were you following me?"

"Not everything's about you, Kale. Elegy's a popular restaurant." Sheesh.

Something buzzed behind me. I spun, scanning the cloudy but drone-free sky.

"Hello?" Kale snapped her fingers. "Are you all right?"

"Huh? Yeah." It had probably been a bumblebee. "I'm fine." Fine for someone who was paranoid.

Kale tapped one paint-spattered tennis shoe. "You saw us at Elegy?"

"Um..." I studied the airspace above the nearby buildings. Twilight had turned the clouds the color of burnt charcoal, glowing with heat around the edges. "Right."

"And?"

"What?" I met her gaze. It wasn't friendly. "Sorry," I said. "It's just that you two looked close. It surprised me, all things considered."

"He *is* my landlord. It pays to be nice."

"He tried to set your house on fire," I said. "While you were inside."

She shrugged.

"You hosed him down with a fire extinguisher."

"I've always wanted to do that." The artist grinned. "Not to Peretti, of course. And it worked. He took me out to dinner to make peace. At least, that's what he said."

A silver Lincoln drifted past. The middle-aged driver glared at us, no doubt impatient for my spot.

"But he had another motive?" *This should be good.*

"He wanted to sell my paintings in Italy."

Well, phooey. That jibed with Peretti's story – minus the art con. "What are you really doing here?" Was she after getting information or giving it? In either case, I trusted her about as far as I could dead lift her, and I darted another glance at Brik's empty truck. Not that I was worried she'd choke me into submission and bash my head against a parking block.

"I was getting some money from the ATM," she said, "and I saw you. Look, Peretti's off his rocker. If he's starting to obsess over you—"

"Obsess?" I took a casual step away from the artist.

"Why else would he come to your tearoom and start screaming?"

"One of our new neighbors told you that? Who?" Brik hadn't been kidding about the neighbors bugging him. Would I have to soundproof the walls?

"Peretti cut off my water supply somehow," she said, ignoring my question. "Which by the way, is totally illegal. But I guess a guy willing to commit arson wouldn't worry about a little thing like that. He's dangerous, Abigail."

I hurled caution to the wind. "Dangerous because he told me you were an art forger?"

She snorted. "He would say that. He's insane. I'll bet he killed his wife." She stepped closer, lowering her voice. "And I think he tried to drive me off the road today."

"You *think*?" I asked, wary.

"There aren't that many red Alfa Romeo's in this area. Look, if he's harassing you, you should call the police."

"If he tried to drive you off the road, *you* should call the cops." First Peretti wanted me to call the cops about Kale, and now she wanted me to report him. These two were made for each other.

She tossed her braids. "Well. Sure, I will."

"But you haven't yet. You're afraid if you sic the cops on Peretti, he'll tell them about the forgeries?"

"They're not forgeries." Kale leaned toward me, and I stepped backward, bumping into my open car door.

A door slammed. Brik locked the tearoom and ambled to his truck.

"Okay," I said lightly. "They're not forgeries."

She retreated. "I don't like it when— I'm proud of my work. It goes to private collectors."

I glanced toward Brik. He set something in the bed of his pickup.

Her lips curled, covetous. "Good looking guy." Her gaze flicked from my sandals to the top of my head. "And I see I'm not the only one who's noticed. Someone's making an extra effort."

"For Brik? Since he's working for me, that would be inappropriate," I said unconvincingly. It wasn't as if I'd chosen this outfit to seduce him. Though it hadn't exactly been the best home-supply-store gear.

My mouth parted, the puzzle pieces meshing into place as neatly as clockwork gears.

She waved her hand in front of my face. "Hello! You there?"

I started. "What? Oh, right." Hurriedly, I opened my car door. "I've got to go. Thanks for the warning." Without waiting for a response, I started the car and drove home.

Inside my bungalow, I dumped my junk on the dining room table, made myself a cup of tea, and called Detective Chase.

Who wasn't available.

I paced in front of my entertainment center and left a message. "This is Abigail Beanblossom." This wasn't the sort of thing you left a message about though. My theory was thin, but it made *sense*. "Um, Kale Halifax and Gino Peretti both came to see me. Independently. I think there may be some trouble there." *Tell him, tell him, tell him.* "There's also something I remember about the murder. Well, not the murder, but about the people involved. It might not be important. Or maybe it is. Anyway, I'm home for the evening if you want to—"

A beep. A dial tone.

"—call me."

Great. But he knew to call me. Assuming he picked up his messages on a weekend, and I didn't sound like a complete ditz.

A burst of music thundered from next door, and I groaned. "Brik!"

In spite of the noise, I opened the French door to the backyard. Storm clouds darkened the sky. A warm breeze tossed my curtains and carried the scent of rain on dry earth.

I glanced at the gaming headset on my couch. A rumble of thunder rattled the windows. I needed to do something to get my mind off murder.

My stomach grumbled in a hungry echo.

Right. Scones.

I turned on the oven and let it heat while I laid out the ingredients for apricot and almond scones on my granite counter. My recipe didn't rely solely on almonds for its almond-y flavor. I also added almond paste and almond extract.

I love almonds.

And apricots.

I mixed a soft dough. Head bopping to Brik's music, I put it in the freezer to chill and washed dough from my hands.

Fortunately, the almonds and apricots I'd snuck during the mixing process had tided me over, or I might not be able to wait for the scones.

I boiled another cup of tea — my own blend of chamomile, lemongrass, lemon verbena, and spearmint to calm the tension in my gut. Brushing flour from one sleeve of my black blouse, I adjusted my silver necklace and walked onto the back porch.

The storm hadn't broken yet, but wind tossed the branches of the dogwood tree, scattering petals. The sky was the color of cinder. Brik was playing an eighties song I liked, and I discovered my irritation had evaporated. The music was actually kind of fun.

Mug warming my palms, I tilted my face to the sky and inhaled, scenting eucalyptus and jasmine and dogwood on the breeze.

I sipped the tea and returned inside.

All would be well. I'd tell Detective Chase my crazy theory. Well, part of it was fact, but there was guesswork involved too. Chase would catch the killer, and Hyperion and I would start our Tea and Tarot room.

I rounded the corner into the kitchen. "Oh, crap."

Diana stood, one arm extended toward me. In her hand, a butcher knife gleamed dully.

CHAPTER THIRTY-ONE

"SERIOUSLY?" NOW I WAS just mad. Why had I played coy with Detective Chase? I was going to be one of those dumb saps who got killed because I knew too much and hadn't told anyone. How stupid could I get?

The knife in Diana's hand didn't waiver. She stalked toward me, her loose, gray tunic and slacks swaying in stately fashion. A bolero necklace dangled against her chest. Her close-cropped gray hair stood up on the top, giving her a Spike-the-Vampire look.

Or maybe it was the butcher knife that made her look insane. Yeah, definitely the butcher knife.

Heart pounding, I backed into the living room. My sandals made flapping sounds on the bamboo floor, and my mind retreated into details. The whisper of silk against my arms. The cinch of my belt, a little too tight around the waist of my shorts.

Brik's music had changed to a Depeche Mode song. Partiers whooped in his yard next door.

If I screamed, no one would hear. And no one would see, either. My boarded-up front window assured us of a nice, private murder. "What are you doing? You shouldn't be here."

"And you shouldn't have had your doddering grandfather flash my and Reince's photo around Elegy."

"He's not doddering," I said. And more weakly, "You heard about that?"

"You wouldn't leave it alone." She walked through the entry into the living room. "I'm sorry for this, because persistence is a trait I admire. There's lots that's admirable about you. I think we could have been friends."

"I couldn't be friends with a murderer, even if Reince did jilt you."

She blanched. Her forward motion paused. "How did you know?"

My gaze darted around the room, looking for a weapon. But the fire-place poker was too far, against the far wall. And I doubted the throw pillows and game controllers on the sofa would provide more than a quick distraction. If only I hadn't plunked for the wi-fi controllers, maybe I could have strangled her with a cord.

"The weight loss," I said. "The new clothes. Reince was one sweet talker, especially when it came to women. You were having an affair and getting in shape."

"So, you *guessed*?" her brows shot skyward. "Well, you guessed wrong. I wasn't losing weight for him. I was losing weight for myself."

And denial ain't just a river in Egypt. "Not entirely a guess. The waiters at Elegy confirmed they'd seen you and Reince together. Still, if you'd stopped at killing Reince, I wouldn't have figured it out. But you panicked. You came after me. You couldn't resist knowing what I was doing." She'd kept at it the same way I had. Did we have something in common after all?

I swallowed. "Sending the office's drone after me — that *was* you, wasn't it?"

She shrugged. "We use the drone for aerial shots of the homes we sell."

"What exactly happened with Reince?" *Stall.* And then maybe my brain would move beyond non-existent cables and to a way to save myself.

"Peretti tracked down Reince when he returned from Italy," she said. "Unfortunately, Florence was with Reince at the time. At that point, she was already suspicious of him. She told me about the unauthorized rental of Peretti's house, and that Reince's numbers weren't quite right. When I went to confront him, I found Reince pulling money out of the ATM. He was going to run. Well, of course he was going to run. What choice did he have at this point?"

The knife gleamed wickedly.

I did a doubletake. Dammit, was that *my* knife? It was! I'd paid over eighty dollars for that knife. That just pissed me off.

"And then?" I asked. *Keep her talking.* Though I had a sick feeling Diana was a multitasker and could talk and stab at the same time.

A muscle twitched in her jaw. "I lost my temper and swung at him. I was aiming for his jaw, but I hit him in the neck instead. He choked, stumbled backwards, and fell. It was the fall that killed him, not me. He hit his head on one of those concrete parking blocks. It wasn't my fault."

"But killing Florence was no accident." Heart banging, I edged backward. "How did she find out about your affair?"

She paced closer. "I was sloppy. After all I'd done for her, I trusted Florence." Her expression hardened. "And she betrayed me."

"With blackmail?" My hip nudged the dining table. "I wondered about the timing of her bonus. You talked your husband into giving it to her as a payoff, didn't you?"

Her lips curled. "He always does what I tell him. So simple. Not like—" Her mouth quivered.

"Not like Reince," I finished for her.

"Oh, Florence was clever about it." Light from the hanging lamp glinted off the blade. "Like you. Dropping little hints here and there. She never came straight out and said she wanted money. Maybe I was wrong to give her the bonus. I told Cyrus at the time it was because of everything she'd done for him and the trouble she was going through over Reince."

"You're probably right. You shouldn't have. The bonus must have made Florence even more suspicious – of you." I bumped into a dining chair. Staying close to the table, I edged around it. "She followed you the night you set fire to the tearoom, didn't she? The police never called her about a fire. Following you was the only way she could have known about the arson so quickly."

"And that night she called me. I could see where this was headed. The bonus wouldn't be enough. I'd be in her power until she died. But everyone dies. She was getting old. I simply decided to give her a little push. She was stupid, like so many women. I tried to help her, I really did. But I couldn't let her have that sort of power over me. I can't let you have that either. I'm not going to jail. Not for a man like Reince."

I sidled away, my left hand gliding along the edge of the tabletop. Past my phone. Past my purse.

"Why set the fire at all?" I asked.

"Two reasons. First, you and that Tarot reader were almost as bad as the police, skulking around the realty and asking about Reince's love life. Second, Reince's death behind your building was an accident, but I decided to use it, move the focus of the police away from the realty and to your wannabe tearoom."

"You were multitasking?" *Delay, delay, delay.* There was a way out of this. There had to be. "Then why sabotage my front step? Why the drone?"

"I am sorry about your grandfather. That was meant for you."

"Yeah. Thanks for the apology flowers, by the way. They were lovely. But why come after me at all?" I had to stay calm. I had to *think*. But no brilliant escapes sprang to mind.

I was no detective, and I was no fighter. And I noticed now the muscle tone beneath her drapey clothes. She was stronger and faster than me. She'd been strong enough to kill two people.

"Why were you unsurprised to see me here?" she asked.

"Believe me, I was surprised." I should never have left my French doors open. She must have come in while I was in the kitchen and hidden in my bedroom before surprising me.

"But you suspected me," she said, "and that had to be about more than my weight loss."

"Those flowers. My grandfather's accident wasn't in the papers. You shouldn't have known about his fall. That suggested you were watching when it happened. With the company drone?"

She nodded.

"But why come after *me*?" I asked.

"Why me? Why me?" She mock whined. "When I first met you in that diner and learned you'd lost a six-month deposit to Reince, I realized you'd make a perfect fall guy. Sorry, fall gal. I mean, who pays six months' rent up front? It's unheard of. So, I started watching you. And the more

I watched, the more worried I became. You might be gullible, but you're determined."

My jaw clenched. "In other words, you panicked." I edged around the corner of the table, toward the open French door. Even if I made a break for it, she'd be on me. She was too close, and she knew it. "You don't do well in panic mode, Diana. Coming here was a mistake."

"I'm not panicked. I don't *want* to kill you, but you've driven me to it, just like Florence. None of this is my fault. I tried to warn you off, but like Florence, you just wouldn't stop. Now tell me. What was it really that tipped you off?"

Diana wanted to make sure no one else knew. She wanted to cover her tracks. "There's no point in killing me," I said. "It will be just another trail to cover."

"Too late to back out now. And then I'll have to pay your grandfather a condolence visit. He's in such a fragile, weakened state after his fall."

Thunder cracked. A gust of rain splattered the windows. Shrieks rose from the partygoers next door.

"No!" I grabbed the nail gun off the table and aimed for her chest. "Back off!"

She lunged, her tunic rippling in her wake.

I pulled the trigger. The nail gun clicked, shuddered in my hands. I gaped at the jammed gun. *Seriously?*

And then she barreled into me, the knife blade arcing downward.

I shrieked and swung the nail gun. It connected with the side of her wrist, knocking the knife sideways. A ribbon of heat scorched my left bicep. I stumbled backwards.

Diana kept coming, her arm swinging back and down in a terrifying loop.

Again, I squeezed the trigger. It clicked, useless.

I smacked her hand away, threw the nail gun, turned, and ran for the open French door. My feet skidded on a throw rug, but I kept moving forward, in a staggering crouch. I wouldn't die here. I wouldn't let her hurt my grandfather.

Diana's breath was loud in my ears. I imagined I could feel its heat on the back of my neck. The muscles between my shoulders ratcheted tighter. I tensed, expecting the blade in my back. I plunged past the curtains, whipping in the wind, and hurtled into the rain.

Detective Chase leapt up the deck steps and knocked me sideways. I tripped, falling gracelessly on my side.

He tackled Diana. The two slid across the wet porch. The knife skittered across the redwood planks and beneath the outdoor table.

Detective Chase rolled the swearing, struggling Diana onto her stomach. He clicked handcuffs around her wrists.

"Let me go!" she shouted.

"I don't think so, ma'am."

Gasping, I staggered to my feet. "You... How?" My knees wobbled. Heedless of the rain dripping down my face, I dropped onto a deck chair.

"Your business partner called."

"Hyperion?"

"He said you were in danger, something about ten swords."

I gaped. "And you came?"

Spots of red appeared high on his cheekbones. "He said he'd meet me here."

"And you came?" I repeated.

"And when I checked my phone, I saw your message. You sounded funny, so I tried calling you. But you didn't pick up, and I had a bad feeling." He yanked Diana to her feet and looked around. "I guess your partner's not here yet."

Shakily, I rose and wiped the water from my face. My phone lay inside, on the dining room table. I hadn't heard it in the kitchen. Hadn't heard it over the noise of Brik's party. If I had picked it up, told the detective what I'd suspected, he wouldn't have come. And if Hyperion hadn't... And Diana would have...

My mouth went dry. "That's..." Lucky, I'd been lucky. I'd nearly died tonight. And then my grandfather... I swayed, dizzy, and grasped the back of the wet chair for balance. We'd come so close.

Hold on. Where *was* my super-psychic business partner? "Hyperion's late for my rescue?" I asked indignant.

The detective's cowboy hat, stained dark with water, lay near my feet. I stooped to pick it up and to hide my sudden need to scream. When I'd mastered myself, I straightened and held out the hat.

"Thanks." One hand gripping Diana's forearm, he took it from me and clapped it on his head. Water coursed down his chiseled face. "I think you had something to tell me?"

"Yeah. Diana's..." The killer. Captured. Done.

It was over.

The rain pattered down, a steady, cleansing stream.

EPILOGUE

GRAMPS AND TOMAS SHUFFLED through Tea and Tarot's open front door. Between them, the older men carried a large, rectangular object wrapped in brown paper.

Peking, now three-months old, waddled behind them. His yellow down had been replaced with brown feathers, graying at the side. Teal and purple bands ringed his wings. The duck had taken to following Gramps everywhere.

"Where do you want it?" Gramps asked.

"Whatever it is, just put it down." I leaned on my broom. "Er, what is it?"

Gramps and Tomas maneuvered between the white tabletops. They set the package against the elegant reclaimed-wood counter, with its white quartz top.

Tea and Tarot was nearly done. Antique-looking drawings of herbs hung from the walls. Books on tea and fortune telling lined a shelf against the brick.

Hyperion and I were cleaning the place for our grand opening next week. Bastet sat on the counter and supervised, his tail lashing. He gave the duck a hard stare, then lay down, head on his paws, and closed his eyes.

Peking quacked once and shook his tail feathers.

Gramps stooped and tore the open paper, revealing a wooden sign. It looked like something from an old British pub: *Beanblossom's Tea and Tarot*.

I bit my bottom lip. Hyperion and I were still arguing over the name of the shop. It wasn't fair that my name alone was on the sign.

"Oh, Gramps, it's beautiful," I said, keeping an eye on the cat. He didn't seem interested in Peking, but you never could tell. "But Hyperion—"

"Is it here?" Hyperion brushed dust from his skinny, olive green slacks and black t-shirt and strode into the room. He stopped short and stared at the sign. "Abbykins!"

"Hyperion, we don't need to use—"

He clapped his hands together. "It's perfect."

"But your name's not on it," I said. "I didn't know—"

"I knew," Hyperion said. "Your grandfather kept asking me about the name for the sign. We agreed Beanblossom's is a good witchy/fairy name, that suits both Tea and Tarot. Besides, my name will be all over our website." He lowered his chin and stared at me. "*All* over it."

Consider me warned. "Are you sure?" I asked

"He's sure," Gramps said, wry. "He only agreed when Tomas agreed to show him the bottlecap trick."

"The bottlecap...?"

Tomas pulled a bottlecap from his pocket. There was a blur of motion. The cap thunked into the reclaimed wood counter and stuck there.

"Damn," Hyperion said. "You really can kill a man with a bottlecap."

Tomas dropped a newspaper on one of the white tabletops. "That woman's trial starts next week."

I would be a witness for the prosecution, and even in handcuffs and an orange jumpsuit, Diana was terrifying. But the prosecutor was confident she had enough evidence to convict. Weirdly, I felt a little guilty about my role in sending Diana to jail, even if she did deserve it. And she really did.

"It's too bad she doesn't know where your money went," Tomas said.

"No." I'd mostly given up hope of getting it back, and that burned. For all I knew, Reince had buried it somewhere. "Poor Florence."

"Poor Florence?" Tomas's graying eyebrow rose. "She was a blackmailer."

I shook my head. "I'm not entirely sure she was. Even Diana admitted Florence never came straight out and asked for money. I'll never be able to prove it, but I think Florence just liked knowing Diana's secret.

Diana had given her so much help, and that put Diana in a position of dominance. Knowing about Diana and Reince gave Florence power."

"Still sounds like blackmail to me," Gramps said.

I sighed and leaned against the counter. "Maybe."

Brik walked inside, and I straightened off the white quartz. Hastily, I smoothed my hair. But I couldn't do much about the sweat and dirt streaking my face and worn t-shirt.

"Hi," I said. "What are you doing here?"

"I came to help with the sign." He jerked his thumb toward the open door, painted a shiny black. Sunlight glittered off the stained-glass lily in its top. "I brought a ladder."

"I can do it." Gramps lowered his brows.

"But I'm here," Brik said easily. "And it's my ladder."

Tomas nudged my grandfather. "Liability issues."

"All right," Gramps said, his head pulling back. "There it is."

Brik measured the sign, nodded, and strode outside. The door swung slowly shut behind him.

Hyperion whistled. "Now, how did Brik know we were putting the sign up today?"

I felt myself blushing. "It wasn't me. I didn't even know Gramps was coming over today."

"Your contractor friend stopped by for a beer last night," Gramps said. "I might have showed it to him then."

"And you didn't invite me?" Hyperion pressed his palm to his chest in mock outrage.

"Stopped by for beer?" I parroted. Brik was hanging out with my grandfather?

"He's not a bad guy." Gramps winked at me. "You could do worse."

"I know," Hyperion said, rueful. "But I'm pretty sure he's straight."

My face grew hotter. "We're just neighbors."

"Sure, you are," Gramps said. "I'm certain that business about opposites attracting is bogus."

"Hello?" Kale's next-door neighbor, the curvy and curly-haired brunette, poked her head through the door. "I saw your flyers around town. I thought this tearoom might be yours."

Peking quacked a hello. Bastet opened one irritated eye and glared at the duck.

"Tea and Tarot," Hyperion said.

"Hi!" I motioned her inside. "This is my grandfather, Frank, and my friend Tomas, and I think you know Hyperion. And this is Allyson."

"Allyson with a y." She shook hands, beaming. "Not that you'll ever need to spell it. This place looks fantastic. Will it have wi-fi?"

"Absolutely not," Hyperion said. We'd agreed we didn't want people sitting here for hours nursing a single cup of tea.

"Perfect." She dumped her oversized purse on a table. "The internet's a horrible distraction. By the way, I have a new neighbor — Peretti's wife! He didn't murder her after all," she said indignantly. "She's divorcing Gino and taking the house. You should see the guy who's moved in with her." She fanned herself. "Hubba hubba."

"What about Kale?" I asked.

"She disappeared, didn't you hear?" She lowered her voice. "The police think she was an art forger."

"Imagine that," Hyperion said.

"Apparently," Allyson continued, "she created new works by dead California artists, copying their styles. Reince was helping her sell them. That's definitely going in a book."

"Allyson's a writer," I explained to Gramps and Tomas.

Brik strolled into the tearoom. "Frank, can you give me a hand with the sign?"

"Sure, I can." The two of them carried the sign onto the walk, and we trailed behind them.

I touched the poppy doorknob for good luck.

Brik climbed the ladder, and Gramps handed up the sign. He steadied it from below while the contractor screwed its chain into the overhang. He frowned. "This wood is a little loose here. Someone hand me the nail gun."

I trotted inside and returned with the gun. He pressed it against the wood and grinned at me. "And why wouldn't the gun fire when you tried to shoot that lunatic?"

"Because it only works when the barrel's pressed against something," I said dryly. It had been pressed against Hyperion's thigh when I'd shot him. I just wished Brik would have made that point more clear when he'd been giving me nail gun lessons.

Hyperion snapped a picture with his phone. "That's going on social media."

"The sign or the hot blond?" Allyson muttered. Then, "Oh, here, give me your phone. This is an occasion. Let me take a picture of you all."

Grinning, we clustered around the ladder, and she snapped three photos.

"Perfect!" She handed Hyperion the phone.

His dark eyes sparkled, and he stretched his arms wide. "This is it. This is happening." His gaze met mine. "I told you, the cards are never wrong. Never."

I didn't know about that — opening our shop was a risk, and so was partnering with Hyperion. But in that moment, it didn't matter. I had everything I needed.

<<<<>>>>

Can't wait to read more? Read book 2 in the series, !

Author's Note

I got lucky with this book. A good friend of mine worked in a tearoom and has dreams of starting one of her own. So, I got lots of good intel on tearoom operations... which I mostly use in the *next* books in the series, since Beanblossom's only got off the ground in the epilogue.

Abandonment by a parent is not an easy thing to get over, and it's an issue Abigail will continue to struggle with in the next books. Change and forgiveness takes time, but I'm confident that with a little help from her friends, Abigail will manage it. She's a tough cookie, but she isn't *hard*. And of course, there will be more mystery and murder for Abigail and Hyperion to grapple with.

What's Next?

A *picture containing person*

Description auto-matically generated

ABIGAIL AND HYPERION UNCORK *a murder...*

Tea and Tarot room owner Abigail Beanblossom is used to running interference for her socially-awkward former boss, tech billionaire Raz-zzor. So when he invites her on a stakeout to investigate the sale of counterfeit wine from his latest venture – an upscale winery – she barrels on in. But the two stumble across the corpse of a wine merchant, and new wine in old bottles is now the least of their problems.

Good thing amateur detectives Abigail and her partner, tarot reader Hyperion Night, have a nose for murder. Their investigation takes them from elegant wine cellars to chic tea parties on the California coast. But just as the investigation starts to get its legs, Abigail discovers there's more than wine at the bottom of this crime...

Hostage to Fortune is book two in the Tea and Tarot cozy mystery series, and has tearoom recipes in the back of the book.

Click here to get your copy of *Hostage to Fortune* so you can start reading the series today!

Turn the page to read the first chapter of *Hostage to Fortune*.

Sneak Peek of Hostage to Fortune

I OWED RAZZZOR.

I was also, possibly, going to kill him.

"Is the Tesla too obvious?" Razzzor crumpled the bag of organic dried cherries. Before I could object–because you don't steal a woman's stake-out snacks–he reached into my bag of tortilla chips. Razzzor jammed a fistful into his mouth.

My ex-boss choked, sputtering. "Augh. Abigail! What are these?"

"This is why I partitioned our food. They're chemical-coated, lime-flavored tortilla chips. And no, a Tesla is not too obvious." God help us all. We'd already spotted three of the luxury sports cars zipping past the high-end wine store we were watching.

Across the street, the shop's windows glowed. Its interior overhead lights sparkled off the wine bottles. Twilight cast purple shades across its white stucco front.

The shadows seemed to shift, and I forced myself to relax. Nothing was going to happen. This was just for fun. A way to reconnect with an old friend outside of an online gaming platform. A way to repay a debt I never really could repay.

"Not organic?" Razzzor wiped his mouth with the back of his hand. "How can you eat this garbage?" He motioned at the bags littering the front of the sleek car.

"It's easy. I don't want to go through life thinking about all the good food I missed."

"You make organic tea and scones and you eat this?"

"I'm complicated."

"You're not thinking this through." He patted his abs through the front of his hoodie. "You've only got one body. Gotta take care of it."

My gaze traversed his lanky frame, his pale face. "You're one to talk. The only parts you exercise are your fingers."

Razzzor shot me his cheerful, boy-next-door grin. "Untrue. I have a personal trainer now."

"Meh. Flat abs are nice, but have you tried these donuts?" I raised a pink box. "They put candy bar pieces on top."

He frowned.

I sighed and set the box on the burled wood dash. After nearly a decade working as his executive assistant, I knew how far I could push.

As if reading my mind, he said, "You should come back to work for me. I've got a great new project—"

"No."

"It's world-changing tech—"

"No."

One corner of his mouth quirked upward, his expression softening. "We haven't done so badly together, have we?"

I didn't respond. When he'd sold his tech firm, I'd done well. Without him, I wouldn't have been able to open Beanblossom's Tea and Tarot.

But I owed him for a lot more than that.

Hence the stakeout.

Also, I hadn't exactly had any better offers this evening.

Tourists in board shorts and tank tops wandered east, away from the beach. Whirligigs and windsocks fluttered beneath a nearby awning. Lights twinkled on the hillside, cascading down to the Pacific.

San Borromeo was tiny but had a to-die-for location, just south of Santa Cruz. The tourists crowded in. As a new small business owner, I said *huzzah* to that. Tourists meant afternoon teas and Tarot readings. But it was starting to feel a little crowded.

"How did you know the bottle was counterfeit?" I asked, changing the subject.

Razzzor, in addition to being my best friend, ex-employer, and favorite gaming partner, was now a proud winery owner. In Silicon Valley, a vineyard was the ultimate accessory. Aside from the latest Tesla.

"Because I tasted it." He adjusted his wire-frame glasses. "It wasn't my pinot." The twilight deepened, setting his handsome face in shadow, but I could see the angry set to his mouth.

"Huh." He'd sent me a bottle once, as a gift. (There was no way I could afford his wine.) The bottle had been near-black, elegantly mysterious, and damned heavy. "Explain again why you haven't gone to the police?"

"I just want to check things out a bit first," he said vaguely.

I shifted in the Tesla to get a better look at him. There wasn't a whole lot of room for moving around, and I banged my elbow on the window. "Ow." I winced.

"What are you doing?"

"Trying to figure out what you're hiding." Because he was definitely hiding something. His reluctance to talk to the cops was about more than his libertarian tendencies. And when my ex-boss got sneaky, all sorts of bad things happened.

He straightened, then abruptly slumped lower, his knees jamming beneath the wheel, his hoodie riding up over his neck. Another weird fact about Silicon Valley rich dudes? Being able to dress down is a sign of success.

"Someone's going inside," he said.

I pressed the binoculars to my eyes. A willowy blonde with long, coiling hair and a leather portfolio strode into the wine store. She looked a lot like me, but taller. And her fashionable but no-nonsense red pantsuit looked expensive.

I glanced down at my own outfit—a rose-colored split skirt and loose white cotton tank. Mine looked more comfy.

She stepped outside a few minutes later, still carrying the portfolio. The woman strode down the street.

"Suspicious," I teased. "She didn't buy any wine."

Razzzor grunted.

"And what *was* in that portfolio?" I asked in a deeper, TV-announcer voice.

He stared after the blonde, his mouth compressing.

I threw a handful of organic popcorn at him. "Earth to Razzzor."

A bike messenger skidded to a halt in front of the store. He ducked inside. The man emerged even faster than the blonde, hopped on his bike, and cycled off.

Frowning, I leaned across Razzzor and watched the messenger disappear down the narrow street. "That's weird."

His head whipped toward me. "What?"

"He didn't take anything into the store, did he?"

"I don't know," Razzzor said. "I wasn't watching that closely."

"Because he didn't take anything out either."

"Do you think—"

"That I've figured out the flaw in this stakeout? Yes. There's nothing odd or unusual about people going into a wine store. What exactly are we watching for here?"

"Fine," Razzzor huffed. "I can see you're not taking this seriously." He opened the Tesla's door and stepped out.

"Where are you going?"

"Inside."

"Wait." I scrambled to escape the sports car. This was harder than it sounded. Tesla's don't have handles. They have buttons. But it's hard to remember that when you're not used to riding in one. My hands fumbled, gliding across the door's smooth surface. Finally, I found a button.

The window glided down.

"Oh, come on."

Razzzor strode across the street. His long shadow vanished beneath a streetlight. An unreasoning panic flashed through me.

Grabbing a lamp post for balance, I scrambled out the window and bolted after him.

"I'm sorry." I panted. "I am taking this seriously. But if you really think someone's counterfeiting your wine, you should call the police."

He grabbed the wine shop's door handle and pulled it open. A bell jangled overhead. We stepped inside.

Long aisles lined with wooden shelves stretched toward the back of the narrow store.

"The pinots are over there." Razzzor turned a corner and vanished down an aisle.

An oversized, black paper tag dangled from a bottle, pulled slightly out of one of the shelves. Since it looked like something out of *Harry Potter*, I glanced at the tag. In neat, silvery script, it read: "This inky Cot pairs well with barbecued pork and burgers with blue cheese."

"Not with *my* burgers." I shoved the bottle deeper onto the shelf. Razzzor had disappeared, and I suddenly felt very alone. "Razzzor?"

"Over here."

I turned a corner.

Razzzor rotated a black wine bottle in his hand. "It's one of mine."

"Is it fake?" I asked.

"I don't think so, but I'd have to taste it to be sure. It's a different year than the counterfeit bottle I found last week."

"Does that matter?"

"Maybe. I don't know." He started to put the bottle back onto the shelf.

I laid a hand on his. "Hold on. Why don't we ask the owner where he bought this one?"

"You know I hate direct confrontations."

Boy, did I. I'd spent the better part of my twenties helping him evade them. "Who said anything about a confrontation? You're a vintner. He's a wine seller. It's just a friendly chat."

We walked to the rear of the shop, where an old-fashioned cash register stood on a glass-topped wooden counter. A bell sat beside the register. I tapped it, and it pealed through the wine store.

"So," Razzzor said in a low voice. "Who should we be?"

"Be?"

"Our stakeout personas. Should we be boyfriend and girlfriend?"

"Maybe we should stick with something closer to reality," I whispered. "I can be your admin assistant."

His head dipped, his shoulders hunching. "Whatever you say."

We waited.

Razzzor frowned and dinged the bell again.

We waited some more.

Razzzor rubbed the back of his neck.

"Something could be wrong." I grinned. Even though I was just a lowly tearoom co-owner, I kind of liked playing detective. "As good citizens, we should check." Good citizens and totally not two gaming geeks.

He canted his head. "Maybe we should wait some more."

"I'm your fake assistant, remember? It's my job to make sure your time isn't wasted." I strode around the counter. "Hello?" I called.

A door behind the counter stood open. I peered inside. Cases of wine made unsteady towers on the floor and blocked a simple wooden desk.

I stepped into the doorway and stopped short, sucking in a harsh breath.

Razzzor bumped into me. "What? What's wrong?"

A man lay prone on the wood floor. Blood pooled around his head, turned toward the desk.

I gaped like a koi fish, my heart knocking against my chest. "Oh my God." I hurried forward, cursing guiltily. Dammit. I hadn't *really* thought someone was hurt.

"Call an ambulance," I said.

I stepped around the odd arrangement of boxes to the fallen man's side. "Sir?" I asked loudly and pressed two fingers to the side of his neck. I didn't feel a pulse, but I wasn't exactly a pulse-taking expert.

I glanced at Razzzor, standing behind the wooden desk. His fists clenched at his sides.

"Fine," I said, "I'll call an ambulance." I rummaged in my purse for my phone.

"No." Greenish, Razzzor steadied himself on a stack of wine boxes.

I paused, phone gripped between my hands. "No? What are you talking about?"

He gulped, his Adam's apple bobbing. "His eyes..." He pointed. "Call the police. He's dead."

Click here to get your copy of *Hostage to Fortune* so you can keep reading this series today.

Cinnamon-Chip and Coconut Scones

INGREDIENTS:

3 ¾ C flour

¼ C sugar

3 T baking powder

1 tsp cinnamon

¼ tsp salt

8 T cold unsalted butter

1 ¼ C milk

2 C coconut (dry)

1 C Hershey's cinnamon chips

Heat oven to 375 degrees F.

Mix flour, sugar, baking powder, cinnamon and salt in a medium-sized bowl. Cut butter into cubes and mix into the flour mixture with your fingers, crushing the butter, until the mix is coarse and sandy.

Add milk and stir until almost combined. Add coconut and cinnamon chips and mix in. You may need to add extra milk, a tablespoon at a time, until the mix is incorporated.

Knead dough in the bowl. Roll out to 1" thick. Cut circles 2 ½ inches in diameter, or cut into triangular wedges 2 ½ inches at the base. Bake on ungreased cookie sheet until light golden brown. Circles take approximately 15 minutes. Triangles will usually take 20-25 minutes.

Almond and Apricot Scones

INGREDIENTS

4 ½ C all-purpose flour

½ C sugar

1 T + 1 tsp baking powder

¾ tsp salt

¾ C + 2 T almond paste (7 ounces)

½ C butter, chilled

1 C chopped dried apricots

½ C chopped toasted almonds

½ C chopped untoasted almonds

1 C milk

½ C heavy cream

½ tsp almond extract

Line two cookie sheets with parchment paper.

Mix flour, sugar, baking powder and salt in a large-sized bowl. Cube butter and almond paste. Add to dry mixture and using your fingers, mix it in, crushing the almond paste and butter, until the mixture is coarse and sandy. Mix in the apricots and almonds.

In a medium-sized bowl, whisk the remaining liquid ingredients. Slowly add to the dry mixture, folding the liquid in until everything is mostly combined.

Use your hands again to make sure all the dry ingredients are combined with the wet. Gently knead ingredients in the bowl into a ball of dough.

Divide dough in half. Flatten each half to a round approximately ¾" to 1" thick. Place on the parchment lined cookie sheets and freeze for 1 hour.

Preheat oven to 375 degrees F.

Remove dough from freezer and cut each disc into 8 triangles, like you're cutting a cake. Space each scone approximately 1" apart on the lined cookie sheets and bake for 20-25 minutes until golden brown.

"Earl Grey" Tea Blend

1 CUP CHINA BLACK tea leaves

3-inch strip of dried bergamot peel

A pinch lavender (too much and it tastes like soap)

Mix the herbs. Lavender can be overpowering, so you only want to use a grain or two. Add 1 tsp of the mixture to tea strainer and steep in a mug of hot water for 5-10 minutes.

Rosemary and Horsetail Tea for Hair and Nails

INGREDIENTS

1 tsp dried horsetail (2 parts)

½ tsp dried rosemary leaves (1 part)

Add herbs to tea strainer and steep in a mug of hot water for 10-15 minutes. Remove strainer and enjoy!

Note: Most herbal recipes are given in "parts". I've hopefully simplified by using teaspoons.

More Kirsten Weiss

THE PERFECTLY PROPER PARANORMAL Museum Mysteries

When highflying Maddie Kosloski is railroaded into managing her small-town's paranormal museum, she tells herself it's only temporary... until a corpse in the museum embroils her in murders past and present.

If you love quirky characters and cats with attitude, you'll love this laugh-out-loud cozy mystery series with a light paranormal twist. It's perfect for fans of Jana DeLeon, Laura Childs, and Juliet Blackwell. Start with book 1, *The Perfectly Proper Paranormal Museum*, and experience these charming wine-country whodunits today.

The Tea & Tarot Cozy Mysteries

Welcome to Beanblossom's Tea and Tarot, where each and every cozy mystery brews up hilarious trouble.

Abigail Beanblossom's dream of owning a tearoom is about to come true. She's got the lease, the start-up funds, and the recipes. But Abigail's out of a tearoom and into hot water when her realtor turns out to be a conman... and then turns up dead.

Take a whimsical journey with Abigail and her partner Hyperion through the seaside town of San Borromeo (patron saint of heartburn sufferers). And be sure to check out the easy tearoom recipes in the back of each book! Start the adventure with book 1, *Steeped in Murder*.

The Wits' End Cozy Mysteries

Cozy mysteries that are out of this world...

Running the best little UFO-themed B&B in the Sierras takes organization, breakfasting chops, and a talent for turning up trouble.

The truth is out there... Way out there in these hilarious whodunits. Start the series and beam up book 1, *At Wits' End*, today!

Pie Town Cozy Mysteries

When Val followed her fiancé to coastal San Nicholas, she had ambitions of starting a new life and a pie shop. One broken engagement later, at least her dream of opening a pie shop has come true.... Until one of her regulars keels over at the counter.

Welcome to Pie Town, where Val and pie-crust specialist Charlene are baking up hilarious trouble. Start this laugh-out-loud cozy mystery series with book 1, *The Quiche and the Dead*.

A Big Murder Mystery Series

Small Town. Big Murder.

The number one secret to my success as a bodyguard? Staying under the radar. But when a wildly public disaster blew up my career and reputation, it turned my perfect, solitary life upside down.

I thought my tiny hometown of Nowhere would be the ideal out-of-the-way refuge to wait out the media storm.

It wasn't.

My little brother had moved into a treehouse. The obscure mountain town had decided to attract tourists with the world's largest collection of big things... Yes, Nowhere now has the world's largest pizza cutter. And lawn flamingo. And ball of yarn...

And then I stumbled over a dead body.

All the evidence points to my brother being the bad guy. I may have been out of his life for a while—okay, five years—but I know he's no killer. Can I clear my brother before he becomes Nowhere's next Big Fatality?

A fast-paced and funny cozy mystery series, start with Big Shot.

The Doyle Witch Mysteries

In a mountain town where magic lies hidden in its foundations and forests, three witchy sisters must master their powers and shatter a curse before it destroys them and the home they love.

This thrilling witch mystery series is perfect for fans of Annabel Chase, Adele Abbot, and Amanda Lee. If you love stories rich with packed with magic, mystery, and murder, you'll love the Witches of Doyle. Follow the magic with the Doyle Witch trilogy, starting with book 1, *Bound*.

The Riga Hayworth Paranormal Mysteries

Her gargoyle's got an attitude.

Her magic's on the blink.

Alchemy might be the cure... if Riga can survive long enough to puzzle out its mysteries.

All Riga wants is to solve her own personal mystery—how to rebuild her magical life. But her new talent for unearthing murder keeps getting in the way...

If you're looking for a magical page-turner with a complicated, 40-something heroine, read the paranormal mystery series that fans of Patricia Briggs and Ilona Andrews call AMAZING! Start your next adventure with book 1, *The Alchemical Detective*.

Sensibility Grey Steampunk Suspense

California Territory, 1848.

Steam-powered technology is still in its infancy.

Gold has been discovered, emptying the village of San Francisco of its male population.

And newly arrived immigrant, Englishwoman Sensibility Grey, is alone.

The territory may hold more dangers than Sensibility can manage. Pursued by government agents and a secret society, Sensibility must decipher her father's clockwork secrets, before time runs out.

If you love over-the-top characters, twisty mysteries, and complicated heroines, you'll love the Sensibility Grey series of steampunk suspense. Start this steampunk adventure with book 1, *Steam and Sensibility*.

Get Kirsten's Mobile App

Keep up with the latest book news, and get free short stories, scone recipes and more by downloading Kirsten's mobile app.
Just click HERE to get started or use the QR code below.
Or make sure you're on Kirsten's email list to get your free copy of the Tea & Tarot mystery, *Fortune Favors the Grave*.
You can do that here: KirstenWeiss.com or use the QR code below:

Connect with Kirsten

You can download my free app here:

https://kirstenweissbooks.beezer.com

Or sign up for my newsletter and get a special digital prize pack for joining, including an exclusive Tea & Tarot novella, *Fortune Favors the Grave*.

https://kirstenweiss.com

Or maybe you'd like to chat with other whimsical mystery fans? Come join Kirsten's reader page on Facebook:

https://www.facebook.com/kirsten.weiss

Or... sign up for my read and review team on Booksprout:

https://booksprout.co/author/8142/kirsten-weiss

About the Author

I WRITE LAUGH-OUT-LOUD, PAGE-TURNING mysteries for people who want to escape with real, complex, and flawed but likable characters. If there's magic in the story, it must work consistently within the world's rules and be based in history or the reality of current magical practices.

I'm best known for my cozy mystery and witch mystery novels, though I've written some steampunk mystery as well. So if you like funny, action-packed mysteries with complicated heroines, just turn the page...

Learn more, grab my **free app**, or sign up for my **newsletter** for exclusive stories and book updates. I also have a read-and-review tea via **Booksprout** and is looking for honest and thoughtful reviews! If you're interested, download the **Booksprout app**, follow me on Booksprout, and opt-in for email notifications.

bookbub.com/profile/kirsten-weiss

goodreads.com/author/show/5346143.Kirsten_Weiss

facebook.com/kirsten.weiss

instagram.com/kirstenweissauthor/

TREATMENT FIDELITY IN STUDIES OF EDUCATIONAL INTERVENTION

Treatment Fidelity in Studies of Educational Intervention is a detailed guide to the increasing emphasis on methodological rigor and implementation fidelity in educational research. A timely contribution to the field, this book offers practical guidance and systematic research on the nature of implementation fidelity in experimental settings, and provides strategies for combining fidelity-related data with other data types to evaluate a program's impact in schools and other educational settings. With contributions from leading scholars in the area of research methods in education, *Treatment Fidelity* synthesizes recommendations for current measurement practices, case studies of recent or ongoing research programs, and technical evaluation reports on studies that measure and model fidelity as part of estimating a treatment's impact. Intended for scholars, professionals, and graduate students interested in school-based intervention, this volume presents information on how to address implementation in applied research.

Greg Roberts is Associate Director of the Meadows Center for Preventing Educational Risk at the University of Texas at Austin.

Sharon Vaughn is Manuel J. Justiz Endowed Chair in Education and Executive Director of the Meadows Center for Preventing Educational Risk.

S. Natasha Beretvas is Professor in the Department of Educational Psychology at the University of Texas at Austin.

Vivian Wong is Assistant Professor in the Curry School of Education at the University of Virginia.

TREATMENT FIDELITY IN STUDIES OF EDUCATIONAL INTERVENTION

*Edited by Greg Roberts, Sharon Vaughn,
S. Natasha Beretvas, and Vivian Wong*

Routledge
Taylor & Francis Group

NEW YORK AND LONDON

First published 2017
by Routledge
711 Third Avenue, New York, NY 10017

and by Routledge
2 Park Square, Milton Park, Abingdon, Oxon, OX14 4RN

Routledge is an imprint of the Taylor & Francis Group, an informa business

© 2017 Taylor & Francis

The right of Greg Roberts, Sharon Vaughn, S. Natasha Beretvas, and Vivian
Wong to be identified as editors of this work has been asserted by them
in accordance with sections 77 and 78 of the Copyright, Designs and
Patents Act 1988.

Library of Congress Cataloging in Publication Data
A catalog record for this book has been requested

ISBN: 978-1-138-83850-5 (hbk)
ISBN: 978-1-138-83851-2 (pbk)
ISBN: 978-1-315-73426-2 (ebk)

Typeset in Bembo
by Deanta Global Publishing Services, Chennai, India

Printed and bound in the United States of America by Publishers Graphics,
LLC on sustainably sourced paper.

CONTENTS

ACKNOWLEDGMENTS

Greg Roberts and Sharon Vaughn were supported in part by grant P50 HD052117-07 from the Eunice Kennedy Shriver National Institute of Child Health and Human Development, and by grant R305F100013 from the Institute of Education Sciences, U.S. Department of Education. The content is solely the responsibility of the authors and does not necessarily represent the official views of the Eunice Kennedy Shriver National Institute of Child Health and Human Development, the National Institutes of Health, or the Institute for Education Science.

1

IMPLEMENTATION FIDELITY AND EDUCATIONAL SCIENCE

An Introduction

Greg Roberts

The funding of *experimental* research in education has grown four-fold over the last 15 years (IES, 2014; NIH, 2015). One by-product of this more focused funding model is a greater interest in *implementation fidelity*, generally defined as the extent to which an intervention is delivered as intended by end users in authentic education settings (ibid.). Increasingly, funders (ibid.), consumers, and conductors of education research identify fidelity as a necessary feature of well-designed experimental inquiry. However, there is a relative lack of practical guidance and even less systematic research on the nature of implementation fidelity in experimental settings (Cordray, 2007) or on strategies for combining fidelity-related data with other data types to evaluate a program's impact in schools and other educational settings. This book takes a step toward building the knowledge base in this area.

Chapters in this volume address the measurement and statistical modeling of implementation fidelity in studies designed to estimate the causal effect of an educational treatment (we use "program," "intervention," and "treatment" interchangeably throughout this introduction). The book presents the work of a handful of scholars who have begun to grapple with these issues, and it builds on the efforts of others working in this and related areas. Several chapters are prescriptive; they recommend current practice related to the measurement or the statistical modeling of fidelity. Others present case studies of recent or ongoing programs of research with a focus on their fidelity-related aspects. These chapters offer first-hand accounts of efforts to introduce implementation fidelity into the conduct of experimental research. The remaining chapters report on studies that measure and model fidelity as part of estimating a treatment's

impact. Papers in this category are organized like peer-reviewed journal articles or technical evaluation reports.

The book presents sophisticated content in "plain language." Our purpose is to make the information available to a wider readership than might be otherwise possible. Mathematical formulae and more advanced statistical constructs are provided as footnotes for interested readers. Our objective is to build an intuitive understanding of the material and the ideas on which it is based rather than to be technically precise. Accordingly, this book is intended for: (1) scholars doing intervention and evaluation research in schools and other educational settings; (2) professionals working within and across substantive areas, including individuals in research consulting firms; (3) funders of intervention research; and (4) graduate students who are training for careers as substantive or applied researchers in areas related to school-based intervention. Researchers doing substantive research on quantitative methods will have an interest as well because the volume describes the types of challenges faced by scientists working in applied areas, suggesting areas for potential methods-related inquiry.

Purposes of This Chapter

The main purpose of this introduction is to discuss the implications of introducing a third concern into the relationship between research design and causal inference. Specifically, how does implementation fidelity figure into the design/inference relationship; what assumptions do we make about fidelity and how do they relate to the assumptions that underlie the causal designs that characterize intervention research; and what design and analytic strategies are available for including implementation fidelity in the treatment/outcome "equation"? We focus on content that may help readers as they navigate one or more of the book's chapters. Additionally, we address these topics in the context of intervention *development*. Development is *not* the book's focus, but it represents the starting place for many programs of research that focus on an intervention and on its impact on important outcomes.

Implementation Fidelity

There is little consensus on what is meant by "implementation fidelity" (Cordray, 2007). For many, it describes the degree to which users of a program adhere to its intended use. The relevant question is "to what extent is a treatment used (or participated in or taken up) according to its intent or design?" In this sense, implementation fidelity is part of the *translation of scientific results into practice* rather than the doing of science itself. The assumption is that evidence-based protocols work best when deployed or used according to their intent or design, and implementation fidelity describes the alignment

between a treatment's actual use in a community or practice setting and its intended or validated use, where "validated" in this case refers to the scientific consensus about the program's usefulness, efficacy, or effectiveness. Concerns about randomization, treatment diffusion, compliance, or efficacy are generally not part of the discussion when talking about implementation fidelity in a translational context.

However, with the advent of school-based, large-scale randomized studies in the late 1990s, implementation fidelity was repurposed and its use extended beyond translational contexts to include adherence in experimental studies. This repurposing introduced confusion about the term's precise meaning (Hulleman & Cordray, 2009), particularly when used to describe aspects of experimental design. Adherence is still part of the equation in randomized trials. However, both its purpose and the consequences of non-adherence differ when considered in an experimental context versus a translational context, and the primary difference centers on the inference-making agenda of experimental research.

Chapters in this book vary somewhat on the precise meaning of implementation fidelity. These differences translate into diverse recommendations on fidelity's role in the design of research, the analysis of data, or the interpretation of findings, which is unsurprising given the general lack of clarity that characterizes fidelity-related questions in an experimental context. This book was proposed as a forum for illustrating this diversity as a first step toward a general framework for making evidence-based recommendations about implementation fidelity in experimental science. The chapters contribute to an ongoing and important conversation, one that deserves greater attention and a more focused approach to defining important terms, articulating methods, and specifying best practices as they relate to experimental research in schools and classrooms.

That said, there are areas of relative consensus. In the sections that follow, we touch upon these. Our primary purpose is to provide readers with knowledge that may be necessary to fully appreciate one or more chapters. We also use these sections to introduce each chapter and to situate it within the larger context of this volume. As described earlier, we introduce constructs in the context of program development, because implementation fidelity is so closely aligned with the developmental aspects of intervention research and with the theory-building process that characterizes the early stages of program evaluation.

Implementation Fidelity and Intervention Development

A new intervention emerges when a potential program developer has compelling ideas about how better to meet a currently unmet or poorly met need. A first step in developing a new program is to define its key elements (a *program model*, as described later in this chapter). Many suggest that a *minimum* of three

components is necessary: the *program's activities*, its *theory of change*, and its *intended outcomes*. In this context, activities represent "what" program users do or should do when using the program (as well as "what" evaluators or researchers look for when evaluating the fidelity with which the program is used). The program's activities include the materials, procedures, decision rules, grouping schemes, scheduling requirements, and other elements suggested by the *theory of change* and presumed to be necessary to improved outcomes. The theory of change (sometimes called the *theory of action*) describes "why" the indicated activities are thought to cause improved outcomes. Program developers base assumptions about program-related change on general theories of learning, behavior, social cognition, motivation, and effective teacher practice. A theory of change for an emerging program applies a general theory or theories from one or more of these areas (or other areas, as necessary) to craft activities that theoretically lead to valued outcomes. Outcomes represent the anticipated benefits of having done the indicated activities. In an experimental context, outcomes represent changes associated with one set of program activities over and above any changes associated with a set of different program activities, including those associated with typical practice.

Several chapters in this volume address implementation fidelity in the context of program development. In Chapter 7, Jill Allor and Lynne Stokes argue that the products of scientific inquiry—a process defined by development, efficacy trials, replication, and effectiveness trials—should include not only an efficacious and effective intervention but also reliable measures of its implementation. Their case study provides recommendations in this respect. In Chapter 2, Frank Gresham notes that programs with complex activities are more difficult to implement with fidelity than interventions with simpler designs. He further points out that measurement of implementation fidelity becomes more error prone as interventions increase in complexity—for a given program implementer, the *true* level of fidelity and the *measured* level of fidelity will be less similar, on average, for more complex interventions compared to simpler programs. Consistency across raters is more difficult to establish and maintain in the context of complex treatments, as well. Gresham's general point is that interventions should be only as complex as necessary to realize anticipated outcomes. Unnecessarily complex interventions are difficult to implement and their implementation, such as it may be, is difficult to measure reliably. Finally, in Chapter 4, Roberts et al. suggest that development of a new program can be augmented by understanding typical practice in the schools and classrooms where the treatment will be implemented. They suggest that typical practice may represent an intervention, similar to a newly developed program, and that while the two interventions (newly developed and current practice) may have elements in common, it is their differences that hypothetically cause changed outcomes, particularly in the context of experimental studies. Roberts et al. recommend that the differences in two programs

(the experimental program and current practice) be carefully specified when developing a new intervention as a means of *differentiating* the two and as a prelude to developing measures of fidelity.

Differentiation

Theory of change is fundamental to the notion of *differentiation*. As suggested, a new program arises in response to currently unmet or poorly met needs. In schools, the perceived need often relates to student learning or behavior, teacher practice, or both. Developers propose a new program because it represents a different way of doing things, and in theory, a more effective way of meeting the targeted need. Differentiation represents the distinction(s) between typical or current practice and the practices offered by the new treatment. Of course, doing things differently simply because they diverge from existing practice is not a sufficient reason to propose change. Absent a compelling theory of change, the new components of a proposed program are simply new; there is little reason to suppose they are better than existing practice and no reason to invest the money necessary to test the impact of such differences. In this sense, a theory of change is what justifies the program's proposed activities, and a compelling theory expertly operationalized into feasible program activities often warrants the investments required for systematic scientific inquiry. The new program may share features with existing practice; however, it also includes features that are necessary (hypothetically, at this point) to its improved impact and *necessarily unique to the proposed new program*.

In Chapter 2, Gresham follows Perepletchikova et al. (2014) in describing differentiation as a *process* whereby critical differences in the treatments being compared are explicitly identified. His example involves three treatments for anxiety, each based on a different "macro theory" (social learning theory, cognitive behavior theory, and respondent conditioning model). Accordingly, they differ in their theories of change and in their activities. By identifying the underlying theories and the related theories of change, the programs can be differentiated along important dimensions. These differences provide a basis for hypothesizing about the relative effects of each program. They (the differences) also represent the domain of program-related behaviors (or activities) from which investigators can sample to develop measures of implementation fidelity. In an experimental context, the new program is expected to outperform current practice because of the features that set it apart, not because of the features it shares with typical practice. Like Gresham, Allor and Stokes conceptualize differentiation as the product of an ongoing process that includes not only program development, but efficacy and effectiveness trials as well. Implicit in their reasoning is the idea that programs evolve from the point of initial conception to final "rollout," that the differences between a new program and existing practice will change accordingly, and that reliable measures of fidelity align with the evolving nature of the new program.

Differentiation is inherent in the achieved relative strength (ARS) index described by Murrah et al. in Chapter 3. In their evaluation of a program that prepares parents to talk with their adolescents about the importance of Science, Technology, Engineering, and Mathematics (STEM), they found that teenagers whose parents participated in the program reported more conversations with their parents about STEM than did teenagers in the control condition. In Murrah et al.'s theory of change, increased communication about STEM between parents and their teenaged students was associated with greater student awareness about STEM, which was in turn associated with increased course taking. The evaluation tested the validity of this line of reasoning in comparison to a group of untreated teenagers and their parents. Murrah et al. used *program models* to depict points at which the new program departed from typical school practice (i.e. differentiation). Murrah et al. also used program models to represent the hypothetical cascade of effects (e.g. increased communication leads to increased interest which leads to increased course taking) associated with participation in the parent training program.

Program Model

A program model describes a treatment's components and illustrates important interrelationships. It identifies the key activities and depicts the chain of effects they hypothetically trigger, culminating in improved outcomes. A program model helps users implement the intended program and it provides researchers with a standard against which to compare the program as implemented for purposes of evaluating fidelity. It also serves as a road map for investigators when developing questions, identifying measures, and interpreting results. Further, to the extent that typical practice can be depicted in model form (i.e. a program model for typical practice), differences between a new program (when used as intended) and usual practice (when used) can be pinpointed, suggesting very specific contrasts beyond those associated with main treatment effects. Using program models to differentiate new and existing programs (or alternatives of a new program, or more than one new program) prior to testing the experimental treatment provides a means of fine tuning the new program, establishing pertinent research questions, and designing a study of the treatment's effect and the factors that may influence that effect.

The application of program models is featured in several chapters. In Chapter 3, Murrah et al. argue that program models and a focus on differentiation, as described later, improves the reliability and sensitivity with which fidelity is measured. Implementation fidelity is an inherently difficult construct to measure with sensitivity. By depicting the new program's core features and the mechanism(s) thought to animate those features (the "what" and the "why"), a program model "unpacks the black box" and offers a framework for identifying program elements that are thought necessary for improved outcomes.

In Chapter 7, Allor and Stokes, though in a different context, also stress the importance of engaging with the fidelity question in the context of developing a program's model.

In Chapter 4, Roberts et al. consider fidelity in the context of a treatment effect, which depends not only on fidelity by those implementing the new program but also on the quality of practice by individuals or groups in the comparison. They suggest that program models may be relevant for the experimental program as well as for the typical practice that the new program is designed to replace, particularly in settings where current models of practice are relatively strong. There is evidence that typical practice has improved in several content areas over the last 10 years (Lemons et al. 2014) because it has become increasingly aligned with the findings of experimental research (it is "evidence-based"). Existing practice in these cases not only poses a more robust comparison for a newly developed intervention than might be the case otherwise; it is likely to represent a more coherent alternative, as well—one with activities driven by a theory of change which is in turn based on prevailing theories about learning and effective teaching. In other words, the *program model* for existing practice in select cases can be depicted with a level of detail similar to the new program because existing practice represents "yesterday's new program" (i.e. an earlier and recent iteration of evidence-based practice). Modeling typical or current practice as part of developing a new intervention highlights the differences between the experimental treatment and existing practice, which yields more sensitive measures of fidelity to the extent that differences in the two models are a key focus of measurement. In turn, more sensitive and focused measures of fidelity provide additional information with which to evaluate treatment's effect. When usual practice represents a compelling alternative, a straight-up contrast with a newly developed treatment may be less useful for refining ongoing practice than a contrast that focuses on the *differences* between existing and newly developed programs.

In Chapter 5, Keith Zvoch suggests that data on the extent to which a treatment is actually delivered and received as intended can help to contextualize a study's results by identifying program-related sources of variation in the treatment's effect. In this sense, Zvoch takes a more expansive approach to program modeling than the three-part approach described elsewhere, adding contextual variables as considerations when estimating a program's effect. Zvoch reminds readers that site-based (i.e. schools, school districts, etc.) and population-level differences in outcomes may help to identify conditions under which a program is particularly effective (or less so). His larger argument is that observed variation in implementation fidelity creates natural contrasts that can be exploited to identify for whom and under what conditions a program "works." In prospective studies, where the research design is established prior to implementation, site-based or population-level differences are built-in features of the study, and data are collected purposively to address related questions. In program evaluation studies, which are often less structured by necessity, differences in these

respects are explored analytically, as a means of "mining" the data to understand its underlying structure. Whether prospective or post hoc, the possibilities described by Zvoch require that *contextual variables* be included in the program's model. The modeling of contextual variables introduces the notion of *statistical moderation*.

Contextual Factors and Moderation

Program models can range from the fairly simple to the extremely complex, depending on the program and on the model's purpose(s). Many program models include components in addition to the activities, theory of change, and outcomes that we describe (e.g. *outputs* and *resources*, *short-term outcomes*, and *long-term outcomes*). For educational programs, *contextual factors* are important when the intervention is tested in more than one school or classroom or across different populations of students. Contextual factors, when included in a program model, are not the target of intervention, because they are non-malleable (i.e. unchangeable) or, if malleable, because changes in contextual variables may be outside of the program's focus or beyond its scope. Instead, contextual factors often denote *moderators* of a program's effect, and they are included in the model because they potentially influence the treatment's impact on outcomes or because they alter the fidelity with which the program can be implemented. In an experimental context, moderators represent dimensions along which a program's effect on outcomes varies—they describe when, for whom, and under what conditions a program works or works differently.

Moderating variables can influence the development process if the program is designed to accommodate differences in the settings where it will be used or if multiple program models are developed that differ in their activities (and/or theories of change) based on differences in school, teacher, and student-level contextual factors. For example, a program developer may tailor an intended program to one or more subgroups of schools, teachers or students represented by a moderator or moderators (for example, schools with high percentages of English Learner students, beginning teachers, or struggling students). Alternatively, developers may add features that, based on the theory of change, increase the program's immunity to the effects of moderating influences. By recognizing the potential impact of important moderators, program activities can be added or modified so that the intended model can be comparably implemented across a variety of classrooms or schools with similar effect, independent of differences in those tasked with implementation (schools and teachers), differences in those who are supposed to benefit from participation (students), or differences in structural aspects of the settings where the program is being implemented (prior achievement or existing resources in the participating schools or classrooms).

In Chapters 2 and 3 respectively, Gresham, then Murrah et al. discuss a related issue. Though they describe their thinking from different perspectives, both make points about statistical conclusion reliability and the threat of confusing variation in fidelity across implementers of a program with differences in the program's "true" impact. Even in studies that randomly assign participants to different treatment groups, a program that is implemented differently by users can disguise the cause or causes of observed differences in outcomes. Zvoch assumes a moderation model to address questions about whom and under what circumstances a program may work. In essence, he explores the potential differences in treatment's impact for different levels of moderating, or contextual, factors. Roberts et al. make a related point in Chapter 4 by acknowledging not only the necessity of documenting practice in comparison settings but also the importance of being clear about what "practice" one is and is not documenting in the alternative. They remind readers that the implementation of program features in comparison settings that are unique and specific to the experimental treatment complicates the interpretation of observed outcomes, particularly when their use is unmeasured.

Levels of Intervention and Benefit

Models serve as an organizing tool for program developers and as a road map for program users. For evaluators and researchers, a program model provides a basis for developing relevant hypotheses, framing research questions, selecting measures, and establishing a baseline for monitoring fidelity. A program model also provides a tool for identifying factors that may influence the program's performance. Finally, a model can represent the level(s) at which a program intervenes and the level(s) at which benefits are expected to accrue. In educational studies, participants may be students, teachers, or others who contribute to or benefit from the educational process. In many cases, teachers are the intended users of a new educational program, and students are its beneficiaries. The treatment in this context is delivered by teachers and students are the intended recipients; teachers use the program and students presumably benefit. These data can be described as *multilevel* and the relationship among the levels is described as nested or clustered. In this example, students are nested in classrooms and classrooms are nested in schools. A failure to properly account for nested data can lead one to conclude *falsely* that a new intervention is more effective than typical practice.

In Chapter 6, Unlu et al. fit a series of three-level models with students nested in classrooms and classrooms nested in schools. Roberts et al. present a relatively novel model, where students are nested in classes (or sections of American History) and classes/sections are nested in teachers. Zvoch represents his data as students nested in schools (i.e. a two-level model). The intervention is a

school-based summer literacy program, where teachers were not involved in its implementation. While different in their details, these three teams of investigators address the same underlying requirement—the adjustment of standard errors and degrees of freedom to account for the effects of nested or clustered data. By modeling the nested structure of their data, Unlu et al., Zvoch, and Roberts et al. conduct unbiased tests of group differences.

Treatment Dosage

A treatment effect, in practical terms, is the difference at posttest of two otherwise comparable groups. A treatment that is fully implemented as intended can yield unbiased estimates of the program's effect. However, if business-as-usual participants receive some or all of the treatment, or if the treatment-assigned participants receive something less than the full program as designed and intended, estimates of a treatment's effect may be a less than reliable indicator of its "true" effect or its efficacy. In this scenario, Roberts et al. describe the amounts of experimental treatment received on average by the treatment group and by the business-as-usual group as *dosage*, although others approach this construct a little differently.

For example, Gresham, in Chapter 2, frames dosage as part of a more general construct labelled *treatment receipt* (Bellig et al., 2004), which he describes as participants' comprehension of and responsiveness to the treatment. Dosage, for Gresham, represents the amount of treatment received by participants assigned to treatment. He operationalizes dosage as the number of times per day or week that a participant is exposed to the program, or the duration of a treatment regimen given a specified need. The Achieved Relative Strength indices described by Murrah et al. in Chapter 3 represent estimates of dosage and relative dosage, which they describe as average fidelity and absolute fidelity. They also introduce binary complier indices that categorize individuals as compliers or non-compliers based on actual treatment received. In Chapter 4, Roberts et al. use latent variables to model the dosage of unique treatment components available to participants in both treatment and business-as-usual. They conceptualize relative dosage as the difference in dosage for the treatment-assigned group (i.e. adherence) and for the business-as-usual group (i.e. diffusion). They estimate this difference as part of the structural models they use to calculate treatment effects. Allor and Stokes (Chapter 7) propose an interesting study that manipulates levels of dosage as part of a larger program of intervention research. Randomly assigning participants to a "low dose" of treatment, a "high dose" of treatment, and a business-as-usual condition would address a number of questions about fidelity, its variation across program users, and its effects given different contextual factors.

Zvoch's recommendations in Chapter 5 represent a dose-response approach to modeling an intervention's impact. He also describes the three commonly used approaches to estimating treatment effects summarized in a subsequent

section. Unlu and her colleagues examine several approaches for estimating fidelity in multi-site studies where levels of implementation fidelity vary by site. In Chapter 6, they propose a "cut off" method and a "matching" method for statistically manipulating fidelity, which they conceptualize as dosage, as a means of estimating program impact for different dosage profiles. In practice, this involves comparing the outcomes of two otherwise comparable groups, where their only difference, on average, is the exposure to treatment.

Recommended Reading: An Abridged Primer on Research Design, Causal Inference, and Potential Outcomes

This section briefly summarizes the relationship of research design and causal inference making. It is intended as a reference for readers who may be new to causal inference and research designs in educational settings.

We describe the work of Donald Campbell and his colleagues (Campbell & Stanley, 1966; Cook & Campbell, 1979) and touch on the ideas of Donald Rubin and others (Imbens & Rubin, 2015; Neyman, 1934) who work from a potential outcomes perspective. Campbell's work and Rubin's potential outcomes framework provide the modern context for thinking about causal inference. Campbell's work is intuitive and accessible. It is well-suited to the needs of substantive researchers who want to investigate a program's role in *causing* observed change. However, many interventionists have only a passing acquaintance with his thinking.

Like Campbell, Rubin tackles the challenges associated with making reliable judgments about the cause or causes of observed change. Rubin's work is influential. Indeed, federal funders of experimental studies in education define a *causal* effect as the difference in the *potential outcomes* for a common set of units under different conditions (IES, 2014; NIH, 2015). Unfortunately, the knowledge base on potential outcomes is relatively obscure, due partly to the complexity of its presentation. This is unfortunate given its consequences for intervention research. We introduce elements of Rubin's framework in a "reader-friendly" format, under the assumption that investigators doing intervention research on education-related questions will benefit from greater awareness of the logic that underlies the causality-related questions that drive their work. We outline key implications of potential outcomes for the fidelity construct as well. Entire textbooks are devoted to experimental design, and most of these describe Campbell's work and Rubin's thinking in considerable detail. *We focus primarily on the elements of these two traditions that bear directly on implementation fidelity as presented in one or more chapters in this volume.*

We focus our discussion on *experimental* research. *Experimental* describes the category of designs that allows one to infer a treatment's causal relationship with outcomes. For experiments conducted in educational settings, the comparison of ultimate interest is between outcomes experienced by the same student

(or teacher, etc.) when exposed to two or more different programs at the same point in time (Imbens & Rubin, 2015). This comparison, of course, is not possible (as long as individuals are constrained by time and space)—either we observe the outcome for an individual when exposed to treatment *or* we observe that individual's outcome when he or she is not exposed to treatment (or when he or she is exposed to another treatment such as typical school practice). We cannot observe both outcomes for the same individual at the same time (Holland, 1986). We can, however, estimate the potential (or likely) outcomes that cannot be observed directly, allowing for inferences about the cause of an observed effect. This is the aim of experimental research.

Internal Validity

Campbell classified research designs as pre-experimental, quasi-experimental, or experimental based on the extent to which an investigator can confidently conclude that the treatment, *rather than alternative causes*, is responsible for change. Experimental designs, versus pre-experimental or quasi-experimental designs, offer the greatest confidence, because they eliminate (or at least minimize) otherwise compelling alternatives as causes of observed outcomes. Campbell and Stanley (1966) (see also Cook & Campbell, 1979) describe eight alternative hypotheses, which they discuss as threats to a study's *internal validity*. Of these, *selection bias* is the most recognized.

Selection bias in experimental research is likely when the groups differ, on average, prior to beginning the treatment. In the presence of bias, differences at posttest may simply be differences that were present prior to providing the intervention. The *selection* (i.e. assignment) model that is least prone to bias is the randomized design. In a randomized design, every sampled participant has an equal probability of being assigned to every condition or group. Two groups are likely to be comparable (or statistically non-different), on average, when each sampled participant has the same chance of being assigned to each condition.[1]

A randomized design is the most reliable means of minimizing a selection's threat to internal validity. Creating comparable groups prior to treatment eliminates selection as an alternative cause of or explanation for later differences; group differences at posttest are likely due to causes other than already existing differences. However, internal validity also requires that a randomized design—the groups' comparability at pretest in all respects except treatment condition—remain uncompromised across the study's duration. This generally means that the two groups experience similar amounts and similar patterns of attrition over the course of the study (Campbell and colleagues label this *experimental mortality*). Ideally, of course, all participants are present for the duration. In school settings this is seldom the case. Participants in school-based studies may move to another school, they may drop out of school altogether, or they

may simply decline to continue participating in the study. Fortunately, a study's internal validity can withstand a degree of attrition to the extent that first, the participants who leave are similar to those who complete the study, and second, the proportion of students leaving the study is comparable across the treated and non-treated groups and across important subgroups within each condition (i.e. no *differential attrition*). The level of threat due to attrition depends on the amount of overall attrition *and* on the degree of differential attrition—as levels of overall attrition increase, lower levels of differential attrition are tolerable. The What Works Clearinghouse (http://ies.ed.gov/ncee/wwc) provides guidelines for evaluating the threat due to overall attrition, the threat due to differential attrition, and the conditional threat of differential attrition at different levels of overall attrition.

Minimizing the threats posed by selection bias and by attrition and differential attrition bias helps to limit threats related to *history, maturation,* and *statistical regression.* History and maturation do not threaten validity to the extent that two otherwise comparable groups are exposed to similar historical events and mature according to typical (or comparably atypical) patterns. However, if one treatment group is disproportionately affected by an unforeseen and unpreventable event, a validity threat is introduced. Testing is a threat to the extent that the two groups are exposed to different measures or to the extent that the same measures are administered in non-standardized ways. However, poor instrumentation is a threat even in randomized designs. If one's measures are prone to error, the equal distribution of that error across two conditions (i.e. randomizing error) may not sufficiently control the threat and may introduce threats unrelated to internal validity.

Statistical regression or regression to the mean, the fourth of Campbell and Stanley's (1966) threats, is a complex, often misunderstood, concept. It occurs when data are collected on more than one occasion (e.g. pretest/posttest) on a non-random sample (non-randomly sampled from a population) using two measures that are imperfectly correlated. In general, when observing repeated measures in a group, relatively high (or relatively low) observations are likely to be followed by less extreme values nearer the true mean, independent of participation or lack of participation in treatment. The more extreme the sampled group is from its population at pretest, the greater the regression at posttest. Also, less correlated measures at the two time points (e.g. pretest/posttest) are associated with greater statistical regression than measures that are highly correlated, even if the same measure is administered on the two occasions. The impact of regression to the mean can be quantified and there are strategies for addressing it analytically (Trochim 2000). It can also be managed by randomly assigning participants to groups, so that statistical regression is comparable across conditions.

The last threat in Campbell and Stanley's (1966) taxonomy is *diffusion of treatment,* which describes the situation where participants assigned to a no-treatment

group or a comparison group receive some or all of the experimental intervention. Diffusion threatens internal validity by making the groups more comparable in the one area where differences matter—exposure to the treatment. In a perfect world, participants assigned to the comparison would participate in none of the treatment and those assigned to treatment would receive the full intervention (all of its components, as designed, and according to plan). In applied settings, and especially in schools and classrooms, this is seldom the case. Participants assigned to the treatment group often receive different amounts of the program or variations of the intended program, whereas those in the comparison may participate in some or all elements of the experimental intervention.

A study with high internal validity provides strong evidence that an intervention *causes* observed change (or fails to cause change). Eliminating, controlling, or managing threats to internal validity increases the chance that the treatment is the legitimate cause of change. By randomizing groups, discouraging diffusion, and standardizing measures, a researcher can maximize a study's internal validity and produce unbiased estimates of the treatment's effect. A researcher-controlled study with a focus on internal validity is described as an *efficacy trial*. In an efficacy trial, the study's purpose is to estimate the treatment's effect; thus, the researcher is interested in participants remaining in the condition to which they were assigned and ensuring that the conditions faithfully represent the two extremes for which they were organized—full exposure to the treatment as intended and no exposure to the treatment (Mowbray et al., 2003). In this context, measures of implementation fidelity represent tools for monitoring and improving adherence to the program's intended use in sites or with units that have low fidelity. When used at sites or with units assigned to the non-treated condition, the same measurement tools can identify instances of treatment diffusion, providing the intervention researcher with information to manage the efficacy trial. Fidelity data can also be used in dosage models as described elsewhere in this book.

External Validity

External validity describes the extent to which the impact for an efficacious program can be realized in larger populations. *Effectiveness trials* are randomized studies that implement an efficacious program "at scale" in authentic settings. The treatment is a "known" quantity; there is prior evidence of its impact from internally valid efficacy studies. The purpose of testing the intervention "at scale" is to determine the extent to which it affects outcomes when used "as implemented" rather than "as intended." Unlike efficacy trials, where dosage is monitored and managed (to the extent possible), effectiveness studies are characterized by no support for implementation beyond the initial training that adopters of the program would receive as part of typical use. In effectiveness trials, fidelity and diffusion are allowed to vary (Mowbray et al., 2003), and this variation can be

modeled to better understand the contexts in which a treatment is more likely to be implemented, the conditions under which a comparably-implemented treatment is likely to have a greater effect, and the settings where a similarly-effective treatment is more effective for some students than others or better implemented by some teachers compared to others.

Potential Outcomes

The Campbell tradition represents an intuitive approach to questions about causality. For intervention researchers working in substantive areas, it provides an informal framework for thinking about research design and the inferences one can make about treatment's causal role in changed outcomes. The potential outcomes framework offers a formal explication of the logic that underlies causal inference-making. It also provides a basis for thinking more broadly and systematically about the nature of causality and the application of research design in educational science. More so than Campbell's approach, potential outcomes offer a way forward for intervention researchers who work in settings or with populations where fully randomized designs are not possible or with randomized data that are compromised due to noncompliance, attrition, or other unforeseen challenges. We briefly describe the paradigm, the assumptions on which it relies, and its implications for treatment fidelity.

As indicated, funders of education research define a treatment effect as the difference in the *potential outcomes for one common set of units under different conditions*. As described above, the fundamental problem with causal inference (Holland, 1986) is that the outcome for an individual can be observed when exposed to treatment *or* that individual's outcome can be observed when not exposed to treatment (or when he or she is exposed to typical practice), but observing both is not possible. In this sense, the potential outcomes approach becomes a missing data problem (e.g. .50 of the required outcomes are missing), and the purpose of research design and data analysis is to replace missing values with reasonable estimates. Randomized designs represent the most reliable means of estimating missing outcomes, for many of the reasons outlined in the discussion of Campbell.[2] Both approaches invoke the notion of exclusion. For Campbell, the idea is to exclude causes of outcomes that represent alternatives to the treatment. A randomized design is more likely than not to yield groups that are comparable in important respects and when the only difference in these otherwise comparable groups is their exposure to treatment, threats to internal validity are excluded. For Rubin, a randomized design yields estimates for outcomes the treated group (or the *common set of units*) would have likely experienced had they not been assigned to participate in the treatment. In this context, a randomized design is a substitute for the contrast on which a fully unbiased effect depends—the outcomes for a common group of participants exposed both to treatment and to comparison at the same point in time. Designs other than randomized assignment may also approximate the fundamental

comparison that underlies potential outcomes. These require relatively strong assumptions, many of which qualify as exclusion restrictions, and we discuss these more fully in a later section. However, before doing so, we introduce these other assignment mechanisms.

Assignment Mechanisms

The randomized design represents only one means *of assigning units to conditions*, and it generally represents the "experimental" design. However, other assignment models have been proposed for situations where random assignment is not possible or where a randomized design is compromised during its implementation. We briefly describe two examples —propensity score matching and instrumental variable models. These are increasingly mentioned in education research and they are illustrated in one or more chapters of this book. Both derive from Rubin's operational framework. They treat potential outcomes as missing data and they apply design and analytic strategies to calculate an average treatment effect. Otherwise, they differ in a number of ways, with their distinguishing feature being the mechanism by which cases are *assigned* to condition.

Propensity score matching separates observed differences into two categories—differences due to participants' characteristics that may influence their likelihood of receiving or participating in a treatment and differences due to the treatment itself. If observed covariates are used to model the first possibility (differences in the probability of being assigned to treatment), the second (differences due to treatment) can be estimated. In a randomized design, the assumption is that all covariates are evenly distributed across the groups. Propensity score matching replicates this balance when randomization is not possible, allowing for causal estimates of effects when using well-populated extant databases that include large numbers of salient covariates. It can also enhance the benefits of an experimental study when factors beyond the investigator's control (i.e. attrition) compromise the design. In Chapter 6, Unlu et al. apply propensity scores to create subgroups of teachers in the comparison condition that are high and low implementers of a literacy initiative. They use known implementation-related values from treatment teachers to identify comparable cases in the comparison group. They compare the utility of a "matching approach" and a "cut off" approach for linking levels of implementation fidelity to student outcomes.

A strong instrument (as in "instrumental variable") is a randomly assigned variable (Z) that has its effect on Y *only* through X. Specifically, it predicts X and it is uncorrelated with errors in the regression of Y on X. Instrumental variables (IV) are common in economics research, where they are sometimes discussed in the context of "natural experiments." They also have a novel application in randomized designs when treatment compliance is imperfect. In this context, the

assignment to condition, versus the receipt or uptake of treatment, represents a strong instrument (Angrist et al., 1996; Heckman & Robb, 1985) because it does not cause outcomes in the absence of X (it is uncorrelated to treatment receipt), but it does predict compliance—presumably, units assigned to the treatment condition are more likely to receive treatment than those assigned to a comparison or to a typical practice condition. *Receiving* a treatment cannot be randomly assigned when noncompliance is possible; in school settings, perfect compliance is an unreasonable expectation because access to and receipt of treatment at the student level often depends on a third party, teachers most commonly. Treatment assignment in a randomized trial provides a powerful instrument for adjusting a treatment effect to account for lack of compliance, including limited access to a school-based, teacher-delivered treatment. In Chapter 5, Keith Zvoch uses assignment to condition as an instrument to estimate the effects of summer school on oral reading fluency.

Estimands

Assignment represents how treatments are assigned to cases. An estimand is the target of inference or the "thing" about which we wish to infer; it is often the effect of the treatment under study. The estimand is not directly observed (per the nature of inference); instead, an estimand is approximated using an estimator that is specific to the assignment mechanism in use. Several estimands are common when working from a potential outcomes perspective. We describe the three most common. First, the *average treatment effect* is the expected gain for a randomly selected unit from the population. Recall that this cannot be known *directly* because we only observe one of two potential outcomes for any given case. It can only be estimated. When data are randomized and when compliance is perfect, the estimator for the average treatment effect is the difference in means for the treatment and comparison groups (or, alternatively, the beta weight for the indicator of treatment status from ordinary least squares regression). As an estimator, it represents an unbiased estimate of the average causal treatment effect assuming that the errors are independent and identically distributed across groups. The variance of the average treatment effect can be calculated as well using the sample variance from the treatment and comparison groups. Variation in this case represents the variety of average treatment effects one would obtain if the experiment were done repeatedly.

When noncompliance occurs in the context of randomized assignment, access to or receipt of treatment is no longer independent of potential outcomes and confounders. For example, in a school context, teachers who implement a new program with very high fidelity often differ from low and non-implementers in other ways (e.g. experience, willingness to consider and adopt new practices, etc.), some of which affect outcomes over and above the effect of treatment itself.

In the presence of noncompliance, a contrast of the means for treatment and comparison no longer estimates the average treatment effect. Instead, it provides an intent-to-treat effect (ITT) which represents the effect of an opportunity to receive or participate in treatment. In essence, ITT is the effect of being assigned to a treatment, regardless of one's participation in, access to, or uptake of the treatment regimen.

The complier average causal effect (CACE), sometimes called the local average treatment effect (LATE), represents the effect of treatment for cases that actually take up the treatment, not just those who were given an opportunity to participate. As with ITT, the receipt of treatment is not independent of potential outcomes; however, assignment to treatment does remain independent. To the extent that random assignment had a positive effect on the probability of receiving treatment, it represents a strong instrument to identify the treatment effect on cases that comply with assignment, as discussed earlier. CACE (as the estimand) can be conceptualized as the ratio of the ITT estimand and the effect of assignment (the instrument) on treatment compliance; as compliance approaches perfection, the CACE and the ITT effects converge. Compliance in IV can be coded categorically (Angrist et al., 1996) into 3 groups. Compliers represent the group that take up or participate in the intervention if assigned to do so or do not take up the intervention if assigned to a comparison group. Never-takers are those that do not take up the treatment regardless of assignment, whereas always-takers take up the intervention independent of assignment. For Campbell, always-takers represent a threat to a study's internal validity (treatment diffusion). Never takers, or non-compliers, can be conceptualized in terms of treatment diffusion, to the extent that typical practice constitutes the non-treated condition and to the extent that typical practice represents a "treatment." In this scenario, never-takers are essentially always-takers of the non-experimental treatment. In either case, they threaten biased estimates of a treatment's effect.

Assumptions

The rigor of a causal inference depends on the mechanism used to assign participants to treatments. Campbell and Rubin agree that random assignment is best in this respect. Campbell argues that random assignment creates comparable groups for purposes of comparison. Rubin argues that it provides the best estimate of the outcomes for the treated group if the group had not, in fact, been treated (i.e. their potential outcomes). However, by characterizing a treatment effect in terms of potential outcomes rather than observed outcomes, Rubin's approach provides a means for describing and defending assignment mechanisms other than randomized designs that support causal inference-making, including strategies that apply to data that is usually described as observational. However, the potential outcomes approach makes several key assumptions.

The stable unit treatment value assumption (Imbens & Rubin, 2015) is paramount in this respect. Generally known by its acronym, SUTVA assumes that there is no interference between common units (Cox, 1958)—a change in the outcome for any given unit (student, teacher, etc.) cannot depend on whether another unit receives the treatment. This means that the value of the outcome for a given unit when exposed to a treatment will be the same regardless of the treatments that other units receive. In this sense, SUTVA represents a type of exclusion restriction, much like Campbell's threats to internal validity. Both seek to exclude causes other than treatment as the mechanism for change. SUTVA also assumes that differences in the approach to assignment do not represent unique treatments. This is a subtle point. In essence, Rubin argues that one's approach to answering a scientific question does not affect the "true" answer (as opposed to a given solution). As an example, he suggests that how a person with a headache decides to take an aspirin (or not to take an aspirin) has no effect on the pain they report under either treatment. Whether the person's decision was based on a coin toss or on simple convenience, the effect of the aspirin will be the same for that individual. How we investigate that effect may vary, and the quality of our inferences about aspirin's effect may fluctuate accordingly, but the true effect of the aspirin for a given individual is independent of our inference-making efforts in that respect. His larger point is that scientific inquiry, while systematic, only approximates the reality of things. Being clear about one's assumptions, regardless of the mechanism, estimand, or estimator in question, are necessary to responsible inquiry. Assumptions should be articulated and caution should be taken.

Final Comments

This section provides a brief summary of what is likely a semester's worth of content on the theoretical underpinnings of modern research design. Readers who desire a more thorough treatment of the topic are encouraged to consult the references for this section or one of many excellent book-length treatments of this topic. The purpose of this primer is to acquaint readers with content that is central to several chapters in this book.

Notes

1 Note that *selection bias* also appears in discussions of survey research and other single-group (or pre-experimental) designs, where it generally refers to choosing a subgroup of cases from a larger group such that the sample (the subgroup) represents the population (the larger group). A random procedure is often useful when addressing this task (e.g. random sampling), but selection bias when sampling from a population differs from selection bias in the context of randomly assigning members of a sample to one or more groups for purposes of controlling selection bias in an experimental context. In an

experimental context, matters related to sampling from a population are often discussed as *sampling bias*, which threatens a study's *external validity* (which is the confidence one can have that an internally valid treatment effect generalizes to the larger group from which the sample was selected) rather than its internal validity. Selection (and selection bias) in the experimental context concerns the creation of two (or more) comparable groups for the purpose of protecting the study's internal validity.

2 Both traditions borrow heavily from the early work by Fischer (1925) on randomization and causality.

References

Angrist, J. D., Imbens, G. W., and Rubin, D. B. (1996). Identification of causal effects using instrumental variables. *Journal of the American Statistical Association*, 91(434), 444–455.

Bellig, A., Borrelli, B., Resnick, B., Hecht, J., Minicucci, D. S., Ory, M., Ogedegbe, G., Orwig, D., Ernst, D., and Czajkowski, S. (2004). Enhancing treatment fidelity in health behavior change studies: Best practices and recommendations from the NIH Behavior Change Consortium. *Health Psychology*, 23(5), 443–451.

Campbell, D. T. and Stanley, J. C. (1966). *Experimental and Quasi-Experimental Designs for Research*. Chicago, IL: Rand McNally.

Cook, T. D. and Campbell, D. T. (1979). *Quasi-Experimentation: Design and Analysis for Field Settings*. Chicago, IL: Rand McNally.

Cordray, D. (2007). Fidelity of intervention implementation. Presentation at The IES Summer Training Institute on Cluster Randomized Control Trials, 17–29 June, Nashville, TN. Available online at https://ies.ed.gov/ncer/whatsnew/conferences/rct_traininginstitute

Cox, D. R. (1958). *Planning of Experiments*. Oxford: Wiley.

Fisher, R. A. (1925). Theory of statistical estimation. *Mathematical Proceedings of the Cambridge Philosophical Society*, 22(5), 700–725.

Heckman, J. J. and Robb, R. (1985). Alternative methods for evaluating the impact of interventions: An overview. *Journal of Econometrics*, 30(1), 239–267.

Holland, D. W. (1986). Statistics and causal inference. *Journal of the American Statistical Association*, 81, 945–960.

Hulleman, C. S. and Cordray, D. S. (2009). Moving from the lab to the field: The role of fidelity and achieved relative intervention strength. *Journal of Research on Educational Effectiveness*, 2, 88–110.

IES (Institute for Educational Sciences) (2014). Available online at https://ies.ed.gov/IES

Imbens, G. and Rubin, D. (2015). *Causal Inference for Statistics, Social, and Biomedical Sciences*. New York: Cambridge University Press.

Lemons, C. J., Fuchs, D., Gilbert, J. K., and Fuchs, L. S. (2014). Evidence-based practices in a changing world: Reconsidering the counterfactual in education research. *Educational Researcher*, 43, 242–252.

Mowbray, C. T., Holter, M. C., Teague, G. B., and Bybee, D. (2003). Fidelity criteria: Development, measurement, and validation. *American Journal of Evaluation*, 24(3), 315–340.

Neyman, J. (1934). On the two different aspects of the representative method: the method of stratified sampling and the method of purposive selection. *Journal of the Royal Statistical Society*, 97(4), 558–625.

NIH (National Institutes of Health) (2015). Available online at http://www.nih.gov

Perepletchikova, F., Hagermoser, S., and Lisa, M. (2014). Assessment of treatment fidelity in psychotherapy research. In T. Kratochwill (Ed.), *Treatment Integrity: A Foundation for Evidence-Based Practice in Applied Psychology*. School Psychology Book Series. Washington, DC: American Psychological Association. 131–157. Available online at DOI.org/10.1037/14275-008

Trochim, W. M. (2000). The research methods knowledge base. Available online at www.anatomyfacts.com/research/researchmethodsknowledgebase.pdf

2

FEATURES OF FIDELITY IN SCHOOLS AND CLASSROOMS

Constructs and Measurement

Frank M. Gresham

The concept of treatment fidelity (integrity) is important across a diversity of fields that are involved with providing treatments or interventions to individuals. In medicine, the concept of treatment compliance or treatment adherence is an important and problematic issue. In the field of nutrition, the concept of dietary adherence is important for successful outcomes. In the fields of rehabilitation and substance abuse, the term program implementation captures the concept of treatment fidelity. Finally, in the field of applied behavior analysis, the concept of procedural reliability is commonly used to refer to treatment fidelity. Despite variations in terminology across these diverse fields, the concern that treatments or interventions are delivered as prescribed or intended is of paramount importance to document that changes in individuals' functioning (medical, nutritional, psychological, or behavioral) are due to treatments and not from uncontrolled, extraneous variables.

Treatment fidelity refers to the methodological strategies used to monitor and improve the reliability and validity of academic and behavioral interventions in schools. From a research methodology standpoint, a fundamental goal is to demonstrate that changes in a dependent variable are due to systematic, manipulated changes in an independent variable and are not due to extraneous variables. An independent variable in this sense means an active, manipulated treatment or instructional variable designed to improve or enhance performance on some meaningful outcome variable. In short, researchers must be able to state that their interventions were implemented as planned or intended and were not modified or otherwise changed substantially by those responsible for implementing the treatment.

From an educational practice standpoint, treatment fidelity is crucial in documenting that changes in academic or social behavior are due to an intervention. For over 10 years, schools have promulgated and increasingly adopted a *response*

to intervention (RTI) model of service delivery (Gresham, 2002; Jimmerson et al., 2007). RTI can be defined as the change in behavior or performance as a function of intervention. An RTI approach uses students' lack of response to an evidence-based intervention that is implemented with *fidelity* as the basis for intensifying, modifying, or changing an intervention. Obviously, one cannot unequivocally conclude that changes in students' behavior or performance were due to an intervention without in some way documenting that the intervention was implemented as planned or intended.

The purpose of the present chapter is to discuss the concept of treatment fidelity within the context of evidence-based interventions. Various methods of measuring treatment fidelity are described and evaluated. The chapter concludes with a discussion of various threats to valid inference making within the context of evidence-based interventions.

A number of task forces within education and psychology have called for an increasing emphasis on treatment fidelity. For example, the Task Force on Evidence-Based Practice in Special Education of the Council for Exceptional Children stated that the integrity of intervention implementation is critical in single-case designs because the independent variable is implemented continuously over time (Horner et al., 2005). Similarly, other task forces within the American Psychological Association on evidence-based treatments such as Divisions 12 (clinical psychology), 16 (school psychology), 17 (counseling psychology), 53 (clinical child and adolescent psychology), and 54 (pediatric psychology) have called for the assessment and monitoring of treatment fidelity. Furthermore, researchers who submit efficacy grants to the Institute of Educational Sciences (IES) using randomized control trials or single case experimental designs now must describe how treatment fidelity will be measured, frequency of assessments, and what degree of variation in treatment fidelity will be accepted over the course of the study (IES, 2012). These recommendations have also been made by the National Institutes of Health (NIH, 2015). Specifically, the NIH Behavior Change Consortium recommended that treatments be monitored and reported and that treatment agents be trained and supervised in the delivery of treatments (Bellg et al., 2004).

Dimensions of Treatment Fidelity

The treatment fidelity concept is presently conceptualized as a multidimensional construct rather than earlier unidimensional conceptualizations that considered it to only adhere to an established treatment protocol (Gresham, 1989; Peterson et al., 1982). *Treatment adherence* reflects a quantitative dimension of treatment fidelity because it can be measured in terms of the number or percentage of critical treatment components that are implemented over the course of a particular treatment. Treatment adherence can be conceptualized as the *accuracy* and *consistency* with which a treatment is implemented over time. In this conceptualization,

there are two aspects of treatment adherence: First, treatment component adherence, and second, session/daily adherence. Table 2.1 illustrates an example of how one might present data on these two dimensions of treatment adherence for a Good Behavior Game intervention implemented each school day for one week. As can been seen in Table 2.1, the average daily adherence to the intervention was 72.5% but the average component integrity was only 58.75%. Two components had 60% integrity (reminding students of the game, rules, and consequences, and verbally acknowledging rule violations). One component had only 40% integrity (immediately resuming teaching after rule violations) and another component had only 20% integrity (providing verbal praise for acceptable behavior).

Table 2.1 allows one to assess two dimensions of treatment adherence (daily adherence and component adherence). It should be noted that each of the eight components of the Good Behavior Game are assumed to be *equally weighted* which may not be true in terms of any given component's importance in creating behavior change. Presently, we do not have an adequate knowledge base to know how components in any treatment should be weighted and thus we are forced to equally weight each component of a given treatment.

Recently, other dimensions of treatment integrity have been discussed in the literature: *interventionist competence* and *treatment differentiation* (Nezu & Nezu, 2008; Perepletchikova et al., 2007). Interventionist competence refers to the skills and

TABLE 2.1 Treatment Adherence for Good Behavior Game Implemented 5 Days per Week

	Day					
Component	*Monday*	*Tuesday*	*Wednesday*	*Thursday*	*Friday*	*%*
Classroom rules posted	Y	Y	Y	Y	Y	100
Teams are posted	Y	Y	Y	Y	Y	100
Teacher reminds students of game, rules, and consequences	Y	Y	N	Y	N	60
Teacher verbally acknowledges rule violations	N	Y	N	Y	Y	60
Teacher tracks rule violations on scoreboard	Y	Y	Y	Y	Y	100
Teacher immediately resumes teaching after each rule violation	Y	N	N	N	Y	40
Teacher provides verbal praise for acceptable behavior	N	N	Y	N	N	20
Teacher provides reward to team with 5 or fewer marks	Y	Y	Y	Y	Y	100
	75%	75%	62.5%	75%	75%	
Daily Fidelity: 72.5%	Component Fidelity: 58.75%			Overall Fidelity: 65.63%		

experience of the interventionist in delivering the treatment. Competence might be best conceptualized as a qualitative dimension of treatment fidelity because it reflects judgments of how well a treatment is delivered. Treatment differentiation represents theoretical distinctions between different aspects of two or more treatments and how those theoretical differences are represented in treatment delivery. For example, social learning theory posits that observational learning or viewing an adaptive response in the presence of anxiety-provoking stimuli might reduce an anxiety response. A common technique based on social learning theory is coping modeling, in which the model initially demonstrates an anxiety response and then gradually becomes more comfortable in the presence of anxiety-provoking stimuli.

In contrast, cognitive behavior theory hypothesizes that the mechanism accounting for the reduction of anxiety is how an individual perceives or thinks about anxiety-provoking situations and responses. A common technique in cognitive behavior therapy is to challenge thoughts that magnify negative outcomes related to these situations and to replace them with more effective, realistic thoughts. A third approach to the treatment of anxiety is based on the respondent or classical conditioning theory of anxiety maintenance. In this model, it is assumed that escape from anxiety-provoking stimuli serves to maintain the anxiety response. Treatment for anxiety is typically based on *exposure* to anxiety-provoking stimuli and preventing the individual from escaping these stimuli. Based on the respondent conditioning model, this should result in extinction of the anxiety response due to respondent extinction.

Treatment differentiation involves a process whereby treatments being used differ from each other along critical dimensions (Perepletchikova, 2014). In my example for the three different treatments for anxiety, one would have to differentiate procedures unique to social learning theory from those unique to cognitive behavior theory from those unique to the respondent conditioning model. In practice, this may be difficult to do because it is likely that a cognitive behavior therapist might use some procedures from social learning theory and respondent conditioning and vice versa. Waltz et al. (1993) suggested that treatment adherence and treatment differentiation are closely related because measure of treatment adherence may be sufficient to determine whether treatments are distinct from one another.

Distinguishing between treatment adherence and interventionist competence can be confusing because competence presupposes adherence, but adherence does not presuppose competence. One may adhere to a treatment with perfect adherence but do so in an incompetent manner. For example, a classroom teacher might be instructed to deliver contingent praise for appropriate classroom behavior in an intervention using differential reinforcement of alternative behavior (DRA). This teacher may do this with perfect adherence, but do so with poor, insincere quality that is not reinforcing to the student. A breakdown in treatment fidelity in this case would suggest training, practice, and feedback to ensure a more competent

delivery of the treatment. This breakdown in treatment adherence would require performance feedback and training in implementing key components of a treatment plan (Noell & Gansle, 2014).

An additional dimension of treatment fidelity is *treatment receipt* (Bellg et al., 2004). Treatment receipt can be conceptualized by exposure/dose of the treatment, participant comprehension of the treatment, and participant responsiveness to the treatment. Exposure or dose of a treatment refers to the amount of treatment received by the participant. For example, "dose" of a treatment might be the number of times per day or week the participant is exposed to the treatment. Exposure to a treatment can also be conceptualized as the *duration* of a treatment regimen for a particular problem. Some problems might require only three weeks of exposure to a treatment, whereas other problems might require a considerably longer time to remediate the problem (10–15 weeks). Participant comprehension refers to the degree to which a participant understands or comprehends the content of a treatment. For example, a teacher's understanding of the difference between attention-maintained and escape-maintained behaviors would constitute participant comprehension. Participant responsiveness refers to the extent to which a participant is engaged in a treatment and finds it relevant.

Measurement Issues in Treatment Fidelity

A continuing and unresolved issue in treatment fidelity research and practice is the accurate assessment and measurement of the treatment fidelity construct. There have been minimal developments in designing feasible and efficient treatment fidelity assessments that have acceptable psychometric qualities (Sanetti & Kratochwill, 2009). Assessment of the treatment adherence dimension of treatment fidelity requires that treatment components be objectively specified and measured. Measurement issues in treatment fidelity can be conceptualized in terms of classical test theory in which components can be viewed much like items on a test or scale. The degree to which each component of the treatment is implemented can be thought of as the reliability or consistency with which a component is implemented over the course of a treatment. This can be viewed as the stability of each component's implementation over time, much like test-retest reliability.

Some researchers have suggested that the reliability of treatment fidelity measures could be evaluated using internal consistency indices such as coefficient alpha, item-total correlation, and/or factor analysis (Schulte et al., 2009; Sheridan et al., 2009). This is a dubious recommendation for establishing the reliability of treatment adherence measures. There is little or no evidence that would indicate that the various components of a treatment should correlate with each other (i.e. the "internal consistency" of the treatment). Consider the eight components of the Good Behavior Game intervention presented in Table 2.1. There is little reason to believe that Step 1 (Classroom rules posted) should correlate with Step 7 (Teacher provides verbal praise for acceptable behavior),

and it is doubtful that each step of the intervention should correlate with the intervention's total score, such as would be done in calculating item-total correlations. Moreover, a factor analysis of these eight components would probably yield a single factor that might be labeled total treatment fidelity, which would be meaningless in a psychometric sense. Baer (1977) made a similar argument in commenting on the reliability of direct observations of behavior using interval-based recording procedures.

Perhaps a more useful and relevant psychometric principle in evaluating treatment fidelity is the concept of measurement *accuracy*. Measurement accuracy can be defined as the degree to which any given measurement reflects the correspondence between measured behavior and the true value of that behavior (Cone, 1988). The requirement for establishing accuracy is the existence of an incontrovertible index or standard against which measures of behavior can be compared. If the "true" value of behavior is known, then different methods for measuring that behavior can be compared.

Specifying treatment components in standard and absolute terms and computing percent accuracy can establish the accuracy of any assessment method. Peterson et al. (1982) suggested that the true value of a dependent variable (target behavior) in nature is not possible because some portion of the variability in a dependent variable may be influenced by fluctuations in functional relationships between unmeasured and unknown environmental events. As such, the true value of a dependent variable cannot be known a priori.

In contrast, the "true" value of an independent variable (i.e. the treatment) in nature can be operationally defined as the value specified by the researcher and thus can be known a priori. The extent to which implementation of the independent variable matches or approximates this pre-specified value corresponds to its accuracy of implementation. Accuracy can be computed across different observers over time, using different assessment methods in research and practical applications of treatment fidelity assessments.

It appears that the field needs to develop a science of treatment fidelity assessment using a series of studies that use multiple methods of fidelity assessment across multiple interventions. This would indicate that the convergent validity of these assessment methods should be assessed using direct observations, self-reports, permanent products, and interventionist interviews. Currently, there is no systematic program of research on this topic and the field of intervention science would benefit greatly from this line of research.

Methods of Treatment Fidelity Assessment

Treatment fidelity can be assessed using either direct or indirect assessment methods. The distinction between direct and indirect assessment methods is based on the extent to which treatment fidelity is being measured at the *time* and *place* of the actual implementation of a treatment. As such, a direct assessment of treatment

fidelity is based on direct observation of a treatment as it is being implemented. An indirect assessment of treatment fidelity would be based on an assessment of the fidelity of a treatment *after* its actual implementation. There are advantages and disadvantages of using either direct or indirect methods of treatment fidelity assessment.

Direct Assessment

Direct assessment of treatment fidelity is identical to the systematic observation of behavior in applied settings. Several considerations should be entertained in the selection and design of direct observation systems, such as the content of the observations, the number of treatment components observed, the number of times fidelity will be observed, and the quality of the data produced by the observations.

The goal of any direct observation assessment is to generate data that accurately represent the behaviors of interest. Content validity is the most important type of validity for direct observation assessment. Representativeness of observational data depends on both the number of observation sessions (content sampling) and the length of each observation session. Generally speaking, the greater amount of data collected on representative behaviors, the more representative the data will be of the content domain.

There has been surprisingly little research attention that has been devoted to the question of the amount of direct observation data that is required to produce a representative sample of treatment fidelity. Researchers and practitioners do not know how to produce a representative sample of treatment fidelity because they do not know how many times per day, how long, or over how many days one must observe to produce a representative picture of the level of treatment fidelity with which a treatment is being implemented. A potentially valuable approach to determine the representativeness of fidelity data would be to conduct studies using the logic of Generalizability Theory (G Theory) (Cronbach et al., 1972). G Theory is concerned with the dependability of behavioral measures and the accuracy of generalizing from an observed score to the average score that could be obtained under all possible conditions of measurement. Unlike classical test theory, G Theory can simultaneously evaluate multiple sources of error, called *facets*, in any given measurement.

A generalizability study of treatment fidelity could evaluate multiple facets that influence treatment fidelity, such as number of times per day it is assessed, duration of a treatment, number of days in a treatment, and the setting in which treatment takes place. These facets were evaluated in a study by Hintz and Matthews (2004) and showed that an unacceptably high number of observations are required to obtain a dependable result. This methodology has been applied to various behavioral assessment methods including systematic direct observations (Hintze & Matthews, 2004), direct behavior ratings (Chafouleas et al., 2007), and behavior rating scales (Bergeron et al., 2008).

Threats to Reliability of Fidelity Measurement

An informative way of conceptualizing various threats to the measurement of treatment fidelity is to use Kazdin's (1977) conceptualization of reliability using direct observations of a dependent variable. Although Kazdin's article focused on threats to the measurement of a dependent variable, these same threats apply to the measurement of an independent variable (i.e. the treatment). One major threat in the measurement of an independent variable is *reactivity* of observations; that is, an interventionist is usually aware that they are being observed while implementing a treatment. As such, the interventionist may deliver the treatment with better integrity than would be the case if they were not being observed. Knowledge of being observed while implementing a treatment affects the reliability of direct observations of treatment fidelity. Peterson et al. (1982) recommended that fidelity assessments be spot checked on a random schedule to correct, in part, to reduce this reactivity effect.

Another threat to the reliability of fidelity measurement is *interventionist drift* that reflects the fact that interventionists sometimes "drift" away from the original treatment protocol. For numerous reasons, interventionists change the way in which they apply a given treatment over time. If uncorrected, the treatment may bear little correspondence to the planned or intended treatment. Periodically debriefing interventionists and providing performance feedback is one way to prevent drift (see Noell & Gansle, 2014).

Another threat to the reliability of fidelity measurement is the *complexity* of a given treatment. Treatments that are complex, contain numerous steps, and are difficult to implement may threaten the reliability of treatment implementation. One way of ensuring greater reliability of treatment fidelity is to design treatments with a minimal number of steps and still maintain effectiveness. It is likely that simpler treatments are implemented with greater reliability than more complex treatments.

A final threat to the reliability of treatment fidelity is *interventionist expectancies* and *feedback*. Several studies from the treatment acceptability literature indicate that teachers who expect a treatment to be effective are more likely to implement that treatment with better integrity than teachers that have lower expectancies of treatment effectiveness (Elliott, 1988). A systematic line of research also has shown that interventionists who are provided with consistent, specific performance feedback on their implementation of treatments had much greater integrity than when not provided with this feedback (Burns et al., 2008; Duhon et al., 2009; Noell et al., 1997; Witt et al., 1997). Research has consistently demonstrated that performance feedback that includes a review of graphic presentation of implementation data has sustained higher levels of treatment fidelity (see review by Noell & Gansle, 2014).

Treatment Fidelity and Threats to Valid Inference Making

Threats to drawing valid inferences in behavioral research can be created by the failure to ensure the fidelity with which those treatments are delivered

(Gresham, 1997; Moncher & Prinz, 1991; Shadish et al., 2002). Experimental research attempts to isolate and measure the effects of independent variables on dependent variables. Failure to control extraneous factors operating in the experimental situation prevents definitive conclusions from being drawn regarding the effects of independent variables. The extent to which any given research design is successful in ruling out plausible rival hypotheses is not absolute but rather of degree. Four types of validity are usually considered: internal validity, external validity, construct validity, and statistical conclusion validity.

Internal validity describes the extent to which changes in a dependent variable can be unequivocally attributed to systematic, manipulated changes in an independent variable. Internally valid experiments allow the researcher to rule out alternative explanations for obtained results. If significant behavior change occurs as reflected in the dependent variable and if no data concerning the accuracy or degree to which the independent variable was implemented are presented, the internal validity of the experiment is compromised. In a similar vein, if significant changes in a dependent variable do not occur and if treatment integrity is not monitored, differentiating between an ineffective treatment and a potentially effective treatment implemented with poor integrity is impossible (Gresham, 1989). Alterations, changes, or deviations from an established treatment protocol have been called therapist drift, discussed earlier in this chapter. Therapist drift may produce positive effects, negative effects, or no effects at all; however, unless treatment fidelity is monitored and measured, such drift precludes definitive conclusions regarding what may have been responsible for treatment outcomes.

External validity refers to the inferences about the extent to which a causal relationship can be generalized over variations in settings, individuals, treatments, treatment agents, and outcomes (Shadish et al., 2002). Poorly defined, inadequately described, and idiosyncratically implemented treatments make replication and evaluation of treatments difficult (Moncher & Prinz, 1991). The absence of information concerning treatment definition and fidelity limits the generalizability of treatments across settings, situations, participants, and treatment implementers (Kazdin, 1992).

Construct validity describes explanations of the causal relation between independent and dependent variables (Shadish et al., 2002). Whereas internal validity involves the demonstration that an independent variable was responsible for changes in a dependent variable, construct validity deals with the interpretation or explanation of the causal relation. Construct validity is close to the statistical concept of *mediation*, which describes the manner or the mechanism by which an independent variable produces a given effect (Baron & Kenny, 1986).

An intervention designed to improve reading comprehension provides a useful illustration. Suppose a practitioner implements a cognitive strategy intervention and hypothesizes that this intervention would improve the student's working memory and thus improve reading comprehension. Treatment fidelity data

might reveal that the treatment actually involved teaching the student an explicit problem-solving strategy, with mastery teaching of each step in the strategy and specific correction procedures for student errors (i.e. direct instruction). The manner in which this intervention was carried out is more consistent with a direct instruction causal explanation that, with a cognitive strategy explanation, aimed at enhancing working memory. The failure to present treatment fidelity data in this case would prevent an interventionist from reaching this conclusion.

Statistical conclusion validity describes those aspects of the quantitative evaluation of a study that influence the conclusions drawn about the effect of independent variables (Shadish et al., 2002). One threat to statistical conclusion validity is the variability with which treatments are implemented. For instance, in an investigation comparing Treatment A with Treatment B, a researcher would like to conclude that differences between these two treatments were due to true differences between these two treatments and not to extraneous factors. In calculating an effect size, the denominator includes a measure of variability that is operationalized as the standard deviation. Whatever differences exist between the effects of Treatment A and those of Treatment B are, in part, a function of the variability in the experiment. This variability may be due to within-group differences of participants in the two treatments, random variability of dependent measures, and/or differences in how the experimenter implemented the two treatments (i.e. treatment fidelity differences). Inconsistent application of or deviations in how treatments are implemented can increase the variability in an experiment. Increased variability can result in lower effect sizes and thereby create a threat to statistical conclusion validity of a study.

Summary

Some investigators might argue that the imprecise application of treatments does not pose threats to the validity of conclusions that might be drawn about the relationship between independent and dependent variables. These investigators may maintain that changes in the dependent variable imply the stable and accurate application of the independent variable. This assumption is not justified because changes in the dependent variable could be due to some unrecognized and unmeasured collection of "third variables" or to modifications in treatment protocols that went undetected.

Some researchers might also argue that explicit assessment and demonstration of treatment fidelity is not a necessary condition for intervention research because errors in experimental control are protected by replications within and across participants in experimental research, particularly in single-case design research. Johnston and Pennypacker (1993: 266–267) noted,

> Merely replicating control and experimental conditions (and reproducing their effects), regardless of their similarity to the original version,

provides only very indirect and tenuous support for the influence of the independent variable. Direct and convincing evidence can only be obtained by conducting manipulations that clearly rule out all possible extraneous factors, while identifying the necessity of the variables constituting the independent variable.

This same advice holds true to researchers using group experimental designs as well. One cannot make a causal inference with direct and unequivocal evidence that an intervention has been implemented as intended.

Factors Related to Treatment Fidelity

Historically, the emergence of treatment fidelity can be traced to an influential paper by Yeaton and Sechrest (1981). This paper provided a clear conceptualization of treatment fidelity, in which several key issues involved in its definition, measurement, and evaluation were detailed. These authors hypothesized reciprocal relationships among the strength, integrity, and effectiveness of treatments. In this conceptualization, the strength of treatments implemented with poor integrity is decreased because active treatment ingredients are diluted and the effectiveness of those treatments is reduced. Treatment integrity is important for evaluating the strength and effectiveness of treatments for different behaviors, in different settings, for different individuals, and across different treatment implementers.

On the basis of a logical and intuitive analysis, Gresham (1989, 1997) identified several factors or variables that might be related to treatment fidelity. These variables can be classified into two categories: (1) variables related to the intervention and (2) variables related to the interventionist.

Variables Related to the Intervention

Three variables are related to an intervention: (a) complexity of the intervention, (b) materials/resources required to implement the intervention, and (c) ease of implementation of the intervention. The complexity of a treatment is directly related to the degree of treatment fidelity (Yeaton & Sechrest, 1981). Wolf (1978) suggested that the failure to replicate the effects of the achievement place model (a behavioral intervention for delinquent youth) was due to a lack of treatment fidelity. The achievement place model is a highly complex token economy system of behavior change requiring consistent and systematic application of numerous behavioral principles. Similar problems have been noted with the correct application of the direct instruction model (an intervention for academic skills). Becker and Carnine (1980) noted difficulties with maintaining high levels of treatment fidelity using the direct instruction model. Generally speaking, the more complex the treatment, the lower the fidelity of the implementation of that

treatment will be. This is particularly problematic in treatments implemented by third parties (teachers and parents). Without frequent checks on the fidelity of treatments implemented by third parties, one must tenuously assume the treatment was implemented as planned.

Treatments that require additional materials and resources beyond those commonly found in school, home, or community settings are likely to be implemented with poorer integrity than are treatments requiring no special resources. Many treatments require equipment and resources that are either expensive or difficult to access. For example, functional magnetic resonance imaging (FMRI) has been used in reading research to track changes in brain function of individuals undergoing intensive remedial reading interventions (Shaywitz, 1996). FMRI equipment is exorbitantly expensive, not commonly available, and requires highly trained personnel to operate and interpret.

Researchers and practitioners designing treatments requiring specialized resources and materials are likely to experience problems in establishing and maintaining adequate levels of treatment fidelity. The use of expensive reinforcers (rewards), substantial changes in environmental ecologies, technical equipment, and unusual privileges not readily available in most environments is likely to result in lower levels of treatment fidelity. At the same time, however, this same equipment and supplies may be required to produce treatments of sufficient strength to change certain problem behaviors.

The relative ease with which a given treatment can be implemented can affect the fidelity of that intervention. That is, interventions requiring a high degree of response effort in their implementation are likely to be implemented with poorer fidelity. For example, restitutional overcorrection is sometimes used to decrease the frequency of undesirable behaviors. Restitutional overcorrection involves having an individual repair the damage or return the environment to its original state and subsequently engage in behaviors to bring the environment to a condition vastly better than it was prior to misbehavior. Restitutional overcorrection requires an extremely high degree of response effort (i.e. physical guidance through the process is often necessary) and this often results in lapses in treatment fidelity (Azrin & Besalel, 1999). Compare the response efforts required for implementing restitutional overcorrection versus differential reinforcement of alternative behaviors (DRA) interventions. Clearly, a DRA intervention requires much less response effort than overcorrection and is likely to be implemented with greater fidelity because it does not involve a physical-guidance component.

Variables Related to the Interventionist

Treatments requiring more than one treatment agent may be implemented with lower integrity than treatments requiring only one treatment agent. Generally speaking, treatments requiring more than one treatment agent are likely to be more

complex and have more "moving parts" to keep up with than single treatment agent treatments. A good example of this type of treatment is Multisystemic Family Therapy (MST) that addresses five major categories of interventions: family interventions, peer interventions, school interventions, individually oriented interventions, and psychiatric interventions (Henggler et al., 1996). Maintenance of treatment fidelity is critical for MST to produce beneficial outcomes. This program emphasizes the promotion of high levels of treatment fidelity to achieve desired outcomes. Treatment fidelity is ensured by a 5-day overview of the MST model, participation in weekly group supervision meetings, weekly consultation with MST consultants, and quarterly on-site consultant booster sessions. Without this intense level of fidelity monitoring, it is unlikely that the MST program would have adequate treatment fidelity.

Treatments that are perceived by treatment consumers or treatment agents to be effective may be implemented with greater integrity than treatments perceived to be ineffective. Some researchers have suggested that treatment fidelity is the central element linking the acceptability and use of treatments (Witt & Elliott, 1985; Yeaton & Sechrest, 1981). This is based on the assumption that acceptable treatments are more likely to be implemented with greater fidelity than less acceptable treatments. In turn, these treatments are more likely to be effective in changing behavior. Perceived effectiveness or the degree to which treatment agents are presented with positive outcome information on treatments has been shown to influence treatment acceptability ratings by teachers (Von Brock & Elliott, 1987). Additionally, treatments that produce rapid behavior change may be continued with even greater fidelity than slower acting treatments. That is, the fidelity of a treatment may be reinforced and maintained by the immediacy of behavior change (Gresham, 1997).

There is little empirical research addressing the relationship between treatment effectiveness (perceived and actual) and treatment fidelity. Currently, we lack knowledge of which treatments are more effective with what behaviors and how this effectiveness data moderates or mediates the subsequent fidelity of treatments. This represents a fruitful avenue for future research.

The motivation of treatment agents to invest their efforts into a behavior change treatment may impact the fidelity with which that treatment will be implemented. Teachers may request consultation in designing an intervention plan to improve academic performance in the classroom. Their real motivation, however, may be to have the child tested for special education and removed from the classroom rather than implement an intervention plan with fidelity to improve academic performance. Parents may verbally commit to an intervention plan that involves parent training sessions and implementation of behavioral techniques to change noncompliant behavior. In some cases, there may be little correspondence between what parents say they will do and what actually gets done. The lack of motivation on the part of parents may cause serious threats to the fidelity of parent training interventions.

Conclusions and Recommendations

One unresolved issue in the treatment fidelity literature is determining the extent to which each component of a treatment should be weighted. Clearly, all treatment components are not equally important, with some being crucial for effectiveness and others being somewhat less important. Given this state of affairs, it would appear that rigid adherence to a treatment protocol may not necessarily be required or desirable. There is probably a ceiling effect above which treatment fidelity improvement may not be necessary or cost beneficial. The problem the field faces in this respect is that we do not know what level of fidelity is necessary with what treatments in order to produce beneficial outcomes. We also do not know how far we might drift away from a treatment protocol and still have positive effects.

It would seem to be the case that the level of adherence to treatment protocols depends on the type of research study being conducted. Rather stringent adherence to a treatment protocol would be required for *efficacy studies* because these studies seek to establish intervention effects under tightly controlled conditions (i.e. under conditions of high internal validity). It also seems reasonable that less rigid adherence to treatment protocols would be required for *effectiveness studies* because these studies seek to establish intervention effects under less controlled conditions (i.e. under conditions of high external validity). There are a number of examples in the psychotherapy literature with children and adolescents where researchers have recommended flexibility in delivery of treatment protocols (Henggeler & Lee, 2003; Kazdin, 2003; Kendall et al., 2003). Interventions designed and delivered via the consultation process do not have similar evidence regarding flexibility in the delivery of treatments.

There is not a reliable database to guide researchers and practitioners in deciding the optimal levels of treatment fidelity for different treatments. For some problems, treatment fidelity of 70% might be sufficient. For other problems, 90% or greater treatment fidelity might be required. A potentially useful avenue for future research is based on the notion of *treatment effect norms*. A treatment effect norm refers to the average outcomes of a given intervention or family of interventions whose purpose is to alleviate a problem. Meta-analysis has been used extensively as a means of quantifying what effects, on average, might be produced with what interventions, with which clients, and under what conditions.

In a similar vein, one could establish and catalog *treatment integrity effect norms* by quantifying what levels of treatment integrity, measured by what methods, with what intervention procedures, produce what level of treatment outcomes. For instance, in using the Good Behavior Game as a Tier 1 intervention, we might find that, on average, 80% integrity as measured by direct observations is required to produce socially valid reductions in disruptive behavior measured by direct observations. It might be that lower levels of treatment integrity using this intervention do not produce socially valid effects. Similar treatment integrity effect

norms could be established across multiple tiers on interventions. This endeavor would perhaps require collaboration across multiple sites to build a sufficient database for the construction of these norms.

The failure to define and measure the degree to which treatments are implemented as planned or intended compromises the development and progression of the science of evidence-based interventions. The importance of treatment fidelity spans multiple fields of endeavor involving the provision of treatment services to individuals, including medicine, education, psychotherapy, and applied behavior analysis. Experiments conducted in the laboratory can easily control sources of extraneous influence that affect the phenomenon of interest. In applied settings, controlling all possible sources of extraneous influence affecting the phenomenon of interest can be difficult. One thing that can and should be controlled is the fidelity with which any given treatment is implemented.

References

Baer, D. (1977). Reviewer's comment: Just because it's reliable doesn't mean you can use it. *Journal of Applied Behavior Analysis*, 10, 117–120.

Baron, R. and Kenny, D. (1986). The moderator-mediator distinction in social psychological research: Conceptual, strategic, and statistical considerations. *Journal of Personality and Social Psychology*, 51, 1173–1182.

Becker, W. and Carnine, D. (1981). Direct instruction: A behavior therapy model for comprehensive educational intervention with the disadvantaged. In S. Bijou and R. Ruiz (Eds.), *Behavior Modification Contributions to Education*. Hillsdale, NJ: Erlbaum. 145–210.

Bellg, A., Borelli, B., Resnick, B., Hecht, J., Minicucci, D., Ory, M., and Czajkowski, S. (2004). Enhancing treatment fidelity in health behavior change studies: Best practices and recommendations from the NIH Behavior Change Consortium. *Health Psychology*, 23, 443–451.

Bergeron, R., Floyd, R., McCormack, A., and Farmer, W. (2008). The generalizability of externalizing behavior composites and subscale scores across time, rater, and instrument. *School Psychology Review*, 37, 91–108.

Burns, M., Peters, R., and Noell, G. (2008). Using performance feedback to enhance implementation fidelity of the problem-solving team process. *Journal of School Psychology*, 46, 537–550.

Chafouleas, S., Christ, T., Riley-Tilman, C., Briesch, A., and Chanese, J. (2007). Generalizability and dependability of direct behavior ratings to assess social behavior of preschoolers. *School Psychology Review*, 36, 63–79.

Cone, J. (1988). Psychometric considerations and the multiple models of behavioral assessment. In A. Bellack and M. Hersen (Eds.), *Behavioral Assessment: A Practical Handbook*. New York: Pergamon. 42–66.

Cronbach, L., Gleser, C., Nanda, H., and Rajaratnam, N. (1972). *The Dependability of Behavioral Measures*. New York: Wiley.

Duhon, G., Mesmer, E., Gregerson, L., and Witt, J. (2009). Effects of public feedback during RTI team meetings on teacher implementation integrity and student academic performance. *Journal of School Psychology*, 47, 19–37.

Elliott, S. N. (1988). Acceptability of behavioral treatments in educational settings. In J. Witt, F. Gresham, and S. Elliott (Eds.), *Handbook of Behavior Therapy in Education*. New York: Plenum. 121–150.

Gresham, F. M. (1989). Assessment of treatment integrity in school consultation and prereferral intervention. *School Psychology Review*, 18, 37–50.

Gresham, F. M. (1997). Treatment integrity in single-subject research. In R. Franklin, D. Allison, and B. Gorman (Eds.), *Design and Analysis of Single-Case Research*. Mahwah, NJ: Erlbaum. 93–117.

Gresham, F. M. (2002). Responsiveness to intervention: An alternative approach to the identification of learning disabilities. In R. Bradley, L. Danielson, and D. Hallahan (Eds.), *Learning Disabilities: Research to Practice*. Mahwah, NJ: Erlbaum. 467–519.

Henggeler, S. and Lee, T. (2003). Multisystemic treatment of serious clinical problems. In A. Kazdin and J. Weisz (Eds.), *Evidence-Based Psychotherapies for Children and Adolescents*. New York: Guilford. 301–324.

Henggeler, S., Pickrel, S. Brondino, M., and Crouch, J. (1996). Eliminating treatment dropout of substance abusing or dependent delinquents through home-based multisystemic therapy. *American Journal of Psychiatry*, 153, 427–428.

Hintze, J. and Matthews, W. (2004). The generalizability of systematic direct observations across time and setting: A preliminary investigation of the psychometrics of behavioral assessment. *School Psychology Review*, 33, 258–270.

Horner, R., Carr, E., Halle, J., McGee, G., Odom, S., and Wolery, M. (2005). The use of single-case research to identify evidence-based practice in special education. *Exceptional Children*, 71, 165–179.

IES (Institute of Educational Sciences) (2012). Requests for Applications: Special Education Grants (CFDA No. 84-324A). Washington, DC: US Department of Education.

Jimmerson, S., Burns, M., and VanDerHeyden, A. (Eds.) (2007). *Handbook of Response to Intervention: The Science and Practice of Assessment and Intervention*. New York: Springer.

Johnston, J. and Pennypacker, H. (1993). *Strategies and Tactics of Behavioral Research* (2nd edition). Hillsdale, NJ: Erlbaum.

Kazdin, A. (1977). Artifact, bias, and complexity of assessments: The ABCs of reliability. *Journal of Applied Behavior Analysis*, 10, 141–150.

Kazdin, A. (2003). Problem-solving skills training and parent management training for conduct disorder. In A. Kazdin and J. Weisz (Eds.), *Evidence-Based Psychotherapies for Children and Adolescents*. New York: Guilford. 241–262.

Kendall, P., Aschenbrand, S., and Hudson, J. (2003). Child-focused treatment of anxiety. In A. Kazdin and J. Weisz (Eds.), *Evidence-Based Psychotherapies for Children and Adolescents*. New York: Guilford. 81–100.

Moncher, F. and Prinz, R. (1991). Treatment fidelity in outcome studies. *Clinical Psychology Review*, 11, 247–266.

Nezu, A. and Nezu, C. (2008). Treatment integrity. In D. McKay (Ed.), *Handbook of Research Methods in Abnormal and Clinical Psychology*. Thousand Oaks, CA: Sage. 351–366.

NIH (National Institutes of Health) (2015). Available online at http://www.nih.gov

Noell, G. and Gansle, K. (2014). The use of performance feedback to improve intervention implementation in schools. In L. Sanetti and T. Kratochwill (Eds.), *Treatment Integrity: A Foundation for Evidence-Based Practice in Applied Psychology*. Washington, DC: American Psychological Association. 161–184.

Noell, G., Witt, J., Gilbertson, D., Ranier, D., and Freeland, J. (1997). Increasing teacher intervention implementation in general education following consultation and performance feedback. *School Psychology Quarterly*, 12, 77–88.

Perepletchikova, F. (2014). Assessment of treatment integrity in psychotherapy research. In L. Sanetti and T. Kratochwill (Eds.), *Treatment Integrity: A Foundation for Evidence-Based Practice in Applied Psychology*. Washington, DC: American Psychological Association. 131–158.

Perepletchikova, F., Treat, T., and Kazdin, A. (2007). Treatment integrity in psychotherapy research: Analysis of studies and examination of associated factors. *Journal of Consulting and Clinical Psychology*, 75, 829–841.

Peterson, L., Homer, A., and Wonderlich, S. (1982). The integrity of independent variables in behavior analysis. *Journal of Applied Behavior Analysis*, 15, 477–492.

Sanetti, L. and Kratochwill, T. (2009). Toward developing a science of treatment integrity: Introduction to the special series. *School Psychology Review*, 38, 445–459.

Schulte, A., Eaton, J., and Parker, J. (2009). Advances in treatment integrity research: Multidisciplinary perspectives on the conceptualization, measurement, and enhancement of treatment integrity. *School Psychology Review*, 38, 460–475.

Shadish, W., Cook, T., and Campbell, D. (2002). *Experimental and Quasi-Experimental Designs for Generalized Causal Inference*. New York: Houghton–Mifflin.

Shaywitz, S. (1996). Dyslexia. *Scientific American*, 275, 98–104.

Sheridan, S., Swanger-Gagne, M., Welch, G., Kwon, K., and Garbacz, S. (2009). Fidelity measurement in consultation: Psychometric issues and preliminary examination. *School Psychology Review*, 38, 476–495.

Von Brock, M. and Elliott, S. N. (1987). The influence of treatment effectiveness information on the acceptability of classroom interventions. *Journal of School Psychology*, 25, 131–144.

Waltz, J., Addis, M., Koerner, K., and Jacobson, N. (1993). Testing the integrity of a psychotherapy protocol: Assessment of adherence and competence. *Journal of Consulting and Clinical Psychology*, 61, 620–630.

Witt, J. and Elliott, S. (1985). Acceptability of classroom management strategies. In T. Kratochwill (Ed.), *Advances in School Psychology* (Volume 4). Hillsdale, NJ: Erlbaum. 251–288.

Witt, J., Noell, G., LaFleur, L., and Mortenson, B. (1997). Teacher use of intervention in general education settings: Measurement and analysis of the independent variable. *Journal of Applied Behavior Analysis*, 30, 693–696.

Wolf, M. (1978). Social validity: The case for subjective measurement or how applied behavior analysis is finding its heart. *Journal of Applied Behavior Analysis*, 11, 203–214.

Yeaton, W. and Sechrest, L. (1981). Critical dimensions in the choice and maintenance of successful treatments: Strength, integrity, and effectiveness. *Journal of Consulting and Clinical Psychology*, 49, 156–167.

3

A FRAMEWORK FOR INCORPORATING INTERVENTION FIDELITY IN EDUCATIONAL EVALUATION STUDIES

William M. Murrah, Jeff Kosovich, and Chris Hulleman

The randomized controlled trial (RCT) is considered by many researchers to be the gold standard for rigorously evaluating the efficacy and effectiveness of interventions (IES, 2014). While the RCT is a crucial tool for understanding the average causal impact of an educational intervention, it is less useful for understanding the processes by which an intervention impacts outcomes. In fact, many have described the information about causal effects provided by randomized experiments as a "black box" (Cook, 2003; Imai et al., 2011). In order to open this black box there is growing interest in collecting data on intervention fidelity to inform our understanding of how, and under what conditions, interventions work (Bloom, 2005).

Assessing intervention fidelity will help researchers understand and interpret impact estimates, as well as assess the generalizability of these results to other conditions in which the treatment is implemented. However, if fidelity measures are added to evaluation studies ad hoc and without careful planning, they may fail to capture information about the implementation of the intervention under investigation and the nature of the treatment contrast in study conditions. These measures may not be psychometrically reliable and valid to provide interpretable information. Another concern is that without carefully planned assessment of fidelity, researchers may not be able to evaluate and further develop the conceptual models of the intervention. The five-step framework helps address these concerns by guiding the evaluator in assessing intervention fidelity, starting in the early stages of planning an intervention evaluation and continuing through analyses of results.

Although funding agencies and education researchers have generally come to accept the importance of both assessing intervention fidelity and linking fidelity

assessments to outcomes of interest (IES 2014), there is little information available to educational researchers about the appropriate procedures for accomplishing these goals (Nelson et al., 2012; O'Donnell, 2008; Weiss et al., 2014). The purpose of this chapter is to present a framework to help researchers conceptualize, measure, and analyze the fidelity of specific interventions. First, we describe the framework conceptually, explaining each step. We then give a more detailed example of an intervention evaluation using the framework to give readers a more nuanced understanding of how this framework can be used.

Five-Step Model of Intervention Fidelity

The five-step framework focuses on explicating the intervention by breaking it into its primary processes and measuring those processes effectively to evaluate intervention fidelity. As such, it provides a useful guide for educational researchers to consider when designing their RCTs in a way that is sensitive to measurement of fidelity. To be most useful, educational researchers must begin thinking about intervention fidelity early in the development of the intervention study. For more detailed descriptions and discussion of the five-step fidelity assessment framework, we refer readers to the writings of Hulleman and colleagues (Hulleman et al., 2013; Nelson et al., 2012). Below, we offer a brief description of the framework followed by a relevant example.

Step One: Define the Intervention Logic Models

Without specifying what is happening inside the black box of the intervention, researchers and evaluators are left wondering what mechanisms explain a successful intervention, or what factors contributed to a failure. As presented in Figure 3.1, unpacking the black box involves specifying two types of processes: intervention and psychological. *Intervention processes* are the core components of the intervention theorized to drive changes in participants and thus impact key psychological processes within the participants. *Psychological processes* refer to the proximal changes in participants, such as depth of knowledge and attitudes that lead to the desired outcome, such as increased learning and achievement. Often, changes in the psychological processes are the goal of the intervention. While identification of outcomes as proximal and distal may depend on the particular analysis being considered, for clarity in this chapter we consider psychological processes as proximal outcomes, and all other outcomes impacted by the proximal outcomes as distal outcomes. Researchers can begin by creating a logic model, which is a graphical depiction—similar to a path diagram—of the core components of the intervention (Nelson et al., 2012). The *change logic model* is a conceptual representation of the intervention organized in the hypothesized causal order of events. This model should include the intervention core components, psychological processes and intervention outcomes. Once defined, the change model aids researchers in developing an *operational logic model* that identifies which indicators the researchers

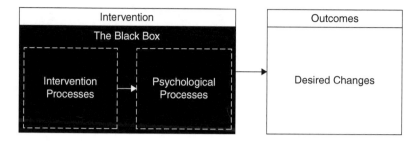

FIGURE 3.1 The Intervention Black Box. Adapted from Kosovich (2013).

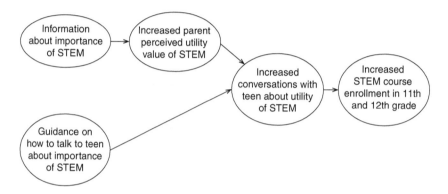

FIGURE 3.2 Change Logic Model for the Parent Intervention (Study 1). See Kopp et al. (2012) for more information.

deem important for measuring the core components (Knowlton & Phillips, 2009; Nelson et al., 2012). Development of the operational model involves the specification of each core component and associated subcomponents.

For example, in a randomized experiment of parents by Harackiewicz et al. (2012), parents were targeted with an intervention designed to increase their high school student's course-taking in science and mathematics. As presented in Figure 3.2, the intervention contained two core components: providing information about the importance of Science, Technology, Engineering, and Mathematics (STEM), and providing guidance on how to talk to teens about STEM topics. There were also two psychological processes targeted: perceived value of STEM to their teens' lives, and the number of conversations about the value of STEM. The information about the value of STEM was theorized to increase parents' perception of the value of STEM for their teens, and together with guidance on how to talk to their teens, was theorized to increase the conversations that parents had with teens about the value of STEM. This would in turn increase course taking in high school. Figure 3.3 presents the operational logic model for the parent intervention. The boxes represent the measures or information collected for each of the hypothesized core intervention components, as well as proximal and distal

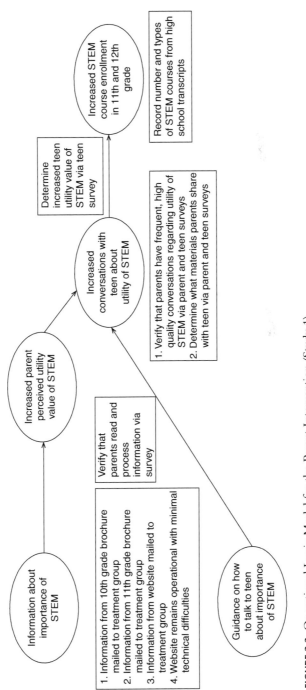

FIGURE 3.3 Operational Logic Model for the Parent Intervention (Study 1).

Note: Boxes represent components to be measured. See Kopp et al. (2012) for more information.

outcomes. Thus, the operational model clarifies which aspects are important to measure and what types of measures need to be developed in order to understand the level of intervention fidelity. It is crucial to capture these elements in both the treatment and control conditions so that actualized treatment strength can be ascertained (Hulleman & Cordray, 2009).

Logic models are meant to guide researchers, implementers, and evaluators toward the ideal version of the program of interest. The models specify critical aspects that define each condition (i.e. control, treatment, alternative treatment) as well as the common aspects that span conditions. When theory-based interventions are developed, they are thought to work through very specific mechanisms. Fidelity assessment is meant to measure variation in those mechanisms within and between different groups. A point to note is that aspects of the control group or alternative treatment group may promote psychological processes targeted by one or more core components of the intervention. This could result in attenuation of expected treatment effects related to these components. This possibility highlights the importance of measuring fidelity in the control group as well as the treatment group (Cordray & Pion, 1993).

Step Two: Identify Fidelity Measures

After specifying core components and the operational logic model, it is necessary to compile measures of each component (Nelson et al., 2012). The change and operational models provide researchers with a map and an organized inventory of what needs to be measured during the intervention. Direct or indirect measures should be obtained or developed for each component. Each fidelity indicator can be measured through observational data (e.g. live, video-recording, permanent product), self-report data (from implementers or participants), data logs, or any number of other instruments. These measures need not be limited to a single level of setting. In fact, fidelity may operate at every level of an institution; students, teachers, administrators, and schools are all candidates for fidelity measurement. Including this step allows researchers to keep in mind those measures that are necessary for their study, and in which groups they should be measured. For example, if researchers suspect that business-as-usual practices may expose participants to core components of the intervention, they should plan to measure these core components in both groups. As identified in Figure 3.3, fidelity measures in this study included using computer logs (information about importance of STEM), self-report surveys (increased parent perceived utility value of STEM), interviews (increased conversations), and academic transcripts (increased STEM course enrollment in 11th and 12th grade).

Step Three: Conduct Psychometric Analyses

Once measures are identified—but before being incorporated within the analysis of treatment variation—dimensionality and reliability evidence should be gathered

for the different fidelity measures (Hulleman et al., 2013; Kosovich, 2013; Nelson et al., 2012). If the decisions related to how to combine fidelity indicators is not consistent with their dimensionality, analyses including these measures can impact the validity of results. Researchers must first determine how the individual fidelity indicators will be combined into scales. Will there be a single, overall measure of fidelity, where all indicators contribute to one index? Or, instead, will there be sub-scales of fidelity that correspond to the core components and subcomponents, to the measures (e.g. self-report, observation), or based on the dimension of fidelity (i.e. exposure, adherence, quality, responsiveness)? The choice of combined indicators should be based on both theoretical and empirical grounds. These combinations should be useful to the goals of the fidelity assessment, but should also reflect the empirical relationships between the indicators. Empirical methods, such as factor analysis, can help evaluators decide how best to combine items (Abry et al., 2012; Brown, 2006; Hulleman et al., 2013), but a strong conceptual framework about how the items should be grouped is essential (Marsh & Hau, 2007). Loss of information and the measurement scale of the indicator should also be considered when combining indicators. Combining indicators typically results in a loss of detailed information; specifically, when combining indicators into a scale, it is common to either average or sum the indicators to create a total composite score. If some indicators are more important than others to the construct, then these distinctions are lost because all indicators are equally weighted. In addition, combining indicators can be challenging because of different metrics. For example, it would be improper to average a binary (0, 1) indicator and a continuous indicator from a nine-point scale because the two indicators would be contributing drastically different amounts of information to the composite.

Once the appropriate dimensions of fidelity have been determined, then the researcher can focus on scale reliability. As with any measure, the use of instruments that produce reliable and valid scores is absolutely critical to generating useful data. The importance of reliability cannot be overstated; good reliability increases the confidence that scores produced are consistent and replicable (Traub & Rowley, 1991). Poor reliability of fidelity measures can lead to bias in models that include fidelity measures as covariates or mediators. Without good reliability, the scores produced cannot be interpreted as accurate representations of focal constructs.

Step Four: Conduct within- and between-Group Fidelity Analyses

If the fidelity measures have been deemed psychometrically acceptable, researchers can then begin the fidelity analyses. Within-group descriptive analyses involve investigating the variation in fidelity within each experimental condition. These analyses give researchers a rich description of how well the intervention was implemented as well as how implementation may have varied across individuals and groups (e.g. classrooms) within the experimental conditions. For example,

fidelity can be calculated by computing the average value of a particular fidelity measure, or by computing the proportion of fidelity relative to the total possible fidelity on that measure. Once the basic descriptive statistics have been examined, researchers can then conduct more sophisticated analyses that contrast the treatment and control groups. Such between-group contrasts can be conducted through the use of an Achieved Relative Strength index (ARS) (Hulleman & Cordray, 2009; Hulleman et al., 2013). ARS values are useful in a number of different ways, but are primarily used for comparing a group's level of measured fidelity to other groups or some absolute standard. For example, we might expect students who receive a value intervention to experience more exposure to value concepts than students who don't. Alternatively, we might be interested in how far the group is from some ideal standard (e.g. a maximum fidelity value or an important benchmark). The specific index of fidelity should depend on the research or substantive question at hand.

Achieved Relative Strength Indices

Several different methods are available for calculating ARS. The easiest method is to compare average differences between components. Another method involves comparing binary complier indices, which can be calculated based on a cut score chosen by the researcher. Finally, researchers can calculate absolute fidelity indices, which determine the achieved proportion of total possible fidelity to a component (i.e. what proportion of participants reached maximum fidelity for a component). Comparing ARS values allow researchers to determine the treatment strength of an intervention. For example, in the parent intervention teenagers reported having more conversations with their parents about STEM than those in the control condition in both 10th grade ($d = .26$) and 11th grade ($d = .39$) (Kopp et al., 2012). In this example, the intervention effect was expected to be stronger in 11th than 10th grade because the second intervention dose was not delivered until early fall of 11th grade. The within- and between-group fidelity analyses are the foundation of intervention fidelity assessment. This step in the framework allows researchers to determine whether or not their intervention was implemented at an acceptable level of fidelity.

Step Five: Link Fidelity to Outcomes

As has been demonstrated, a significant amount of work can be done to analyze fidelity without investigating the relationship to outcomes. However, Step Five is critical for fidelity assessment to be used to its full potential—it allows a researcher to determine if fidelity matters for an intervention. Theoretically, the impact of an intervention on outcomes should increase as fidelity increases and result in appropriate correlations between fidelity measures and outcomes. Linking indices to outcomes can provide several pieces of useful information, including whether

the measured components actually affect outcomes in the expected manner, whether fidelity mediates the effect of the intervention (MacKinnon et al., 2002), or whether there are differences in which intervention components are important for groups characterized by demographic factors (i.e. moderated mediation). Fidelity indices could be added into the statistical model used to predict program outcomes (e.g. Abry et al., 2014; Abry et al., 2012; Kopp et al., 2012). For example, in the parent intervention, a series of logistic regressions could be used to examine the relationship between each of the fidelity indices and both proximal (number of conversations between parents and teens) and distal outcomes (number of STEM courses taken). It may be possible that participants with high levels of incoming value are more likely to exhibit high levels of fidelity. This type of analysis can provide additional diagnostic information for determining how effective an intervention may be in the future. In this way some interventions may be able to identify risk factors for participant noncompliance. However, researchers must be careful in how they interpret analyses that include measures of fidelity. Because fidelity indices are typically collected after random assignment, the strong causal interpretation afforded by randomization requires much more stringent assumptions. Instead, researchers may wish to use fidelity measures in exploratory analyses that complement the intent-to-treat analyses.

Summary

The five-step fidelity assessment framework provides a useful and systematic way to assess intervention fidelity in educational settings. It also helps to clarify the conceptual model of an intervention, and allows researchers to organize and identify indicators needed to measure fidelity. The framework also emphasizes the investigation of reliability and validity information to maximize the usefulness of measures. The common need to combine indices further emphasizes the need for good measurement practice and psychometric techniques. Finally, if the first four steps have been effectively executed, the fifth step allows researchers to test whether or not fidelity affects outcomes. As a result, the five-step framework combines theoretical, methodological, and analytical approaches to bolster the validity arguments made about an intervention's effectiveness. We present a summary of the five-step model in Table 3.1.

Applying the Five-Step Model

The example in this section uses data from a motivation intervention designed to aid student success in classrooms. This intervention helps students see the relevance and usefulness of the topic they are learning (i.e. utility value) (Eccles et al., 1983) for their current or future goals (Hulleman & Harackiewicz, 2009). One implementation of the intervention delivered in a laboratory (Study 1) (Hulleman et al., 2010) with college undergraduates yielded a significant main effect of

TABLE 3.1 The Five-Step Framework of Fidelity Assessment

Step	Description	Key Terms
1. Define the intervention logic models	Users describe the theory of change through which the intervention is expected to operate. This includes all of the core and common components intervention.	Intervention processes Psychological processes Change logic model Operational logic model Core intervention components Common components of educational settings
2. Identify fidelity measures	Users identify one or more measures for each of the core and common components.	
3. Conduct psychometric analyses	Users demonstrate that data collected is consistent and meaningful for final analyses.	Dimensionality Reliability
4. Conduct within- and between-group fidelity analyses	Users determine if fidelity levels for each group are adequate and compare levels across groups to determine if they are sufficiently different from one another.	Achieved relative strength (ARS)
5. Link fidelity to outcomes	Users determine if variation in fidelity is related to variation in outcomes—typically higher fidelity should lead to more desirable outcomes.	

condition—participants in the treatment group reported significantly higher perceptions of utility value than participants in the control group ($\beta = .19, p = .05$). However, another implementation of the intervention delivered in a classroom (Hulleman & Harackiewicz, 2009) produced a much weaker effect—there was almost no difference between the control and treatment groups ($\beta = .08, p = .12$). Whereas student perceptions of utility value increased dramatically in the lab study (Hulleman et al., 2010), increases in perceptions of utility value in the field were minimal (Hulleman & Harackiewicz, 2009). Without measuring fidelity (i.e. intervention processes), it was difficult to conclude whether the intervention worked or not because evidence supported both conclusions. In fact, post hoc investigation of intervention fidelity in the two studies (Hulleman et al., 2010; Hulleman & Harackiewicz, 2009), revealed that fidelity to the intended design was 58% for the lab study and 25% for the field study (Hulleman & Cordray, 2009). These differences corresponded with differences in outcome where the utility intervention had a larger effect in the lab ($g = 0.45$) than in the field

(g = 0.05; Hulleman & Cordray, 2009). These findings suggest that degradation in fidelity is one possible reason results in the field interventions were weaker.

In the following example, we use the five-step framework to evaluate an online version of the utility intervention just described. This replication was implemented as a randomized field experiment in an introductory psychology course over a 15-week semester (complete details about this study, including analyses of outcomes, can be found in Hulleman et al., under review). Students were randomly assigned to one of two different conditions: control (C_x) or treatment (T_x). Each student was asked to write two essays (one during week 4 and one during week 8) based on their experimental condition. As reported in Hulleman et al. (under review), however, the treatment yielded small effect sizes.

How Well Was the Intervention Implemented?

The fact that this intervention was conducted within an experimental framework means that fidelity measures can be compared within and across conditions by assessing treatment strength (Hulleman & Cordray, 2009). Fidelity indices are used to calculate achieved relative strength (ARS), which provides researchers with useful information about how effectively an intervention is implemented.

Sample and Procedure

As reported in Hulleman et al. (under review), the intervention was conducted in an introductory psychology course during a 15-week semester. The sample included 206 students. Eligible students completed both surveys and were 18 years old or older (N = 298; 74.2% Female, 61% freshman, 84% non-psychology majors, 84% White, 5% African American). The mean age of participants was 18.7 years. Data were collected throughout the semester. A self-reported measure of utility value (the key psychological process of the intervention) was administered before, during, and after completion of the intervention. During the second week of the class, participants filled out a motivation survey (Time 1 motivation). During the fourth week participants took the first exam (Exam 1). The first intervention essay was assigned after students completed Exam 1, and the second essay was assigned during the eighth week of the semester. During the fourteenth week of the semester, students completed another motivation survey (Time 2 motivation). Finally, during the fifteenth week, students completed their final exams.

Intervention Essays

Fidelity data were collected from student essays and self-report responses and were aggregated across the two intervention essays. In both essays, students were asked to respond to writing prompts that focused on the relevance of course material to their lives (utility value condition) or a summary of course material that they were

currently learning (control condition). Specifically, the utility value prompted, "Choose a topic from above that is personally useful and meaningful to you (it may be the same topic as before). In 1–2 paragraphs (75–125 words), describe how learning about this topic will be beneficial to you in the future (e.g. education, career, daily life)." Although similar in format, the control prompts simply asked students to identify a topic in class and summarize it in 75–115 words.

Step One: Identify Logic Models

Recall that the logic models refer to two types of conceptual path models used in presenting fidelity assessment plans. As such, they lay out the theoretical logic of the intervention. The change model is used to represent what the researcher believes is the causal flow of the intervention by its core components. The operation model is used to operationalize the core components by specifying what can be measured that will represent each component.

Defining the Change Model

In deriving the change model from the utility intervention, one core component was identified. The major core component is relevance. As discussed, asking students to consider new material in the context of old material may facilitate increased utility value. Because both quantity and quality of relevance are plausibly important to the development of increased utility value, each was included. Furthermore, because the essays are expected to anchor new material to personal relevance, the number of personal pronouns included in an essay may also indicate relevance. Finally, participants were asked to write a specific amount in each essay. It is possible that students who wrote less in their essays were less likely to produce useful relevance compared to students who wrote more.

Figure 3.4a shows the change model for the summary condition which suggests that summarizing information should lead to typical performance. Figure 3.4b shows the change model for the utility condition and specifies that participation in the utility essay should lead to increased writing about the relevance of psychology to students' lives, which will then increase their self-reported perceptions of utility value for the course. Ultimately, this will lead to increased interest and course performance.

Defining the Operational Model

After defining the core components, subcomponents need to be identified. The core component (relevance) comprises five facets: number of connections, connection specificity, connection personalization, the number of personal pronouns, and number of other pronouns. Together, these facets operationalize the subcomponents of the change model (see Figure 3.5). As a set, the indicators of each

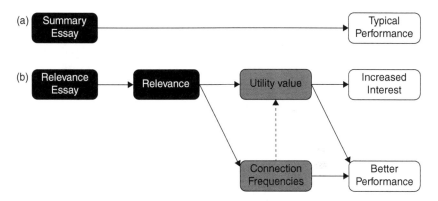

FIGURE 3.4 Conceptual Logic Model for the Utility Value Intervention. Accurately assessing fidelity requires a strong understanding of the theory of change underlying the intervention. The control group (a) and treatment group (b) may have different theories of change. The models themselves are considered conceptual logic models because they convey the individual pieces of the intervention groups as well as the theorized causal path.

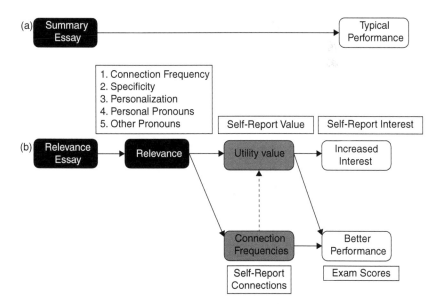

FIGURE 3.5 Operational Logic Model for the Utility Value Intervention. After settling on a conceptual model, it's necessary to identify measurable aspects (or subcomponents) of the intervention. The operational logic model adds a description of the subcomponents of each major point of the intervention. For example, the major core component of the example intervention is "Relevance" which is operationalized through five subcomponents: connection frequency, specificity, personalization, personal pronouns, and other pronouns. In this figure, black-rounded boxes represent the intervention processes, gray-rounded boxes represent psychological processes, and white-rounded boxes represent outcomes.

component give us an idea of the fidelity to that particular component as well as diagnostic information. They provide more detailed information about specific components which can serve to focus attention when modifying the intervention in the future.

Step Two: Identify Appropriate Fidelity Measures

After defining the conceptual framework of the intervention, it was necessary to identify and develop measures of the various facets of fidelity. In the focal intervention, a number of measures relied on the qualitative analysis of student essays, which necessitated the development of a coding rubric (see Kosovich, 2013 for the full set of measures).

Of the five relevance writing facets, the first three were measured using the coding rubric. First, the number of relevance connections was counted. A connection was considered to exist when a distinct relationship between course material and unrelated material is discussed. For example, a connection was "Now that we have learned about encoding, short term memory and long term memory, I studied very differently for this exam than I would have in the past." Second, connection specificity was included as a gauge of response depth and was measured on a seven-point (with half-point increments) ranging from 0 (Essay contained no connections) to 3 (Essay connections are specific—it explicitly states that two or more things—e.g. events, topics—are related and provides a specific example). For example, a specific connection would be:

> What made me the most nervous about being a freshman in college was being able to pick-up good study habits. After learning and reading about how memory works I decided to try and study a few days before our first exam. On the night before our exam I went back and reviewed everything I had been studying the previous days before and it had felt like I could recall everything very well.
>
> *(Intervention participant, Specificity Rating 3/3)*

Third, connection personalization was also measured. It was included because connecting material to personal topics may be more useful than connecting to abstract topics. The connection personalization dimension is also measured on a seven-point scale and ranges from 0 (Essay contained no connections) to 3 (Essay contained strong personalization—it provides a specific instance or example of the topic's personal relevance to the person or significant other—e.g. mother, sibling, friend—rather than general for everyone—why the content is important for this person in particular). For example, a personalized connection would be:

> This material is relevant to my life because a large part of it consists of ways to improve memory and retain information. As a freshman, this can be very

important to me because I am adjusting to college classes and how I study the concepts and information from these courses.

(Intervention participant, Personalization Rating 2.5/3)

One important characteristic to note from the set of essays in the current study is that specificity and personalization tended to occur together. Although some essays with high personalization and low specificity did occur, they were uncommon.

The fourth and fifth facets incorporated in the relevance components were drawn directly from essay text. The fourth facet was the number of personal pronouns in the essays. Personal pronouns were all instances of "I," "Me," "My," and "Mine." The fifth facet was the number of other pronouns in the essays. Other pronouns were defined as all instances of "We," "Our," "Us," and "Ours."

In addition to the two intervention-related components, an additional pair of measures was included for assessing group similarity. Both of these measures provided an opportunity to measure components that should have been roughly equal between the treatment and control groups. Thus, they served a dual purpose of assessing group differences in fidelity analyses (see Step Four) and as covariates for outcome analyses (see Step Five). First, the average relevance essay word count (as opposed to the goal setting essay word count used above) was used to determine if similar amounts of writing are being done in all conditions. Second, essay writing quality was also included on the coding rubric described earlier. Writing quality was rated on a seven-point scale, half points are used, ranging from 0 (No Response) to 3 (Essay contains groups of sentences that are logically related and clearly understandable). Although writing quality can be represented with a much more detailed set of indicators, this indicator was only meant to provide a measure of drastic differences in writing quality, rather than more subtle nuances.

Step Three: Conduct Psychometric Analyses

Evaluating the Psychometric Properties of the Fidelity Measures

Step Three of the five-step framework specifies that the psychometric properties of any measures used must be examined. Because the primary focus of the current study is fidelity analysis, reliability and validity evidence for the fidelity rubric is of primary importance. Inter-rater reliability, using adjacent percent agreement (i.e. ratings were within one point of each other), was calculated to estimate how consistent raters were at reliably producing ratings of essay elements. As with scale items, determination of reliability is necessary for assessing whether or not raters can dependably produce ratings. Poor reliability results in scores that are not interpretable because the values depend on situational factors rather than intervention factors. Table 3.2 contains descriptive statistics for the various fidelity measures.

Fidelity indices that required reliability estimates include (a) the number of relevance connections, (b) the specificity of those connections, (c) the degree of

TABLE 3.2 Fidelity Descriptives by Experimental Condition

		M	*SD*	*Min*	*Max*
Summary	Word count	136.39	41.29	21.50	256.00
(control)	Personal pronouns	0.55	1.37	0.00	7.00
(n = 102)	Other pronouns	1.51	1.95	0.00	9.00
	Writing quality	2.55	0.41	0.50	3.00
	Connections	0.02	0.16	0.00	1.50
	Specificity	0.04	0.23	0.00	1.50
	Personalization	0.04	0.21	0.00	1.50
	*Relevance**	*−1.23*	*0.16*	*−1.26*	*−0.06*
Utility	Word count	175.88	50.81	36.00	345.50
(n = 104)	Personal pronouns	12.36	5.08	2.50	23.50
	Other pronouns	1.27	1.53	0.00	10.50
	Writing quality	2.62	0.40	1.00	3.00
	Connections	2.48	0.80	0.50	4.75
	Specificity	2.29	0.47	0.75	3.00
	Personalization	2.33	0.53	0.50	3.00
	*Relevance**	*0.62*	*0.31*	*−0.56*	*1.24*

Note: * Indicates that the variable is a composite. Composites were calculated by standardizing and then averaging the relevant facets resulting in possibly negative values. Relevance is a composite of personal pronouns, other pronouns, connections, specificity, and personalization.

personalization of those connections, and (d) writing quality. The other fidelity indices (word count, number of personal pronouns and other pronouns) do not require reliability estimation because they are observed variables and are assumed to have no measurement error; these measures were counted using a computer.

A total of 750 essays were rated during the course of this study. Due to the number of essays, every essay could not be rated by two people. Instead all of the essays were rated by at least one rater, and a series of random samples—totaling 20% of the essays—was drawn from the population of essays and rated by three additional raters. Overall, adjacent percent agreement across raters was acceptable by commonly reported reliability values (Stemler, 2004; Frick & Semmel, 1978) suggesting that different raters could consistently agree about 87% of the time within one point (on a seven-point scale) on the fidelity elements.

Step Four: Conduct within- and between-Group Fidelity Analyses

How Well Was the Intervention Implemented Based on Different Indexes of Achieved Relative Strength (ARS)?

Table 3.3 contains basic descriptive statistics for the fidelity measures for each group. To determine how well the intervention was implemented in the study, achieved relative strength was examined in three ways using average, absolute,

TABLE 3.3 Average Achieved Relative Strength (ARS) Indices

Achieved Relative Strength[1]		Average ARS				Absolute[2]	Binary Complier[3]
		Δ_f	Δ_1	D	g		
Utility[a]	Word count	0.78	0.96	0.85	0.85	0.27	0.46
vs	Writing quality	0.16	0.16	0.16	0.16	0.13	0.05
Summary[b]	Personal pronouns	2.32	8.62	3.17	3.15		
	Other pronouns	−0.16	−0.12	−0.14	−0.14		
	Connections	3.07	15.04	4.26	4.22	0.96	3.18
	Specificity	4.73	9.72	6.02	5.98	0.51	3.72
	Personalization	4.29	11.10	5.66	5.62	0.67	2.98
	Relevance	*2.17*	*6.50*	*2.86*	*2.83*		

Notes: Word count and writing quality are common components. Δ_1 and Δ_f (an average ARS index) represent Glass's Δ using the summary and utility standard deviations respectively. Delta is included because it is suggested for best-practice reporting of effect sizes in experimental designs where distributions and variances are not equivalent across conditions. When employed in a design such as this study, the denominator for Δ should be the standard deviation for the group most representative of fidelity, rather than the control group as is conventionally used. Absolute and binary complier indices were only calculated for variables that had meaningful absolute or complier values.

[1] Positive values indicate that the utility condition mean was higher than the summary condition mean.
[2] Individuals were considered to have absolute fidelity if: Word count ≥ 250, writing quality $= 3$, connections ≥ 3, specificity $= 3$, and personalization $= 3$.
[3] Individuals were considered compliers if: Word count ≥ 150, writing quality ≥ 2, connections ≥ 2, specificity ≥ 2, and personalization ≥ 2.
[a] n = 104
[b] n = 102

and binary complier indices to compare the treatment and control groups. In particular, ARS comparisons were made for: word count, writing quality, number of connections, specificity, and personalization. Table 3.3 contains average, absolute, and binary complier contrasts for all five of the fidelity measures. Figure 3.6 compares the common components (e.g. writing quality and word count) to fidelity components (e.g. connections, specificity, and personalization) in standard deviation units. This comparison demonstrates that group differences on the important intervention fidelity factors are 3 to 5 times larger than differences on the common components.

Average Fidelity

The first analysis is the average ARS which compares experimental group means to determine differences in fidelity. Previous research utilizing ARS indices suggested using Hedges' g (Hulleman & Cordray, 2009), which is an effect size measure from the family of standardized mean differences. Hedges' g is calculated using the pooled standard deviation of the two groups being compared; however, its

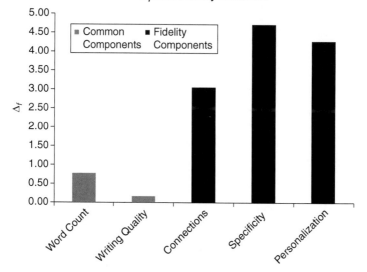

FIGURE 3.6 Comparing common components (e.g. writing quality and word count) to fidelity components (e.g. connections, specificity, and personalization) makes it possible to assess treatment differentiation. As is preferable, the Tx and Cx differences presented in the figure demonstrate that group differences on the important intervention factors are 3–5 times larger than common components. Note that values are in standard deviation units.

calculation assumes relatively similar standard deviations and distributions (Kline, 2004). Experimental designs are particularly problematic for such assumptions because treatments can cause different distributions and variances resulting in a pooled standard deviation that does not represent either group effectively. To account for such problems, an alternative to g, Glass's Δ, was proposed (Smith & Glass, 1976). Glass's Δ uses the standard deviation of the comparison group rather than a pooled standard deviation because it assumes that the typical standard deviation in non-experimental settings is more like that of the comparison group. For outcome effect sizes, Δ uses the standard deviation from the control group, thus approximating the distribution of a group without any treatment. Kline (2004) suggests reporting Δ using each of the groups' standard deviations because the selection of a comparison group can cause drastically different values. For example, in an experiment that has three conditions Δ_1, Δ_2, and Δ_3 would be calculated using the standard deviations of Group 1, Group 2, and Group 3 respectively.

Intervention fidelity is a special case of experimental comparison because it focuses on adhering to conditions that are different from normal. Because fidelity researchers are interested in the relative difference in fidelity between the treatment and control groups, rather than comparing treatment to a baseline condition, the logic of Δ becomes reversed. That is, the appropriate baseline condition for

understanding adherence to the intervention model is the intervention condition rather than the control condition. Thus, the standard deviation of the intervention group will be used in the calculation of the achieved relative strength effect size resulting in delta-fidelity:

$$\Delta_f = \frac{\overline{M}_{tx} - \overline{M}_k}{s_f}$$

Where $\overline{M}_{tx}$ is the mean of the treatment group with the highest expected fidelity, $\overline{M}_k$ is the mean of any comparison group (either other treatment or control groups), and s_f is the standard deviation of the highest-order treatment condition (the group expected to have the highest fidelity of all treatment conditions). In cases of hierarchically ordered intervention groups, researchers should consider calculating Δ using the standard deviation of the group with the most core components rather than the standard deviation of the control group. The important distinction between Glass's Δ and Δ_f can be made at a conceptual level. The effect size, Δ, was designed to test the departure of a condition from a theoretical baseline. For typical experiments, researchers are testing departure of a treatment group from a control group. For fidelity analyses, however, researchers are testing for infidelity from the intervention. Because the ideal intervention does not exist, Δ_f treats the highest order condition as the best approximation of the theoretical intervention. Therefore, Glass's logic was adapted for the fidelity framework to produce Δ_f (Kosovich, 2013). As a side note, these effect size measures should not be considered with the same treatment-counterfactual logic that governs intervention outcome analyses. ARS contrasts take a step outside of strong causal inference in an effort to describe and explore potential pathways where intervention mechanisms operate. It is worth repeating that the interpretation of Δ_f differs from Glass's Δ because we are now interested in departure from fidelity rather than departure from a control, counterfactual, or baseline.

Table 3.3 contains the several different methods for calculating average ARS contrasts. Of primary interest are the effect sizes contained in the Δ_f column; the other effect sizes are supplied for comparative purposes (see also Figure 3.6). As expected, the utility condition had drastically higher values on the three major fidelity indices than the control group: connections ($\Delta_f = 3.07$), specificity ($\Delta_f = 4.73$), and personalization ($\Delta_f = 4.29$). The utility condition was also somewhat higher on word count ($\Delta_f = 0.78$) and writing quality ($\Delta_f = 0.16$). Although there was a sizeable difference between the control and treatment groups on word count, it appeared that the difference was an artifact of the intervention prompt rather than intervention effects. During the first dose of the intervention, participants in the control group were asked to write "about 1 or 2 sentences" per topic (4 topics) presented to them whereas participants in the treatment conditions were asked to write one or two paragraphs about a single topic. The differences in prompt instructions appear to be the culprit for word-count differences because

the differences between groups vanished in the second intervention dose which indicated a word range. Unsurprisingly, the utility group ($\Delta_f = 6.5$) had drastically higher relevance than the summary group as expected.

Absolute Fidelity

As a secondary measure of local fidelity, a subset of absolute fidelity indices were also calculated using a variant of Hedges' g adjusted for proportions (Hulleman & Cordray, 2009). Absolute fidelity was determined by comparing proportions of students in the treatment and control groups who achieved a maximum value on the particular measure being examined. For example, writing quality, specificity and personalization all had maximum values of three. With indices without an absolute value, an empirical or theoretical absolute was used instead of an actual maximum value. For connection frequency, we chose three connections or higher based on the frequency distribution of responses. For word count, we used the directions given to students as a guide (i.e. 250 words).

Binary Complier

Similar to absolute fidelity, binary complier indices require categorization of individuals as compliers or non-compliers. In other words, the researchers or evaluators create a theoretically and/or empirically driven standard for which *minimally acceptable fidelity* has been achieved. This particular type of index allows researchers or evaluators to potentially detect if a critical mass of intervention participation has occurred. In this case, the users must set a cut-off value that identifies individuals as compliers. For example, individuals in the current example were considered writing quality compliers if they achieved a rating of at least 2.5—this was the point in the scale where the writing was expected to be a coherent idea. Similarly, specificity, personalization and number of connections were all assigned a value of two as indicating minimally acceptable fidelity. Both specificity and personalization used two as a cut-off because that is the point in which the individuals clearly articulated an experience, whereas more than a 2 indicated some greater degree of elaboration (which was desirable but not necessary). Similarly, number of connections used a value of two because the activity required at least two connections to be made (again, more was desirable but not necessary). Finally, word count used 150 words as a cut-off because that was the minimum recommendation for the activity in both groups—thus 150 words or more was an indicator that the individual was following directions.

Step Five: Link Fidelity to Outcomes

Because most of the subsequent chapters in this volume are examples of linking fidelity measures to outcomes, we only briefly describe this step for our current

example. Using the example data, we restricted our analysis to the intervention group because the control-group variance was essentially zero. In prior studies of the utility value intervention, students' self-reported perceptions of utility value mediated the effect of treatment assignment on self-reported interest. In Step Five of the fidelity framework, we are interested in testing if variation in treatment uptake can predict differences in outcomes. To this end, we conducted a mediation analysis of the effect of fidelity on student interest as it is transmitted by utility value (Togfighi & MacKinnon, 2011). Using multiple regression, we first tested the effects of our fidelity components on self-reported utility value. This model included all of our fidelity measures, but was restricted to the intervention group. Ultimately there was a positive relationship between rated connection frequency and utility value ($b_a = .22, p = .03$). We then tested the effects of our fidelity components on self-reported interest. This model was similar to the first, except that it also included utility value as a predictor. In this case, there was only a significant effect of utility value on interest ($b_b = .60, p < .001$). We then computed the indirect effect of rated connection frequency on interest by multiplying the two regression coefficients together and calculated confidence intervals for the effect size. This analysis revealed that the effect of fidelity on self-reported interest was mediated by utility value ($b_a * b_b = .13, 95\% \text{ CI } [0.03, 0.25]$). This analysis provides two important pieces of information. First, that variation in treatment fidelity (i.e. number of connections written) predicts variation in the theoretical mechanism of the intervention (i.e. perceptions of utility value). Second, it shows that this effect is transmitted to our more distal outcome, interest, through its impact on utility value. Thus, for the example presented, we can say confidently that our treatment and control groups were highly differentiated, and that variation in treatment uptake related to improved outcomes.

Conclusions

The intent-to-treat analysis will remain the gold standard for program evaluation, by providing evidence for *whether* an intervention works. However, the precise measurement of intervention fidelity is critical for evaluating *how* and *under which conditions* these interventions work. Analyses of fidelity data complements the strong causal inferences afforded by the intent-to-treat analyses. The five-step framework for assessing intervention fidelity provides evaluators with crucial guidance on how to assess intervention fidelity. To be effective, this framework should be used early in the process of developing intervention evaluations. There are many reasons why well-crafted interventions may or may not work. The rigorous assessment of intervention fidelity is critical for understanding either outcome.

In this chapter we have described the five-step framework for intervention fidelity. Many of the subsequent chapters focus on linking fidelity measures to outcomes, which is Step Five in our framework. The intent of this chapter was to clarify why Steps One through Four are critical for the effectiveness of any

method used for this purpose. Without a clear understanding of how the intervention should work, careful consideration of the instruments measuring the core components, an understanding of the psychometric properties of those instruments, and an understanding of the levels of fidelity measured by those instruments both within and between the treatment and control groups, the role of fidelity in understanding outcomes of an intervention are dubious at best.

References

Abry, T., Hulleman, C. S., and Rimm-Kaufman, S. E. (2014). Using indices of fidelity to intervention core components to identify program active ingredients. *American Journal of Evaluation*, 36(3). Available online at DOI:10.1177/1098214014557009

Abry, T., Rimm-Kaufman, S. E., Hulleman, C. S., Thomas, J., and Ko, M. (2012). *The How and for Whom of Program Effectiveness: Dissecting the Responsive Classroom® Approach in Relation to Academic Achievement.* Paper presented at the Spring Conference for the Society of Research on Educational Effectiveness, Washington, DC.

Bloom, H. S. (Ed.) (2005). *Learning More from Social Experiments: Evolving Analytic Approaches.* New York: Russell Sage Foundation.

Brown, T. A. (2006). *Confirmatory Factor Analysis for Applied Research.* NY: Guilford Press.

Cook, T. D. (2003). Why have educational evaluators chosen not to do randomized experiments? *The Annals of the American Academy of Political and Social Science*, 589(1), 114–149.

Cordray, D. S. and Pion, G. M. (1993). Psychological rehabilitation assessment: A broader perspective. In R. Gluechauf, G. Bond, L. Sechrest, and B. McDonel (Eds.), *Improving Assessment in Rehabilitation and Health.* Newbury Park, CA: Sage. 215–240.

Eccles, J. S., Adler, T. F., Futterman, R., Goff, S. B., Kaczala, C. M., Meece, J. L., and Midgley, C. (1983). Expectancies, values, and academic behaviors. In J. T. Spence (Ed.), *Achievement and Achievement Motivation.* San Francisco, CA: W.H. Freeman. 74–146.

Frick, T. and Semmel, M. I. (1978). Observer agreement and reliabilities of classroom observational measures. *Review of Educational Research*, 48(1), 157–184.

Harackiewicz, J. M., Rozek, C. S., Hulleman, C. S., and Hyde, J. S. (2012). Helping parents to motivate adolescents in mathematics and science: An experimental test of a utility-value intervention. *Psychological Science*, 23(8), 899–906.

Hulleman, C. S. and Cordray, D. S. (2009). Moving from the lab to the field: The role of fidelity and achieved relative intervention strength. *Journal of Research on Educational Effectiveness*, 2(1), 88–110.

Hulleman, C. S. and Harackiewicz, J. M. (2009). Promoting interest and performance in high school science classes. *Science*, 326, 1410–1412.

Hulleman, C. S., Godes, O., Hendricks, B. L., and Harackiewicz, J. M. (2010). Enhancing interest and performance with a utility value intervention. *Journal of Educational Psychology*, 102(4), 880–895.

Hulleman, C. S., Rimm-Kaufman, S. E., and Abry, T. D. S. (2013). Whole-part-whole: Construct validity, measurement, and analytical issues for fidelity assessment in education research. In T. Halle, A. Metz, and I. Martinez-Beck (Eds.), *Applying Implementation Science in Early Childhood Programs and Systems.* Baltimore, MD: Paul H. Brookes Publishing Co. 65–93.

Hulleman, C. S., Kosovich, J. J., Barron, K. E., and Daniel, D. B. (under review). Enhancing interest and performance with a utility value intervention: A replication and extension.

Imai, K., Keele, L., Tingley, D., and Yamamoto, T. (2011). Unpacking the black box of causality: Learning about causal mechanisms from experimental and observational studies. *American Political Science Review*, 105(04), 765–789.

IES (Institute of Education Sciences) (2014). WWC procedures and standards handbook: What works clearinghouse (Version 3.0). Washington, D.C. Available online at http://ies.ed.gov/ncee/wwc/pdf/reference_resources/wwc_procedures_v3_0_standards_handbook.pdf

Kline, R. B. (2004). *Beyond Significance Testing: Reforming Data Analysis Methods in Behavioral Research.* Washington DC: American Psychological Association.

Knowlton, L. W. and Phillips, C. C. (2012). *The Logic Model Guidebook: Better Strategies for Great Results.* Los Angeles, CA: Sage.

Kopp, J. P., Hulleman, C. S., Harackiewicz, J. M., and Rozek, C. (2012). Applying the five-step model of fidelity assessment to a randomized experiment of a high school STEM intervention. *Society for Research on Educational Effectiveness.*

Kosovich, J. J. (2013). *Assessing Intervention Fidelity in a Randomized Field Experiment: Illuminating the Black Box.* Unpublished master's thesis, James Madison University: Harrisonburg, VA.

MacKinnon, D. P., Lockwood, C. M., Hoffman, J. M., West, S. G., and Sheets, V. (2002). A comparison of methods to test mediation and other intervening variable effects. *Psychological Methods*, 7(1), 83.

Marsh, H. W. and Hau, K.-T. (2007). Applications of latent-variable models in educational psychology: The need for methodological-substantive synergies. *Contemporary Educational Psychology*, 32(1), 151–170.

Nelson, M. C., Cordray, D. S., Hulleman, C. S., Darrow, C. L., and Sommer, E. C. (2012). A procedure for assessing intervention fidelity in experiments testing educational and behavioral interventions. *The Journal of Behavioral Health Services & Research*, 39(4), 374–396.

O'Donnell, C. L. (2008). Defining, conceptualizing, and measuring fidelity of implementation and its relationship to outcomes in K–12 curriculum intervention research. *Review of Educational Research*, 78(1), 33–84.

Smith, M. L. and Glass, G. V. (1977). Meta-analysis of psychotherapy outcome studies. *American Psychologist*, 32(9), 752–760.

Stemler, S. E. (2004). A comparison of consensus, consistency, and measurement approaches to estimating interrater reliability. *Practical Assessment, Research, and Evaluation*, 9(4), 1–19.

Tofighi, D. and MacKinnon, D. P. (2011). RMediation: An R package for mediation analysis confidence intervals. *Behavior Research Methods*, 43(3), 692–700.

Traub, R. E. and Rowley, G. L. (1991). Understanding reliability. *Educational Measurement: Issues and Practice*, 10(1), 37–45.

Weiss, M. J., Bloom, H. S., and Brock, T. (2014). A conceptual framework for studying the sources of variation in program effects. *Journal of Policy Analysis and Management*, 33(3), 778–808.

4

IMPLEMENTATION FIDELITY

Examples from the Reading for Understanding Initiative

Greg Roberts, Nancy Scammacca Lewis, Anna Maria Fall, and Sharon Vaughn

Implementation fidelity in experimental settings is a priority for funders of educational research. However, there is little guidance on how to include fidelity-related data in efficacy or effectiveness studies conducted in classrooms and schools. In this chapter, we describe strategies for *measuring fidelity* and *including fidelity-related data* in randomized trials of innovative educational practice. We illustrate our recommendations using recent experiences from the Promoting Acceleration of Comprehension and Content through Text (PACT) project, conducted by the Meadows Center for Preventing Educational Risk at the University of Texas with funding from IES' Reading for Understanding initiative (see http://files.eric.ed.gov/fulltext/ED551445.pdf). PACT comprised a series of studies, many of which were efficacy-focused and group-randomized. For this subgroup of studies, we describe the program model, the study design, and the measurement strategy. The PACT work operationalized fidelity as treatment *dosage*, which we define in terms of *adherence* and *crossover* (or *diffusion*), where *adherence* is teachers' use of the intended program when in treatment-assigned classes and *crossover* is teachers' use of the intended program in business-as-usual classes. Finally, we discuss the use of structural equation models to estimate dosage as a mediator of the effect of assignment on outcomes.

Promoting Acceleration of Comprehension and Content Through Text

Promoting Acceleration of Comprehension and Content through Text (PACT) represents a variation of team-based learning applied to middle school history instruction. The original team-based model, used primarily in college and graduate-level classrooms (Sisk, 2011; see also Johnson & Johnson, 1987), is characterized by four

features: (1) instructor-assigned groups of five to seven students with diverse skills, (2) individual responsibility for out-of-class assignments and preparatory homework, and (3) incentives for working effectively as a team during (4) in-class group application exercises (Sweet & Michaelsen, 2012). Vaughn et al. (2013, 2014, 2015) embedded the team-based approach into a discourse-oriented intervention that targeted content acquisition and content-area reading comprehension in eighth-grade American history classes (i.e. the PACT model).

The PACT model addresses students' use of discipline-specific text to think critically about content, to exchange ideas, to defend perspectives, and to build knowledge through discussion and collective elaboration on core constructs. PACT supports collective problem solving by promoting, modeling, and managing content-driven discourse (Swanson & Wanzek, 2014). It includes five components in addition to its team-based dimensions: (1) a structured introduction to each curricular unit as a means of activating background knowledge and providing a general framework around which to organize details (*Comprehension Canopy*), (2) instruction and iterative review of words and concepts related to the curricular unit (*Essential Words*), (3) reading of primary and secondary text sources as a means of acquiring knowledge (*Critical Reading*), (4) ongoing discussion of newly learned information with an emphasis on student explanation and elaboration (*Team-Based Learning (TBL) Knowledge Application*), and (5) checks at the individual and group levels to encourage accountability and to foster collaborative discussion, respectively (*TBL Comprehension Check*).

These program activities can be represented as a normative program model (Figure 4.1). The activities, implemented over a 10-day interval, are designed to engage students in structured discourse-based interactions around standards-based social studies content, on the assumption that students' understanding of written language and their retention of print-based information improves by increasing their purposeful engagement with text, their collaborative discussion using text, and their elaboration on different perspectives embedded in text. The program

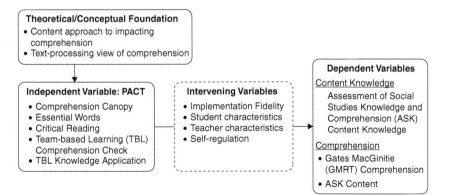

FIGURE 4.1   Normative Model for PACT.

activities were replicated across three 10-day cycles to teach American history content on different aspects of the American Revolution.

We do not present PACT's theoretical aspects in Figure 4.1, though they are often included in logic models as mediators or moderators of a program's effects. Instead, we focus on the tangible behaviors that a teacher engages when implementing PACT because in a fidelity-related context, what a program implementer (or user) is supposed to do and what he or she actually does are the most salient data points. The normative model represents the standard against which actual practice is evaluated. It serves as the basis for measuring fidelity and for modeling its role in improved student outcomes (Funnell & Rogers, 2011).

PACT Research Design and Measurement

Although research design is not a primary focus of this chapter, the proposed measurement and modeling strategies make more sense when described in the context of the design within which the data were collected. Accordingly, we begin with an overview of the completely group-randomized block design.

Completely Randomized Block Design

A fundamental purpose of intervention research is to estimate the *effect* of a new or potentially innovative program. In a potential outcomes framework (Imbens & Rubin, 2015), *effect* is defined as the difference between the average outcomes for a participant receiving the intervention and the average outcomes for the same individual had he or she been assigned to a non-treated condition. These latter outcomes, for treated participants had they not been treated, cannot be observed directly because the participants are engaged with the intervention (thus their designation as *potential* outcomes); however, they can be estimated. One way of estimating potential outcomes for a group is to observe individuals who are similar in every respect with the exception of their participation in treatment. Randomly assigning units (individuals, classrooms, schools, etc.) to one or more conditions is the most efficient way to estimate potential outcomes, a necessary condition for making strong inferences about the causal relationship of an experimental treatment and observed outcomes.

To create comparable groups for the PACT project, we randomly assigned *classes* (i.e. groups) to one of two conditions—PACT or business-as-usual. Further, we randomly assigned classes *within* teachers; each participating teacher agreed to teach about half of her Social Studies sections using the PACT materials and methods. For the other half, the teacher used her usual materials and methods. The same content was taught in both conditions; only the methods and materials differed. This represents a completely group-randomized block design, because each block includes all conditions. In this case, teacher was the blocking variable, class was the randomized unit, and all teachers taught PACT classes and business-as-usual

classes. In a blocked design, there is generally less error or "noise" to contend with because standard errors are based on the variability within each block. Between-block variability is not included in the error variance. An effect is estimated for each block (each teacher represents her own "mini" randomized study) and the overall effect is the average effect across blocks.

Block designs are widely used; blocking on teacher, however, is a relatively novel approach to creating comparable groups at pretest. We based our decision on several considerations. First, we wanted to manage the effect of "teacher" as a way of disentangling teacher effectiveness from treatment effects. PACT's discourse-based approach requires teachers to initiate and manage student discussion, to entertain and encourage contrary perspectives, and to possess a deep knowledge of the content area as a vehicle for helping students identify trends and their causes and effects. Pilot data on the PACT intervention suggested that teacher differences in these areas are *not* trivial, that such differences correlate with teacher effectiveness in the business-as-usual condition, and that these types of teaching competencies are very difficult to measure reliably. Our work prior to PACT suggested that a reliable metric for capturing teacher effectiveness (one that predicts differences in student outcomes) must be so broadly conceived (e.g. "excellent, average, or poor") that it generally fails to contribute to a deeper understanding of student-level outcomes and their relationship to instructional behavior.

We elected to "neutralize" teacher effectiveness by including it as a blocking variable in the research design, allowing us to estimate a treatment effect for each teacher as the difference in class-level performance between her PACT classes and her business-as-usual classes. We were also able to calculate a standard error for each "study" or teacher. Tests of a treatment effect's statistical significance are more efficient under these conditions, and they represent the impact of the intervention controlling for differences in teacher effectiveness. Randomizing classes within teachers also allowed us to model the variation in effect estimates across blocks. Again, by conceptualizing each teacher as her own mini study, we were able to create a distribution of independent treatment effects (dependence due to school was not statistically significant) that could be further analyzed. Fidelity as a predictor of variation in treatment effects was of particular interest in this respect.

Definitions for Fidelity

Fidelity has been defined along a number of dimensions, as described elsewhere in this book. Three dimensions were of particular interest in the context of a within-teachers design: (1) *adherence* and *crossover*, (2) *differentiation*, and (3) *dosage*. We define *adherence* as the degree to which teachers in treatment classes adhere to the program's normative model. *Crossover* represents the presence of intervention-unique elements (the components that *differentiate* the experimental intervention from alternatives) in the business-as-usual condition. In educational settings, an

experimental intervention may target student outcomes such as improved reading or math achievement or improved classroom behavior. Teacher behaviors, like improved instructional practice, are outcomes as well, and increasingly, normative models in educational science combine student and teacher outcomes, because many educational interventions depend on changed teacher behavior to improve student outcomes.

We include *differentiation* in the discussion of fidelity, although it is often a feature of intervention development and the early stages of pilot testing. In our work, differentiation represents the substantive differences between the normative model and business-as-usual. The normative program model may include components that are present in many educational settings because they represent expected or evidence-based practice. It is difficult, perhaps even unethical, to ask teachers or other implementers to refrain from such practices. However, a well-articulated model also contains elements that are unique to the experimental intervention, either in addition to already present evidence-based practices or in place of practices that lack an evidence base. As we describe elsewhere, for the PACT model, the unique elements include *Comprehension Canopy, Essential Words, Critical Reading, Team-Based Learning (TBL) Knowledge Application,* and *TBL Comprehension Check* along with the features of team-based learning. These are not typical, but represent the added value of PACT (over and above usual practice). When well implemented, they are the hypothesized cause of improved outcomes in randomized studies of the intervention.

We typically focus on *adherence* and *differentiation* when considering questions about teachers' use of a new program and the extent to which the program represents a feasible, unique, and potentially powerful alternative to usual practice. Work of this type often coincides with the pilot phase of a research program and with initial studies of the program's efficacy. Also, because *adherence* and *crossover* define *dosage* in our scheme, the program planning stage and early efficacy studies represent opportunities to "calibrate" *adherence* and *crossover* in the settings where the program will be evaluated, an undertaking that requires knowledge of teachers' usual practice, details on researchers' intended practice (as represented by the normative model), and a careful plotting of the points along which the two differ. This underscores the importance of documenting business-as-usual, both generally and in the local settings where the efficacy trial will be conducted. Recall that a treatment effect is essentially the difference between the outcomes associated with the new program and the outcomes that result from usual practice. Program planning that leverages the potential added value of a new intervention—the extent to which it is differentiated from usual practice—is more likely to yield programs that realize that value. Likewise, fidelity frameworks that acknowledge the importance of usual practice in understanding a given *effect* may be more successful in establishing a new treatment's efficacy.

In a completely group-randomized design, *dosage* represents differences in *adherence* and *crossover* within each block or teacher. Specifically, *dosage* describes the relative amounts of treatment available in treatment-assigned classrooms and in business-as-usual classrooms. *Dosage*, in our scheme, acknowledges that some amount of the treatment may *crossover* into business-as-usual classrooms, a real possibility in a within-teacher design, where teachers in business-as-usual classes have direct access to treatment materials and knowledge about their intended use. Our scheme also recognizes that *adherence* may not be 100%—some teachers may never implement all activities of the normative model in their treatment classes, some may always implement only a subset of activities, and some may always implement a subset of activities but occasionally implement others. If *adherence* is less than perfect and/or *crossover* is present for a given teacher, then a less-than-full *dosage* of treatment has been administered when averaged across classes and conditions within teachers. Likewise, a full dose is present for purposes of modeling student outcomes when *adherence* is 100% and when there is no *crossover* of treatment activities into business-as-usual classrooms. *Crossover* and *adherence* are of particular interest in a within-teacher randomized design.

We define *dosage* as the degree to which teachers adhere and crossover relative to a given *program model*. In this definition, *dosage* does not drive the effect; *the program model determines the effect. Dosage* only represents the degree to which the model is fully represented in a study of the treatment's efficacy or effectiveness. A program model that is ineffectual (its "true" effect is 0) will be disappointing no matter how perfect its implementation or how high its *dosage*. *Dosage* provides an index for understanding the extent to which the intended program model was in fact evident and properly allocated across groups and for understanding how less-than-perfect implementation may relate to a pattern of observed outcomes.

Measurement of Fidelity

Fidelity data in the PACT studies were collected by audio recording all participating teachers' classes across all instructional sessions (we used recording lanyards to collect and transmit the data). We favored audio recordings over direct observation for several reasons. First, most school districts, like those in which the PACT project was implemented, require that classroom visits be scheduled in advance for a specific day and time. Teaching behavior in the presence of a guest may represent a typical day's worth of instruction; however, on average, individuals behave differently when observed, particularly if an evaluative purpose is implied. Given this, we generally describe data collected using direct observation as indicative of what a teacher *can* do as much or more than what he or she in fact *does* do on a daily basis, whether in treatment classrooms or in the business-as-usual classes.

For example, teachers in the PACT project were fully aware of and reconciled to the reasons for not using PACT-unique methods and materials in their business-as-usual classes. A scheduled observation to a business-as-usual classroom

would likely discover an absence of PACT-unique instruction, even if PACT materials and methods are used on days previous to and subsequent to the visit. Likewise, in treatment classes, teachers may be more likely to engage in PACT-friendly behaviors when they know such are expected and when they know the day and time on which a visitor will be looking for these behaviors. We are not suggesting that this is true in all cases or for all teachers, only that it is more likely than not, and for purposes of measuring *adherence, crossover,* and ultimately *dosage,* it introduces a source of systematic error. Further, we are not suggesting that direct observation be avoided altogether. For PACT, we augmented recorded data with the occasional visit as a means of informally validating the audio recordings. Additionally, the research team had weekly access to the audio-recorded data and was able to intervene if necessary to deal with *crossover.* The lanyard itself created a disincentive to use the PACT materials and methods in business-as-usual classes. It provided teachers with a tangible reminder of the reasons for maintaining the study's randomized design, a legitimate aim in an efficacy context.

A second benefit of audio recording every instructional session is that it yields the population of teaching behavior for each participating professional. It is not necessary to code all of the data. Reliable samples can be drawn (and redrawn) from the population of behavior depending on one's research question and the necessary analyses. For example, in the PACT studies, *dosage* was conceptualized as a mediator of the effect of class-level assignment on student-level *outcomes* (more on this in a later section). This required the estimation of a cross-level product term, the analysis of which involved fairly demanding assumptions about the measurement properties for *dosage* compared to less complicated models. We were able to draw and code a larger sample of teacher behavior than we might have otherwise, and the records were coded more comprehensively than is typical as a means of more precisely estimating *adherence* and *crossover.* The objective was to derive highly accurate estimates of *adherence* and *crossover* to derive precise estimates of *dosage.*

A third advantage to audio-recording all sessions is that inter-rater reliability is more easily monitored and maintained. Because the record of teacher behavior is permanent, the accuracy of coded records can be checked at points in time, and records can be recoded as necessary. In the PACT work, initial inter-rater reliability on the fidelity instrument was established using a gold standard method (Gwet, 2012). To avoid observer drift, the coding team re-established reliability at points subsequent to the initial session. Further, if using a sample of audio-recorded teacher data as described in this chapter, the confirmatory factor measurement model can be estimated for different subsamples, with contrasts across the multiple measurement models providing a strong test of the measure's underlying reliability.

We matched PACT and business-as-usual classes within teachers by day of the week and drew a 30% simple random sample of matched pairs. Our reasoning was that the non-PACT-related elements of instruction might vary in both conditions by day of the week. The matching was done to minimize this variation. For

each sampled pair of instructional sessions, coders rated the extent to which the teacher implemented the elements that comprised each PACT-unique component. We rated *adherence* and *crossover* on the PACT-specific components using a four-point Likert-type scale. If the component was not required or expected for the sampled day, it was rated as not applicable. The same protocol was used to code PACT and business-as-usual classes. Coders were blind to treatment condition. We did not code teaching behaviors beyond the PACT-unique components. Instead, we assumed that required or evidence-based practices other than PACT-unique teaching behaviors would be comparably prevalent for each teacher regardless of condition.

We sampled matched pairs of recordings using a simple random approach. We considered alternatives, such as restricting the sample to the later stages of implementation or weighting transcripts of audio-recorded sessions to over-represent instruction from later stages of implementation, based on the likelihood that teachers would improve their use of PACT materials and methods given opportunities to practice such that teacher *adherence* on day 30 of the intervention would be greater than *adherence* on day 1, on average. However, because *dosage* represented PACT's availability, on *average*, we decided to sample randomly across the 30-day treatment interval. In a pilot setting, where a program's feasibility is the focus, a sampling plan stratified on the phases of implementation (e.g. day 1 versus day 30, or early versus late) would be reasonable. However, for an efficacy trial with *dosage* operationalized as a mediator, we decided to define *dosage* in terms of the entire 30-day cycle.

Fidelity (Dosage) as a Mediator

We analyzed PACT data using structural equation models (SEM). SEM is characterized by two sub-models, a measurement model and a structural model (Bollen, 1987; Byrne, 2012; Geiser, 2012; Hancock & Mueller, 2006). The measurement sub-model uses confirmatory factor analysis (CFA) to estimate hypothetical *latent* constructs based on observed data. Often, CFA uses scores from multiple tests to estimate values for a *latent* factor (e.g. reading comprehension could be conceptualized as a latent factor that predicts scores on the Gates-McGinnitie Reading Comprehension test, the Comprehension subtest from the Woodcock Johnson Reading Mastery Test, and the high-stakes reading measure used in the state where a study is staged). When a CFA is fit at the item level, the latent construct accounts for each item's contribution to the latent variable's estimate. For example, student responses on items from the Gates-McGinnitie Reading Comprehension test can be used to establish each item's difficulty and to estimate each respondent's reading comprehension level (for details on item-response models, see De Boeck & Wilson, 2004).

We estimated *dosage* in the measurement model of the general SEM using audio-recorded item-level data to estimate latent factors for *adherence* and *crossover*

within each block or teacher. *Dosage* described differences in the amount of PACT-specific behavior in a teacher's treatment classes (*adherence*) and the amount of PACT-specific behavior in her business-as-usual classes (*crossover*). In several studies, we used the mean of difference scores between *adherence* and *crossover* across classes within each block as the estimator of *dosage*. In other cases, we estimated *adherence* and *crossover* as latent factors using audio-recorded data from each class within blocks and conditions, and *dosage* was the differences between these latent factors. We also estimated *dosage* as a higher-order factor that predicted both *adherence* and *crossover* within blocks. The three models are increasingly ambitious and complex. They vary depending on the quality of the data with which we were working and the research questions of interest. However, as a general rule, including *dosage* and its constituent parts directly in the model (estimated as parameters with random components) increases the options for understanding how fidelity influences outcomes.

The other sub-model in SEM is the structural model. The structural model is a path analysis that represents the inter-relationships of the model's factors, whether observed or latent. In a single-level context, coefficients of each path in a model can be estimated using a series of regressions. In a multilevel model, the underlying math is more complex. However, the purpose remains the same—to explain patterns of systematic variation among a group of variables. Figure 4.2 depicts the general model that we fit using SEM, including the measurement sub-model (the arrows from *dosage* to the boxes labeled x_1 to x_6) and the structural model, which represents the inter-relationships of *assignment, dosage, outcomes*. The model is fit within each teacher or block. *Assignment* and *outcomes* are manifest variables and *dosage* is latent. The structural model, in this case, represents statistical mediation, with *dosage* mediating the effect of *assignment* on *outcomes*.

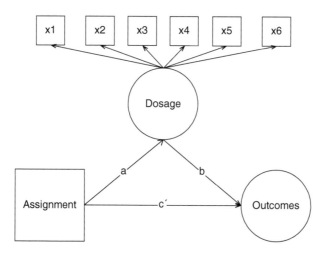

FIGURE 4.2 Structural Equation Model.

Statistical mediation (Hayes, 2013; MacKinnon, 2008) is used to model the influence of a third variable on the relationship of an independent and dependent variable. The application of statistical mediation in our PACT work is summarized in Figure 4.2, where path *a* and path *b* represent the indirect effect, and the product of *a* and *b* ($a \times b$) defines the *magnitude* of the mediation effect. The *c'* path represents the direct effect of assignment on student outcomes when the indirect effect is modeled (the "leftover variance" after accounting for the a*b mediation effect). Path c, not presented in Figure 4.2, is the total effect, which is merely the sum of the direct and indirect effects [(a*b) + c']. The statistical significance of the indirect effect can be determined in one of several ways. *Bootstrapping* is generally regarded as the most appropriate approach for evaluating whether an indirect effect differs from 0 (Cheung & Lau, 2008). Earlier approaches failed to acknowledge that the distribution of *a*b* is not known and is not necessarily normal, even if *a* and *b* are normally distributed. Bootstrapping uses a resampling-with-replacement method to create a sampling distribution for the indirect effect, producing robust standard errors for tests of statistical significance.

Recall that path *c'* is the direct effect of treatment when the indirect effect is also modeled. When the indirect effect differs statistically from 0 *and* when *c'* does not differ statistically from 0, the indirect effect has completely displaced the effect of *assignment* on *outcomes* in Figure 4.2. This scenario can be described as complete mediation. Partial mediation occurs when both the indirect effect, a*b, and the direct effect *c'* differ statistically from 0. Direct, indirect, and total effects can be calculated for the total sample and for different groups within the sample, and effects can be compared across groups of interest. In the PACT studies, the salient groups were classes assigned to treatment and classes assigned to business-as-usual.

Statistical Modeling

We discuss statistical mediation in the context of Figure 4.2. For illustrative purposes, we assume that the "true" treatment effect for PACT is .20. In Figure 4.2, this means that the total effect of *assignment* on the *outcome*, or the difference between treated students and untreated students, equals 20% of the sample's standard deviation (i.e. $c = .20$). We assume full *adherence* and no *crossover* because the "true" effect of a treatment presumes a full dose. We further assume that the mediating effect through *dosage* fully accounts for the total effect, which implies that there are no unmeasured confounding variables. Finally, we assume that dosage is reliably measured. Of course, in a "real world" setting, we do not know the effect of *assignment* on *dosage*, nor do we know the effect of *assignment* on *outcomes* or the mediating effect of *dosage* until the study is implemented and the data are collected and analyzed. We assume foreknowledge of these values here as a means of illustrating the inter-relationship and interdependence of *assignment, dosage,* and *outcomes* in an analytic context. We describe this fully known model as the "population model". In random-effects modeling, sample statistics from a given

study represent estimates of these population-level parameter values. Multiple replications of the study might yield different estimates of the treatment's effect (or different estimates of model parameters other than treatment effect); however, as the number of replications approaches infinity, the mean for a given parameter across iterations converges on the "true" or population value.

Thus, for the population model in this example, path b represents the total effect of treatment ($b = c$) assuming perfect *adherence* and no *crossover* ($a = 1$), and full mediation ($c' = 0$). Further, to the extent that *dosage* is reliably and fully measured, its effect on *outcomes* (i.e. path b) represents an upper limit for the effect of the treatment in question (recall that *dosage* and treatment are distinct), at least in the context of the business-as-usual that typifies the schools in which the study was conducted. If those in treatment received a full dose of the program and if those in comparison were completely unexposed to the treatment, then *dosage* may be at its maximum and the coefficient for path b may estimate the program's "true" effect for units similar to those where the study was conducted. This reduces to an intent-to-treat approach; with full compliance, complete implementation in treatment classes, and no crossover in the comparison, *assignment* and *dosage* are redundant. However, any given sample is only one of many possible samples for a given population of studies (again assuming random effects), meaning that any given analysis seldom if ever represents its population model with perfect accuracy. The more information one can gather about the relationship of *assignment* and *outcomes* beyond each unit's treatment assignment, the more fully one can identify the effect of treatment.

Deriving an estimate of the *dosage* participants received provides a key piece of information that improves our knowledge of the relationship between assignment and outcomes. Given that dosage rarely is 100%, what is the impact on the sample estimate of PACT's population-level effect if participants receive less than a full dose? In the PACT projects, implementation was typically characterized by imperfect though strong *adherence* and by limited but nontrivial *crossover*. In other words, path a was less than one because assignment to condition did not perfectly predict a teacher's use of the normative program model and thus it did not fully account for students' exposure to the PACT treatment. Table 4.1 summarizes the

TABLE 4.1 Normative Model for PACT

	Path a	Path b	Indirect Effect	c' (% of population effect)
Model 1	.90	.20	.18	.02 (90%)
Model 2	.80	.20	.16	.04 (80%)
Model 3	.70	.20	.14	.06 (70%)
Model 4	.50	.20	.10	.10 (50%)

Note: c' (% of population effect) represents the percentage of the population effect (the "true" effect) that is captured by the sample estimate.

consequences of less than perfect implementation. We hold the value for c constant at .20, because we assume that .20 is the total effect in the population model. We hold b at .20 as well, because that is the population value when implementation is perfect, and we manipulate values for path a to represent different levels of *adherence* and *crossover*. We have already stipulated that c' is 0 in the population model, so any nonzero value for c' in a given sample's data can be characterized as "uncaptured" variance in the total effect. c' represents the proportion of the total population-level effect that is not realized. Table 4.1 demonstrates that as *adherence* diminishes and/ or *crossover* increases, so too does the proportion of the population effect captured by the sample estimate. For example, when path a is .90, the indirect effect is .18 ($a*b$), which represents a loss of about 10% of the total effect in the population model (c' in the population is 0 but c' in the sample is .02). When path a equals .80, c' is .04, which means that 20% of the population total effect is uncaptured. Again, the population model presumes that $c = .20$ and that b fully explains this effect when implementation is perfect and *dosage* is reliably measured.

What is the impact on the sample estimate of PACT's population-level effect for different levels of *adherence* and *crossover*? Recall that we used a completely group-randomized design in the PACT studies, with classes randomized to treatment or business-as-usual within teachers. Teachers were treated as "blocks", and each block represented its own "mini" randomized study. Recall also that we used several approaches to calculate *dosage*, although they were increasingly sophisticated variations on a difference score between estimated values for *adherence* and *crossover* within each block. Table 4.2 displays several scenarios using different combinations of *adherence* and *crossover*. The values are means across all blocks. For convenience, we interpret these as the proportion of PACT-specific components present in treatment (*adherence*) and business-as-usual (*crossover*) classes. Note also that the values are presented as coefficients for path a.

Model 1 represents the ideal case and 100% of the "true" total effect is recovered in this sample. Model 4 represents the situation where the teacher uses the same amount of PACT-unique methods and materials in her treatment and business-as-usual classes. Path a (or *dosage*) in this case is 0 because assignment is unrelated to the amount of PACT students receive. Model 2 represents a likely

TABLE 4.2 Structural Equation Model

	Adherence	Crossover	Path a	c' (% of population effect)
Model 1	1.0	.00	1.00	.00 (100%)
Model 2	.80	.10	.70	.06 (70%)
Model 3	.80	.50	.30	.14 (30%)
Model 4	.50	.50	.00	.20 (0%)

Note: c' (% of population effect) represents the percentage of the population effect (the "true" effect) that is captured by the sample estimate.

scenario in a "real world" setting. Students in the treatment classes received a great deal of the PACT program and students in the business-as-usual received a bit of the PACT-specific instruction. Under these conditions, we expect to "recover" about 70% of the population effect or "true" effect; assuming the known-model described earlier, the treatment effect in the sample for Model 2 would be .14. For Model 3, the treatment effect would be .06, meaning that we have failed to retrieve most (70%) of the true effect. We assume that Model 4 is the worst of possible scenarios because it is unlikely that a teacher would make greater use of PACT materials and methods in her business-as-usual classes than in her treatment classes, short of a simple misunderstanding about assignment.

What impact does differences in the degree of use of PACT program components have on the measurement of dosage? Recall that we estimate *dosage* as part of the measurement model in SEM. In Figure 4.2, the observed data on which the measurement model is based are represented in squares. These are the coded audio-recorded data. Each square represents a PACT component and the arrow from dosage to each square represents the extent to which that component contributes to the estimation of dosage and ultimately to the sample estimate of the total treatment effect. Given such, hypotheses about the relative impact of one or more program components can tested. This would involve manipulating parameters in the measurement model, a topic that is beyond the technical scope of this paper. However, at a conceptual level, it is fairly straightforward to see how estimates of the path coefficients in the measurement model provide a means for evaluating the relative impact(s) of one or more program components. As a simple example, assume that *dosage* is relatively robust (.80) and that PACT's *Comprehension Canopy* (x_1 in Figure 4.2) accounts for 80% of the sample estimate of *dosage*. In a very simple rendering of Figure 4.2, *Comprehension Canopy* would account for about 64% of the sample estimate for the total treatment effect, assuming all of the earlier provisos related to the population model parameters. Again, this is provided for illustrative purposes only. It does not represent actual SEM results.

Final Observations and Several Recommendations

A well-designed plan for collecting fidelity data on a program's essential elements is an important first step in accounting for the degree to which a program is implemented as intended. However, using these data merely to report the extent of implementation (as is often seen in published studies) is an underuse of valuable and costly information. Failing to account for factors such as *adherence, crossover,* and *dosage* in the analysis of outcome data yields results based on the usually false assumption of perfect adherence, no crossover, and full dosage. As described in this chapter, modeling the extent to which *dosage* mediates *outcomes* better accounts for the true effect of the unique program elements that differentiate the instruction received in the treatment and business-as-usual conditions. Incorporating fidelity data in the analytical approach also allows for the detection of the program

elements that are key drivers of student outcomes, allowing for further refinement of the program's normative model for greater efficacy.

The practices outlined in this paper were part of a well-funded program of research. Some of the recommendations may not be feasible in other settings. However, there are a handful of practices that we think are feasible and necessary in most if not all efficacy contexts.

1. Focus implementation-related measurement on the points at which the normative treatment model and local business-as-usual differ. This requires knowledge of typical practice in schools where efficacy trials will be implemented. It also requires a well-specified program model that has been subject to iterative pilot studies.
2. Adopt a well-defined model of implementation fidelity and specify how implementation fidelity conditions the relationship of treatment and outcomes. We introduce adherence, crossover, and dosage within the context of a SEM analysis, with *dosage* modeled as a mediator. Other conceptual models are possible and may be more appropriate given circumstances other than those that we encountered in the PACT studies. The important point, in our view, is to be thoughtful about how implementation fidelity is likely to operate in the context of one's research design (including the assignment mechanism), one's research questions, and the analytic approach that one will use to estimate treatment effects. For example, *dosage* was a key construct in the PACT work because it aligned with the program's research questions. In another context, it may be less important than other fidelity-related constructs. Differences in this respect should be carefully considered during the earliest stages of the project planning process.

Technical Notes

In this section, we provide additional comments on several topics in Chapter 4. These include: (1) completely randomized block designs; (2) estimation of multi-level mediation models; (3) interpretation of mediation models; and (4) a generalized form of the estimand used to estimate dosage.

1. Several assumptions apply to completely randomized block designs. Randomly assigning groups to one or more treatments allows inferences about the causes of observed outcomes. However, these inferences can be biased if several key assumptions are unmet or unaddressed during analysis. First, the logic that underlies inferential models assumes (1) that a *population* of observations (i.e. observations for the same study if it was replicated on a very, very large number of occasions) accumulate according to a probability function (some observations are more probable than others); (2) that this probability function can be described as a distribution with a mean, standard deviation, and

other attributes; and (3) that the occurrence of a given observation within the distribution does not increase the probability of another observation's occurrence. We assumed that teacher-level effects are normally and independently distributed, which means that the distribution of coefficients for b_j is symmetric (i.e. equal area under the curve on either side of the mean value) with a population mean of μ and variance of σ^2 and that the occurrence of any given value in this distribution of effects does not influence the probability of other values occurring (however, note that research designs in schools violate the independence assumption because students in the same classroom or teachers in the same school are more likely to be similar to others in their classroom or school than other classrooms or schools; we discuss this possibility in the section on nested data in this volume's introduction). The same assumptions are required for the errors, ε_{ij}, in a randomized complete blocks design. Further, because the study involves observations on a handful of variables, rather than a single variable, the multivariate variation for these assumptions applies. In other words, we assumed that the distribution for these multiple variables was normal and that observations in this multivariate "space" were independent. These assumptions are often overlooked or underemphasized. However, they are necessary for making unbiased inferences about a treatment's role in *causing* observed differences at posttest.

2. In multilevel mediation with cross-level mediating effects, conflating the two variance components (between- and within-groups) that comprise the b path into a single estimated b biases estimates on both the between and within levels, if the effects at these two levels in fact differ (Preacher et al., 2010). The direct path from assignment to the outcome is labeled c; when adjusted for the indirect effect, this path is generally relabeled c'. In complete mediation, the product of a and b entirely displaces the c path. To avoid conflating slopes for path b, we separated variance in the observed relationship into latent between- and within-groups components which were modeled separately but simultaneously to estimate relationships at each level (Muthen & Muthen, 2014; Preacher and Kelly, 2011; Preacher et al., 2010).

3. In the context of randomized designs, mediation can be described in several ways. In SEM, mediation is often characterized as causal when the independent variable has a significant effect on the outcome, when the independent variable has a significant effect on the mediator, which is path a in Figure 4.2, and when the product of coefficients for X on Y through the mediator differs statistically from 0 (Muthen & Asparouhov, 2009; Pearl, 2001). In our case, assignment to PACT or business-as-usual predicted the amount of PACT-related materials and methods a teacher used in a given class (the amount of *adherence* or *crossover* depending on condition) which in turn predicted the dosage of PACT available to students in that class, path b in Figure 4.2. The causal argument is reasonable if the mediator occurs subsequent to the independent variable and if errors in the mediator are

uncorrelated with errors in the outcome. However, it is important to note that the relationship of the mediator and the outcome in such models is technically a covariance. The mediator does not cause changes in outcomes because we did not manipulate (or randomize) levels of *dosage* within the two treatment conditions. However, a mediator-randomized design is seldom feasible (where the mediator is randomized within levels of the independent variable), and it is not necessary to the "naïve" approach (Muthen & Asparouhov, 2009) that generally characterizes mediation models in education science.

4. In the potential outcomes (or causal inference) framework, mediation depends on four assumptions: (i) no unmeasured confounding of the treatment-outcome relationship; (ii) no unmeasured confounding of the mediator-outcome relationship; (iii) no unmeasured treatment mediator confounding; and (iv) no mediator-outcome confounder affected by treatment (Valeri & VanderWeele, 2011). Random assignment to condition satisfies assumptions (i) through (iii) for purposes of estimating direct effects. However, in a potential outcomes framework, assumption (iv) is necessary. Sometimes described as sequential ignorability, it is generally assumed, and to the extent that the assumption holds, mediated causal effects can be identified. The alternative to assuming (iv) is to randomize the mediator within levels of the independent variable, an approach that generally falls beyond the realm of feasible research designs.

    The widely accepted alternative (sometimes called the SEM approach—Pearl [2001]) is to adopt a naïve (Muthen & Asparouhov, 2009) stance related to mediation, where x is shown to cause y and x is shown to cause m, given a randomized design. However, causal indirect effects are assumed if the product of coefficients for x on y through m differs statistically from 0. Note as well that in a potential outcomes framework, random assignment meets criteria for an instrumental variable, meaning that it can be used as an exogenous proxy for treatment status to estimate local area treatment effects (or complier average causal effect), a class of causal effects in the potential outcomes framework.

5. In the present example, we estimate the relationships in Figure 4.2 to determine the extent to which the data support the hypothetical model. The relationship between *assignment* and *dosage* can be modeled using a dummy-coded variable (0/1) or effects coding (−.5/+.5) to represent treatment and business-as-usual. Sometimes called a MIMIC model, this approach requires the assumption of (or test for) no difference at posttest in the covariances for the two groups. Alternatively, multi-group models can be fit. Multi-group approaches estimate the same model in the treatment and business-as-usual conditions. The assumption of covariance equivalence does not apply for the structural elements of the model (the three main variables and paths a, b, and c) because the covariance matrices are separately but simultaneously

modeled for each group. However, equivalence (termed *measurement invariance*) has to be established in the measurement model for the multi-group approach (see Cheung and Rensvold, 2012 for a discussion of measurement invariance). In Figure 4.2, we depict *assignment* as a dichotomous variable. We estimated *dosage* as a continuous *latent* variable in the measurement model. Latent variables are one of the advantages of SEM, because they represent more precise estimates of a given construct compared to observed measures of the same construct. In Figure 4.2, x_1 through x_6 are observed (or "heard") data for each of the 6 program components in the PACT program model. We do not show the error terms in Figure 4.2 for the sake of parsimony.

6. The estimating equation for the *structural* model in Figure 4.2 can be written as:

$$Y_{ijk} = \gamma_{000} + \gamma_{010\,tjk} + \gamma_{020\,mjk} + \gamma_{030\,cjk} + \varepsilon_{ijk} + r_{1jk} + \mu_{00k} + \mu_{01k} + \mu_{02k} \tag{1a}$$

$$m_{jk} = a_{00k} + a_{01ktjk} + r_{2jk} \tag{1b}$$

$$\begin{aligned} = \gamma_{000} + \gamma_{010\,tjk} + \gamma_{020} \left(a_{00k} + a_{01ktjk} + r_{2jk} \right) + \gamma_{030\,cjk} + \varepsilon_{ijk} + r_{1jk} + \\ \mu_{00k} + \mu_{01k} + \mu_{02k} \end{aligned} \tag{2}$$

$$\begin{aligned} = \gamma_{000} + \gamma_{010\,tjk} + \gamma_{020}\,a_{00k} + \gamma_{020}\,a_{01ktjk} + \gamma_{020}\,r_{2jk} + \gamma_{030\,cjk} + \varepsilon_{ijk} + \\ r_{1jk} + \mu_{00k} + \mu_{01k} + \mu_{02k} \end{aligned} \tag{3}$$

where γ_{000} is the is the grand mean for student outcomes, γ_{010} is the average direct effect of treatment, $\gamma_{020}\,a_{00k}$ is the average indirect of treatment via mediator m, and γ_{030} is the average effect associated with the level-2 covariate, c. Person-level residuals, ε_{ijk}, and cluster-level residuals, r_{0jk}, are assumed normally distributed with means of 0, and variances of δ^2 and τ_π variance between clusters and within sites, respectively. The terms, μ_{00k}, μ_{01k}, and μ_{02k} represent random effects associated with each site-level mean, with each site-level treatment effect, and with each site-level mediating effect, respectively. We assume that γ_{030} is constant across sites. Though not represented in (3), we specify variance between site means as τ_{b00} and variance between site-level treatment effects as τ_{b11}. The coefficient τ_{b01} represents covariance between site-level means and site-level treatment effects. The total effect, which can be conceptualized as the average treatment effect, is the sum of the direct and indirect effects.

Acknowledgement

The research described here was supported by Grant R305F100013 from the Institute of Education Sciences, U.S. Department of Education. The opinions expressed are those of the authors and do not represent views of the Institute or the U.S. Department of Education.

References

Bollen, K. A. (1987). Total, direct, and indirect effects in structural equation models. *Sociological Methodology*, 17, 37–69.

Byrne, B. M. (2012). *Structural Equation Modeling with Mplus: Basic Concepts, Applications, and Programming*. New York: Routledge.

Cheung, G. W. and Rensvold, R. B. (2002). Evaluating goodness-of-fit indexes for testing measurement invariance. *Structural Equation Modelling*, 9(2), 233–255.

Cheung, G. W. and Lau, R. S. (2008). Testing mediation and suppression effects of latent variables: Bootstrapping with structural equation models. *Organizational Research Methods*, 11, 296–325.

De Boeck, P. and Wilson, M. (2004). *A Framework for Item Response Models*. New York: Springer.

Funnell, S. C. and Rogers, P. J. (2011). *Purposeful Program Theory: Effective Use of Theories of Change and Logic Models*. San Francisco, CA: Jossey-Bass.

Geiser, C. (2012). *Data Analysis with Mplus*. New York: Guilford.

Gwet, K. L. (2012). *Handbook of Inter-Rater Reliability* (3rd ed.). Maryland: Advanced Analytics, LLC.

Hancock, G. R. and Mueller, R. O. (2006). *Structural Equation Modeling: A Second Course*. Greenwich, CT: Information Age Publishing.

Hayes, A. F. (2013). *An Introduction to Mediation, Moderation, and Conditional Process Analysis*. New York: Guilford.

Imbens, G. W. and Rubin, D. B. (2015). *Causal Inference in Statistics, Social, and Biomedical Sciences*. New York: Cambridge University Press.

Johnson, D. W. and Johnson, R. T. (1987). *Learning Together and Alone: Cooperative, Competitive, and Individualistic Learning*. New Jersey: Prentice-Hall, Inc.

MacKinnon (2008). *Introduction to Statistical Mediation Analysis*. New York: Lawrence Erlbaum Associates.

Muthén, B. and Asparouhov, T. (2009). Multilevel regression mixture analysis. *Journal of the Royal Statistical Society: Series A (Statistics in Society)*, 172(3), 639–657.

Muthén, L. K. and Muthén, B. O. (2014). *Mplus User's Guide: Statistical Analysis with Latent Variables*. Available online at www.StatModel.com

Pearl, J. (August 2001). Direct and indirect effects. In *Proceedings of the Seventeenth Conference on Uncertainty in Artificial Intelligence*. San Francisco, CA: Morgan Kaufmann Publishers Inc. 411–420.

Preacher, K. J. and Kelley, K. (2011). Effect size measures for mediation models: Quantitative strategies for communicating indirect effects. *Psychological Methods*, 16(2), 93–115.

Preacher, K. J., Zyphur, M. J., and Zhang, Z. (2010). A general multilevel SEM framework for assessing multilevel mediation. *Psychological Methods*, 15(3), 209–233.

Sisk, R. J. (2011). Team-based learning: Systematic research review. *Journal of Nursing Education*, 50(12), 665–669.

Swanson, E. A. and Wanzek, J. (2014). Applying research in reading comprehension to social studies instruction for middle and high school students. *Intervention in School and Clinic*, 49, 142–147.

Sweet, M. S. and Michaelsen, L. K. (Eds.) (2012). *Team-Based Learning in the Social Sciences and Humanities: Group Work that Works to Generate Critical Thinking and Engagement*. Sterling, VA: Stylus.

Valeri, L. and VanderWeele, T. J. (2013). Mediation analysis allowing for exposure–mediator interactions and causal interpretation: Theoretical assumptions and implementation with SAS and SPSS macros. *Psychological Methods*, 18(2), 137–150.

Vaughn, S., Swanson, E., Roberts, G., Wanzek, J., Stillman-Spisak, S. J., Solis, M., and Simmons, D. (2013). Improving reading comprehension and social studies knowledge in middle school. *Reading Research Quarterly*, 48, 77–93.

Vaughn, S., Roberts, G., Swanson, E. A., Wanzek, J., Fall, A.-M., and Stillman-Spisak, S. J. (2015). Improving middle school students' knowledge and comprehension in social studies: A replication. *Educational Psychology Review*, 27, 31–50.

Wanzek, J., Vaughn, S., Kent, S. C., Swanson, E. A., Roberts, G., Haynes, M., and Solis, M. (2014). The effects of team-based learning on social studies knowledge acquisition in high school. *Journal of Research on Educational Effectiveness*, 7(2), 183–204.

5

INTENT-TO-TREAT AND TREATMENT TAKE-UP EFFECTS OF SUMMER SCHOOL ON THE LITERACY OUTCOMES OF STRUGGLING EARLY READERS

Keith Zvoch

Interest in establishing the causal effects of social and educational interventions has drawn attention to the application of the randomized control trial (RCT) in field-based settings (Murnane & Willett, 2011). As in the laboratory, use of a probabilistic assignment mechanism has the advantage of equating study groups in expectation, and thereby offers a straightforward means for providing control over the universe of potential confounding variables. The ease and strength of the inferential logic on which the RCT rests (Heckman, 2005; Holland, 1986; Rubin, 1974) and the historic dearth of RCTs in school-based settings (Cook, 2002) has led to a recent change in the emphasis that federal funding agencies place on applicants seeking extramural support for educational research (IES, 2014; NSF, 2013). By encouraging applicants to propose and implement stronger inferential designs, an increase in the number of small and larger scale RCTs has been realized (see Spybrook, 2013; Spybrook et al., 2013). The results of these investigations have begun to provide sorely need empirical evidence of "what works" in a variety of academic, behavioral, and social domains. However, many questions currently remain regarding the strength and nature of the inference that can be drawn when a field-based RCT is impacted by treatment non-compliance and failures in program implementation (Raudenbush et al., 2012; Sagarin et al., 2014; Weiss et al., 2013).

Despite recognition as the most direct method for supporting causal inference, the RCT can often be difficult to correctly implement in practice. In both the lab and the field, the occurrence of a variety of design breakdowns (e.g. treatment non-compliance, participant attrition) may compromise the inferential strength of an otherwise well-designed experimental investigation (Puma et al., 2009; Shadish et al., 2002; U.S. Department of Education, 2013). The threat of a design

breakdown is summarily increased outside the laboratory as treatment providers and participants often have greater latitude regarding the extent to which treatment protocols are followed. In an applied context, treatment providers may choose to forgo delivering some or all of the active intervention components and intended program recipients may opt to take-up different amounts of the treatment that is offered. In other cases, providers may intentionally or unintentionally deliver aspects of the treatment to the control group and/or control group members may actively seek out and obtain varying amounts of the intervention (Murnane & Willett, 2011). A variety of organizational and contextual constraints may also conspire to limit the amount of treatment that is delivered to and received by program participants (Durlack & DuPre, 2008; Fixsen et al., 2005).

For field-based researchers and program evaluators, the potential for a breakdown in design protocol makes the collection and use of treatment take-up and implementation data a necessary component in virtually all applied intervention studies. The availability of data on the extent to which a treatment was actually delivered and received as intended can aid in contextualizing study results and in some cases, may preserve some of the inferential strength of the original design (Hulleman & Cordray, 2009; Weiss et al., 2013; Zvoch, 2012). For example, the ability to explicitly define the obtained contrast in conditions and examine site-based differences in participant outcomes offers the researcher and evaluator opportunity to identify the extent to which treatment effects vary across and in relation to the operational characteristics at each site (Bloom et al., 2014; Schochet at al., 2014). Treatment implementation data may also provide insight into the conditions that support a high-fidelity delivery of protocol and can be useful in identifying if the treatment is differentially effective for certain population subgroups (Bloom & Michalopoulos, 2013; Schochet et al., 2014; Weiss et al., 2013; Zvoch, 2009). In light of the value offered by measurement and analysis of unintended deviations from design protocol, the purpose of this paper is to discuss and demonstrate the application of several methodological approaches for incorporating treatment implementation data in field-based RCTs. The overarching goal is to present an example that contains many common participant non-compliance and field-based treatment fidelity issues and highlight the inherent tradeoffs that are associated with statistical models that aim to integrate fidelity data into the estimation of treatment effects.

Method

Demonstration Context

The applied example involves the delivery of supplemental instruction in a school-based summer literacy program. As described in detail elsewhere (Zvoch, 2012; Zvoch & Stevens, 2013, 2015), supplemental instruction was delivered to struggling readers over the course of 5-weeks during the 3-month summer

vacation period in one central school site. Students received 2.5 hours of direct literacy instruction in whole and small group settings 4 days a week throughout the intervention period, for a total of 50 additional hours of school-based literacy instruction (2.5 hours/day * 4 days/week * 5 weeks). Other than the increased time available for instruction, the summer literacy model was analogous to that delivered during the academic year. Each day, teacher-directed instruction in the critical beginning reading skills of phonemic awareness (oral blending and segmentation) and alphabetic understanding (letter-sounds, decoding, phonic analysis, and fluency/automaticity [speed and accuracy in reading connected text]) was provided to students. The direct modeling of core literacy skills and the provision of multiple opportunities for practice with corrective feedback reflected the evidenced-based instructional approaches that best facilitate early childhood literacy development (National Reading Panel, 2000).

Historically, the summer program was offered to early elementary students who scored below benchmark performance on a spring literacy assessment. For students completing first grade, the basis for a summer school invitation was the production of less than 30 words correct per minute (WCPM) on the Test of Oral Reading Fluency (TORF) (Children's Education Services, 1987). In 2010 and 2011, the district worked with a research team at a local university to add a randomized component to the traditional need-based assignment practice. During these two summers, in addition to the most severely struggling readers, a group of moderately at-risk readers were identified and randomly assigned an offer to participate in the 5-week summer school program. In 2010, a pool containing 48 first grade students who scored in an interval (30–50 WCPM) just above the traditional cutpoint for receipt of a summer school invitation were identified. In 2011, the assignment pool included 53 students.[1]

In total, the random assignment pool consisted of 101 students from the district's seven elementary schools. Demographically, the pool was 76% non-Latino White ($n = 77$) and 56% male ($n = 57$). Sixty-nine percent of the sample received a free or reduced price lunch ($n = 70$) and 10% were identified as English language learners ($n = 10$). Once assigned, the treatment and control groups were comprised of relatively equal percentages of students from special populations. Free lunch recipients (71%, 68%), English language learners (10%, 10%), and students from ethnic minority groups (23%, 25%) characterized the treatment and control groups respectively.

Study Purpose and Plan

The purpose of randomizing a group of moderately at-risk readers to summer school was to identify the effect of the district's supplemental instructional program on a policy-relevant population subgroup. The random assignment of a summer school offer was employed to control for the universe of potential confounding variables, thereby enabling a post-intervention contrast in group

outcomes to be plausibly attributed to the differential treatment conditions experienced by study participants. The intervention was designed to provide a 50-hour instructional contrast between the treatment (50 hours of summer instruction) and control (0 hours of summer instruction) conditions. Logistically, treatment assignment occurred in conjunction with the administration and scoring of the spring TORF assessment. After spring TORF scores were obtained, the research team constructed the assignment pool, randomly assigned students to conditions, and provided district colleagues with a list of students (via study identification numbers) that were assigned to treatment. Recruitment of assigned students was then immediately begun by district literacy coordinators. Students and their families were notified of the summer school invitation in mid-May, approximately 4 weeks prior to the end of the school year.

Treatment Fidelity Issues

As in the laboratory, combining random assignment with uniform delivery and take-up of treatment enables one to draw a strong inference regarding treatment impact. However, the strength of the inference available from a field-based RCT is weakened to the extent that there is non-compliance with treatment assignment and/or when treatment is not delivered and received according to program design. In the current study, several deviations from design protocol served to impact identification of the summer school effect as not all students who were offered a summer school invitation chose to participate and students who were assigned and enrolled in summer school did not always attend fully. The manner in which the change in summer literacy was measured also resulted in the capture of varying amounts of academic year instruction in the summer learning estimate.

Treatment Non-Compliance

Non-compliance with treatment assignment was the first fidelity-related issue that threatened the validity of the RCT. Treatment non-compliance occurs when those assigned to treatment refuse to participate or when those assigned to the control condition seek out and become members of the treatment group. The self-selection into or out of treatment has the potential to compromise RCT treatment effect estimates as the assignment mechanism may no longer be ignorable given endogenous manipulation of group composition by study participants. In the example under consideration, while the summer school offer was randomly assigned, summer school participation was voluntary and a number of students/families chose not to accept the offer. In 2010, 24 of 48 students from the random assignment pool were offered a summer school placement; in 2011, 37 of 53 students received an invitation. In spite of extensive recruitment efforts, only 71% (17 of 24) of students offered a summer school placement in 2010 and

59% (22 of 37) of invited students in 2011 chose to attend. Although none of the students assigned to the control condition sought out and became a summer school participant, with 22 of 61 students refusing the summer school offer, the overall non-compliance rate was 36%.

In addition to the students who refused to comply with their treatment assignment, several students who accepted the summer school invitation did not attend each session. Days of summer school attendance ranged from a low of five to a high of 20 (i.e. perfect attendance), with an overall mean of 17.21 ($SD = 2.97$). The imperfect attendance rate also ensured that some summer school students did not receive a full dose of supplemental instruction.

Measurement Timing

The intended treatment contrast (i.e. 50 hours of school-based summer literacy instruction for the treatment group, zero for control) was also indirectly impacted by the manner in which the summer learning outcome was measured. As is common in the summer school literature, students' summer learning was indexed on the basis of the difference between their last available test score in the academic year prior to summer vacation and the first available test score in the following academic year (Alexander et al., 2001; Cooper et al., 2000; Zvoch & Stevens, 2015). In the current example, the spring oral reading fluency assessment that serves as one half of the basis for calculating the change in summer learning was administered approximately 4–5 weeks prior to the end of the first grade academic year. As a result, both treatment and control students experienced approximately 20 days of instruction (4 weeks × 5 days) after the first grade spring assessment. A similar problem was not realized with the second grade fall assessment however, as all students were screened during the first week of classes.

Instructional Exposure

The misalignment between the spring measurement schedule and the summer vacation period resulted in a non-trivial amount of post-assignment academic year literacy instruction being delivered to study participants. The specific amount of instruction experienced by students was contingent upon two factors: academic year supplemental instruction status and the number of year-end absences. In the district where the study was conducted, all first grade students receive 1 hour of daily literacy instruction. An additional 0.5 hours of supplemental literacy instruction is also provided to students who receive "Tier II" services in conjunction with the district's Response-to-Intervention (RtI) instructional program. Tier II students therefore could have received up to an additional 30 hours (20 instructional days × 1.5 hours of daily instruction) of academic year literacy instruction after the spring oral reading fluency assessment. The actual instructional dosage was determined by the number of student absences that occurred during the final

4 weeks of the academic year (see below). Over this time period, students missed an average of 0.86 days of school ($SD = 1.29$; $X_{min} = 0$, $X_{max} = 7$).

Treatment Fidelity Measures

To facilitate the analysis of outcome data, two types of fidelity measures were constructed. Dummy codes were first used to form several dichotomous summer status indicators that were applied in statistical models designed to estimate and compare the summer reading fluency outcomes of the study subgroups. A continuous measure of students' post-assignment instructional exposure was also constructed. The instructional exposure measure was used to index the total amount of "summer" instruction received by study participants. The index served as a basis for describing subgroup differences in instructional receipt and for computing the actual contrast in treatment conditions (i.e. the instructional hour difference) that was realized at each site during the course of the study. As is described in more detail below, the school-level treatment contrast offered a means for examining site-based variation in treatment effects.

Compliance Indicators: Dichotomous

The first dummy-coded indicator variable distinguished between students who were randomly assigned to summer school (whether they attended or not) and their peers who were in the assignment pool, but did not receive an invitation to attend (i.e. the control group). This contrast provided an Intent-to-Treat (ITT) estimate of the effect of assignment to summer school. A second set of dummy codes was then used to distinguish between treatment participants, refusers (i.e. "no-shows"), and students in the control group. Two dummy codes were used to represent the three groups with the control group serving as the referent. The separation of students who did not accept the summer school offer from those who did facilitated a group-specific contrast between treatment participants and controls and between treatment refusers and controls. The distinction between participant and non-participant groups yielded an As-Treated (AT) estimate of treatment receipt. A final indicator distinguished between those who participated in summer school and those who did not regardless of their treatment assignment. The reassignment of non-compliers to the control condition was used to account for participation status in an instrumental variable (IV) model used to estimate the effect of treatment receipt.

Student-Level Instructional Exposure Index: Continuous

In addition to the dichotomous summer status indicators, an instructional exposure index was constructed to examine reading fluency change as a direct function of instructional dose. The exposure index was assembled by combining

Instrumental variable (IV) methods were then used as another approach to account for treatment non-compliance. An instrument is a variable or set of variables that is correlated with an outcome only through its effect on other variables. For example, as random assignment has a direct impact on treatment group status, but can only be related to a treatment outcome through its effect on inducing treatment participation, random assignment can be used as an instrument to derive an unbiased estimate of the effect of treatment receipt (Angrist et al., 1996; Heckman & Robb, 1985). In the current example, random assignment of the summer school offer enables one to derive unbiased estimates of the effect of assignment on summer TORF change (i.e. ITT) and summer school participation (i.e. did or did not attend). The effect of treatment receipt is obtained by regressing the two outcomes on the dummy-coded treatment status indicator and computing the ratio of the two estimates (i.e. ITT estimate/proportion of compliers) or by estimating a two-stage least-squares regression model.

An estimate of the local effect of treatment recept was also obtained using model-based Complier Average Causal Effect (CACE) methods. A CACE analysis allows unbiased estimation of the effects of an intervention by modeling unknown compliance status as missing data (Imbens & Rubin, 1997; Little & Yau, 1998). More specifically, while the compliance status of students assigned to summer school was known (i.e. assigned students were either participants or refusers), the compliance status of students assigned to the control group was unknown or latent. The CACE method estimates the compliance status of control group members and generates a treatment effect estimate for the complier group (Jo, 2002; Jo & Muthén, 2001).

Figure 5.1 presents the CACE model path diagram. In the figure, boxes are used to represent observed variables, including the independent variable, assignment status and the dependent variable, TORF summer change. A circle with an embedded box is used to represent compliance status, a partially unobserved categorical latent variable (i.e. compliance status is known in treatment group, but is estimated in the control group). The path from assignment status to TORF summer change estimates the summer school effect while the intersecting arrow from compliance status denotes that the treatment effect varies by compliance status. The path from compliance status to summer TORF change indicates that the intercept also varies across compliance class. Demographic covariates (e.g. gender, ethnicity, free lunch status, etc.) are also specified as a set of observed predictors of compliance status and TORF summer change. The latent mixture CACE analysis was performed within a structural equation modeling framework using Mplus 6.11 (Muthén & Muthén, 2010).

The final set of inferential analyses were designed to estimate and model site-based variability in treatment effects. The examination of site-to-site differences via multilevel modeling techniques (e.g. Raudenbush & Bryk, 2002) should only be considered demonstrative and exploratory however, given design limitations that do not fully support a robust multilevel analytic framework. These limitations

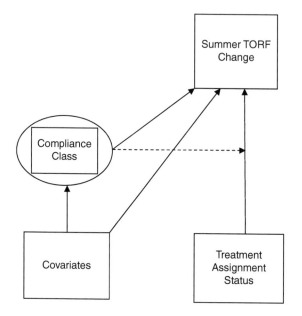

FIGURE 5.1 Summer School CACE Model.

include the student-level assignment to conditions, the post hoc identification of a partially nested data structure (i.e. the academic year nesting of students within schools vs. the central school site for summer school participants), as well as the relatively small number of students and schools in the sample.

In the multilevel analyses, the dummy-coded treatment/control assignment indicator was specified as a site-centered, student-level predictor of summer reading fluency change. The associated parameter was allowed to vary across school sites. This specification generated an ITT estimate for each school. At level-2, variance in the ITT estimates was modeled as a function of the achieved treatment contrast in each school location (i.e. the instructional hour difference between treatment and control students). To control for the total amount of instruction received by sampled students at each site, mean instructional hours were specified as a predictor of school mean reading fluency change. Equation 1 presents the within-school model, where Y_{ij} is the change in summer reading fluency for student i in school j, β_{0j} is the mean change in reading fluency in school j, β_{1j} is the ITT effect for school j, and r_{ij} is a student level residual term. Equations 2a and 2b present the between-school model where the intercept and slope coefficients estimated at level-1 become outcomes predicted by level-2 school variables and associated residual terms (u's).

$$Y_{ij} = \beta_{0j} + \beta_{1j} \text{ (Assignment Status)} + r_{ij} \qquad (1)$$
$$\beta_{0j} = \gamma_{00} + \gamma_{01} \text{ (Mean Instructional Hours)} + u_{0j} \qquad (2a)$$
$$\beta_{1j} = \gamma_{10} + \gamma_{11} \text{ (Treatment Contrast)} + u_{1j} \qquad (2b)$$

Results

Table 5.1 presents the pretest, posttest, and summer change TORF means and standard deviations for each of the groups. A comparison of means on the pre-program spring literacy assessment revealed that the treatment and control group formed by assignment $F(1, 99) = 3.28$, $MSR = 87.82$, $p > .05$ and the student groups (i.e. participants, refusers, controls) formed by treatment non-compliance, $F(2, 98) = 1.68$, $MSR = 88.62$, $p > .05$ did not statistically differ at the point at which treatment assignment occurred.

Intent-to-Treat (ITT)

In the ITT model contrasting summer TORF outcomes for students randomly assigned to treatment or control, the average change in summer oral reading fluency for control students was a statistically non-significant 3 WCPM loss in fluency ($b_0 = -3.20$, $SE = 1.72$, $p = .06$). In contrast, the coefficient associated with the between-group comparison was positive and statistically significant ($b_1 = 6.25$, $SE = 2.21$, $p < .05$). For those randomly assigned to summer school, the average change in summer oral reading fluency was estimated as a 3 WCPM gain (i.e. $6.25 - 3.20 = 3.05$).

Compliance-Adjusted ITT/Instrumental Variable (IV) Analysis

The application of correction factor for non-compliance with treatment assignment resulted in an upward adjustment to the ITT estimate. Weighting the ITT estimate by the proportion of treatment-group members who accepted the treatment offer and actually received school-based summer instruction, the estimated summer-school effect was approximately 10 additional WCPM for summer

TABLE 5.1 Oral Reading Fluency and Instructional Hour Means and Standard Deviations by Treatment Status

Variable	Participants		Refusers		Controls	
	M	SD	M	SD	M	SD
Spring TORF Grade 1	44.82	9.87	44.00	6.75	47.98	10.16
Fall TORF Grade 2	49.64	13.59	43.91	12.45	44.78	13.46
Summer TORF Change	4.82	9.41	−0.09	10.40	−3.20	12.13
Instructional Hours	68.11	8.25	22.82	5.15	24.42	4.86
N	39		22		40	

Notes: Participants and refusers were students who were randomly assigned to summer school. Students who were not randomly assigned to summer school were controls.

school participants (i.e. 6.25/0.64 = 9.77) or a 6.5 WCPM summer fluency gain (9.77 − 3.20 = 6.57). An analogous treatment effect estimate was obtained in the two-stage least squares IV model, $b = 9.77$, $SE = 3.46$, $p < .05$.

As-Treated (AT)

In the AT model that reassigned students on the basis of their achieved treatment status, the average change in summer oral reading fluency for the control group was again a statistically non-significant 3.20 word-per-minute loss in fluency ($p = .06$). The contrast between treatment refusers and control students was also not statistically significant ($b_1 = 3.11$, $SE = 2.87$, $p > .05$). However, contrasting treatment participants with students randomly assigned to the control group revealed a statistically significant between-group treatment difference of 8 WCPM ($b_2 = 8.02$, $SE = 2.42$, $p < .05$) or an approximate 5 WCPM gain (8.02 − 3.20 = 4.82) over the summer. When the regression was rerun with the group of treatment participants serving as the referent group, the summer gain for participants (i.e. $b_0 = 8.02$, $SE = 2.42$) was statistically different from zero ($p < .05$).

Complier Average Causal Effect (CACE)

To further evaluate the effects of summer school, a latent mixture model for randomized trials with treatment non-compliance (Jo, 2002; Jo & Muthén, 2001) was estimated. In the CACE model, compliance status was represented by a categorical latent variable identifying compliance class (see Figure 5.1). CACE results revealed a statistically significant effect of treatment for compliers ($b = 12.32$, $SE = 5.35$, $p < .05$), with compliers outperforming non-compliers by 12 WCPM. For non-compliers, the average change in summer oral reading fluency was estimated as a statistically non-significant 7.50 WCPM loss ($p = .14$). It should also be noted that within the relatively homogenous sample of moderately at-risk readers, none of the demographic covariates were predictive of compliance-class membership or summer-fluency outcomes.

Table 5.2 provides a summary of results from the dichotomous treatment status models. In Table 5.2, it can be seen that the larger WCPM estimates were obtained when methods that accounted for non-compliance with treatment assignment were applied. Relative to the ITT estimate, compliers (or those who would have complied if assigned) were estimated to outperform their peers by 6–12 WCPM over the study period. However, with the exception of the AT estimate, the standardized effect of treatment remained relatively constant across the models. Overall, the treatment group was estimated to outperform the control group by .5-.7 of a standard deviation depending on the analytic model applied.

TABLE 5.2 Treatment Impact Estimates

Analytic Model	Estimate	SE	ES
Intent-to-Treat (ITT)	6.25*	2.21	0.57
Instrumental Variable (IV)	9.77*	3.46	0.59
As-Treated (AT)	8.02*	2.42	0.74
Complier Average Causal Effect (CACE)	12.32*	5.35	0.48
Multilevel ITT	6.23*	1.95	0.57

Notes: Results based on data from 101 students
SE = standard error
ES = Effect Size
$* = p < .05$

Instructional Dose and Treatment Contrast

After examining summer reading fluency change as a function of treatment group-status indicators, summer learning was then evaluated with respect to the actual dosage of instruction received over the study period. The simple bivariate relationship between instructional dosage and reading fluency change ($r = .31$) was positive, indicating that on average students who received more instruction had better learning outcomes. The linear relationship between instructional hours and summer reading fluency change was statistically significant at a conventional alpha level, $p < .05$.

In addition to identifying the simple dose-response relationship between instructional receipt and summer learning, the availability of the continuously measured instructional dose variable also enabled investigation of the size of and variability in the achieved treatment contrast. When examined as a function of assigned treatment status, the intended 50-hour treatment contrast was not achieved. On average, students assigned to summer school received 51.77 hours of literacy instruction ($SD = 23.09$) between the spring and fall TORF assessments while students assigned to the control condition received 24.42 instructional hours ($SD = 4.86$), $F(1, 99) = 54.37, MSE = 332.49, p < .05$. The 27-hour difference reflected a 45% reduction in the intended treatment contrast. When examined by achieved treatment group status, summer school participants experienced an average of 68.11 ($SD = 8.25$) instructional hours while summer school refusers ($M = 22.82, SD = 5.15$) and control students ($M = 24.42, SD = 4.86$) had less instructional exposure. The group mean differences were statistically significant, $F(2, 98) = 565.76, MSE = 41.48, p < .05$. Tukey's post hoc tests revealed that summer school participants experienced a statistically greater number of instructional hours than summer school refusers and control students. The mean difference between refusers and controls was not statistically significant.

Site-Based Variability

As the student sample was obtained from seven elementary schools that varied in terms of mean reading fluency change and in the mean amount of post-assignment instruction received by students, it was possible to further examine within and between site outcome variance with multilevel modeling methods. In particular, the site-based variability provided an opportunity to describe the extent to which the instructional hour treatment/control contrast varied by school building and to inferentially examine whether estimated treatment effects varied as a function of the size of the obtained contrast at each school site.

Descriptive results indicated that school mean reading fluency change ranged from −5.41 to 6.00 WCPM ($M = 0.00$, $SD = 4.54$) and that the treatment contrast was as low as 17 hours at one school site and twice as large at 34 hours at another ($M = 27.05$, $SD = 5.80$). Specification of a two-level model (i.e. students within schools) with the ITT indicator variable's effect modeled as randomly varying across schools revealed the presence of a statistically significant mean difference in summer reading fluency change and site-to-site variability in the size of the ITT effect. Across schools, students assigned to treatment outperformed their peers in the control group by 6 WCPM, $\beta_1 = 6.23$, $SE = 1.95$, $p < .05$. The size of the ITT effect ranged from a two to an eleven WCPM gain depending on school site, $\tau_B^2 = 20.11$.

In an attempt to account for the variability in ITT effects, the treatment contrast index was entered into the model as a unit level predictor. Controlling for the mean level of instruction, results demonstrated that school sites that achieved a larger contrast in the number of instructional hours delivered to treatment and control students had a larger average ITT effect ($\gamma_{11} = 0.82$, $p < .05$). For every 1-hour increase in the treatment contrast, the size of the treatment effect was estimated to increase by approximately one WCPM. On average, schools with larger instructional hour contrasts had a treatment effect that was two to four times greater than schools with the smallest contrast. Figure 5.2 presents a caterpillar plot of the ordered ITT effect estimates. Different line styles are used to represent the magnitude of the achieved treatment contrast. The broken line pattern reflects a below average treatment contrast (<27 hours) whereas the solid line pattern indicates an above average contrast (>27 hours). In Figure 5.2, it can be seen that when there was a larger contrast in the amount of instruction delivered to treatment and control students, the ITT effect tended to be greater than when the contrast was smaller. The one exception was the school site with the largest estimated ITT effect. At this site, a relatively large treatment estimate (~11 WCPM) was obtained despite an average instructional contrast between the treatment and control group (25 hours). Overall, the steep site-to-site increment in ITT effects demonstrates in part how much treatment outcomes varied across sites, but the overlap in the confidence bands nonetheless does not permit sharp distinctions in site performance.

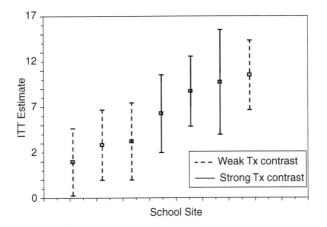

FIGURE 5.2 ITT Effect as a Function of School Site and Achieved Treatment Contrast.

Discussion

The use of field-based RCTs offers researchers and policymakers the opportunity to carefully estimate and evaluate the effect of educational and social interventions (Murnane & Willett, 2011). However, the implementation challenges that arise in applied settings can often undermine the precision and validity with which treatment effects are estimated. As a result, one aim of the current chapter was to identify and measure the unintended deviations from design protocol that arose within the context of a summer school RCT. The identification and indexing of design breakdowns common to applied experimental research (e.g. non-compliance with treatment assignment, treatment delivery, and receipt variance) provided a basis for completion of the second study aim, demonstrating the use of analytic methods that provide alternative or supplemental estimates of treatment impact.

In the current example, the implementation of a school-based summer literacy intervention was affected by non-compliance with treatment assignment and a variety of administrative and participant-related design breakdowns. In all, 36% of students who received a summer school offer refused the invitation and many of those who accepted a summer school placement did not attend fully. The misalignment of the measurement schedule also resulted in the control group's exposure to a non-trivial amount of "summer" literacy instruction. Application of several different analytic methodologies (e.g. IV, CACE) designed to adjust for non-compliance with treatment assignment revealed that estimated summer WCPM literacy gains were larger when the take-up of treatment was explicitly distinguished from receipt of the treatment offer (i.e. ITT). Moreover, when examined with respect to the size of the site-based treatment contrast, results indicated that summer reading fluency outcomes tended to be more positive in

contexts where there was greater instructional differentiation between the treatment and control group.

Results indicating a larger WCPM gain when adjustments were made for treatment non-compliance suggest that the value of many voluntary school-based summer instructional interventions may often be underestimated (e.g. Borman & Dowling, 2006). Yet it is important to recognize that an inferential cost is unavoidable when supplemental compliance adjustment procedures are used to further contextualize an ITT estimate. In general, more stringent assumptions are required to support less generalizable inferences as the size and scope of the implementation failures increase. For example, adjustments for treatment non-compliance necessarily shift the estimable quantity from the average causal effect to the local effect (of treatment) for the subpopulation of compliers. The procedures for compliance adjustment also notably rest on the exclusion assumption that holds that the treatment can affect the outcome only through the treatment received and that treatment effects be homogenous across participants. In addition, a monoticity assumption requires that no individuals purposively defy their assignment by seeking out treatment if assigned to the control condition or refuse treatment if assigned to the intervention group. While the monoticity assumption will likely be satisfied in many cases, the plausibility of meeting the exclusion assumption is more questionable as a treatment offer may non-randomly induce greater engagement among participants who could benefit the most (e.g. initially higher achieving students with strong familial support). Alternatively, the refusal of treatment may be predicated on the differential availability of a somewhat exclusive and potentially more advantageous opportunity (e.g. a summer enrichment camp).

Despite the inferential limitations that follow from non-compliance with the treatment offer, naturally occurring variation in treatment take-up and implementation may nonetheless be useful for gaining additional insight into site-to-site differences in treatment outcomes and the contextual and operational conditions that are associated with treatment effect variance (Weiss et al., 2013). As described above, the construction of an index that captured the total amount of instruction experienced by treatment and control students served to reflect in part the fidelity with which the main program component (i.e. direct literacy instruction) was delivered (and received) by study participants. The subsequent identification of a positive relationship between the magnitude of the treatment contrast and the size of the ITT effect tentatively suggests that a distinction in the amount of instruction experienced by treatment and control students closer to intended design protocol (i.e. a 50-hour contrast) would be associated with a larger impact estimate. In principle, this type of result could serve to reassure school leaders about the value of optimizing the delivery of a targeted program of support. However, the non-experimental nature of the observed relationship and other design constraints nonetheless place a limit on the inference that can currently be drawn regarding an incremental increase in the provision of supplemental summer reading instruction. To more thoroughly test whether an increase in the size of

the treatment contrast results in stronger learning outcomes, a multisite RCT that includes tighter design controls (e.g. an assessment schedule that is contiguously aligned with summer intervention period) and involves random assignment to different treatment levels (i.e. instructional hours) is required (Bloom et al., 2003; Weiss et al., 2013).

While data on treatment compliance and the delivery and receipt of the intervention program can be useful estimating and exploring variability in treatment effects and/or minimizing bias under imperfect design conditions, it is important to acknowledge that the current demonstration had other limitations that are also germane to the interpretability of the analytic results. Of particular concern was the confounding of the summer and academic year school sites. Although the instructional model was analogous in both settings, refusers and control students received their "summer" literacy instruction in one of seven schools at the end of the academic year whereas summer school participants received instruction in their local school during the academic year and at a central school site during the summer. The misalignment between the assessment and academic calendar serendipitously enabled the exploratory investigation of unit-level variability in learning outcomes, but coupled with the small number of schools and student-level assignment to conditions, strong conclusions regarding school contributions to summer learning are not warranted.

Other design limitations follow from the lack of data on instructional quality differences and the level of student engagement in each of the daily lessons. More specifically, instructional exposure (i.e. the absolute amount of instruction experienced) does not directly speak to the quality of the pedagogy or students' attentiveness and active interaction with the instruction offered. The potential for treatment and control members to seek out additional or alternative treatments was also not addressed. Within the context of a summer literacy intervention, participation in alternative summer enrichment activities and the frequency and amount of independent summer reading completed by treatment and control students are obvious factors that can serve to further modify the treatment context. For example, summer school participants can proactively increase their treatment dosage through supplemental daily reading activity while control group members and treatment refusers may be able to attain a treatment dosage comparable to their peers who attend summer school by attending an academically focused summer camp and/or through intensive self-directed summer reading engagement. Lacking complete measures on instructional delivery and receipt and the summer learning activities of all study participants, it was not possible to thoroughly index and take into account the full "dose" of summer instruction experienced by each student.

Despite the potential for implementation breakdowns, the more frequent use of the randomized experiment across different samples and diverse contexts offers a straightforward and unbiased means for estimating the size and variability of ITT effects in school-based interventions. However, as non-random

selection into and out of treatment may undermine the assignment mechanism in a wide range of RCTs, researchers and evaluators will need to pay particular attention to the number and characteristics of students who fail to comply with their treatment assignment. It is thus recommended that ITT as well as various compliance-adjusted estimates be presented in any report that is based on a randomized design with non-compliance. When implementation breakdowns and deviations from design protocol are also likely, attention will also need to be paid to recording the extent to which the intervention is actually experienced by treatment and control group members. In these cases, examination of outcomes as a function of the achieved treatment contrast and with respect to contextual conditions is also advised. By coupling a robust a priori measurement strategy with thorough modeling of implementation data and reporting of implementation-related results, educational leaders will be better positioned to consider the local impact of adopting a new or alternative educational program or innovation.

Note

1 Six students (two treatment, four control) transferred out of the district prior to the start of second grade and were excluded from all analyses. The two transfer students who were assigned to the treatment group did not attend summer school.

References

Alexander, K. L., Entwisle, D. R., and Olson, L. S. (2001). Schools, achievement, and inequality: A seasonal perspective. *Educational Evaluation and Policy Analysis*, 23(2), 171–191.

Angrist, J. D., Imbens, G. W., and Rubin, D. B. (1996). Identification of causal effects using instrumental variables. *Journal of the American Statistical Association*, 91, 444–455.

Bloom, H. S. (1984). Accounting for non-compliers in experimental evaluation designs. *Evaluation Review*, 8, 225–246.

Bloom, H. S. and Michalopoulos, C. (2013). When is the story in the subgroups: Strategies for interpreting and reporting intervention effects for subgroups. *Prevention Science*, 14(2), 179–188.

Bloom, H. S., Hill, C. J., and Riccio J. A. (2003). Linking program implementation and effectiveness: Lessons from a pooled sample of welfare-to-work experiments. *Journal of Policy Analysis and Management*, 22(4), 551–575.

Bloom, H. S., Raudenbush, S. W., and Weiss, M. (2014). *Using Multi-Site Evaluations to Study Variation in Effects of Program Assignment*. MDRC: Author.

Borman, G. D. and Dowling, N. M. (2006). The longitudinal achievement effects of multiyear summer school: Evidence from the Teach Baltimore randomized field trial. *Educational Evaluation and Policy Analysis*, 28, 25–48.

Children's Educational Services (1987). *Test of Oral Reading Fluency (TORF)*. Eden Prairie, MN: Children's Educational Services.

Cook, T. D. (2002). Randomized experiments in educational policy research: A critical examination of the reasons the educational evaluation community has offered for not doing them. *Educational Evaluation and Policy Analysis*, 24(3), 175–199.

Cooper, H., Charlton, K., Valentine, J. C., and Muhlenbruck, L. (2000). Making the most of summer school: A meta-analytic and narrative review. *Monographs of the Society for Research in Child Development*, 65(1), Serial No. 260.

Durlack, J. A. and DuPre, E. P. (2008). Implementation matters: A review on the influence of implementation on program outcomes and the factors affecting implementation. *American Journal of Community Psychology*, 41, 327–350.

Fixsen, D. L., Naoom, S. F., Blase, K. A., Friedman, R. M., and Wallace, F. (2005). *Implementation Research: A Synthesis of The Literature*. Tampa, FL: Louis de la Parte Florida Mental Health Institute, University of South Florida (FMHI Publication #231).

Gennetian, L. A., Morris, P. A., Bos, J. M., and Bloom, H. S. (2005). Constructing instrumental variables from experimental data to explore how treatments produce effects. In H. S. Bloom (Ed.), *Learning More from Social Experiments: Evolving Analytic Approaches*. New York: Russell Sage Foundation. 75–114.

Heckman, J. J. (2005). The scientific model of causality. *Sociological Methodology*, 35(1), 1–97.

Heckman, J. J. and Robb, R. (1985). Alternative methods for evaluating the impact of an intervention. *Journal of Econometrics*, 30, 239–267.

Holland, P. (1986). Statistics and causal inference. *Journal of the American Statistical Association*, 81, 945–970.

Hulleman, C. S. and Cordray, D. S. (2009). Moving from the lab to the field: The role of fidelity and achieved relative intervention strength. *Journal of Research on Educational Effectiveness*, 2(1), 88–110.

Imbens, G. W. and Rubin, D. B. (1997). Bayesian inference for causal effects in randomized experiments with non-compliance. *The Annals of Statistics*, 25, 305–327.

IES (Institute of Education Sciences) (2014). Request for Applications: Education Research Grants. Washington, DC: US Department of Education.

Jo, B. (2002). Estimation of intervention effects with noncompliance: Alternative model specifications. *Journal of Educational and Behavioral Statistics*, 27, 385–409.

Jo, B. and Muthén, B. O. (2001). Modeling of intervention effects with noncompliance: A latent variable approach for randomized trials. In G. A. Marcoulides and R. E. Schumacker (Eds.), *New Developments and Techniques in Structural Equation Modeling*. Mahwah, NJ: Lawrence Erlbaum Associates. 57–87.

Little, R. J. and Yau, L. H. Y. (1998). Statistical techniques for analyzing data from prevention trials: Treatment of no-shows using Rubin's causal model. *Psychological Methods*, 3, 147–159.

Murnane, R. J. and Willett, J. B. (2011). *Methods Matter: Improving Causal Inference in Educational and Social Science Research*. New York: Oxford University Press.

Muthén, L. K. and Muthén, B. O. (2010). *Mplus User's Guide* (6th edition). Los Angeles, CA: Muthén & Muthén.

National Reading Panel. (2000). *Teaching Children to Read: An Evidence-Based Assessment of the Scientific Research Literature on Reading and Its Implications for Reading Instruction*. Rockville, MD: National Institutes of Health (NIH Pub. No. 00-4754).

NSF (National Science Foundation) (2013). Proposal and Award Policies and Procedures Guide (NSF 14-1). Arlington, VA: National Science Foundation.

Puma, M. J., Olsen, R. B., Bell, S. H., and Price, C. (2009). *What to Do When Data Are Missing in Group Randomized Controlled Trials* (NCEE 2009-0049). Washington, DC: National Center for Education Evaluation and Regional Assistance, Institute of Education Sciences, and U.S. Department of Education.

Raudenbush, S. W. and Bryk, A. S. (2002). *Hierarchical Linear Models: Applications and Data Analysis Methods* (2nd edition). Thousand Oaks, CA: Sage.

Raudenbush, S. W., Reardon, S. F., and Nomi, T. (2012). Statistical analysis for multisite trials using instrumental variables with random coefficients. *Journal of Research on Educational Effectiveness*, 5(3), 303–332.

Rubin, D. B. (1974). Estimating causal effects of treatments in randomized and nonrandomized studies. *Journal of Educational Psychology*, 66, 688–701.

Sagarin, B. J., West, S. G., Ratnikov, A., Homan, W. K., Ritchie, T. D., and Hansen, E. J. (2014). Treatment noncompliance in randomized experiments: Statistical approaches and design issues. *Psychological Methods*, 19(3), 317–333.

Schochet, P. Z., Puma, M., and Deke, J. (2014). *Understanding Variation in Treatment Effects in Education Impact Evaluations: An Overview of Quantitative Methods* (NCEE 2014–4017). Washington, DC: U.S. Department of Education, Institute of Education Sciences, National Center for Education Evaluation and Regional Assistance, Analytic Technical Assistance and Development.

Shadish, W. R., Cook, T. D., and Campbell, D. T. (2002). *Experimental and Quasi-Experimental Designs for Generalized Causal Inference*. Boston, MA: Houghton Mifflin.

Sheiner, L. B. and Rubin, D. B. (1995). Intention-to-treat analysis and the goals of clinical trials. *Clinical Pharmacology and Therapy*, 57, 6–15.

Spybrook, J. (2014) Detecting intervention effects across context: An examination of the precision of cluster randomized trials. *Journal of Experimental Education*, 82(3), 334–357.

Spybrook, J., Lininger, M., and Cullen, A. (2013). From planning to implementation: An examination of changes in the research design, sample size, and statistical power of group randomized trials launched by the Institute of Education Sciences. *Journal of Research on Educational Effectiveness*, 6(4), 396–420.

U.S. Department of Education (2013). *What Works Clearinghouse: Procedures and Standards Handbook* (Version 3.0). Available online at http://ies.ed.gov/ncee/wwc/pdf/reference_resources/wwc_procedures_v3_0_standards_handbook.pdf

Weiss, M. J., Bloom, H. S., and Brock, T. (2013) *A Conceptual Framework for Studying the Sources of Variation in Program Effects*. MDRC: Author.

West, S. G. and Sagarin, B. J. (2000). Participant selection and loss in randomized experiments. In L. Bickman (Ed.), *Research Design: Donald Campbell's Legacy* (Volume 2). Thousand Oaks, CA: Sage. 117–154.

Zvoch, K. (2009). Treatment fidelity in multisite evaluation: A multilevel longitudinal examination of provider adherence status and change. *American Journal of Evaluation*, 30(1), 44–61.

Zvoch, K. (2012). How does fidelity of implementation matter? Using multilevel models to detect relationships between participant outcomes and the delivery and receipt of treatment. *American Journal of Evaluation*, 33(4), 541–559.

Zvoch, K. and Stevens, J. J. (2013). Summer school effects in a randomized field trial. *Early Childhood Research Quarterly*, 28(1), 24–32.

Zvoch, K. and Stevens, J. J. (2015). Identification of summer school effects by comparing the in- and out-of-school growth rates of struggling early readers. *Elementary School Journal*, 115(3), 433–456.

6

LINKING IMPLEMENTATION FIDELITY TO IMPACTS IN AN RCT

Fatih Unlu, Laurie Bozzi, Carolyn Layzer, Arthur Smith, Cristofer Price, and Richard Hurtig

Introduction

Simple experimental studies randomize study participants into two groups: a treatment group that includes participants who receive the offer to participate in a program or intervention, and a control group that includes participants who do not receive that offer. Such studies primarily address questions about the program impacts on the average outcomes of participants. While the corresponding results are highly policy relevant as they can be used to make inferences about the effectiveness of the program or intervention as it is offered, the average impact estimate often masks the fact that it is actually averaged across program units or sites which often implement the intervention to varying degrees of fidelity.

Program developers, researchers, and policy-makers often look at the variation in implementation across study sites and wonder how the average impact estimate would change if all sites implemented all or most of the program components. They can become even more motivated to explore this question when researchers find null average impact estimates for programs that developers and policy-makers believe work well. In such cases, a finding that there is no relationship between fidelity of program implementation and impacts (e.g. the impact is null even in sites where the program is fully implemented) would have different implications for future implementations of the program and research than a finding that there is a positive relationship between fidelity and impacts (e.g. the impacts are higher in sites with higher implementation fidelity).

Unfortunately, conventional analytic methods that have been used to address these types of questions have been limited and flawed. Except in planned variation studies, these questions cannot be addressed directly within the standard experimental framework because study participants are not randomly assigned to specific implementation

fidelity or dosage levels, and fidelity and dosage are not observed in the control group. These challenges have limited researchers to conventional approaches such as comparing a portion of the treatment group (higher or lower implementers) to the entire control group or correlating implementation measures with outcomes only within the treatment group. While such approaches allow for exploring variation in implementation variation, they cannot support strong causal conclusions about the relationships between implementation fidelity and program impacts.

The contribution of this chapter to the program-evaluation literature is twofold. First, we conceptually describe how two analytic methods that have been developed to examine potential associations between program-related factors and impacts can be adopted to explore the link between implementation fidelity and impacts with more rigor than the conventional methods described above. Second, we demonstrate the application of these methods in the evaluation of the Breakthrough to Literacy (BTL) program, where stakeholders wanted to know whether the impacts on student outcomes were greater in classrooms in which BTL was implemented with higher fidelity than those with lower fidelity.

The two methods used to address this question are based on the work of Schochet and Burghardt (2007) and Peck (2003), and will herein be referred to as the "cut-off method" and the "matching method." These approaches use the following common steps: construction of an implementation index measuring the fidelity of program implementation in the treatment group; fitting a regression model to treatment teachers' data to predict implementation fidelity as a function of baseline school, teacher, and student characteristics; and the calculation of predicted implementation ratings for both BTL and control teachers using this model. As a result, each treatment teacher has a predicted and an actual observed implementation rating, and each control teacher has a predicted implementation rating.

The two methods differ in how the predicted implementation ratings are employed. Specifically, the cut-off method divides BTL and control teachers into two subgroups using the predicted rating: higher predicted implementers and lower predicted implementers. The impact of BTL is then estimated separately for each subgroup and the resulting impacts are compared. The matching method matches each BTL teacher with a control teacher with the most similar predicted implementation rating. The matched BTL and control teacher pairs are then divided into high and low implementer groups using the actual implementation rating of the BTL teachers and separate impacts are estimated for each subgroup. It is important to note that both of these methods examine whether there is any variation in the BTL impacts that could be attributable to variation in implementation fidelity. This is in contrast to treating fidelity as a mediator that would examine the direct and indirect effect of BTL that may have been realized through implementation fidelity. The subgroup impacts yielded by the two methods likely consist of a mix of direct and indirect effects. It is also important to note that the two methods rely on different identifying assumptions, which are subsequently discussed in more detail in the technical appendix.

In the BTL context, the two approaches yielded similar substantive conclusions. We believe these are promising approaches for studying the relationships between aspects of the implementation of a program and its effects and are attractive because they rely primarily on exogenous baseline characteristics, rather than actual implementation measures, which are endogenous.

The organization of this chapter is as follows. Section 2 presents the summary of the BTL evaluation and motivates the analyses described in this chapter. Section 3 provides a summary of the existing research and theory for studying implementation fidelity and its relationship with impacts in evaluations studies. Section 4 describes the data and analytic approaches used to explore the relationships between the implementation fidelity of the BTL program and impacts on their students' literacy outcomes. Section 5 presents the corresponding results. The chapter ends with a discussion of the strengths and limitations of the two approaches and recommendations for future work.

Study Background

Breakthrough to Literacy

The data used in this chapter were originally collected in the study *Breakthrough to Literacy in the Chicago Public Schools: A Large-Scale Evaluation* (CLIMBERs), a five-year study investigating the impacts of Breakthrough to Literacy (Wright Group/McGraw-Hill) in a sample of Chicago public preschool and kindergarten classrooms. BTL is a comprehensive literacy curriculum designed to be incorporated into classroom instruction throughout the school day across topic areas and developmental activity centers. It is designed to support the development of children's vocabulary, oral language, and comprehension skills throughout the classroom curriculum with five "daily essential practices": listening to and discussing stories; reading; writing; individualized software instruction; and talking, reading and writing at home.

BTL instruction is organized around a weekly theme that is centered on a book read aloud daily by the teacher. Each *Book of the Week*[1] is part of a theme and was deliberately chosen to be part of BTL for didactic reasons (e.g. promoting understanding of vocabulary and basic concepts such as colors and sizes). The book of the week is read aloud to the whole class by the teacher daily, and she or he promotes active discussion with children, asking questions and making connections between the book and children's experiences and ideas. Throughout the discussions, the teacher promotes the understanding of text, as well as vocabulary, reading comprehension, motivation, and concept development.

In addition to interactive book readings, BTL also incorporates computer use into its activities. BTL software presents the book of the week as well as associated interactive activities and other books for students to use at their own pace. Kindergarten-age children are expected to spend about twelve to fifteen

minutes per day using the individualized, self-paced BTL literacy activities on the computer. The software is also loaded with a tracking program that allows teachers to monitor their students' progress in a variety of early literacy subskill areas. Teachers are expected to provide children with numerous and diverse writing opportunities (e.g. keeping journals, answering questions about the book of the week, dictating text to teachers, etc.). In addition, BTL offers materials for children to use at home.

Impacts of Breakthrough to Literacy

In the BTL evaluation, 45 schools were randomly assigned to either receive the BTL intervention or to continue with their regular instructional practices as part of the control group; 23 schools were randomized to the treatment condition while the control group included 22 schools. The analysis of kindergarten impacts used 134 teachers and 3,107 students from two cohorts from the 2005–06 and 2006–07 school years.[2] Many of the classrooms in the study included dual-language learners, and while several bilingual classrooms were included in the evaluation, schools expected that instruction would generally be provided in English.

Impacts on Teacher Measures

The impact of BTL on teachers' instructional practices were estimated using two-level Hierarchical Linear Models (HLM) models (classrooms nested within schools) that included several covariates (e.g. sample stratifiers, outcome year, and schools' percentage of minority students) to address two research questions pertaining to the impacts of BTL on kindergarten teachers' instruction and classroom environment at the end of the first year of implementation and the end of the second year of implementation. We found that that after one year of implementation, BTL had substantial and statistically significant impacts on kindergarten teachers' use of instructional practices that supported children's oral language development and print motivation as well as the amount of time they spent in literacy activities and having children use computers. The estimated effects were statistically significant and their magnitude was over 0.2 standard deviations, which suggested that the findings had substantive importance.

Most of these impacts were not evident at the end of the second year of BTL implementation. The only statistically significant impact in year 2 was that BTL teachers provided more computer activity time than the control teachers. Because the intervention itself provided computers to treatment classrooms, however, this finding is less meaningful.

Impacts on Student Measures

The BTL evaluation also examined the impacts of the intervention on students' literacy development using three-level HLM models that nested students within

classrooms, which were nested within schools. Covariates used included sample stratification and cohort indicators, school-level average pretest scores, and the school percentage of minority students.

Overall, the study found no statistically significant differences between the BTL and control students on any of the four tests of early literacy skills administered at the end of kindergarten (*Expressive One-Word Picture Vocabulary Test* [Brownell, 2000], and three subtests of the *Woodcock Reading Mastery Test: Revised/Normative Update* [Woodcock, 1998]: Letter Identification, Word Identification, and Word Attack). The absence of student impacts was particularly surprising because it contrasted with the results from a similar earlier RCT evaluating the impacts of BTL and two other early literacy curricula on preschool children in child-care centers in Florida (Project Upgrade). In that study, BTL had a large impact on teachers (e.g. effect size of 0.91 standard deviations on literacy instructional practices) and on students (i.e. effect sizes of 0.31–0.60 standard deviations on early language and literacy).

At first glance, the differences between the results of the two studies were surprising because both were experimental studies examining the same intervention in early childhood classrooms. However, there were many differences in classrooms, school settings, and teacher backgrounds across the two studies that likely led to the differences in the results. Project Upgrade consisted of full-day (8 hours per day), center-based preschool classrooms while CLIMBERs classrooms were in Chicago's State preschools in which classes met for 2.5 hours daily, with feeding programs. Classrooms in Project Upgrade supported bilingual learners' use of their first language, while only a few CLIMBERs classrooms did so. Finally, although most of the Project Upgrade teachers were not certified and had lower educational credentials than those in CLIMBERs, they were more amenable to change their practices in response to professional development.

We speculated that differences between the students in the levels of BTL implementation could be an important factor. In Project Upgrade, the professional development was more intensive and more consistent. Coaches in Upgrade met weekly to discuss their work and visited teachers 30 times over 15 months— once or twice a month, depending on the particular teacher's need; whereas those in CLIMBERs visited schools eight times over 18 months and had no consistent central meetings. In Upgrade, the same coaches continued working with the same teachers through the 2 years of the intervention, whereas in CLIMBERs, the publisher changed the terms of the coaches' contract in the middle of the implementation, and seven different coaches visited sporadically on an externally-set schedule rather than in response to the teachers' individual needs. In the CLIMBERs context, a smaller proportion of teachers met implementation benchmarks in all but three sub-categories[3] compared with the Upgrade classrooms.

This led to the question of whether some CLIMBERs classrooms implemented BTL at a higher level and whether student impacts for such classrooms were also larger than those with lower implementation fidelity. The analyses reported in this

chapter address this question employing two methods that predict implementation fidelity using baseline school, teacher, and classroom characteristics and assess the association between the predicted implementation fidelity and impacts.

Prior Research on Studying Implementation Fidelity

The relationships among aspects of implementation of a program and its impacts are often of interest to researchers and policy-makers trying to determine the most effective ways to improve educational outcomes for students. Past research has tried varied approaches to understanding links between implementation and impacts with varying degrees of success. Studying these links requires an under-standing drawn from two sets of literature relevant to the topic: studies of the *efficacy* of faithful implementation (i.e. those examining whether or not a program was implemented as intended) and studies of the *effectiveness* of faithful imple-mentation (i.e. those investigating whether high implementation led to improved outcomes [O'Donnell, 2008]). Important elements of these two sets of literature are summarized below.

The first step in relating program implementation to impacts is measuring program implementation, which has been addressed in numerous ways. For exam-ple, Domitrovich et al. (2010) identified four measures of implementation in a study of an intervention that trained teachers on instruction methods: (1) dosage: the number of times the intervention was used; (2) fidelity: defined narrowly as adherence to prescribed program elements; (3) generalization: using the program elements in other areas of teaching; and (4) child engagement: an estimation of the number of children engaged in the activity. Hamre et al. (2009) and Knoche et al. (2009) each labeled three similar aspects of implementation. Durlak (2010) discusses *eight* aspects of program implementation including fidelity, dosage, qual-ity, participant responsiveness, program differentiation, monitoring of control or comparison conditions, program reach, and adaptation.

In addition to the variation in the measurement of program implementation, there have been diverse approaches to usage of these measures. Durlak (2010) found that implementation varies over the course of a study and it tends to increase over time for more difficult interventions with support and to decrease over time for easy-to-implement programs that are not reinforced. As a result Durlak (2010) recommended the use of multiple measures of implementation over time. This can make relating the resulting measures to outcomes or program impacts challenging as the latter tend to be captured less frequently. Hamre et al. (2009) addressed this issue by taking an average of the observed implementa-tion measures and examining its relationship to outcomes (finding mixed results). Odom et al. (2010) generated a multiplicative composite measure out of two dif-ferent types of implementation, structural (adherence) and process (quality), and found that there were significant and positive relationships between outcomes and both the quality and composite measures (with mixed results for adherence).

When it comes to relating implementation to outcomes (or program impacts), two methods have been commonly utilized. The first method entails splitting the treatment group into subgroups such as "higher" and "lower" implementers and the outcomes of each subgroup are then compared to that of the entire control group (e.g. Durlak & DuPre, 2008). This is problematic because the entire control group likely includes both types (i.e. "potential higher implementers" and "potential lower implementers" had they been assigned to the treatment group) and it would be more appropriate to compare higher or lower implementers in the treatment group with only their expected counterparts in the control group rather than all control group members.

The second method involves correlating various implementation measures to outcomes within the treatment group alone (Durlak & DuPre, 2008; O'Donnell, 2008). While this approach yields estimates of the association between levels of program implementation and outcomes for treatment group members, the results are likely to reflect inherent (i.e. pre-existing) differences between treatment group members that led to the variation in the implementation fidelity. Due to such confounding these analyses do not provide strong evidence of whether or not an intervention is likely to produce larger impacts if it is implemented with higher fidelity.

Hulleman & Cordray (2009) adopted a different approach to assessing differences in implementation across the treatment and control groups. They modeled program implementation elements in both the treatment group and control group. In the former group program elements are expected to occur as a result of implementing the program while in the latter, they may occur naturally. They concluded that presenting these differences demonstrates how closely the observed treatment-control contrast resembles the hypothesized one. While examining these contrasts is useful in assessing the magnitude of observed impacts, it does not directly address potential relationships between degree of implementation or implementation fidelity and program impacts.

Relating Fidelity of Program Implementation to Program Impacts

The primary aim of the empirical analyses presented in this chapter is to investigate the relationship between teachers' level of BTL implementation and the BTL impacts on their students' achievement. This section describes the data, sample, and measures used in these analyses.

Data and Sample

The analytic sample included 133 kindergarten teachers from the original study sample who had classroom observation and student assessment data from the spring of 2006 or 2007, or both (75 BTL and 58 control teachers).

In addition, all kindergarten students in these teachers' classrooms who had assessment data from the same periods were included (i.e. 1099 BTL and 787 control students).

Many of the teachers had participated in the study for 2 years and had 2 years of classroom observation data which is used to create a measure of BTL implementation. When a teacher had two implementation ratings, only the higher rating of the two was retained (along with the rest of the data associated with that school year, i.e. student outcomes from his/her year with the lower rating excluded from this analysis).[4] We implemented these approach analyses due to a couple of reasons. First, it was congruent with the study's goal to examine student outcomes among BTL teachers who implemented BTL at a high level and we believe each teacher's highest observed implementation rating was considered to be the best measure available of their true highest level of BTL implementation. Second, we considered other strategies of handling teachers with 2 years of data such as retaining the fidelity score from the second year and the associated data with that year or averaging the fidelity rating across the two years.[5] We concluded that we did a much better job of predicting implementation fidelity (which is an integral component of our analytical strategy) when the higher fidelity rating of teachers with 2 years of data was retained over these two alternative approaches.[6]

Of 75 BTL teachers, 35% had two years of implementation data and of the 58 control teachers, 36% participated in the study for 2 years (see Exhibit 6.1). The records for the remaining teachers came from their only year of BTL implementation (first or second year of the study).

Measures

Four types of measures were used in analyses: (1) student literacy outcomes; (2) measures to capture teachers' implementation of BTL; (3) predictors of teachers' BTL implementation ratings; and (4) covariates. These measures are described below.

Student Outcome Measures

Kindergarten students in the study were individually administered four tests of literacy skills at the end of the academic year, which are described below.

Expressive One-Word Picture Vocabulary Test (EOWPVT) (3rd edition) (Brownell, 2000)

This is a standardized, norm-referenced measure of a person's English-speaking vocabulary. Internal consistency reliability coefficients ranged from alpha = 0.92–0.97 (median 0.95); split-half reliability coefficients = 0.93–0.98 (median 0.96).

EXHIBIT 6.1 Baseline Characteristics of the Teachers, Classrooms, and Schools of Sample BTL and Control Teachers

	BTL		Control	
	Mean	*SD*	*Mean*	*SD*
Teacher Baseline Characteristics				
Second year of study participation (%)	34.7%		36.2%	
QUEST language development subscale	2.0	0.4	1.9	0.4
QUEST TV subscale	2.9	0.3	2.8	0.3
QUEST average score (minus language and TV subscales)	1.8	0.3	1.8	0.3
Arnett caregiving rating scale	3.1	0.5	3.0	0.4
School Baseline Characteristics				
Enrollment	1041.3	454.4	801.9	260.1
Mobility rate	22.4	10.2	24.1	8.8
Percentage of students from families with low incomes	91.1%	14.6%	77.7%	27.0%
Percentage of students from minority groups	92.1%	5.2%	87.1%	9.8%
Class baseline characteristics				
Class average pre-CTOPPP score	23.9	5.8	25.0	5.7
Class average standardized PPVT score	81.5	9.3	82.1	11.6
Percentage of students who spoke only English	50.5%	42.7%	47.6%	40.9%
Percentage of students who were girls	50.0%	10.0%	50.0%	10.0%

Notes

[a] Exhibit reads: The data from 34.7% of the BTL teachers and 36.2% of the control teachers came from their second year of study participation.

[b] The sample size was 133 teachers (75 BTL and 58 control teachers). In this table, however, two to four teachers in each of the groups were missing data for the class average Pre-CTOPPP and PPVT scores as well as the proportion of the percentage of students in the class who were girls.

Scores were standardized to have a mean of 100 and standard deviation of 15 points.

Woodcock Reading Mastery Test: Revised/Normative Update (WRMT–R/NU) (Woodcock, 1998)

Three subtests from the standardized, norm-referenced WRMT–R/NU were used to measure students' reading skills: Letter Identification measures children's abilities to identify uppercase and lowercase letters. Word Identification measures children's abilities to identify isolated words that appear in large type on stimulus pages while Word Attack measures children's abilities to apply phonic and structural analysis skills in order to pronounce words (mostly nonsense words) with which he or she is unfamiliar. Internal consistency reliability coefficients ranged from alpha = 0.94 (Letter Identification), 0.98 (Word Identification), 0.94 (Word Attack).

Measures of Teachers' Use of BTL-Like Instructional Practices

The BTL curriculum has five core components which can be utilized through the book of the week: reads & discusses; daily writing; individualized software instruction; classroom culture and management routines; and reads, writes, and talks at home. Fidelity of implementation was not directly measured for these components; therefore, measures of the classroom practices associated with the components were constructed using classroom observation data. The steps taken to construct this measure (called the "implementation index") are described below.[7]

Initially, we worked with the curriculum developer to modify the fidelity checklist used by BTL instructional coaches so that it could serve as an implementation index defining the key elements in the curriculum. We then identified individual data elements collected in the original study using the *Observation Measures of Language and Literacy Instruction* (OMLIT) that could be used to measure teachers' use of BTL practices.

The OMLIT is comprised of the following observation instruments designed to guide observers to record detailed information about classroom activities involving literacy instruction (Goodson et al., 2004b):

1. Snapshot (SNAP): Observers record the number of students engaged in specific activities typical of early education and child care settings every 15 minutes.
2. Classroom Literacy Instruction Profile (CLIP): Captures detailed information on the features of instructional activities incorporating literacy during 10-minute intervals.
3. Read Aloud Profile (RAP): Characterizes instruction and teacher-child interactions observed every time a teacher reads a book aloud to two or more students.
4. Classroom Literacy Opportunities Checklist (CLOC): Records details of the classroom environment and resources that are associated with literacy learning.
5. Quality of Instruction in Language and Literacy (QUILL): Captures global measures of the quality of the literacy instruction observed in the classroom.

For the purposes of this analysis, individual data items recorded using the five instruments were combined to create seven composite indicators measuring teachers' use of instructional practices that were closely aligned to BTL. The resulting seven BTL implementation indicators (presented in Exhibit 6.2) measure conceptual dimensions of classroom practices that map onto the original BTL fidelity checklist's five categories (reads & discusses; writes; individualized software instruction; classroom culture and management routines; and reads, writes, and talks at home).

EXHIBIT 6.2 Comparison of the Dimensions Measured in the Final BTL Implementation Index and the Original BTL Fidelity Categories

Original BTL Fidelity Checklist Categories	*Adapted BTL Implementation Index Dimensions*

Book of the week:
 Reads & discusses
	Comprehension while reading aloud:
	     Comprehension activities conducted as part of shared reading experiences when the teacher was reading aloud with more than one child.
	 Comprehension in non-reading activities:
	     Comprehension activities conducted outside of shared reading experiences.
	 Vocabulary:
	     Activities aimed at fostering vocabulary development.
	 Oral language:
	     Activities aimed at developing children's oral language skills other than oral vocabulary.

Daily writing	Writing: Activities and materials intended to support the development of emergent writing skills
Individualized software instruction	Individualized software instruction: Use of computer for instructional purposes.
Classroom culture and management routines	Classroom culture and routines: Organization and management of the classroom
Reads, writes, and talks at home	Not measured

Each of the seven conceptual dimensions of the BTL implementation index were composed of one to fourteen individual items describing teaching practices that were emblematic of the BLT intervention (presented in Exhibit 6.3). The number of items per dimension was determined by the number of data items from the OMLIT that were closely associated with that dimension. Teachers received one point for each of the teaching strategies or classroom characteristics observed. In addition, many of the activities were intended by the developers to be conducted with children in large groups or as a whole class *as well as* in small groups or as individuals. For these items, teachers were given 2 points if they were observed conducting them in *both* large and small groups (or with individual children).

The individual items within each dimension (presented in Exhibit 6.3) were summed to form seven subscale scores that measured the extent to which teachers implemented the seven dimensions of classroom practices associated with BTL. Each of the subscale scores was standardized and the standardized subscale scores were summed to create an overall index of each teacher's use of BTL-like instructional strategies. The overall index had a moderately low level of internal consistency (alpha reliability coefficient = 0.58).

EXHIBIT 6.3 Items Comprising the Seven Conceptual Dimensions of the BTL Implementation Index

Comprehension While Reading Aloud

The teacher read a book aloud.*

The teacher read aloud a book of the week or a book connected to a class theme.

The teacher used one or more strategies promoting comprehension while reading aloud.*

The teacher made at least one connection between the book being read and children's experiences or class themes.*

The teacher asked book-related questions at the end of the read-aloud.*

The average depth of post-read-aloud discussions or activities was moderate to high (e.g. they lasted at least 5 minutes and/or they extended or reinforced the comprehension of the book).*

Comprehension in Non-Reading Activities

The teacher provided one or more activities that supported the development of comprehension skills outside of read-alouds.*

The average quality of discussions was moderately high or high (e.g. the content or topics were rich, abstract, open-ended, extended beyond the here-and-now, and/or related activities to children's experiences).*

Vocabulary

The teacher emphasized vocabulary in at least one read-aloud.*

The quality of story-related vocabulary instruction during read-alouds was moderate to high (e.g. one or more vocabulary word was discussed and a comprehension support was used).

The teacher provided one or more activities that supported vocabulary development outside of read-alouds (e.g. vocabulary knowledge was provided in the context of explanations, writing, songs, stories, rhymes, language games, discussions, shared reading, emergent writing, and/or child tagging or matching).*

Individualized Software Instruction

The average child used a computer for the amount of time recommended by BTL or longer (12–15 minutes).

Oral Language

The teacher provided at least one literacy activity that afforded students knowledge of oral communication and/or listening skills.

The teacher provided one or more activities that included language games, rhymes, songs, storytelling, or discussion that afforded students knowledge in the comprehension of a text and included an average depth of the discussion that was moderately high or high (e.g. they included turn-taking by students and the teacher elaborated or asked students to elaborate on comments).*

The teacher used one or more instructional strategies that promoted higher-order thinking during or after a read-aloud session (e.g. they asked book-related open-ended questions that required speculation, and/or expanded responses, thinking, or analyses).*

The teacher provided at least a few opportunities for oral language.

The average quality of the oral language activities provided by the teacher was moderate to high (e.g. the teacher provided integrated, higher quality oral language opportunities of varying types for most students individually or in small groups in which the teacher scaffolded or extended discussions with multiple turns that focused on non-management topics).

(*Continued*)

EXHIBIT 6.3 *(Continued)*

Writing

Examples of children's writing were on display in the classroom (other than just names).

Children spent time in journal-writing activities.

The teacher used at least one high-quality activity aimed at developing knowledge of the functions and features of print (e.g. using authentic print materials, graphic organizers, or word webs).

The teacher provided a separate writing area and/or writing materials accessible to children.

In at least some writing activities, the writing was done by the children themselves rather than by adults.

The teacher sometimes, often, or consistently encouraged children to write on their own rather than insisting on conventional letter formation or spelling.

The teacher provided one or more literacy activities that involved emergent writing, copying, or tracing.

Children were engaged in one or more writing activity (including emergent writing, copying, and tracing) that was connected to a class theme during the day.

The teacher worked with most or all of the students in writing activities during the day.

Writing activities and opportunities were sometimes, often, or consistently conducted with individuals or small groups.

The teacher provided two or more opportunities to engage in writing.

The teacher provided three or more types of writing activities.

The teacher provided children with writing opportunities that were sometimes, often, or consistently of higher quality (e.g. emergent writing, captioning, dictating, writing names on work, book-making, and/or writing in journals).

The teacher provided writing opportunities that were sometimes or often integrated into activities with goals other than literacy.

Classroom Culture and Routines

The classroom was well organized and had the space and layout to afford children a variety of independent activity choices, including learning centers (e.g. it had at least one distinct activity center, some materials that were marked, sorted, and stored; the layout allowed for at least two group sizes, some independent choices for students, sufficient space, adequate light, and/or no odors).

The average child spent less than 33% of the time in transitions, routines, and management or being uninvolved in activities.

The average child spent at least 50% of their time engaged in educationally "high value" activities (including: reading, alphabet, oral language, sounds, writing, science/nature, math concepts, dramatic play, creative play, block play, and fine motor play).

The average child spent at least 20% of their time in groups of five or fewer (not including meals, routines, transitions, or management).

Notes

[a] Item scores: For most items, a teacher scored one point if they engaged in the described instructional activity. Items with * were scored as follows: 0 if the teacher never engaged in the instructional activity, 1 if they engaged in the activity with a small or a large group, and 2 if they engaged in the activity with *both* a small and a large group.

[b] Items from the OMLIT (Goodson et al., 2004b).

Predictors of Teachers' Use of BTL-Like Instruction

As discussed in more detail below, an integral component of our analytical strategy is predicting teachers' use of BTL-like instruction, or fidelity of BTL implementation. Given the lack of existing guidance for identifying which characteristics and measures may predict fidelity well in this setting, we utilized all available baseline variables that we hypothesize to predict fidelity, which are described in more detail below.

Baseline School Measures

Seven variables were included in the model that predicted teachers' level of BTL implementation including two random assignment blocking variables (representing school administrative area and whether each school's student population was primarily Spanish speaking) as well as school enrollment and mobility rates, and the school percentage of students from minority groups and/or families with low incomes.

Baseline Teacher Measures

The model also controlled for the following baseline measures of teachers' instructional quality:

- *The Caregiver Rating Scale from the Quality of Early Childhood Care Settings* (QUEST) (Goodson et al., 2004a): The QUEST was administered at baseline to describe main aspects of caregiver interactions with students and yielded three subscales.
- *Arnett Caregiver Rating Scale* (Arnett, 1989): Using this scale, observers rated teachers' supervision, discipline methods, and affective style with children as well as the degree to which they encouraged independence.

Baseline Classroom Measures

Four variables were used to measure baseline classroom characteristics: percentage of female students, percentage of English learners; and two measures from the following baseline students' assessments collected in the fall of the 2005–06 school year:

- *Peabody Picture Vocabulary Test (PPVT–III)* (3rd edition) (Dunn & Dunn, 1997). Measured children's receptive English vocabulary.
- *Print Knowledge Subtest of the Preschool Comprehensive Test of Phonological and Print Processing* (Pre-CTOPPP) (Lonigan et al., 2007). Measured students' early knowledge about written language conventions and form as well as alphabet letters.

Analytic Approach

Examining the relationship between fidelity of program implementation and its impacts is complicated by the fact that program participants self-select into different levels of fidelity, and implementation fidelity is neither defined nor observed in the control group.[8] We addressed these challenges by investigating whether students in the classrooms of teachers who adopted BTL practices at higher (lower) levels ultimately performed better/worse on tests of early literacy skills, on average, than their peers in the control group who had teachers who were *likely* to have implemented BTL at a higher (lower) level had they received the intervention.

As the *potential* or *counterfactual* implementation fidelity for the control teachers is not observed, we needed to predict it, which was carried out through three steps. First, we constructed the implementation index for the BTL teachers. Second, we fit an ordinary least squares regression (OLS) model to the BTL teachers' data that predicted their index as a function of the baseline characteristics described above. Third, we estimated predicted BTL implementation ratings for both the BTL and control teachers using the parameter estimates from this OLS model and teachers' observed values on the baseline measures. We used the predicted values of implementation fidelity in two approaches (cut-off and matching) to compare outcomes of BTL teachers with control teachers who had similar implementation propensities. The cut-off and matching methods were suggested by Schochet and Burghardt (2007) and entail partitioning the BTL and control teachers to (predicted) subgroups of high and low implementers and estimating separate impacts for each subgroup. The two methods differ by how the subgroups are formed. The rest of this section provides a non-technical description of the two methods while the statistical framework underlying these methods and their assumptions is formally described in the technical appendix.

Cut-Off Method

This method is implemented via the following steps:

(i)   Determine a predicted probability threshold that would meaningfully divide the BTL teachers into higher and lower implementer subgroups.
(ii) Divide BTL and control teachers into two groups such that BTL and control teachers whose predicted rating was above or at the threshold are placed in the "predicted higher" implementers group while the remaining BTL and control teachers are placed in the "predicted lower" implementers subgroup.[9]
(iii) Estimate the impact of BTL for the two subgroups by separately fitting the impact regression (see technical appendix), which yields separate impacts for the predicted higher and lower implementing subgroups.

This method allows us to estimate the average impact on students who were taught by teachers with higher or lower predicted fidelity rating. As argued by

Schochet and Burghardt (2007), an appealing feature of this method is producing unbiased impact estimates for the predicted higher and lower implementing subgroups since both the observable and unobservable characteristics are expected to be balanced across the BTL and control units within each subgroup. This is because the two subgroups are portioned from the full sample of BTL and control teachers (which are guaranteed to be balanced in terms of observable and unobservable traits as a result of random assignment) based on an index that is a function of only pre-treatment exogenous measures.

Whether these unbiased impact estimates for the predicted "higher" and "lower" implementer subgroups reflect the relationship between implementation fidelity and impacts, however, depends on how well the covariates used in the prediction regression can distinguish high implementers from low implementers. In other words, a poor prediction model can lead to misclassification of teachers and the resulting impact estimates, while being unbiased, may not pertain to implementation fidelity.

Matching Method

This method is implemented through the following steps:

(i) Divide BTL teachers into two groups of equal size using the *actual* implementation rating scores, yielding two subgroups of higher and lower implementing BTL teachers.

(ii) Using the predicted rating values, match each BTL teacher in the high subgroup with the control group teacher with the closest predicted rating where a control teacher could be paired with more than one BTL teacher (one-to-one matching with replacement).[10]

(iii) Repeat the procedure in the previous step for the BTL teachers in the lower subgroup.

(iv) Estimate separate impact estimates for the two subgroups formed in steps (ii) and (iii) as described in the cut-off method.

This description suggests that while the cut-off approach yields impacts on subgroups that differ by predicted fidelity, this method aims to estimate the average impact of the intervention on students taught by teachers with higher (or lower) *actual* implementation fidelity. Therefore, the classification of BTL teachers as higher or lower implementers is ensured to be without any error since it is based on the actual implementation ratings. However, the resulting subgroup impacts would reflect the effect of experiencing high or low fidelity (but not other differences between the treatment teachers in a given subgroup and their matched counterparts) only if the prediction model is strong such that a treatment teacher with a high actual implementation fidelity is matched with a control teacher who would have implemented the program with high fidelity had she or he been

assigned to the treatment group. In other words, the matching approach yields subgroup impact estimates that may be biased unless matching yields perfectly balanced BTL and matched control teacher pairs in terms of both observable and unobservable characteristics. As mentioned above, the technical appendix presents a detailed description of the assumptions that the two approaches rely on.

Results

Teachers' Predicted BTL Implementation Ratings

We fit an OLS model to all 75 BTL teachers' data and predicted their BTL index rating as a function of their baseline teaching quality and classroom and school characteristics. The parameter estimates from this model are presented in Exhibit 6.4. The equation predicting these estimates was used to model BTL and control teachers predicted BTL implementation ratings.

EXHIBIT 6.4 Parameter Estimates from the Model Predicting BTL Teachers' BTL Implementation Rating as a Function of Baseline Teacher, School, and Classroom Characteristics

	Beta	se(Beta)	Pr > |t|
Intercept	−29.22	14.76	0.053
Teacher baseline characteristics			
Second year of study participation (%)	2.99	1.15	0.012
QUEST language development subscale	−0.42	1.45	0.773
QUEST TV subscale	1.96	1.64	0.237
QUEST average score (minus language and TV subscales)	2.93	2.33	0.213
Arnett caregiving rating scale	−0.61	1.42	0.671
School baseline characteristics			
Enrollment	0.00	0.00	0.171
Mobility rate	−0.03	0.06	0.636
Percentage of students from families with low incomes	0.05	0.06	0.335
Percentage of students from minority groups	0.07	0.15	0.629
Administrative area	−1.87	1.91	0.331
Primary school language	−1.61	2.66	0.547
Administrative area* school language	1.65	2.30	0.476
Class baseline characteristics			
Class average Pre-CTOPP score	0.05	0.13	0.708
Class average standardized PPVT score	0.10	0.08	0.246
Percentage of students who were girls	4.11	3.89	0.295
Percentage of students who spoke only English	−0.04	0.02	0.063

Note
[a] The sample includes 75 BTL teachers.

Subgroup Impact Estimates

Results from the cut-off and matching methods are displayed in Exhibit 6.5. The first panel in Exhibit 6.5 (i.e. "Panel A") presents the full sample impact estimates and the corresponding standard errors, p-values, and effect sizes. The full sample impact estimates are reported here to serve as a reference and inform the results for the subgroup analyses. Panel B of Exhibit 6.5 presents the impact estimates and associated statistics for the predicted higher and lower implementing subgroups formed as a result of the cut-off approach, which yielded 37 BTL and 18 control teachers in the higher group and 38 BTL and 40 control teachers in the

EXHIBIT 6.5 Estimated Impacts for High and Low Implementers

	Impact Estimate	Standard Error	P-Value	Effect Size
Panel A: Impact Estimates (Full Sample)				
Expressive one-word picture vocabulary test	0.69	1.53	0.654	0.04
Word Attack	1.28	0.87	0.149	0.11
Word ID	−0.09	1.44	0.950	−0.01
Letter ID	1.37	1.19	0.257	0.10
Panel B: Cut-off Approach (High and Low Implementers)				
High implementers:				
Expressive one-word picture vocabulary test	4.35	2.38	0.080	0.26
Word Attack	3.11	1.58	0.061	0.27
Word ID	2.24	2.69	0.413	0.14
Letter ID	3.06	2.03	0.145	0.23
Low implementers:				
Expressive one-word picture vocabulary test	−0.86	1.96	0.663	−0.05
Word Attack	0.09	1.43	0.951	0.01
Word ID	−2.00	2.22	0.375	−0.13
Letter ID	0.55	1.79	0.760	0.04
Panel C: Matching Approach (High and Low Implementers)				
High implementers:				
Expressive one-word picture vocabulary test	4.37	2.54	0.098	0.26
Word Attack	2.60	1.56	0.108	0.23
Word ID	1.44	2.77	0.606	0.09
Letter ID	2.80	2.10	0.194	0.21
Low implementers:				
Expressive one-word picture vocabulary test	−3.50	2.72	0.211	−0.21
Word Attack	0.26	1.55	0.870	0.02
Word ID	−2.94	2.58	0.267	−0.19
Letter ID	−0.08	2.00	0.968	−0.01

Note: [a] *Denotes statistical significance at the p = 0.05 level.

lower group. The Panel C of Exhibit 6.5 displays the same statistics for the two subgroups as the preceding panels produced by the matching approach.

First, consider Panel B of Exhibit 6.5. While none of the estimated impacts for the high implementers identified by the cut-off approach are significant at the usual p = 0.05 level, two were significant at the p = 0.10 level (Expressive Vocabulary, p-value = 0.08; Word Attack, p-value = 0.061) and the effect sizes for three measures were larger than 0.20 of a standard deviation (s.d.) ranging between 0.23 and 0.27 (Expressive Vocabulary 0.26 s.d., Word Attack 0.27 s.d., and Letter ID 0.23 s.d.).[11] The impact estimates for the lower implementers, on the other hand, were not statistically significant and small, with effect sizes between −0.13 and 0.04.

Panel C in Exhibit 6.5 shows results from the matching method, which were similar to those in Panel B. In the high implementing subgroup, the effect sizes of the estimated impacts for the same three measures were larger than 0.2 of a standard deviation (Expressive Vocabulary = 0.26; Word Attack = 0.23; and Letter ID = 0.21) while two estimates have p-values around the p = 0.10 threshold. For the lower implementing subgroup, the impacts were small and not significant, again consistent with those presented in Panel B for the cut-off approach.

We also investigated whether the estimated impacts for the higher implementers were statistically different than those for the lower implementers across the two methods (presented in Exhibit 6.6). Panel A of Exhibit 6.6 presents the difference in the estimated impacts for higher and lower implementers identified by the cut-off approach, the effect size of the difference, and its p-value. Panel B displays the same information for the two subgroups determined by the matching method. The results in both panels suggest that higher implementers had a higher average impact than lower implementers and that the difference

EXHIBIT 6.6 Comparison of Impacts Estimated Using the Cut-Off and Matching Approaches

	Difference in Impact	Difference in Effect Size	P-value
Panel A: Cut-off Approach			
Expressive one-word picture vocabulary test	5.21	0.32	0.099
Word Attack	3.02	0.27	0.166
Word ID	4.24	0.27	0.231
Letter ID	2.51	0.19	0.360
Panel B: Matching Approach			
Expressive one-word picture vocabulary Test	7.87	0.48	0.041*
Word Attack	2.35	0.21	0.292
Word ID	4.38	0.28	0.254
Letter ID	2.88	0.22	0.326

Note: [a] *Denotes statistical significance at the p = 0.05 level.

between the impacts in effect size units ranges between 0.19 and 0.48 of a standard deviation. Only one of the differences is statistically significant at the p = 0.05 level (Expressive Vocabulary, matching method, p-value = 0.041) while another one is significant at the p = 0.10 level (Expressive Vocabulary, matching method, p-value = 0.099).

It is important to note that subgroup analyses in cluster RCTs like the ones reported here are subject to potential reductions in statistical power due to the reduced sample sizes (Bloom, 2005). This could be one of the reasons why most of the estimated impacts shown in Exhibit 6.5 failed to attain statistical significance. While it is useful to be cautious, the magnitudes of the estimated subgroup impacts provide some suggestive evidence for a positive relationship between the degree of BTL implementation and the impact of BTL. BTL appears to have a larger impact when it is implemented with high fidelity.

Specification Test for the Cut-Off Approach

Recall that the cut-off approach relies on the following assumption (Equation 3b in the technical appendix): The average outcome of the treatment individuals with high (low) *actual* implementation fidelity is equal to the expected actual/potential outcome of the treatment individuals with high (low) *predicted* implementation fidelity. This assumption can be tested by comparing the average values of the outcome measures for the predicted high (low) implementers identified by the cut-off approach with those for the high (low) implementers identified by their actual implementation ratings (i.e. teachers whose observed implementation score was larger than the median score). This test essentially assesses the predictive power of the covariates used in the prediction model for the implementation rating. Specifically, suppose that the covariates perfectly predicted the high implementers; in this case, we would expect the outcome measures in the predicted high group to be exactly the same as those in the actual high group. Conversely, if the covariates were poor predictors, then we would expect the outcome differences across the two groups to be large (provided that outcomes vary in the sample).

The results from these specification tests are presented in Exhibit 6.7. It presents the average outcome value in the actual and predicted high implementing subgroups, the difference between the two expressed in the natural unit of the outcome measure as well as in effect sizes. As seen in Exhibit 6.7, the differences between the two groups are fairly small (effect sizes range between -0.03 and −0.12).

Note that how well the predictors perform in distinguishing high implementers from low implementers can also be directly tested by estimating the "hit-rate," which captures the percentage of teachers who are identified as a high implementer based on both the actual and the predicted implementation rating. The hit-rate in this study was 72%.

120 F. Unlu, L. Bozzi, C. Layzer, A. Smith, et al.

EXHIBIT 6.7 Specification Tests: Average Outcomes in Actual and Predicted BTL Subgroups

	Mean in Actual	Mean in Predicted	Difference	Standardized Difference
High Implementers				
Expressive one-word picture vocabulary test	83.17	85.08	−1.91	−0.12
Word Attack	102.03	102.45	−0.41	−0.04
Word ID	101.56	102.07	−0.51	−0.03
Letter ID	99.51	100.34	−0.83	−0.06

Conclusion

This chapter presents results from two approaches that aim to investigate the relationship between impacts of BTL, an early literacy intervention, and its fidelity of implementation. The results provide suggestive evidence of a positive association between BTL's impact on students and their teachers' levels of implementation fidelity. The strength of the evidence, however, critically depends on the strength of the association between the baseline measures used to predict teachers' implementation ratings and the methods used to match BTL and control teachers for comparisons.

The strength of the association between the baseline measures used to predict and teachers' implementation ratings was limited in this application for several reasons. The measures available in the data were able to account for some of the variation across schools, a few important baseline classroom characteristics (e.g. children's basic literacy skills at the start of the school year) and some pre-intervention teaching practices. Detailed information about teachers' attitudes, teaching histories, and opinions of the types of teaching practices associated with BTL were not available, however. If these had been available, the model predicting teachers' propensity to implement BTL might have explained more of the variation in teachers' BTL-like practices and produced more precise estimates of their implementation propensities.

Other limitations included having a small number of teachers in the sample and the fact that measures of teachers' classroom practices are from observations conducted at a single time. Finally, the instrument developed to measure BTL implementation was constructed using data collected for other purposes. While the data were carefully molded into a measure that was as close as possible to being representative of BTL, it could not fully measure all of BTL's practices.

For future applications of these methods, it would be important to use an instrument that directly and precisely measured the specific classroom practices associated with a particular intervention. In addition, it would be useful to collect detailed baseline data concerning factors that are hypothesized to be highly correlated with implementation (e.g. in the case of this study such predictors may include information about teachers' computer use, attitudes, and teaching histories, which was not collected).

Despite these limitations, this paper demonstrates that using baseline data and matching methods such as the ones used in the analyses presented here are potentially powerful ways to investigate the relationships between implementation and impacts. On the one hand, it is not possible to directly test these relationships and many social scientists still question whether quasi-experimental methods that rely on such predictions (e.g. propensity score matching) can produce unbiased estimates of program effects (e.g. Smith and Todd, 2004; Dehejia, 2005). On the other hand, the equivalence of the overall treatment and control groups from which the subgroups were constructed in the cut-off and matching approaches (which is guaranteed by random assignment) may increase the credibility of this particular application of matching or subsetting when compared with those that are conducted in observational settings. This is an argument also made by Schochet and Burghardt (2007). Furthermore, Cook et al. (2008) demonstrated that it is possible to replicate experimental findings through a carefully designed and well-implemented matching process in which baseline measures of the outcome of interest are employed in the matching. This was the case for the matching procedures conducted in this chapter.

In future studies utilizing randomized control trial designs, researchers could include plans for conducting exploratory implementation analyses such as the ones presented in this chapter. Planning for these types of exploratory studies will allow researchers to develop data collection instruments to measure detailed baseline characteristics of implementers and interventions. Using these exogenous characteristics and capitalizing on the strengths of randomized control trial designs will provide opportunities for more methodologically rigorous exploratory approaches to understanding the relationship between the implementation and impacts of educational interventions. These have the potential to provide researchers with opportunities to more fully develop these methods and to advance the field of education's knowledge of how teachers' uptake of interventions may (or may not) influence impacts on children.

Notes

1 Published by Wright Group/McGraw-Hill.
2 While the BTL evaluation included preschool and kindergarten classrooms, the analyses presented here are limited to kindergarten classrooms because the preschool sample was much smaller than the kindergarten sample and modeling implementation fidelity was not feasible with that sample.
3 Use of two kinds of questioning during read-aloud (use of comprehension strategies and connecting book to class theme or children's experiences) and support for story-related vocabulary development were three sub-categories in which a greater proportion of CLIMBERs teachers than Upgrade teachers met BTL benchmarks.
4 The record with the highest predicted instructional score was retained for control teachers as well so as not to bias the sample toward high scores for BTL teachers and lower or more varied scores for control teachers.
5 We did not consider retaining both fidelity ratings for a given teacher because most of the baseline variables we used to predict implementation fidelity are time invariant.

6 We used two statistics from the prediction process to compare these approaches: R2 of the regression used to predict implementation fidelity (which is described in more detail below) and the proportion of BTL teachers whose classification as a higher or lower implementer based on the predicted rating matches with their classification based on the actual fidelity rating ("hit rate"). Of the three approaches, the one we chose yielded a higher R2 value and hit rate (R2 = 0.39 and hit rate = 72%) than either of the two alternative approaches of retaining the rating from the second year (R2 = 0.30 and hit rate = 68%) and averaging the two ratings (R2 = 0.31 and hit rate = 65%).

7 Note that these steps were necessitated by the fact that the original analysis plan for the BTL evaluation did not include measuring implementation fidelity or relating it to impacts. Therefore, we had to come up with an alternative approach to capture fidelity.

8 It is possible to create a measure of the implementation of "BTL-like activities" in the control group (which would resemble the fidelity measure for treatment teachers) and then to use this measure as a moderator in the impact regression. This approach would allow us to investigate the relationship between *actual* levels of implementation fidelity and the outcome measures while controlling for observable characteristics of treatment and control teachers and students. One of the assumptions this approach relies on is the equivalence of the treatment and control teachers and students with the same level of the actual fidelity measure once observable differences between the two groups are accounted for. This assumption, however, may not be plausible because treatment and control teachers who have similar values of the actual implementation measure and similar observable characteristics may have different unobservable characteristics.

9 Note that since the threshold was set at the median of the BTL group, the two subgroups included the same number of BTL teachers. The number of control teachers in the subgroups, on the other hand, is determined by the distribution of the predicted rating within the control group.

10 This particular matching method was the best option in this context but there are other ways of conducting the matching, such as one-to-one matching without replacement, k-nearest neighborhood matching, caliper matching, and kernel matching.

11 It is customary to ignore (or not give any value) to findings that do not attain statistical significance at the usual p = 0.05 level. Throughout this section, we deviate from this practice and mention/interpret findings that are insignificant but have large effect sizes. This approach is appropriate here because these are subgroup analyses that suffer from statistical power loss due to substantial reduction in sample size. Furthermore, our primary research purpose entails contrasting impact estimates between higher vs. lower program implementers and the comparison of the magnitude of the subgroup effects (besides assessing and reporting whether the differences between the subgroup effects are significant) is relevant for that purpose.

Technical Appendix

This technical appendix includes two sections. The first section presents the statistical framework underlying the cut-off and matching methods. The second section presents the prototypical hierarchical linear model (HLM) specification used to estimate the subgroup impacts presented throughout Chapter 6.

Statistical Framework

These two approaches can be considered as an application of the principal stratification framework where the predicted high and low implementers are the

principal strata that capture the teachers' fidelity of implementation under the treatment condition (Frangakis and Rubin, 2002). Below, we present the statistical framework underlying these approaches (which is based on Rubin's *potential outcomes framework*) and describe each approach in detail.

Let Y_i^T denote the outcome of individual i under the treatment condition while Y_i^C denotes the outcome of the *same* individual under the control condition. These outcomes are thought of as potential outcomes because both cannot be observed for the same individual, i.e. for those assigned to the treatment condition, we observe Y_i^T but not Y_i^C and for those assigned to the control condition, we observe Y_i^C but not Y_i^T. The impact of the treatment for individual i, I_i is defined as:

$$I_i = Y_i^T - Y_i^C \tag{1}$$

Recall that the research question we aim to address pertains to the BTL impact for treatment students taught by teachers who implemented the program with high fidelity, which is represented by:

$$I^H = E(I_i | T_i = 1, F_i^* = H) = E(Y_i^T | T_i = 1, F_i^* = H) - E(Y_i^C | T_i = 1, F_i^* = H) \tag{2}$$

where T_i denotes whether the student i was in a treatment ($T_i = 1$) or control ($T_i = 0$) classroom while F_i^* denotes the actual fidelity level of the program she or he was exposed to. Without loss of generality Equation 2 sets F_i^* to H corresponding to a high level of fidelity, but similar representations can be constructed for the low fidelity level. $E(Y_i^T | T_i = 1, F_i^* = H)$ represents the expected outcome of treatment students taught by high-implementing teachers while $E(Y_i^C | T_i = 1, F_i^* = H)$ represents the expected (potential) outcome of the same students under the control condition, i.e. their potential outcomes had they been assigned to the control group. The cut-off and matching methods differ by how the two terms in Equation 2 are estimated, which is described in more detail below.

Cut-off Method

Estimation of the impacts on the predicted higher implementing subgroup using the cut-off method can formally be represented by:

$$I^H = E\left(Y_i^T | T_i = 1, F_i^* = H\right) - E\left(Y_i^C | T_i = 1, F_i^* = H\right)$$

$$= E\left(Y_i^T \middle| T_i = 1, F_i^p(X)\right) median\left(F_i^p(X)\right)$$
$$- E\left(Y_i^C \middle| T_i = 1, F_i^p(X)\right) median\left(F_i^p(X)\right)$$

$$
\begin{aligned}
&= E\left(Y_i^T \middle| T_i = 1, F_i^p\left(X\right)\right\rangle median\left(F_i^p\left(X\right)\right)\right) \\
&- E\left(Y_j^C \middle| T_j = 0, F_j^p\left(X\right)\right\rangle median\left(F_i^p\left(X\right)\right)\right)
\end{aligned}
\tag{3}
$$

where $F_i^p(X)$ represents the predicted implementation fidelity for individual i based on baseline covariates X and $median(F_i^p(X))$ represents the median of the predicted implementation fidelity in the treatment group. Also note that in this equation, index i represents students assigned to the treatment group while index j represents those assigned to the control group.

As mentioned in the main text, a nice feature of this method is producing unbiased impact estimates for the predicted higher and lower implementing subgroups since both the observable and unobservable characteristics are expected to be balanced across the BTL and control units within each subgroup. In Equation 3, this observation is implemented by:

$$
\begin{aligned}
&E\left(Y_i^C \middle| T_i = 1, F_i^p\left(X\right) > median\left(F_i^p\left(X\right)\right)\right) \\
&= E\left(Y_j^C \middle| T_j = 0, F_j^p\left(X\right) > median\left(F_i^p\left(X\right)\right)\right)
\end{aligned}
\tag{3a}
$$

where the term on the left, which appears in the second line in Equation 3 and represents "the expected outcome of the treatment individuals whose predicted rating is higher than the median rating had they been assigned to the control condition," is replaced with the term on the right, which appears in the third line in Equation 3 and represents "the average observed outcome of the control individuals whose predicted rating is higher than the median rating." Equation 3a is guaranteed by random assignment and does not require any assumptions. The assumption needed by this approach can be shown by:

$$
E\left(Y_i^T \middle| T_i = 1, F_i^* = H\right) = E\left(Y_i^T \middle| T_i = 1, F_i^p\left(X\right)\right\rangle median\left(F_i^p\left(X\right)\right)\right)
\tag{3b}
$$

$$
E\left(Y_i^C \middle| T_i = 1, F_i^* = H\right) = E\left(Y_i^C \middle| T_i = 1, F_i^p\left(X\right)\right\rangle median\left(F_i^p\left(X\right)\right)\right)
\tag{3c}
$$

Equations 3b and 3c state that the expected actual/potential outcome of the treatment individuals with high *actual* implementation fidelity under the treatment/control condition is equal to the expected actual/potential outcome of the treatment individuals with high *predicted* implementation fidelity.

Matching Method

Recall that the matching method allows us to estimate the average impact of the intervention on students taught by teachers with higher (or lower) *actual*

implementation fidelity. Within the potential outcomes framework, this approach is represented by:

$$I^H = E\left(Y_i^T \mid T_i = 1, F_i^* = H\right) - E\left(Y_i^C \mid T_i = 1, F_i^* = H\right)$$

$$= E\left(Y_i^T \mid T_i = 1, F_i^*\right) median\left(F_i^*\right)\right) - E\left(Y_i^C \mid T_i = 1, F_i^*\right) median\left(F_i^*\right)\right)$$

$$= E\left(Y_i^T \mid T_i = 1, F_i^*\right) median\left(F_i^*\right)\right)$$
$$- E\left(Y_j^C \mid T_j = 0, j \in M\left(i : F_i^* > median\left(F_i^*\right)\right)\right) \tag{4}$$

where $M(i : F_i^* > median(F_i^*))$ denotes the set of control teachers (and their students) matched with treatment teachers whose fidelity rating is higher than the median of the fidelity rating in the treatment group. The second line in Equation 4 shows that being a high implementer in the treatment group is defined as having an actual implementation rating that is higher than the median. That is:

$$E\left(Y_i^T \mid T_i = 1, F_i^* = H\right) = E\left(Y_i^T \mid T_i = 1, F_i^*\right) median\left(F_i^*\right)\right) \tag{4a}$$

$$E\left(Y_i^C \mid T_i = 1, F_i^* = H\right) = E\left(Y_i^C \mid T_i = 1, F_i^*\right) median\left(F_i^*\right)\right) \tag{4b}$$

Equations 4a and 4b do not require any assumptions, i.e. the classification of BTL teachers as higher or lower implementers is ensured to be without any error since it is based on the actual implementation ratings. Instead this method requires:

$$E\left(Y_i^C \mid T_i = 1, F_i^*\right) median\left(F_i^*\right)\right)$$
$$= E\left(Y_j^C \mid T_j = 0, j \in M\left(i : F_i^* > median\left(F_i^*\right)\right)\right) \tag{4c}$$

which states that the expected potential outcome of the treatment students taught by high implementing teachers exposed to the high fidelity version of BTL (right hand side of Equation 4c) by the average outcome of the students taught by control teachers matched to high implementers (left hand side of Equation 4c). This would be possible only if treatment assignment is an ignorable conditional on the covariates that are used to predict fidelity.

HLM Specification

The following three-level hierarchical linear model is estimated separately within the lower and higher implementer subgroups with the cut-off and matching methods:

Level 1 (student)

$$Y_{ijk} = \pi_{0jk} + \pi_{1jk}Cohort_{ijk} + \sum_{n=2}^{N} \pi_{njk}Cov_{ijk}^{n} + \varepsilon_{ijk}$$

where:

Y_{ijk} is the outcome measure for student i, in classroom j, in school k,

$Cohort_{ijk}$ is cohort indicator for student i, in classroom j, in school k. In particular, it equals one if the student is from the second cohort of kindergartners and zero; otherwise,

Cov_{ijk}^{n} is the nth student-level covariate, including gender, age, and ELL status,

π_{0jk} is the covariate-adjusted mean of the outcome measure in classroom j, in school k, and

ε_{ijk} is the residual associated with student i, in classroom j, in school k. All error terms are assumed to be normally distributed and independent of one another.

Level 2 (classroom)

$$\pi_{0jk} = \beta_{00k} + \beta_{01k}PercentELL_{jk} + r_{jk}$$

$$\pi_{njk} = \beta_{n0k} \text{ for n } = 1,2,...,N$$

where:

β_{00k} is the covariate-adjusted mean of the outcome measure in school k,

$PercentELL_{jk}$ is the percentage of ELL students in classroom j in school k. This covariate is also tested for inclusion using backwards elimination, and

r_{jk} is the residual associated with classroom j, in school k.

Level 3 (school)

$$\beta_{00k} = \gamma_{000} + \gamma_{001}BTL_{k} + \gamma_{002}admn_{k} + \gamma_{003}Spanish_{k}$$
$$+ \gamma_{004}A_{k} \times S_{k} + \gamma_{005}pretest_{k} + u_{k}$$

$$\beta_{01k} = \gamma_{010}$$

$$\beta_{n0k} = \gamma_{n00} \text{ for n } = 1,2,...,N$$

where:

γ_{000} is the covariate-adjusted grand mean of the outcome measure for the average control school,

BTL_{k} is an indicator variable equaling 1 for BTL schools and 0 for control schools,

γ_{001} is the estimated impact of BTL, or the difference between the average control school and the average BTL school,

γ_{002}, γ_{003}, and γ_{004} are the effects associated with the stratification indicators used during the random assignment process, and their interaction, to control for the study design,

γ_{005} is the effect associated with school-level pretests, and

u_k is the residual associated with school k.

For the interaction method, the second and third levels (classroom and school level) of the HLM specification above is modified to include the predicted rating and its interaction with the BTRL indicator as follows:

Level 2 (classroom)

$$\pi_{0jk} = \beta_{00k} + \beta_{01k}PRating_{jk} + \beta_{02k}PercentELL_{jk} + r_{jk}$$

$$\pi_{njk} = \beta_{n0k} \text{ for n } = 1,2,3,...,N$$

in which $PRating_{jk}$ is the predicted implementation rating for classroom j in school k.

Level 3 (school)

$$\beta_{00k} = \gamma_{000} + \gamma_{001}BTL_k + \gamma_{002}admn_k + \gamma_{003}Spanish_k + \gamma_{004}A_k \times S_k$$
$$+ \gamma_{005}pretest_k + u_k$$

$$\beta_{01k} = \gamma_{010} + \gamma_{011}BTL_k$$

$$\beta_{02k} = \gamma_{020}$$

$$\beta_{n0k} = \gamma_{n00} \text{ for n } = 2,...,N$$

where:

γ_{010} captures the relationship between the outcome variable and the predicted rating while γ_{011} captures the association between the impact and the predicted rating.

References

Arnett, J. (1989). Caregivers in day care centers: Does training matter? *Journal of Applied Developmental Psychology, 10,* 522–541.

Bloom, H. S. (Ed.) (2005). *Learning More from Social Experiments: Evolving Analytic Approaches.* New York: Russell Sage Foundation.

Bloom, H. S., Hill, C. J., and Riccio, J. A. (2003). Linking program implementation and effectiveness: Lessons from a pooled sample of welfare-to-work experiments. *Journal of Policy Analysis and Management*, 22(4), 551–575.

Brownell, R. (2000). *Expressive One-Word Picture Vocabulary Test (EOWPVT)* (3rd edition). Novato, CA: Academic Therapy Publications.

Cook, T. D., Shadish, W. R., and Wong, V. C. (2008). Three conditions under which experiments and observational studies produce comparable causal estimates: New findings from within-study comparisons. *Journal of Policy Analysis and Management*, 27(4), 724–750.

Dehejia, R. (2005). Practical propensity score matching: a reply to Smith and Todd. *Journal of Econometrics*, 125(1–2), 355–364.

Domitrovich, C. E., Gest, S. D., Jones, D., Gill, S., and Sanford DeRousie, R. M. (2010). Implementation quality: Lessons learned in the context of the head start REDI trial. *Early Child Research Quarterly*, 25(3), 284–298. Available online at DOI:10.1016/j.ecresq.2010.04.001

Dunn, Lloyd M. and Dunn, Leota M. (1997). *Peabody Picture Vocabulary Test, Third Edition* (PPVT-III). Circle Pines, MN: American Guidance Service, Inc.

Durlak, J. A. (2010). The importance of doing well in whatever you do: A commentary on the special section. *Early Childhood Research Quarterly*, 25(3), 348–357. Available online at DOI:10.1016/j.ecresq.2010.03.003

Durlak, J. A. and DuPre, E. P. (2008). Implementation matters: A review of research on the influence of implementation on programs and outcomes and the factors affecting implementation. *American Journal of Community Psychology*, 41(3–4), 327–350.

Frangakis, C. E. and Rubin, D. B. (March 2002). Principal stratification in causal inference. *Biometrics*, 58(1), 21–29.

Goodson, B. D., Layzer, J. I., and Layzer, C. J. (2004a). *Quality of Early Childhood Care Settings* (QUEST). Developed as part of the National Study of Child Care for Low-Income Families, under contract to the Agency for Children and Families, U.S. Department of Health and Human Services.

Goodson, B. D., Layzer, C. J., Smith, W. C., and Rimdzius, T. (2004b). *Observation Measures of Language and Literacy Instruction* (OMLIT). Developed as part of the Even Start Classroom Literacy Interventions and Outcomes Study, under contract ED-01-CO-0120, as administered by the Institute of Education Sciences, U.S. Department of Education.

Griffin, J. A. (2010). Research on the implementation of preschool intervention programs: Learning by doing. *Early Childhood Research Quarterly*, 25(3), 267–269. Available online at DOI:10.1016/j.ecresq.2010.03.004

Hamre, B. K., Justice, L. M., Pianta, R. C., Kilday, C., Sweeney, B., Downer, J. T., and Leach, A. (2009). Implementation fidelity of MyTeachingPartner literacy and language activities: Association with preschoolers' language and literacy growth. *Early Childhood Research Quarterly*, 25(3), 329–247. Available online at DOI:10.1016/j.ecresq.2009.07.002

Hulleman, C. S. and Cordray, D. S. (2009). Moving from the lab to the field: The role of fidelity and achieved relative intervention strength. *Journal of Research on Educational Effectiveness*, 2(1), 88–110.

Knoche, L. L., Sheridan, S. M., Edwards, C. P., and Osborn, A. Q. (2009). Implementation of a relationship-based school readiness intervention: A multidimensional approach to fidelity measurement for early childhood. *Early Childhood Research Quarterly*, 25(3), 299–313. DOI:10.1016/j.ecresq.2009.05.003

Lonigan, C. J., Wagner, R. K., Torgesen, J. K., and Rashotte, C. A. (2007). *Test of Preschool Early Literacy (TOPEL)*. Austin, TX: PRO-ED, Inc.

Odom, S. L., Fleming, K., Diamond, K., Lieber, J., Hanson, M., Butera, G., Horn, E., Palmer, S., Marquis, J., and Children's School Success Project. (2010). Examining different forms of implementation and in early childhood curriculum research. *Early Childhood Research Quarterly*, 25(3), 314–328. Available online at DOI:10.1016/j.ecresq.2010.03.001

O'Donnell, C. L. (2008). Defining, conceptualizing, and measuring fidelity of implementation and its relationship to outcomes in K-12 curriculum intervention research. *Review of Educational Research*, 78(1), 33–84.

Peck, L. R. (2003). Subgroup analysis in social experiments: Measuring program impacts based on post-treatment choice. *American Journal of Evaluation*, 2(24), 157–187.

Schochet, P. Z. and Burghard, J. (2007). Using propensity scoring to estimate program-related subgroup impacts in experimental program evaluations. *Evaluation Review*, 31, 95–120.

Smith, J. and Todd, P. (2005). Does matching overcome Lalonde's critique of nonexperimental estimators? *Journal of Econometrics*, 125(1–2), 305–353.

Woodcock, R. W. (1998). *Woodcock Reading Mastery Test: Revised/Normative Update (WRMT-R/NU)*. Circle Pines, MN: American Guidance Service, Inc.

Wright Group/McGraw-Hill (2004). *Breakthrough to Literacy*. Chicago, IL: Wright Group and McGraw-Hill.

7

MEASURING TREATMENT FIDELITY WITH RELIABILITY AND VALIDITY ACROSS A PROGRAM OF INTERVENTION RESEARCH

Practical and Theoretical Considerations

Jill H. Allor and Lynne Stokes

The long-term goal of educational intervention research is to provide practitioners with interventions that produce desired student outcomes and are feasible to use in common educational settings. Ideally, researchers will also determine what level of implementation is needed to achieve the desired outcomes and establish that it is feasible for educators to implement. Historically, researchers have taken great care to measure outcomes (i.e. dependent variables) with reliability and validity. Increasingly, we are recognizing the need for the intervention (i.e. independent variable) (Gresham, 2014) to be carefully measured as well. Treatment fidelity is a term commonly used in educational research to describe assessment of the independent variable. Defining and sensitively measuring implementation of interventions is complex and researchers are constrained by the availability of appropriate personnel, fiscal resources, and time limits (Spillane et al., 2007; Munter et al., 2014), but necessary to determine (a) whether non-significance is due to failure of the theory or inadequate implementation, (b) the degree of implementation that is required to achieve desired outcomes, and (c) the feasibility of adequate implementation in an authentic setting by practitioners.

The Institute of Education Sciences (IES) defines fidelity of implementation as "the extent to which the intervention is being delivered as it was designed to be by end users in an authentic education setting" (IES, 2014: ii). This statement clarifies the end goal to be that educators implement evidence-based interventions with sufficient fidelity to achieve the desired outcomes. A feasible intervention is one that practitioners can reasonably be expected to implement with this level of fidelity. Intervention researchers, including those funded by IES, must produce the tools and procedures to facilitate this in authentic settings. Thus, a solid program of intervention research should produce, in addition to the intervention itself, a reliable and valid fidelity measurement instrument that practitioners can

use to ensure appropriate implementation. Professional development and ongoing coaching should support practitioners in achieving and maintaining this goal.

The purpose of this chapter is to describe theoretical and practical considerations for measuring fidelity of implementation. It is aimed at providing practitioners with usable and scientifically defensible fidelity measures. We follow the process from the early stages of designing a fidelity instrument all the way through its use in a randomized control trial of the intervention. We identify common challenges and provide a framework for making decisions about how to measure fidelity, while working within the limited resources available. We discuss these considerations as they relate to the varying goals for research studies, specifically addressing the current goal structure of IES research grants (IES, 2014). We divide the program of research into three stages that correspond with the IES grant goal structure (goals two through four) for intervention development and research: development stage, efficacy and replication stage, and effectiveness stage. In Table 7.1 we provide an overview of the expectations about fidelity measures in each stage. For each stage, we identify (a) *planning* issues (i.e. grant proposal requirements), (b) *activities* and procedures, and (c) *products* that should be developed. Although we refer to the IES goal structure and requirements throughout this chapter, the recommendations apply to all intervention research.

We begin with an example describing development of a hypothetical intervention and its fidelity instruments. We first provide an overview of how measures of fidelity were created and implemented across this program of research. Then we discuss theoretical and practical considerations within each stage, focusing on issues related to reliability and validity.

Example Scenario

The hypothetical program of intervention research we describe is an idealized one, but does include some of the challenges commonly faced by researchers as they develop and use fidelity instruments for their interventions. Its purpose is to provide some context and concrete examples to illustrate the more technical and abstract ideas discussed in the remaining sections of the chapter. Though programs of research differ in their details, we focus on the commonalities, using the IES grant goal structure as an example and framework for the discussion. We begin at the end.

A supplemental reading intervention has been developed and studied extensively. It includes lessons that will be implemented by a reading teacher and materials for practice sessions that will be delivered by a paraprofessional. The products of the research include materials for professional development and recommendations for ongoing support and coaching. Included also are several fidelity measures: (a) a form for tracking implementation, or "dosage" (e.g. number of sessions, number of minutes, lessons completed); (b) a checklist to be used independently by the teacher as she makes instructional decisions based on student performance

TABLE 7.1 Overview of Fidelity of Implementation Expectations Across a Program of Intervention Research

	Development Stage	Efficacy or Replication Stage	Effectiveness Stage
Planning (proposal requirements)	Describe/plan for methods to be used for developing fidelity measure(s).	Describe measures to be used to assess fidelity of the intervention and to determine what the comparison group is receiving.	Describe: (1) Measures to be used to assess fidelity of the intervention and to determine what the comparison group is receiving; (2) How fidelity will be maintained at equivalent levels as previous studies.
Activities	(1) Develop prototype fidelity measures *and* refine in pilot or separate study. (2) Implement fidelity measures in pilot. (3) Assess reliability and validity of fidelity measures.	(1) Collect fidelity data in studies. (2) Analyze fidelity data and use to indicate when response to inadequate fidelity is needed.	Collect and analyze fidelity data in studies (Note: In IES grants at this stage, additional resources to respond to inadequate fidelity not allowed.)
Products (outcomes)	Fidelity measure(s) to assess whether the intervention is delivered as intended by the end users in an authentic education setting.	Information needed to guide future research: For studies showing benefit: What level of implementation is needed for replication or new effectiveness studies. For studies not showing benefit: Whether (or how) implementation could be improved in new development studies.	Information needed to guide future research. This includes one of the following: For studies showing benefit: What level of implementation is needed for routine practice For studies not showing benefit: Why results differed from previous studies, and whether future research should be undertaken.

data; and (c) observation instruments to measure implementation by both reading teachers and paraprofessionals. The observation instruments were designed to be used by the teacher and paraprofessional for self-assessment (i.e. by watching videos of instructional sessions to check for key elements and procedures). They are also intended to be used by an instructional coach and/or administrator for ongoing support and evaluation. These observations may be conducted either in person or from a video.

These fidelity instruments were developed in the early stages of the program of research (see Table 7.1) and were refined and implemented across the entire program of research. Early in the *development stage*, researchers created the intervention based on a theory of change that specifically identified key variables theorized to result in desired outcomes. This theory of change was based on prior empirical research, well-established theory, and expert opinions. To ensure that the intervention would be *feasible* to implement with fidelity, the intervention itself was developed with the input of important stakeholders, including administrators, teachers, parents, paraprofessionals, and students. To develop valid fidelity measures, the researchers used the theory of change to clearly specify all components of the intervention that they believed must be adhered to for the intervention to be effective. The expert opinion of the developers is key to ensuring that the fidelity measure is valid. For this first iteration of the intervention, they created a set of measures, including a tracking form for collecting dosage information and an extensive observation instrument whose items were linked directly to the theory of change. Items were chosen that were sensitive to various degrees of implementation. This served a dual purpose. First, the researchers needed to ensure that the critical components of the intervention were being delivered so that a test of its potential effectiveness could be determined. In other words, at this stage, the researchers wanted to conduct an analysis of the actual treatment as envisioned by the researchers rather than an intent-to-treat analysis. The purpose was to create an instrument that validly measures the intervention as it was intended to be implemented. Second, sensitively measuring fidelity would allow researchers in later stages of research to determine "how much" of the intervention is needed to be effective. Without a fidelity measure that could detect implementation differences at a fine scale, this would not be possible. The researchers also developed coaching procedures so they would be prepared to provide support if implementation was poor.

The fidelity instruments were then revised based on initial pilot studies' data. Data were collected and analyzed during the pilot studies to evaluate reliability of the fidelity measures. This analysis led to revisions in the fidelity instrument to improve reliability and validity. The fidelity instrument was also revised to reflect improvements in the intervention and the theory of change to ensure its validity. For example, the first iteration of lessons provided teachers with multiple options for activities as the researchers expected the teachers to prefer this type of flexibility. During a focus group, the teachers indicated that the number of choices

required too much planning time. Further, the format of the lessons was difficult to follow because of these choices. The curriculum was revised to create more consistent instructional routines that minimized planning time and allowed the materials to be easier to follow. The theory of change and the fidelity instruments were revised to reflect these intervention changes. Reliability data were collected throughout the pilot studies.

In the next stage, the *efficacy and replication stage*, the researchers conducted a series of randomized control trials to test the efficacy of the intervention. Each trial was conducted in an authentic setting, but the early trials were heavily supported and well controlled by the researchers as they carefully set expectations, closely monitored implementation and provided extensive coaching. This allowed the researchers to verify that the intervention resulted in desired outcomes when fully implemented. Later trials were less tightly controlled to allow for natural variability in fidelity. This enabled the researchers to study the level of implementation needed to achieve desired outcomes. An additional fidelity instrument was created for these trials that facilitated comparison with the activities in the control group to verify that the control group was not receiving a similar intervention. For example, the lessons in the intervention were designed to allow many opportunities for students to actively respond to instruction. One item on the observation instrument included the amount of practice students received for specific skills (e.g. number of minutes the student spent reading orally from text). During these trials, data from the items on the fidelity instrument were also carefully analyzed to determine which ones were most important and which were redundant. The marginal cost of measuring each additional item was considered against the added information it provided, with the goal of reducing the cost of fidelity data collection for the next stage of research. Determining which items are most correlated to positive outcomes increases the validity of the measure and enables the researcher to streamline the measure. This would also increase the likelihood that it would be practical for school-based personnel to use in an authentic setting. The difficulty of training fidelity data collectors to code with high reliability was also assessed for the same purpose; those items that were too difficult (expensive) to measure accurately might not be feasible to collect on a large scale and would probably not be useful to practitioners.

In the final stage, the *effectiveness stage*, a series of studies was conducted to ensure the effectiveness of the intervention when implemented in authentic conditions. The researchers took advantage of natural variation in implementation to further analyze the degree of implementation necessary to achieve desired outcomes. The end result was a fully-developed intervention that included a complete set of tools (i.e. measures and procedures) to establish and maintain adequate fidelity of implementation. These tools included (a) initial professional development, (b) coaching procedures, and (c) observation instruments for self-assessment, coaching, and evaluation. Next, we will address specific considerations for each stage of research.

Development Stage

It is important to consider fidelity activities during the development stage of a research program because early work on designing and establishing reliability and validity will impact the assessment of fidelity during the later stages of research. When planning to conduct development research, researchers should determine the specific methods they will use to develop fidelity measures. Table 7.1 shows that the primary fidelity-related activities during the development stage are to develop and test fidelity measures and instruments. The testing should include assessment of reliability and validity of the measures. To determine validity, a panel of experts might review and provide feedback on whether the measures would be expected to capture the degree to which the intervention would be implemented as intended. Then the prototype measures should be used to collect fidelity data during pilot studies. Although the goal is to create a set of fidelity measures that will be used by the end user, it is likely that the fidelity instrument will be refined in later stages of the research program (i.e. efficacy and effectiveness stages) as it is tested with a larger number of participants.

Developing Measures of Fidelity

The most informative fidelity measures are those that are (a) specifically linked to the theory of change, (b) sensitive to variability, and (c) include measurements that differentiate between the treatment and comparison group. When the measures have these characteristics, they provide valid information that can be used to determine which components of the theory of change are most related to improved outcomes. Because researchers must try to ensure full implementation during the pilot study, natural variation is less likely to occur at this stage. Therefore, if resources allow, researchers may consider developing short-term studies where they intentionally vary intervention delivery (i.e. variations in fidelity) to determine which components or characteristics are most important and/ or what level of implementation is needed to produce the desired effects. In this way, researchers may be able to modify their theory of change, as well as the intervention and fidelity measure. This type of modification is useful to improve both the effectiveness and the feasibility of the intervention because this process clearly identifies which aspects are essential and which are more likely to be implemented with fidelity. These methods also increase the validity of the fidelity measure. Whether or not it is reasonable for researchers to intentionally vary fidelity will depend on the nature and complexity of the intervention and available resources. Alternatively, natural variation may also be informative, as it could inform the theory of change and lead to more specific studies in the future, even though it would not permit strong causal inferences. This type of analysis could also take place in the next stage of research, as we will discuss later.

For fidelity measures to provide valid information about the *level* of each core component needed to achieve beneficial student outcomes, they must have

certain characteristics. First, they must be at least of ordinal scale (for example a Likert scale) rather than dichotomous. Second, measures of more than one core component should not be combined into a composite score, since the importance of each to the outcome will be confounded. Finally, the units in which fidelity is measured should be objective and universally meaningful. Without this characteristic, the researcher will not be able to communicate to other researchers or potential users of the intervention precisely what level of implementation is required to achieve meaningful results. For example, consider an item that asks how often a teacher has a student read orally from a text. A response set of "never, rarely, sometimes, frequently" can be interpreted differently by different people, while an actual number of minutes or words would be universally meaningful.

There is a tension in the goals of development studies regarding fidelity measures. First, it is recommended in IES grants, for example, that researchers determine whether the level of fidelity observed in the pilot study is sufficient to generate beneficial outcomes. To be able to conclude with confidence what level is sufficient, some variation in fidelity, as well as a measure that can detect the variability, are needed. At the same time, a successful development study will be one that shows that maintaining high fidelity in the pilot is possible, and in fact, includes plans for mitigation if it proves inadequate. This suggests that a successful pilot study should not show much variation in its level of implementation. Thus, a planned study of the measure outside the pilot may be beneficial to ensure that it can detect variations in fidelity that are less than those deemed acceptable. At the end of the study, the researchers should be prepared to discuss whether fidelity was high enough to expect beneficial student outcomes.

For example, suppose that the theory of change identifies that "opportunities to respond" is a core component of a reading intervention. A fidelity measure that records the actual number of responses per student (e.g. how many times the student practiced saying sounds or reading a particular word type) would be better than one which records only whether or not the teacher provided students with "adequate opportunities to respond." First, the checklist approach provides less information than a count about "how much" compliance is needed to achieve benefit. Second, as previously mentioned, the interpretation of "adequate" may not be consistent between the researcher and subsequent users of the intervention. Consider another more complex example. The intervention is designed to make it more likely that a student spends time orally reading text at an appropriate level of difficulty. This is a key component of the theory of change. The intervention does this by providing a large quantity of text that is carefully aligned with instruction and by providing teachers with guidance on how to make data-based decisions about pacing through the curriculum and selecting appropriate text. A fidelity measure could include an item on a checklist that indicates whether or not the teacher "chose an appropriate book that was aligned with the student's current lesson content." This would provide procedural information. But, a more informative measure would be one that observed the amount of time a child spent reading

and the number of errors the child made during that reading. The amount of time could be used as a continuous variable, making it more sensitive to variation. The appropriateness of the book could then be determined based on the rate of errors the student made (e.g. 90% accuracy). This information would allow determination of the level of intervention needed to improve outcomes. Collecting such data well would likely take more time, but would provide key information about *fidelity if* this factor is a critical element of the theory of change.

As we have described, fidelity measures need to be sensitive to variability and explicitly linked to the theory of change so that researchers can eventually determine the level of implementation needed to achieve desired outcomes. This goal is difficult to accomplish during the development stage (when pilot studies are small and researchers are supporting high implementation fidelity), but development of appropriate fidelity measures will enhance the chance of achieving this goal in future stages of the research program.

Assessing Reliability and Validity

Researchers are required to assess the reliability and validity of their fidelity measures as part of the development study. The literature of research methods defines reliability and validity in differing ways (Martinez et al., 2014; O'Donnell, 2008). In this chapter, we use these terms to describe the statistical concepts of variance and bias of a fidelity measurement. This implies an acknowledgement that the measures are subject both to variable and consistent error in the measurement. We define reliability as how similarly identical sessions would be assessed for fidelity by different observers or the same observer on different occasions. Thus, reliability is a measure of variance of the measurement. We define validity to describe a theoretical comparison between the average value a measuring process would produce and the true fidelity of the core component, as conceptualized in the theory of change. The difference in these two values is biased. By analogy, a test that always assesses a person's ability identically would have high reliability, but would have low validity if that assessed value is far from the true ability of the person. Note that the latter could occur either because the test asks questions that measure something other than ability (do not measure core component) or because the test's items are scored consistently either too leniently or too harshly (operational definition is off-target).

Validity is the more problematic of these two to assess for fidelity measures. It requires a judgment of both how well an operational definition captures a concept cited in the theory of change and whether the measurement of the operational definition is unbiased. We will consider how to measure both these aspects of validity. Because the concept in the theory of change is typically abstract and often no perfect measure of the operational definition is readily available, validity is hard to assess. Consider the example described previously for an intervention with the core component requiring that students spend time orally reading text

at an appropriate level of difficulty. Suppose "appropriate level of difficulty" is operationalized by how close the students' reading accuracy rate is to 90%, and that observers assess the fidelity measure by reporting the difference between the percentage of words accurately read and 90%. For the first aspect of validity, we would need to determine if a 90% accuracy rate is the correct standard for "appropriate level of difficulty." For the second, we must determine if the observers are consistently reporting a value for the accuracy rate that is neither too high (because they are too lenient in interpreting what is correct) nor too low (because they are too stringent)?

One common approach to addressing the first aspect of validity is to use a panel of experts to judge the alignment of the concept and the measure. The expert would operationalize this for our example by determining how much time is "adequate" (e.g. 10 minutes of a 20-minute lesson) and how to determine that the level of text is "appropriate" (e.g. 90% accuracy rate for word types from recent lessons). In this case, it is a common opinion of literacy experts that a student must read at least at a 90% accuracy rate for a text to be appropriate for instruction; therefore, it would be likely that a panel of experts would determine that 90% is a valid way to determine if the text was "appropriate." A second approach is to show that the fidelity measure is predictive of a desirable outcome. Of course at early stages of research on an intervention, data to support such an investigation will not be available from your own study, but may be from a study on a similar intervention previously conducted or reported in the literature.

There are typically two approaches used to assess the second aspect of validity, whether the measurement of the operational definition is unbiased. The first is that a superior (more expensive or time-consuming) measure, known in the literature as a gold standard, could be taken as truth. Then a sample of sessions is chosen and the observers' assessments compared to the gold standard. In our example, audio recordings of sessions might be made and a linguist could assess accuracy of the spoken words from a list of words from lessons, and these would be compared with observer reports. A more common approach is to *define* the truth as the average of replicates of the measurement from equally qualified observers. This is most often used when the operational measure relies on the observer's opinion (e.g. judgment of quality) rather than factual measures (e.g. how long or how many). In that case, only the first aspect of the validity measure (how well does the operational definition align with the concept specified as the agent in the theory of change) is relevant, since the operational measure will be unbiased by definition.

When interventions are complex, even these approaches do not always produce satisfying results. Munter et al. (2014) used the intervention's developers as experts to judge validity of their fidelity measures. Expert reviewers were asked to judge recordings to validate the coding scheme that determined the level of fidelity. They found this approach only marginally useful, since "variation among expert raters' rankings and categorizations was too great to provide a gauge of the accuracy of our fidelity results" (ibid.: 102).

Reliability is typically more easily assessed than validity because it is a characteristic of only the operational measure itself, from which data can be directly observed. No access to a gold standard or interpretation of a latent concept is required. As a result, researchers do commonly report reliability of their fidelity measures in their publications. However, there is neither a common metric for reporting reliability nor a universal standard about what level of reliability is acceptable for fidelity measures. Reliability is sometimes reported by measures that are appropriate for nominal data, such as exact match rate or Cohen's kappa (e.g. Munter et al. [2014] and Simmons et al. [2011], respectively). Cronbach's alpha is another reliability measure commonly reported (e.g. Nelson et al., 2012). All measures of reliability require that at least a subset of units on which the measure is made (e.g. students, sessions, videos, or even portions of videos) be assessed by at least two observers. The discrepancy between the two provides information about the variability of the measurement process, hence about its reliability.

We argue that assessment of reliability should be expanded to include not just the variability in the measure of fidelity due to observer discrepancies, but also that due to sampling only a fraction of sessions for fidelity evaluation. The former of these sources of variance contributes to measurement error, while the latter is known as sampling error. If fidelity reported for a particular participant is measured as the average observed value of fidelity over a set of intervention sessions, then there will be sampling error unless all sessions are observed or there is no session-to-session variability in fidelity. To reduce variability of the participant's fidelity measure, both sources of variability (due to measurement and sampling) should be controlled to acceptable levels.

The idea of assessing the combined effect of all sources of error for an estimate into a single quantity is borrowed from the survey methods literature, where it is known as the total survey error (TSE) approach (Weisberg, 2009). A model for total mean squared error[1] of the estimator is constructed, where mean squared error is defined as the average squared difference between the estimated and true values of an important survey estimate. The TSE model is a mathematical expression that contains terms for the variances and biases due to various sources of error, including sampling and measurement error. The most important use of the TSE framework for survey researchers is at the design stage, where they must consider the trade-off between errors and costs in order to decide how to allocate resources available for data collection. According to Groves and Lyberg (2010: 849) "this framework is the central organizing structure of the field of survey methodology."

Because fidelity measurement in most large RCTs is conducted using a sampling process and produces measures subject to both bias and variance, this framework can also provide a principled way to think about efficient fidelity data collection. In order to use it, the impact of the biases and variances we have discussed (due to validity and reliability shortcomings) must be measured on the same scale. The mean squared error scale was chosen for TSE because it

is a convenient one; its square root is in the same units as the estimate itself, so comparisons between the average size of the error and the size of the estimate itself are natural. The measures of reliability that are indices (e.g. Cohen's kappa) are not directly convertible to mean squared error, though they are computed from the same type of data (discrepancies in repeated measures). Thus, an alternative measure for the variance introduced by measurement error is discussed later.

A final advantage of combining the effects of the various errors in the fidelity measure into a single measure of variance is that it facilitates appropriate use of fidelity as part of the data analysis for the outcome itself. When fidelity is to be used as a covariate in the analysis of outcomes, its reliability affects its power (Carroll et al., 2006). Though concerns about power take place at a later stage of research, the groundwork for making power calculations later are begun in the development stage.

Now we give more detail on what data should be collected in the development stage so that estimates of the variance of both sampling and measurement error can be made. We begin with a discussion of sampling error. When fidelity measurement requires observation of sessions in which the intervention is delivered, limited resources typically prevent observing all sessions. Instead, the study designers must decide how many sessions to observe, and how to select them. When fewer than all sessions are observed, sampling error in the fidelity measure is introduced, since some information is missing. The smaller the number of sessions observed, the larger the sampling error because of the larger amount of missing information.

The number of sessions observed for evaluating fidelity varies widely in studies. For example, Simmons et al. (2010) measured fidelity for 3 out of 54 intervention sessions for each of the 48 teachers who participated in the study, while Hulleman and Cordray (2009) report a study in which work samples were collected for every session and evaluated for fidelity. In the latter case, no sampling error remains, although measurement error could still be present. In studies in which the fidelity measure is objective and easy to assess, the reverse may be true.

Little guidance is available from the literature to determine how many sessions should be observed, though it is recommended that they are observed regularly throughout the duration of a study (Gersten et al., 2005). This may be because the "right" number of sessions will vary depending on characteristics of the study. The major factor influencing how many sessions are needed is the session-to-session variance in fidelity received by each subject. To understand why, note that if all sessions are conducted with the same fidelity, a single observation from each will provide all the information needed to correctly assess average fidelity for each participant. But the more fidelity varies across sessions, the larger the number of sessions required to accurately assess the average fidelity delivered over the intervention period. Thus one statistic that should be calculated to aid in future planning is the sample variance of fidelity over sessions for each subject.[2]

However, the researcher must make the decision about how many sessions to sample in the development stage in order to estimate this session-to-session

variance and be in a position to plan sample sizes at later stages. Since the purpose of this stage of research is to determine the promise of the intervention, the accuracy of the estimates for future design planning is of lesser importance. If the intervention shows promise, more rigorous tests of the intervention will be conducted, and at least some data will be available for determining the number of fidelity sessions to observe in the efficacy stage.

As long as at least two observations per subject are available, planning estimates of the session-to-session variance can be computed. Since a goal of the development stage is to assess reliability of all fidelity measures, these data should be collected for each one. The sample of sessions should be chosen in a way that approximates randomness over the period of the pilot test. A reasonable way to select the sample, though not technically a random sample, would be to use a systematic sampling procedure (i.e. to select a sample of k sessions from a total of K sessions select every (K/k)th session across the intervention period) for each participant, depending on the unit on which fidelity is measured.

Now we turn to how to collect data to assess the contribution of observer measurement error variance to total survey error. There are two ways to collect data to calculate this variance. One is to have equally skilled but possibly imperfect observers assess the fidelity of a sample of sessions. These sessions can be either part of the trial itself, or from a supplemental training sample, perhaps from videos. The number of observers used in this process is typically two, but could be a larger number, depending on how many different observers are to be used in the pilot study. Alternatively, if a gold standard (near perfect) measure is available, a sample of sessions could be assessed for fidelity by both the gold standard and the imperfect observer. In either case, the number of sessions each observer assesses can be small at this stage (say five or six), but the types of sessions they observe should be as diverse as possible so that a range of fidelity implementation is included. Either method provides data from which an estimate of measurement error variance can be calculated.[3] If it is 0, then observers are perfectly consistent; the larger it is, the less reliable are the observer measurements.

By combining the data from the fidelity measurements across sessions and the observer discrepancy samples, one can estimate the total variance of the fidelity measure from both sources as well as the fraction of that variance that is from observer variance.[4] If this fraction is close to 0, it means that observer inconsistency is only a small component of the total error in the fidelity measure. If the fraction is close to 1, it means that observer consistency is a major portion of the error. If this occurs, the methods available for improving observer consistency are retraining observers, refining the measures themselves, or improving rubrics for measuring them. It is likely that variance of the fidelity measure over the sessions will be artificially low, compared to the variance over sessions that would occur in a study in which the interventions are deployed in a more uncontrolled environment, as in later stages. As a result, the judgments made about the proportion of variance due to sampling error (which is based on the session-to-session variability) is

likely to be underestimated. More accurate assessments of the variance will have to be made in later stages of research.

Efficacy and Replication Stage

The efficacy stage is typically a series of randomized control trials that serve to evaluate the effectiveness of an intervention under either ideal or routine conditions in authentic settings. Proposals for this stage of research require detailed descriptions of fidelity instruments that will assess fidelity of the intervention as well as comparison to a counterfactual. During efficacy and replication studies, researchers are expected to collect fidelity data, including reliability data, and analyze fidelity data to indicate when response to inadequate fidelity is needed. As before, researchers need to plan for responding to low fidelity. Expected outcomes when this stage is completed include hypotheses regarding (a) the degree of implementation needed to result in desired outcomes (if findings were positive) or (b) how implementation could be improved in future studies (if findings were negative). We would also recommend further refinement and validation of fidelity measures, depending on the work completed during the development stage.

If further work is needed to develop or validate fidelity measures, the procedures we recommended in the previous section should be considered. These include clearly and specifically linking the fidelity measure to the theory of change using expert opinion to judge the alignment of the concept and the measure. It may also be desirable to use the additional data collected at this stage with a larger sample to further streamline the measurement instruments. For example, fidelity data in early efficacy trials can be analyzed to determine if some items are redundant. If so, they can be removed, allowing the researcher to shorten the instrument during later efficacy studies and during the effectiveness studies as well. This will be important to efficiently utilize resources in the effectiveness stage (when the *n* is typically very large) and to ensure that the fidelity instrument can eventually be used by school personnel to maintain fidelity after research studies are complete.

The researcher will have to make decisions about the number of sessions to be sampled for fidelity measurement and whether or how observer reliability needs to be improved in each of the trials at this stage. Recall that the reliability of the fidelity measure depends on both adequately small sampling and measurement error. If fidelity data collected as outlined in the previous section are available from a previous development study, then it can be used to help guide the decision about where resources are needed. If such data are not available, then data collected in early trials in this stage could use the methods as in a development study. Then this information can be used when making decisions about later trials.

The goal is to ensure that the method used for defining fidelity produces a measure that corresponds closely to the concept that the researcher believes drives the theory of change. This means that its total error is small. This is assured

by refining the fidelity measures, if necessary, so that their operational definition captures the concept adequately, reducing bias. It also requires ensuring that the total error due to variance is small. This requires selecting a sample size for the number of sessions that is sufficient to achieve a specified margin of error.[5]

Of course, there will be more than a single measure of fidelity made during any study. The analysis outlined above will likely yield different numbers of sessions required to sample for different measures. Two possible solutions to this dilemma are: (1) select the maximum sample size necessary for any measure and use it for all measures; or (2) determine which fidelity measure is most important, and select the sample size based on its properties, and accept the resulting variance for the remaining measures. Finally, there may be cases in which the sample size required is infeasible because the variability of fidelity is so great. In that case, the measure may need to be dropped or revised.

The data collected during each trial allows new estimates of session-to-session variance to be calculated. As less control is maintained over implementation, their fidelity may become less consistent, resulting in an increase in the variance. Thus it is important to continue monitoring the variance and to use the updated estimates for planning fidelity data collection for each successive trial.

At the end of a successful efficacy study, the researcher may make plans for continuing the research on the intervention into an effectiveness stage. Researchers use a power analysis to determine the projected number of participants needed. If the proposed outcome analysis uses fidelity as a covariate in a test of the intervention effect, as is increasingly common today, the power may be improved. The data collected during the efficacy stage will prepare the researcher to predict how much improvement can be expected.

One outcome of this stage of research is to determine the degree of implementation needed to achieve desired outcomes. The researcher may want to design a series of studies to address this question. As in our previous scenario, an early study in this stage might be very tightly controlled, heavily supporting implementation to ensure high levels of fidelity. This tightly controlled study would then be followed by additional studies in which control was loosened and support was decreased with the goal of allowing for natural variation of fidelity. This would provide data to address the question of what level of fidelity is necessary to achieve desired outcomes. Such data could be used in the analysis of the outcome data by including it as a covariate in the outcome model. The coefficient of the fidelity measure can provide insight into how strongly fidelity is related to outcome. Though this method may be a practical use of resources, it would not, of course, allow for strong causal inferences. Planned and specific variations would be ideal. For example, random assignment to a "low dose" vs. "high dose" vs. "control" would yield the strongest conclusions about dosage as dosage that "naturally varies" might vary along with other factors that would not be controlled for in the former scenario (e.g. stronger teachers might provide the highest dosage and their strengths as a teacher would also influence the findings).

Effectiveness Studies

The goal of effectiveness studies is to determine whether the intervention outper-forms a counterfactual when the intervention is conducted under routine condi-tions in authentic education settings, typically on a large scale with a large number of participants. When planning for the effectiveness stage, researchers must describe fidelity measures, how they will be implemented, and how the researchers plan to maintain adequate fidelity implementation. Information about the reliability of fidelity measures (data collected during previous research) can be used to inform decision making. During effectiveness studies, researchers continue to collect reli-ability data on the fidelity measure and they analyze fidelity data to determine the degree of implementation needed to result in desired outcomes.

It is becoming common now to incorporate fidelity data directly into the statistical analysis of outcomes. The effectiveness stage has a natural advantage in facilitating this type of analysis because natural variation is expected. Even though the intention is to have training and coaching in place that produces ideal imple-mentation, realistically variation is likely to occur given the more typical condi-tions found in schools. This natural variation can become an advantage as it allows researchers to conduct more sophisticated analyses regarding the degree of imple-mentation necessary to result in desired outcomes. Variation may be straightfor-ward if the differences are a matter of dosage (e.g. number of sessions implemented, length of sessions), but implementation may vary along other dimensions as well. This variation could be used to further inform the theory of change. It is possible, for example, that teachers could perceive that one component of the interven-tion is not critical or is simply too difficult or time-consuming to implement. Although not ideal for determining causality, these variations could be explored to determine which intervention components are most correlated to positive out-comes. Researchers could then use this data to develop hypotheses that could be tested purposefully in future studies. This could, conceivably, lead to simpler interventions that are equally effective. Conversely, it could serve to demonstrate to researchers that additional professional development is needed to ensure that the more challenging aspects of the intervention are fully implemented. Another advantage of these large-scale studies is that naturally occurring variation allows researchers to explore secondary research questions that examine conditions and procedures that facilitate full implementation of the intervention. This could also lead to new hypotheses to be tested systematically in future research.

Conclusion

We have discussed in this chapter important theoretical and practical considera-tions for measuring fidelity of implementation across an entire program of research. We divided our discussion into the three stages that are also utilized by IES in its grant goal structure: development, efficacy and replication, and effectiveness

(IES, 2014). In the development stage, we highlighted the challenge of establishing validity. We discussed the need to link measures specifically to a theory of change and using expert judgment. Reliability, though more straightforward, can be time-consuming and expensive to assess. The challenge here is to maximize benefit from existing resources by minimizing error. We recommended using statistical variance as a common scale to estimate error that is due to observer disagreement (i.e. measurement error) and error that is present because we are unable to observe all sessions (i.e. sampling error). Calculating variance can aid the researcher in determining how to minimize error by improving observer agreement (via training or revision of the measurement instrument) or increasing the number of observations or both. The size of the fidelity observation sample in the development stage is set based on the goal of providing a usable estimate of session-to-session fidelity variance for scientific planning of subsequent research studies. At the same time, we acknowledge that the sample variance from the pilot study is likely to be an underestimate due to the tight control of intervention delivery in the development stage. A conservative approach is to double or triple the resulting estimate for future planning, depending on how much teacher coaching and remediation was deployed in the pilot.

Another challenging goal for a development study is to determine the level of fidelity necessary to achieve desired outcomes. We acknowledged that this is difficult in the development stage because there is likely to be little variation in fidelity of implementation as the researchers need to ensure that the intervention is fully implemented. However, creating a sensitive and valid measure will enable researchers to address this issue further along in the program of research.

Findings and data gathered about fidelity measures in the development stage should be used to improve the design of the second stage of research, the efficacy and replication stage. This stage sometimes includes creating fidelity instruments, or further refining ones developed at an earlier stage. In either case, they should use fidelity data as in the development stage for this process. But the primary focus in this stage is on collecting and analyzing the fidelity data, taking steps to improve both fidelity and its measurement, if either is inadequate. The size of the fidelity observation sample in the efficacy stage is set based on the goal of providing a sufficiently reliable estimate of fidelity for each unit on which it is measured (e.g. teacher or student). This is important so that these measures can be used as reliable covariates in an analysis of the outcome data itself. Again the researchers must address conflicting purposes as they strive to demonstrate that the intervention is feasible and effective, which requires reasonable levels of fidelity, while they also need to determine what level of fidelity is needed to result in desired outcomes. In this stage, the researcher may choose to meet this second goal by conducting a series of studies in which they gradually allow more variation of fidelity or they may choose to systematically vary fidelity enabling them to make causal inferences about the degree of implementation needed to be effective. Because the

number of participants is typically higher in this stage than in the development stage, the opportunity to collect reliability data is important. These data can be used to streamline the fidelity instrument by eliminating redundant items and examine variability in order to determine the number of observations needed to reliably estimate fidelity. Also, it is becoming commonplace to use fidelity data as a covariate in determining the effectiveness of interventions in achieving desired outcomes.

Finally in the effectiveness stage of a research program, the number of participants is typically increased, which usually requires researchers to make hard decisions about how best to use resources. If the fidelity data collection program we have outlined is followed, the researcher will have information about fidelity that can be used for improving the efficiency of the study design. This will be possible because the researcher will know how to select a fidelity observation sample design that provides reliable estimates. These estimates can then be used effectively as covariates in the analysis of the outcome data. Because research is conducted in authentic settings with only the amount of support that would be feasible for schools to maintain independent of researchers, varying levels of implementation are to be expected. These models allow increased power by salvaging information from low fidelity units, and also help clarify the degree of implementation necessary for success. This will only be possible if fidelity instruments are valid, reliable, and sensitive to variable implementation. In other words, the success of fidelity instruments ultimately depends on the work completed across an entire program of research.

Notes

1   The mean squared error of an estimator $\hat{f}$ of a parameter f can be written in mathematical form as

$$MSE(\hat{f}) = E(\hat{f} - f)^2 = [E(\hat{f}) - f]^2 + Var(\hat{f})$$

which is the sum of the squared bias and variance of the estimator.

2   The session-to-session variance for each subject can be estimated as $s_f^2 = \Sigma_{i=1}^{k}(f_i - \bar{f})^2 / (k-1)$, where k is the number of sessions observed, f_i is the fidelity assessed for the subject in session i, and $\bar{f}$ is the average fidelity for the subject over all observed sessions.

3   The estimate of measurement error variance σ_e^2 for the first method is $\hat{\sigma}_e^2 = \Sigma_{i=1}^{\kappa}\Sigma_{r=1}^{R}(f_{ir} - \bar{f}_i)^2 / \kappa(R-1)$, where κ is the number of sessions evaluated by each observer and $\bar{f}_i$ is the average fidelity across the R imperfect observers of session i. The estimator for the second method is a measure of MSE and is $\widehat{mse} = \Sigma_{i=1}^{\kappa}(f_{ir} - f_{ig})^2 / k$, f_{ir} and f_{ig} are the fidelities assessed for the ith session by the imperfect and gold standard observers, respectively.

4   The variance of the average fidelity from a sample of size k (out of K) sessions is $V(\bar{f}) = (1 - k/K)\sigma_f^2 / k + \sigma_e^2 / k$ (Cochran 1977: eqn. 13.22), where σ_f^2 and σ_e^2 denote session-to-session and measurement error variance, respectively. An approximately unbiased estimator of this variance is $v(\bar{f}) = (1 - k/K)s_f^2 / k$, since the sample variance s_f^2 captures both sources of variance (Cochran 1973: eqn. 13.25). The fraction of the fidelity measure's total variance that is due to observers can be estimated by $\hat{\sigma}_e^2 / s_f^2$.

5 Suppose that it is desired to sample a sufficient number of sessions that the margin of error for a $1-a$ confidence interval for mean fidelity is less than some specified value d. Then the number of sessions required per participant, k, out of the total number K, can be approximated by $k = (z_{a/2}^2 s_f^2) / (d^2 + z_{a/2}^2 s_f^2 / K)$ (Lohr 2010: eqn. 2.25).

References

Carroll, R. J., Ruppert, D., Stefanski, L., and Crainiceanu, C. (2006). *Measurement Error in Nonlinear Models: A Modern Perspective.* Boca Raton, FL: Chapman and Hall/CRC.

Cochran, W. G. (1977). *Sampling Techniques.* New York: John Wiley and Sons.

Gersten, R., Fuchs, L. S., Compton, D., Coyne, M., Greenwood, C., and Innocenti, M. S. (2005). Quality indicators for group experimental and quasi-experimental research in special education. *Exceptional Children*, 71(2), 149–164.

Gresham, M. (2014). Measuring and analyzing treatment integrity data in research. In L. M. Hagermoser Sanetti and T. R. Kratochwill (Eds.), *Treatment Integrity: A Foundation for Evidence-Based Practice in Applied Psychology* (1st edition). Washington, DC: American Psychological Association. 109–130.

Groves, R. and Lyberg, L. (2010) Total survey error: past, present and future. *Public Opinion Quarterly*, 74(5), 849–879.

Hulleman, C. S. and Cordray, D. S. (2009). Moving from the lab to the field: The role of fidelity and achieved relative intervention strength. *Journal of Research on Educational Effectiveness*, 2(1), 88–110.

IES (Institute of Education Sciences) (April 2014). Request for applications: Education research grants CFDA number 84.305A. Available online at http://ies.ed.gov/funding

Lohr, S. L. (2010). *Sampling: Design and Analysis* (2nd edition). Boston, MA: Brooks/Cole.

Martinez, R. G., Lewis, C. C., and Weiner, B. J. (2014). Instrumentation issues in implementation science. *Implementation Science*, 9(118). Available online at DOI:10.1186/s13012-014-0118

Munter, C., Wilhelm, A. G., Cobb, P., and Cordray, D. S. (2014). Assessing fidelity of implementation of an unprescribed, diagnostic mathematics intervention. *Journal of Research on Educational Effectiveness*, 7(1), 83–113.

Nelson, M. C., Cordray, D. S., Hulleman, C. S., Darrow, C. L., and Sommer, E. C. (2012). A procedure for assessing intervention fidelity in experiments testing educational and behavioral interventions. *The Journal of Behavioral Health Services & Research*, 39(4), 374–96. Available online at DOI:10.1007/s11414-012-9295-

O'Donnell, C. L. (2008). Defining, conceptualizing, and measuring fidelity of implementation and its relationship to outcomes in K–12 curriculum intervention research. *Review of Educational Research*, 78, 33–84.

Simmons, D., Hairrell, A., Edmonds, M., Vaughn, S., Larsen, R., Willson, V., and Byrns, G. (2010). A comparison of multiple-strategy methods: Effects on fourth-grade students' general and content-specific reading comprehension and vocabulary development. *Journal of Research on Educational Effectiveness*, 3(2), 121–156. Available online at DOI:10.1080/1934574100359689

Spillane, V., Byrne, M. C., Byrne, M., Leathem, C. S., O'Malley, M., and Cupples, M. E. (2007). Monitoring treatment fidelity in a randomized controlled trial of a complex intervention. *Journal of Advanced Nursing*, 60(3), 343–52. Available online at DOI:10.11 11/j.1365-2648.2007.04386

Weisberg, H. F. (2009). *The Total Survey Error Approach: A Guide to the New Science of Survey Research.* Chicago: University of Chicago Press.

CONTRIBUTORS

Jill H. Allor
Southern Methodist University

S. Natasha Beretvas
The University of Texas

Laurie Bozzi
Abt Associates, Inc.

Anna Mari Fall
The University of Texas

Frank M. Gresham
Louisiana State University

Chris Hulleman
University of Virginia

Richard Hurtig
University of Iowa

Jeff Kosovich
University of Virginia

Carolyn Layzer
Abt Associates, Inc.

Nancy Scammacca Lewis
The University of Texas

William M. Murrah
University of Virginia

Cristofer Price
Abt Associates, Inc.

Greg Roberts
The University of Texas

Arthur Smith
Abt Associates, Inc.

Lynne Stokes
Southern Methodist University

Fatih Unlu
Abt Associates, Inc.

Sharon Vaughn
The University of Texas

Vivian Wong
University of Virginia

Keith Zvoch
University of Oregon

INDEX